Google Analytics Demystified:
A Hands-On Approach

Google Analytics Demystified: A Hands-On Approach

Joel J. Davis

ISBN-13: 978-1491015995
ISBN-10: 1491015993

Editor. Danna L. Givot

Trademarks. This book makes descriptive reference to trademarks that may be owned by others. All terms mentioned in this book that are known to be trademarks or service marks have been appropriately capitalized. Use of a term in this book should not be regarded as affecting the validity of any trademark or service mark and, additionally, should not be viewed as an intention of trademark infringement. The use of such trademarks within this book is not an assertion of ownership of such trademarks by the author or publisher and is not intended to represent or imply the existence of an association between the author or publisher and the lawful owners of such trademarks. The author is not associated with any product, vendor, organization or individual mentioned in this book.

Limit of Liability/Disclaimer of Warranty. Every effort has been made to make this book as complete and as accurate as possible, but no warranty of fitness is implied. The publisher and author make no representations or warranties with respect to the accuracy or completeness of the contents of this work and specifically disclaim all warranties, including without limitation, warranties of fitness for a particular purpose. No warranty may be created or extended by sales or promotional materials. The information, guidance, sugges-tions, and strategies provided are on an "as is" basis. The author and the publisher shall have neither liability nor responsibility to any person or entity with respect to any loss or damages arising from the information or application of information contained in this book. This work is sold with the understanding that neither the publisher nor the author is engaged in rendering legal, accounting, advertising, marketing, digital design, or other professional services. If professional assistance is required, the services of a competent professional person should be sought. Organizations, individuals and websites referred to in this work are provided for information only and should not be interpreted as an endorsement of the organization or any advise or materials the organization may provide. Readers should be aware that digital references listed in this work may no longer be active or may have changed and that Google Analytics terminology, organization and displays may have changed since the date of publication.

Data. All data is fictitious and is presented for instructional purposes only. Data presented is not intended to be interpreted as an indication of actual performance. Travel and Tour is a fictitious company and online site and is presented for instructional purposes only.

For Danna, Kyle and McKenna.

They know why.

A note on your book

In order to minimize environmental impact by reducing waste, *Google Analytics Demystified* is printed on-demand. When an order is placed, a book is printed. Given this approach, there is a *very slight* chance that there may be a printing problem. If this is the case, we apologize and, if you purchased from Amazon, we encourage you to request a free replacement. To contact Amazon by email, phone, or chat, click the "Contact Us" button from any Help page at http://www.amazon.com/help. If you can't access this feature, use one of the Amazon.com customer service phone numbers: U.S. and Canada (1-866-216-1072) or International (1-206-266-2992).

Brief Contents

Detailed Contents

Section V: The Audience Menu

Section VI: The Behavior Menu

Section VII: Segments

Section VIII: Goals

Section IX: Tracking Downloads

Section X: Events

Section XI: Referral Sources

Section XII: The Social Menu

Section XIII: The Ecommerce Menu

Section XIV: Attribution and ROI

Section XV: Experiments

Section XVI: Data Management

Answers to Practice Exercises

Index

Every website and blog begins with a set of assumptions. We use our best judgment to make decisions related to content, navigation, and visitor flow and behaviors. Once the property is up and running, we have three options:

- We can let the property continue as is and hope for the best (very dangerous).

  Or ...

- We can rely on our judgment or best guess to plan revisions (still dangerous).

  Or ...

- We can monitor visitor characteristics and behaviors to determine the best way to reduce weaknesses and increase strengths (very beneficial).

If you are currently taking the latter approach and are using the full range of Google Analytics to inform your judgment, then congratulations. There is no need for you to buy this book. On the other hand, if you are not familiar with Google Analytics, or if you would like to improve how you use and apply Google Analytics to making better strategic decisions, then this book is definitely for you.

What Google Analytics can do for you

Simply put, Google Analytics helps you work smarter (not harder) so that you can increase the success of your digital property. In this book, we focus on the application of Google Analytics to websites and blogs, for which Google Analytics allows you to answer questions such as:

- How are visitors finding my site and what do they do when they arrive? What are the most common entrance pages? What are the most common exit pages?

- Which content do my visitors find most interesting and motivating? How much of my content is actually being consumed? What do visitors do after they read my content?

- How easily can site visitors find what they are looking for? Is my site content aligned with the search terms visitors use to find content?

- What are the strengths and weaknesses of site interaction? What can I do to improve visitors' experience and facilitate interaction?

- How effective are my campaigns? What efforts result in positive outcomes and help accomplish my goals? How can I make my campaigns more effective?

- How are my site transactions influenced by visitor characteristics, site usage, and other aspects of site engagement?

- How can I conduct tests to optimize my site's layout, content, organization, and navigation?

- How can I identify and examine the characteristics and behaviors of key sub-groups of site visitors?

And best of all, not only will Google Analytics help you answer these questions, it will do so for free as long as your website or blog has less than 10 million hits per month.

A mind-set for analytics

There are several good books that describe the need for analytics and approaches to the analysis of digital data. We don't cover the topics addressed by these authors, and it is recommended that you read at least one of these books to obtain a more detailed perspective on the mind-set for digital analytics. I've found the following very useful:

- *Web Analytics 2.0: The Art of Accountability and Science of Consumer Centricity* by Avinash Kaushik

- *Keeping Up with the Quants: Your Guide to Understanding and Using Analytics* by Thomas Davenport and Jinho Kim

There are also several good books that explain Google Analytics. Unfortunately, these books are either older and don't reflect recent changes or they take a passive rather than an active approach. These authors generally assume that you have your own operational website or blog where you have authorization to implement key concepts and procedures. I think that this approach is limiting. You may want to learn how to apply Google Analytics to your own situation, but you may not have access to a working site or you may have access but don't want to do something that might negatively affect the site itself or the integrity of any data already collected. As a result, this book takes a different approach.

Our approach to helping you learn Google Analytics

We'll supply you with a full working website, free of charge.

We've created a website for a fictitious travel agency. Your use of this site will allow you to implement concepts raised in the book and explore Google Analytics on your own without any fear of ruining a real site or real data.

This approach advances your learning in three important ways. First, you will be an active rather than a passive participant in the learning process. You will be able not only to read about what Google Analytics can do, but you can immediately apply and explore key concepts on a working website. Second, you can explore Google Analytics without risk to existing data. Since mistakes are an important part of the learning process, you can make and correct errors without any harm to your existing website. Finally, because you will have an active site and real data, you can explore on your own, thereby increasing your depth of understanding. We explain how to obtain and personalize this website in Section One.

Moving through the book

Many of the chapters provide stand-alone instruction, so if there is a particular topic of interest you can immediately turn to that chapter. However, the concepts and exercises in the book have been sequenced to allow ideas to build over the course of the book. As a result, we suggest that you move through the book sequentially.

Required technical skills

Our approach to Google Analytics is detailed but not overly technical. While it is important to understand the "what" of Google Analytics, our focus and emphasis is on the "why." We try to help you not only see what the data "is," but we also try to help you extend your skills so that you are better able to determine what the data "means." The ability to draw meaning from Google Analytics data should help you make more informed, better strategic decisions. This, in turn, should lead to higher levels of success for your own digital properties. Nevertheless, your active engagement in learning Google Analytics does require a basic set of technical skills. We assume that you can (or will learn how to) do the following prior to starting with Chapter One:

- transfer files from your computer to an external server

- open a web page and modify the source code

Applying what you learn

We have provided extensive sets of exercises for you to use to apply and extend the discussion of key topics. We encourage you to work through these exercises and then compare your answers to ours (which are provided in the back of the book). You'll notice as you work through the book and exercises that our focus is on helping you obtain meaning from the data - using the data to determine implications for strategic decision-making.

Let's get started.

Organization

Google Analytics Demystified presents sixteen sections of content, organized as follows:

- Section I, Getting Started, consists of five chapters that help you get your website up and running, register with Google search, and collect data for future analysis.

- Sections II through IV help you understand the fundamentals of data characteristics, collection and management. The concepts covered in these sections lay the foundation for the successful use of Google Analytics and for the successful application of Google Analytics data to strategic decision-making.

- Sections V and VI explain two specific types of analytics data: *Audience* (who comes to your site) and *Behavior* (what people do after they arrive).

- Sections VII to X focus on tools and techniques that both broaden and deepen your analytics data and the data's subsequent application to decision-making. These sections explore segmentation and custom segments, the creation and use of website goals, download tracking, and events that help you better understand content consumption and website engagement.

- Sections XI to XIV continue the explanation of analytics data: *Acquisition* and *Social* (how people learn about your site and referral sources, especially social sources), *Ecommerce* (purchase and other conversion behaviors), and *Attribution* (assigning purchase and conversion credit to different referral sources).

- Section XV explains how to use Google Analytics to conduct content-focused experiments.

- Section XVI addresses advanced topics in ongoing data management, specifically: alerts, shortcuts, data exports, and dashboards.

The book concludes with answers to all practice exercises.

A Note on Universal Analytics

Until recently, there were two forms of Google Analytics: Standard and Universal. However, Google has implemented procedures to phase out Standard Analytics and make Universal Analytics the only supported approach. This is to your benefit, as Universal Analytics provides improved data processing and reporting, new and expanded data collection methods, and additional tools for data analysis. In addition, Universal Analytics allows you to connect multiple devices, sessions, and engagement data with a single unique User ID and to track a broad range of digital devices.

So, in what circumstances do you need to worry about Universal Analytics?

- If you have not yet incorporated Google Analytics on your digital property then you will automatically be using Universal Analytics when you add Google Analytics. Similarly, you will automatically be using Universal Analytics when you set up the website provided with this book. You can skip to the next chapter if this describes your circumstances.

- If you have an online property that is already using Google Analytics *and* if you want to apply the concepts from this book to that property, then you'll need to determine which version of Google Analytics is active. It is important that your property be using Universal Analytics because this is the version of Analytics to which the book's procedures and examples apply.

  You can determine your version of Google Analytics by checking the Google Analytics Tracking Code (GATC) currently being used on your site. If you see this line within your GATC code

  var _gaq = _gaq || [];

  then you will need to migrate to Universal Analytics.

While migration procedures are beyond the scope of this book, the following resources should prove useful:

Universal Analytics Upgrade Center	https://developers.google.com/analytics/devguides/collection/upgrade/
Universal Analytics Upgrade Guide	https://developers.google.com/analytics/devguides/collection/upgrade/guide

A Note on Ecommerce

The travel website we provide with this book is a basic ecommerce site. Site visitors have the opportunity to "purchase" a vacation to either the Bahamas or Mexico. Of course, no real vacations are purchased and no payment is received.

The incorporation of ecommerce into the site allows you to use transactions as a terminal event. As such, you can improve your analytical and strategic skills by using Google Analytics to answer questions such as:

- Are some referral sources more important than others in facilitating transactions?

- To what extent are new versus returning site visitors different with regard to transactions?

- How do site visitors move through the site on the way to a transaction? What site characteristics facilitate a transaction? What site characteristics reduce the opportunity for a successful transaction?

- Do transactions differ by browser? By geography?

- How effective are my marketing or other communications in facilitating and encouraging transactions?

Learning how to answer these and related questions will serve you well even if your site or blog is not engaged in ecommerce. Let's say, for example, that you have a website or blog where terminal events relate to content consumption. The prior questions and the skills you'll acquire in addressing these questions still apply - simply substitute "content consumption" for transactions. The skills you learn using ecommerce data should be generalizable to whatever terminal events are appropriate to your website or blog.

Finally, Google Analytics has begun to implement an advanced form of ecommerce tracking: Enhanced Ecommerce. This data collection option allows a deeper understanding of shopping and purchasing behaviors, product and category economic performance, and merchandising success. However, the use of Enhanced Ecommerce does require a considerable level of expertise in shopping cart and product data management and integration. Since we believe that relatively few readers of *Google Analytics Demystified* are likely to implement Enhanced Ecommerce, we direct those interested to the resources shown on the following page.

Better Data, Better Decisions: Enhanced Ecommerce Boosts Shopping Analytics	http://analytics.blogspot.ie/2014/05/better-data-better-decisions-enhanced.html
Overview of Enhanced Ecommerce	https://support.google.com/analytics/answer/6014841?hl=en
Enhanced Ecommerce (UA) Developer Guide	https://developers.google.com/tagmanager/enhanced-ecommerce

Google Analytics Demystified

Section I: Getting Started

As mentioned in the Introduction, we provide you with a free website to use as the basis for your exploration of Google Analytics. The five chapters in this section help you obtain and customize this website so that Google Analytics can collect and report data on visitor characteristics and behaviors.

- Chapter 1 takes you through the steps you will use to get your site up and running. Each step is clearly described and successful completion of these steps requires only the ability to upload/download files and access/modify a web page's HTML code following our directions.

- Chapter 2 verifies that your site is operational and that Google Analytics is collecting and reporting data.

- Chapter 3 registers your working site with Google search while Chapter 4 registers your site with Google Analytics as an ecommerce site.

- The final chapter in this section, Chapter 5, provides directions for populating your travel site with data. This data will provide the basis for your application of the book's concepts and procedures.

Google Analytics Demystified

First Steps

This book takes a hands-on approach to helping you learn Google Analytics. While you can (and eventually should) apply each chapter's concepts to your own website or blog, it is probably better to use the example site that we've created to accompany this book. Any errors you make on this site will not result in the destruction of real, valuable data. Your use of this site also allows us to guide you through each instructional step in a meaningful and relevant way. This first set of activities gets your website operational and tracked by Google Analytics.

> Our example site is a travel agency with ecommerce. While your website or blog may not include an ecommerce option, all of the concepts and techniques discussed throughout this book will still apply to your situation. You can see the site in action at:
> `http://www.googleanalyticsdemystified.com/xqanqeon`

You'll need to accomplish the following in order to get your site operational and tracked:

1. Make certain that you have a Google account, such as that used for Gmail or Google+.

2. Download the travel agency website.

3. Select a unique keyword to identify your site.

4. Acquire a domain name and server space. Make certain that the website is working.

5. Register your website with Google Analytics.

6. Obtain your unique Google Analytics Tracking Code (GATC).

7. Add GATC to each page of your website. Customize your site.

8. Upload your website and confirm that it is working.

9. Confirm access to Google Chrome.

10. Populate your site with data.

If needed, create a Google account

A Google account is required for access to Google Analytics. If you already have a Google account, such as that used for Gmail or Google+, then skip this step and continue with downloading the travel agency site. Otherwise, you'll need to create an account.

Creating a new Google account is very simple. You just respond to the questions asked at:

`https://accounts.google.com/SignUp`

Google will now associate all of your Google Analytics activities with this account. Remember to be signed into this account when you want to access Google Analytics.

Download your travel website

As mentioned earlier, there is no need to create your own website in order to explore Google Analytics. We provide you with the core site which we'll use throughout this book.

The website is contained in a zip file that can be downloaded from:

`http://www.googleanalyticsdemystified.com/resources/bksite.zip`

Download and then unzip the file which will give you a folder named "bksite". You'll rename this folder in the next step.

Select a unique keyword to identify your site

You will need to select a one-of-a-kind name to distinguish your site from others using this book, as well as to facilitate search engine indexing. The unique name for my site is "xqanqeon". If you are at a loss for a unique name, just go to the fantasy name generator at:

`http://www.rinkworks.com/namegen/`

Use the "Simple Interface" to select a name type. Then, pick a name from the displayed list. Before final selection, do a Google search for the name you selected. If you received "no results found" or "similar" results which are not identical, then your name is a good one. If there are exact matches, then modify your name (perhaps by adding an extra "x" or "q") until you obtain "no results found" or "similar" but not identical results.

Once a name is found, rename the "bksite" folder with this new name.

Your site will need to be accessible online so you will need your own domain name and server space. You will also need to be able to transfer files from your computer to that space.

File transfer is accomplished through FTP which is an acronym for File Transfer Protocol. As the name suggests, FTP is used to transfer files between your computer and another computer or, in this case, to the server where your website will be housed. Two common FTP programs are Cyberduck (for Mac) and WinSCP (for Windows). Both programs come with tutorials for using FTP and can be found at:

http://cyberduck.en.softonic.com/mac

http://winscp.net/eng/download.php

There are two options for making your website accessible online.

-   If you already have server space **and** an available domain name **and** FTP authorization, then these can be used to house your travel agency website. Note that the subdirectory name for your website will be the same as the title of the folder containing your website. For example, the domain name (URL) of my travel site is:

    http://www.googleanalyticsdemystified.com/

    The folder that contains my travel site content is named xqanqeon. Thus, the full URL to my travel site is:

    http://www.googleanalyticsdemystified.com/xqanqeon/

-   If you do not have a domain name or server space or FTP authorization, then you will need to purchase these. While there are many, many companies that provide these services, I've had over a decade of excellent service from Hyper-mart.com.

    It is not technically necessary for you to house your travel website in a subdirectory. However, doing so makes it much easier to isolate this site from the remainder of your website content and it makes it much easier to erase the site if/when desired.

Once you have purchased a domain name and server space, upload the entire (renamed) travel site folder. Visit the home page of the site and use the links to make certain that the site is operational.

Now it's time for you sign up for Google Analytics. Registering your site allows Google to collect and report data from your site. **Before visiting the Google Analytics entry page, make certain that you are signed into Google with the account that you want associated with Google Analytics**. Then, create a Google Analytics account as follows:

1. Go to the Google Analytics main page at:

    `http://www.google.com/analytics/`

    Click the **ACCESS GOOGLE ANALYTICS** link on the top right-hand side of the page.

2. On the next page, click the **SIGN UP** button on the right side of the page.

3. You'll now see where you let Google Analytics know your site specifics. The **Website** box is highlighted on the top of the page, . Leave this box as is.

4. Scroll down (if necessary) to **Setting up your account**.

5. In the "Account Name" text box beneath **Setting up your account** type in the name that you will use to identify your Google Analytics master account. Label your account "My Travel Site."

6. Scroll down (if necessary) to **Setting up your property**. In Google Analytics, a web property is the total set of pages on which your tracking code is installed. Every property has a unique ID which you will receive later in the registration process. Name your property "My Travel Website" in the "Website Name" text box.

7. The next text box (labeled "Website URL") asks for your website URL. Type in the full URL (including the subdirectory, if any) at which your website resides. This is the path by which you access the home page of your site. Thus, for my site, I would type in:

    `http://www.googleanalyticsdemystified.com/xqanqeon/`

8. Choose "Other" for **Industry category**.

9. Select your country and time zone from the next pair of pull-down menus.

10. Leave the four boxes on the bottom of the page checked.

11. Click on the blue **Get Tracking ID** button.

12. **Accept** the terms of service. You should then see a "Success" message on the top of the page.

After you have successfully completed the registration process, you'll be taken to the page which provides your unique Google Analytics tracking code. This code appears in the box labeled:

> "This is your tracking code. Copy and paste it into the code of every page you want to track."

For the moment, this is all that concerns us on this page.

My tracking code is as shown below.

```
<script>
  (function(i,s,o,g,r,a,m){i['GoogleAnalyticsObject']=r;i[r]=i[r]||function(){
  (i[r].q=i[r].q||[]).push(arguments)},i[r].l=1*new Date();a=s.createElement(o),
  m=s.getElementsByTagName(o)[0];a.async=1;a.src=g;m.parentNode.insertBefore(a,m)
  })(window,document,'script','//www.google-analytics.com/analytics.js','ga');

  ga('create', 'UA-54675304-1', 'auto');
  ga('send', 'pageview');

</script>
```

Your tracking code will look identical to mine **except** that in the third to last line you will see your unique tracking number (which starts with "UA-" and ends in "1"). You may also see your domain name in place of **'auto'**. Note that this tracking code is only intended for use on websites and on the website which you described in the registration process. A different implementation of the code is required for mobile or app tracking and for different websites or blogs you may wish to track. In this book, we address the most common implementation of Google Analytics: website or blog data collection for a single domain.

Copy and save the GATC in a text file for future use. This is the easiest way to retrieve the code. However, if you need but don't have access to the code at a later date, see the addendum to this chapter for how to retrieve your code.

You should move on to the next step while the analytics tracking code is still displayed in your browser window. This will facilitate the addition of the GATC to each page of your website. If you no longer have access to the page with the GATC, use the code you copy and pasted into a text file.

Your travel website folder contains HTML and other file types and folders. The following non-HTML files/folders are in your travel website folder:

Folders:	brochure
	images
	information
Javascript:	form-tracking-google-analytics-V2.js
	google-analytics-scroll-tracking_ua.js
CSS:	templateo_style.css

You do not need to worry about any of these. These items never need to be modified and need to be uploaded only once to your server.

The remaining files in your travel website folder are HTML files. Each of these files must have the Google Analytics tracking code added to its source code. We'll divide your site's pages into four sets, as each set needs a slightly different customization.

Set 1: Core Pages

The first set of pages contains the following:

> contact.html
> index.html
> information.html
> mediaplay.html
> purchase.html

Each of these pages needs to contain the Google Analytics tracking code. You can achieve this as follows:

1. Copy the Google Analytics tracking code (GATC) into your computer's memory.

2. Open the ".html" page in your selected text or HTML editor.

2. Look at the HTML source code for the page. You'll notice two HTML tags labeled **<HEAD>** and **</HEAD>** near the top of the page's HTML code. Each page will have some code already present between these two tags. Leave this code as is. (Note that the code will differ across pages and will be discussed later in the book.) Look for the closing **</HEAD>** tag.

4. Paste the GATC just prior to the closing **</HEAD>** tag, as shown on the next page.

```html
<head>

<meta http-equiv="Content-Type" content="text/html; charset=UTF-8"/>
<title>xqanqeon - Buy a trip</title>
<meta name="keywords" content="xqanqeon" />
<meta name="description" content="xqanqeon" />
<link href="templatemo_style.css" rel="stylesheet" type="text/css" />

<script>
  (function(i,s,o,g,r,a,m){i['GoogleAnalyticsObject']=r;i[r]=i[r]||function(){
  (i[r].q=i[r].q||[]).push(arguments)},i[r].l=1*new Date();a=s.createElement(o),
  m=s.getElementsByTagName(o)[0];a.async=1;a.src=g;m.parentNode.insertBefore(a,m)
  })(window,document,'script','//www.google-analytics.com/analytics.js','ga');

  ga('create', 'UA-54675304-1', 'auto');
  ga('send', 'pageview');

</script>

</head>
```

Adding the GATC to each of these pages allows the page to send data to Google Analytics. However, we want to maximize the chances for Google and other search engines to list your site in search results. Later on, this will help you better understand how Google Analytics distinguishes organic referral traffic to your website from paid search and other referral sources. In order to accomplish this, it is necessary for you to incorporate your unique site name in key places on *each of these five pages*. This can be accomplished as follows:

Near the top of each page's source code you should see three lines of HTML code similar to that shown below, which was taken from the purchase page of the travel website:

```html
<title>UNIQUE NAME - Buy a tour</title>
<meta name="keywords" content="UNIQUE NAME" />
<meta name="description" content="UNIQUE NAME" />
```

We have already customized the top line of each page to reflect that page's content. This is the title of the page which is displayed on the top of the browser when the page is loaded. In this case, visitors will see your site name and "Buy a tour" when they load this page. What you need to do is customize each core page with the unique name you selected earlier.

On all three lines, replace the phrase UNIQUE NAME (leave the quotation marks if they are present) with the unique, one-of-a-kind name that you've chosen for your site. This will be the same name that appears after the "/" in the URL of your site and is the name that you used to name your travel website folder. Thus, for example, My site's full URL is:

http://www.googleanalyticsdemystified.com/xqanqeon/

As a result, my three lines of code read as follows, where "xqanqeon" has been substituted for "UNIQUE NAME":

```
<title>xqanqeon - Buy a trip</title>
<meta name="keywords" content="xqanqeon" />
<meta name="description" content="xqanqeon" />
```

Customize and save each of the five core pages with your unique name and then move on to the next step.

Set 2: Home page

Follow the prior directions to add the GATC to your home page (`index.html`) and to customize the page with your unique name. Next, your home page contains text which will need to be customized. You'll notice that there are four instances of UNIQUE NAME in the description. As before, replace the phrase UNIQUE NAME with the one-of-a-kind name that you selected for the site (and which you used in the prior step). Since my unique name is "xqanqeon" my block of text reads:

> This is a test site for instruction in Google Analytics. The name of the site is xqanqeon. Hopefully search engines will index this site as xqanqeon so that we can see the search terms used to find the site. For the last time, the name of the site is xqanqeon. We've put the term xqanqeon in the page title to help in indexing.

Save the page when you are done, making certain that it retains its original name and .html suffix.

Set 3: Concept pages

Your folder contains eight pages which will be used later to illustrate specific Google Analytics concepts. These pages are:

chap45.html	events.html
chap47.html	thanks_c.html
chap48.html	information1a.html
chap52.html	information1b.html

All that you need to do with these pages is incorporate the GATC prior to the closing **</HEAD>** tag as you did with the prior pages. Note that some of these pages will contain additional code between the **<HEAD>** and **</HEAD>** tags. Just leave this code unaltered and paste the GATC just prior to the closing **</HEAD>** tag. Beyond adding the GATC, no further customization of these pages is required.

Save each page with its original name when done.

Set 4: Purchase confirmation pages

Your site contains six purchase confirmation pages:

thanks_p2b.html	thanks_p2m.html
thanks_p10b.html	thanks_p10m.html
thanks_p15b.html	thanks_p15m.html

Each page transmits simulated ecommerce data to Google Analytics. Due to the large amount of HTML code on each page, we've created these pages in a way that allows you to customize each page by changing only one line of code. You'll see on the top of the page a group of code immediately after the first **<HEAD>** tag. One of the lines contains the phrase PASTE ACCOUNT NUMBER HERE, as shown below:

<head>

<script>

```
(function(i,s,o,g,r,a,m){i['GoogleAnalyticsObject']=r;i[r]=i[r]||function(){
(i[r].q=i[r].q||[]).push(arguments)},i[r].l=1*new Date();a=s.createElement(o),
m=s.getElementsByTagName(o)[0];a.async=1;a.src=g;m.parentNode.insertBefore(a,m)
})(window,document,'script','//www.google-analytics.com/analytics.js','ga');

ga('create', 'PASTE ACCOUNT NUMBER HERE', 'auto');

ga('send', 'pageview');
```

Replace PASTE ACCOUNT NUMBER HERE with UA and the number from your GATC. Do not remove the ' marks. When this is done, the code will look like this (of course, with your own account number):

<head>

<script>

```
(function(i,s,o,g,r,a,m){i['GoogleAnalyticsObject']=r;i[r]=i[r]||function(){
(i[r].q=i[r].q||[]).push(arguments)},i[r].l=1*new Date();a=s.createElement(o),
m=s.getElementsByTagName(o)[0];a.async=1;a.src=g;m.parentNode.insertBefore(a,m)
})(window,document,'script','//www.google-analytics.com/analytics.js','ga');

ga('create', 'UA-54675304-1', 'auto');

ga('send', 'pageview');
```

Make this change on each of the six purchase confirmation pages, saving each page as it is modified.

Upload and confirm that your newly customized site is working

FTP the entire travel agency folder to your server, that is, **all** files and internal folders. Then, visit via your primary URL. Use the links on the top of the pages to make certain that they work and that all your changes appear as intended. You should see your unique name as part of each core page's title. Your unique name should also be incorporated into the text on the home page. Note that the non-core pages are not reachable through any of the page links. These pages are intended for special use later in the book.

Depending upon what you see, you will need to either redo the prior step or move on to the next step. If you are unsure as to how the site should look, you can view my site at:

http://www.googleanalyticsdemystified.com/xqanqeon/

Make certain you have the Google Chrome browser

If you already have Chrome installed on your computer then you're set. Skip to the next step. If you need to install Chrome follow the instructions at:

https://support.google.com/chrome/answer/95346?hl=en

Populate your site with data

While you can use any browser to generate data on your site, I recommend that you use Google Chrome, in great part because of the ease with which you can erase your browsing history and thus easily (and repeatedly) visit your site as a "new" visitor.

Wait a day from the time you uploaded your final version of the site. Then, using Chrome or another browser, visit your site. Visit every page, fill out and send the contact form (no form will actually be sent) and order a trip or two. Then clear Chrome's browsing history and visit again. Visit just one page. Clear Chrome's browsing history and visit again. Do something different. Continue until you have five or so visits to the site.

Wait a day. Then, go on to the next chapter.

If you are not sure how to clear Chrome's browsing history see the chapter addendum on the next page.

Chapter Addendum 1: Clearing Chrome's Browsing History

1. From the Chrome menu, select **Clear browsing data**.

2. In the dialog box that appears, make certain that "Browsing history," "Download history," and "Cookies and other site and plug-in data" are checked.

3. Select **the beginning of time** to clear your entire browsing history.

4. Click on the gray **Clear browsing history** button to return to your browser.

Chapter Addendum 2: Retrieving GATC

You can retrieve your Google Analytics Tracking Code at any time from the Google Analytics site, as follows:

1. Make certain that you are signed into the Google account associated with your travel website. Then, go to the Google Analytics main page at:

    `http://www.google.com/analytics/`

    Click the **ACCESS GOOGLE ANALYTICS** link on the top right-hand side of the page.

2. On the top of the next page, click on **Admin.**

3. The next page will display three columns, indicating the single account, property, and view associated with the account you set up earlier. In the middle column is a link labeled **Tracking Info**. Click on this link to reveal a new submenu. From this new menu select the top link, labeled **Tracking Code**. When this link is selected, your tracking code will be displayed.

2
Verifying Data Collection

We now need to confirm that Google Analytics is tracking visits and visitor behaviors. Confirmation requires that you visit Google Analytics at:

http://www.google.com/analytics

Make certain that you are signed into the Google account associated with your travel website prior to visiting. If not, sign in and continue.

Viewing your data

When you arrive at the Google Analytics home page, click on **Access Google Analytics** (in the upper right hand corner of the page). You'll then see your Google Analytics home page. Your account, which should be labeled "My Travel Site," will be shown next to a folder icon. Your property is named "My Travel Website." If this property is not displayed, click on the account name to expand the view (see opposite).

Next we want to see the data viewing options for this property. At this point, you'll have just a single option, which will be labeled **All Web Site Data** (see opposite). If this option is not displayed, click on the folder icon next to the property name to see this view. The globe icon next to **All Web Site Data** indicates that data is available through this link.

At the main administrator's page, you'll see an estimate of the number of sessions on the same line as **All Web Site Data.** Several factors may lead to a situation in which the session count reported on this page is lower than your true session count. As a result, It is typically best to use the session count on your starting data reporting page, described next.

Clicking on your data view (in this case, **All Web Site Data)** takes you to your **Audience Overview** page, as illustrated below. Note that the session count of six is reported along with other summary data, such as three users.[1] If all has worked as expected, you should see a page that resembles this, only reporting your website's data. If there is a session count and other data on this page, congratulations, your site is operational and Google Analytics is collecting data. If there is no data, wait a day and check again. If there is still no data (and you confirmed that your GATC can be read), then your tracking code is present but not working properly. Review the steps outlined in the prior chapter and revise/re-upload as necessary.

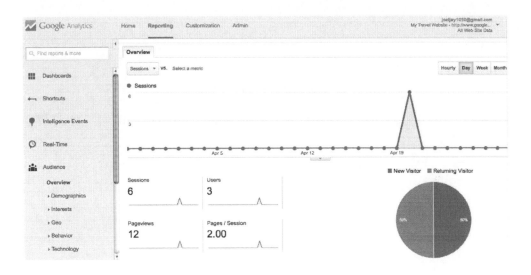

---

[1] For the moment, think of a "session" as a visit to your site and a "user" as a site visitor. More precise definitions are presented later in the book.

3
Registering Your Site With Google

You improve the chances of your site showing up in Google search results when you explicitly bring the site to Google's attention. You bring your site to Google's attention through the following registration process.

1. Go to Google Webmaster Tools at:

    https://www.google.com/webmasters/tools/home

    If necessary sign in using the Google account associated with your travel website.

2. On the "Welcome to Webmaster Tools" page, type your complete site URL in the **Add a Site** box. Make certain that you include the subdirectory name. In my case, for example, the full URL to my site is:

    http://www.googleanalyticsdemystified.com/xqanqeon

    Click **Add a Site** when done.

3. On the next page, leave **Recommended Method** selected and then follow the instructions (similar to those shown below). You will upload the file provided by Webmaster Tools to the root (not the sub) directory of your site. Leave your browser window open to this page while you are following the directions. Click **Verify** when you are done.

    Recommended: HTML file upload

    Upload an HTML file to your site.

    1. Download this HTML verification file. [google9ae1325eeca8ad24.html]

    2. Upload the file to http://www.classmatandread.net/telxqmq/

    3. Confirm successful upload by visiting http://www.classmatandread.net/telxqmq/google9ae1325eeca8ad24.html in your browser.

    4. Click Verify below.

    To stay verified, don't remove the HTML file, even after verification succeeds.

4. If you've done as instructed, you'll see the confirmation page that says "Congratulations." If this is the case, then click **Continue.** If you do not see the "Congratulations" then redo the prior step.

5. The next page (after you click **Continue**) will display menu options on the left-hand side of the page. Click **Crawl** and then **Fetch as Google**.

6. On the next page (shown below) make certain that the displayed URL is correct. If your site is in a subdirectory, type the subdirectory name into the text box. If all looks right, click **Fetch** (which is located on the right-hand side of the page in the orange box).

7. You'll see **Fetch Status** change to Pending.

8. Within the next 1 to 15 minutes, your screen will continue to update. Have patience until the **Pending** label changes to **Success** (see bottom line of figure below). If this hasn't happened within 15 minutes, press **Fetch** again. When you're successful, the screen will look like that shown below, where **Success** is shown beneath **Fetch Status**.

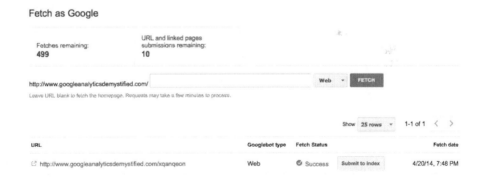

9. Press **Submit to Index**. You'll see the popup window shown on the top of the next page. Select **Crawl only this URL** and click **OK**.

10. A successful submission will change the **Submit to Index** label to **URL Submitted to Index.**

11. After a few minutes, conduct a Google search using your unique identifying keyword. Your results should look similar to this where the home page of my site is listed in the search results for "xqanqeon."

xqanqeon - Home Page Welcome
www.googleanalyticsdemystified.com/**xqanqeon**/ ▾
This is a test site for instruction in Google Analytics. The name of the site is **xqanqeon**.
xqanqeon refers to this site. Hopefully the search engines will index this ...

4

Registering as an Ecommerce Site

Google Analytics needs to be informed if a site is engaged in ecommerce in order to process purchase and related information. We inform Google Analytics of our engagement in ecommerce in one of two ways. Try this approach first:

1. Visit the Google Analytics site at:

    `http://www.google.com/analytics`

    Sign in, if necessary, using the Google account associated with your travel website. You will then see your Google Analytics home page.

2. On the top of the home page, click **Admin**.

3. The next page will display three columns indicating the one account, property, and view associated with the account you set up earlier. The far right column contains a link labeled **Ecommerce Settings**. If you do not see this link, try the alternative approach discussed below.

4. Click on the **Ecommerce Settings** link to reveal a new page. Beneath **Enable Ecommerce** is a slider bar set to "Off." Click on this bar to turn it "On" and then click on **Next Step**.

5. Leave **Enhanced Ecommerce Settings** set to "Off" and press **Submit**. You will then see a message noting "Success" on the top of the page. Click on **Home** on the top of the page to return to your Google Analytics home page.

If no **Ecommerce Settings** option appears in your View column, then turn on ecommerce as follows:

1. Visit the Google Analytics site at:

    `http://www.google.com/analytics`

    Sign in, if necessary, using the Google account associated with your travel website. You will then see your Google Analytics home page.

2. On the top of the next page, click **Admin**.

3. The next page will display three columns indicating the one account, property, and view associated with the account you set up earlier. On the top of the far right column there should be a link labeled **View Settings**. Click on this link to reveal a new page labeled "Reporting View Settings." Scroll down until you see **Ecommerce Settings**. Flip the **Off** switch to **On** and click **Save** on the bottom of the page.

4. You will then see a message noting "Success" on the top of the page. Click on **Home** on the top of the page to return to your Google Analytics home page.

5

Populating Your Site With Data

We will soon lead you through an examination of the types of data available through Google Analytics. This examination and accompanying discussion will be much more meaningful if you are able to apply the discussion to your own data. As a result, it would be valuable for you to populate your site with data. You can do this using one or both of the approaches described below. Both are recommended.

- Populate your travel agency site with data yourself. Here, using your Chrome browser, visit the site and view one or more pages, use the contact form, buy a tour, etc. Clear your browser history after every three or so visits in order to obtain a mix of new and returning users. Do this twenty or thirty times. Your visit can originate either through direct access by typing the desired site page into your browser or by using Google search results, if available.

- Ask your friends to populate the site with data. You can use email or social media to display/send links to your site. Some links can go to the home page while other links may go directly to the purchase or contact page. Encourage your friends to use different links and visit several times over the course of a day or two, engaging differently with the site each time. You can also provide your friends with a search term that they can use to find and access your site via search results.

You can check to see if data is accumulating by following the procedures outlined in Chapter 2.

Google Analytics Demystified

Section II:
Account Management

A prerequisite to the useful acquisition of Google Analytics data is that all administrative functions be understood and completed prior to a significant amount of data being collected. The chapters in this section help you understand Google Analytics account structure and how to apply this structure to ensure that data is being collected and disseminated in the most efficient manner.

- Chapter 6 introduces you to Google Analytics account structure, and explains the characteristics and inter-relationships of accounts, properties, and views.

- Chapter 7 shows you how to create and modify accounts, properties, and views.

- Chapter 8 provides the book's first set of application exercises. You can use these exercises to evaluate how well you understand the concepts in Chapters 6 and 7.

- Chapter 9 explains how to give others access to your data. Chapter 10 provides application exercises related to account access.

Accounts, Properties, and Views

So far, you've set up one Google Analytics account with one property and a single view within that property. You've used this account, property and view to check whether or not Google Analytics was collecting data from your site. This chapter explains accounts, properties, and views, their relationship to each other, and how to expand your options in terms of multiple accounts, properties, and views.

Let's begin with a look at the account, property, and view hierarchy. Then, we'll see how to organize accounts and properties to best meet different types of advertising or business situations.

The account, property, and view hierarchy

Google Analytics is organized around a hierarchy of accounts, properties and views. Any single account can have one or more properties and each property, in turn, can have one or more views. The figure shown below provides a real-life example and also shows how any single Google user ID (such as the email address you use to log into Google Analytics) can have multiple accounts, each of which in turn can have multiple properties and views.

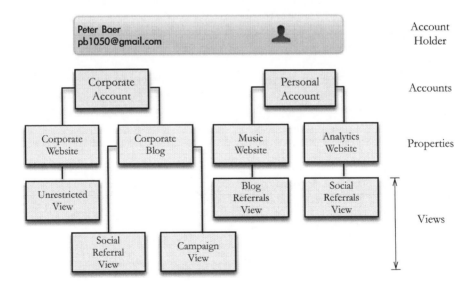

Let's look at this structure.

- Peter is the account holder. He uses his Google ID **pb1050@gmail.com** to log into various Google properties including Google Analytics.

- Peter has access to two accounts at Google Analytics. These accounts reflect his two roles. Since Peter is the analytics manager for his company, the first account he has access to collects data relevant to his company's website. Peter also has a personal account which he manages.

- Peter's company uses Google Analytics to help it understand two of its digital properties. One property is the company website and the second property is the company blog. Peter also uses Google Analytics to help him collect information on two of his personal digital endeavors: a music website and an analytics website. Since the company and personal accounts are set up separately, the data from the two never intermix.

- The chart shows the views, or ways of looking at the data, collected by Google Analytics for each of the properties. One view is shown for the corporate website and two views are shown for the corporate blog. More views are used, but they are omitted so that the amount of clutter in the chart is minimized. Some of the views associated with Peter's music blog and analytics blog are also shown.

With this in mind, the following sections explain the characteristics of accounts, properties, and views.

What is an account?

As can be seen in the prior figure, accounts are at the top of the hierarchy. A Google Analytics account is a way to name and organize how you collect data from one or more properties. Every Google Analytics user has access to at least one account, either the one they created themselves (as you did in Chapter 1) or one that they were given access to by someone else.

The first page you see when you sign into Google Analytics (the home page) provides a listing of all the accounts associated with your Google ID.

I have two accounts: one that I use for instructional purposes, "My Travel Site", and one that monitors my personal web properties, labeled "Personal Accounts" (see opposite).

If the properties associated with an account are not displayed, then clicking on the folder icon to the left of the account name displays all of the properties associated with that account, as shown opposite. In my case, the same as yours, one property is associated with the account set up for this book ("My Travel Site/My Travel Website"). In addition, two properties are associated with my "Personal Accounts." One property monitors my website activity and the other monitors my Wordpress blog.

You **cannot** migrate historical data from one account to another. Thus, if you set up an account for a web property, you cannot later move that property to another account.

What is a property?

A property can be a website, a mobile application, a blog -- any page or screen that receives traffic via the web or mobile app. Within any Google Analytics account, you can identify one or more properties from which you want to collect visitor data. Google Analytics generates the unique tracking code that collects data from each property. As we saw earlier, I have two properties associated with my account labeled "Personal Accounts."

You can tell the relationship between properties and accounts by looking at the Google Analytics identification number that follows each property name. Every account has a unique identification number and, as a result, different identification numbers keep the accounts separate. In my case (as illustrated in the screen capture shown on the top of this page), the primary identification number for "My Travel Site" is "UA-50182280" while the primary identification number for "Personal Accounts" is "UA-50203869". The dashed digit at the end of the identification number is the unique property identifier. Within "Personal Accounts," for example, my blog is one property associated with this account (indicated by the "-1"), while my website is another property within the account (indicated by use of the same account number but followed by a "-2" at the end of the identification number).

When setting up properties within accounts, **never** assign the same property to more than one account as this will seriously affect data integrity and the validity of subsequent analyses.

Relationship between accounts and properties

You can use a one-to-one relationship of *one account/one property*, or you can use a one-to-many relationship of *one account/many properties*. You can also have multiple Google Analytics accounts (as I do), where each of which contains one or more properties.

One Account/One Property

This is the simplest configuration. Here, you've associated a single account with your Google identity and you've created one property to be tracked within that account. This is comparable to having just one corporate website or one corporate blog that you want to track. Your current Google Analytics configuration uses this approach.

One Account/Multiple Properties

Imagine that your situation is a bit more complex: you want to track both a corporate website and a corporate blog simultaneously and you want to keep the data collected from each source independent of the other. You still need only one account, but now you would have two properties (corporate website and corporate blog) associated with a single account. This is similar to what I do with my Personal Accounts.

Multiple Accounts

If you manage Google Analytics for multiple websites that belong to multiple clients, you can create a separate Google Analytics account for each client with as many properties and views as necessary within each account. This type of organization lets you give your clients access to their unique accounts, and ensures that clients are not able to view one another's data.

Once you have set up your accounts and properties, it then becomes necessary to decide the characteristics of the data you want to view. This is where **Views** come in.

What is a view?

Views determine the specific data you see for a property. Whenever you set up a property, Google Analytics sets up an unfiltered view for that property's data which by default is labeled **All Web Site Data**. An unfiltered view means that 100% of the data collected is shown in all of that view's reports.

But, this does not have to be the case. Google Analytics allows up to 50 views for each property and these views can be added at any time. Why, though, would you need more than the unfiltered, complete data view?

You may not need 50 views, but there are some views that you should be certain to create for each property. It's a good idea to create these views early in the process, as the data reported in a view includes only the data collected since the view was created. If, for example, you create a new view on June 1, then you can examine data from June 1 forward, but you will not be able to see any data collected prior to June 1 in that view.

Most views are created by adding filters, where a filter defines what data are included and excluded from a particular view. For now, let's identify the different types of alternative views and filters that underlie good analytics practice. The next two chapters will take you through the steps required to create new accounts, properties, and views with and without filters.

There are four views that every property should have.

Ideally, since views do not report historical data, all four views should be created at the time you initiate analytics data collection . Views only report data onwards from the date they were created.

View 1: Raw, unfiltered data

This is the view we just discussed. It is the easiest view to set up because there are no filters involved. This default view for any property presents 100% of all data collected. This view is important because it is your backup should anything "bad" happen to the other views. For example, if any of your other views have issues with your Google Analytics setup, you will be able to refer to your raw data to get to the bottom of the issue, or if you inappropriately apply a filter to another view, this view will help you recover data that would otherwise have been lost. This is a valuable asset as Google Analytics will not repopulate the data in a view, even if filters are removed or adjusted.

View 2: Internal sources of traffic are eliminated

It's likely that a significant amount of traffic is generated by you or other individuals whose behaviors and characteristics are of no interest. This might include others who work for your company or vendors who are working on the site. Creating this view results in data reports that provide only the traffic you consider relevant, while excluding any traffic you consider irrelevant. You can apply one or more filters to create this view.

View 3: Filters test view

As much as we all try to avoid error, it is nevertheless the case that nearly everyone working with Google Analytics has at one time made a mistake in applying filters. When an erroneous filter is applied to a working data file, the results can be devastating as filtered data cannot be recovered. While this file doesn't eliminate inappropriate or erroneous filters, it does eliminate the disaster associated with these filters. This view is a place to try out new filters before they are applied to the working file of View 2. Try out your new filters here and monitor the results for a week or so. If all seems to be working fine, then apply this filter to the working file, delete this view with its filter, and create a new replacement view file which can be used the next time you want to try out a new filter.

View 4: Experimental test view

This view is similar to View 3 in intent. It is a place for you to test actions related to goals, funnels, custom variables, and other approaches to customizing Google Analytics. (These topics will be discussed in later chapters.) Try out your ideas here before incorporating them into your working view. As with View 3, monitor the results for a week or so. If all seems to be working fine, then apply your new customizations to the working file. Then, when necessary, delete this file and create a new experimental file to allow for the evaluation of future customization attempts.

7
Managing Accounts, Properties, and Views

Chapter Six introduced you to the concepts of accounts, properties, and views. This chapter helps you learn how to create new accounts, properties and views. No actual web presence is required beyond that which you already created earlier in the book. The examples in this chapter are for practice rather than actual data collection.

The activities in this chapter will help you learn how to execute the most common functions related to accounts, properties and views. You will learn how to:

-   Create a new Google Analytics account and property to supplement the account created in Chapter One

-   Add a second property to an account

-   Rename an existing view

-   Duplicate an existing view

-   Delete an existing view

-   Create an entirely new view

-   Delete an existing property

-   Delete an existing account

Accessing Administrative Functions

Make certain that you login to Google Analytics using the same Google ID that you used to create your travel agency account and property.

You create new accounts, properties and views as well as manage these items via the Google Analytics administrator page. To access the administrator's page, click **Admin** at the top of your home page after you have logged into Google Analytics.

There are three columns of information whenever you access this page through the **Admin** link. The left column is labeled **Account**, the middle column is labeled **Property**, and the right-hand column is labeled **View** (see below). Beneath each column label is a pull-down menu through which you access existing accounts, properties and views or create new ones. Your administrator's page should look similar to mine, where the account name is "My Travel Site", the property name is 'My Travel Website" and the view name is "All Web Site Data".

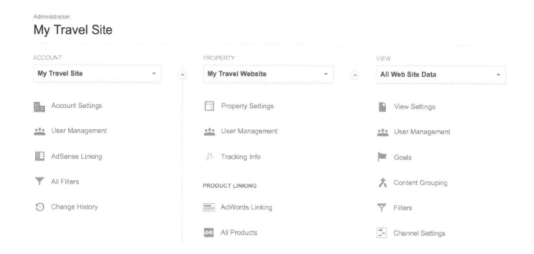

The specific names shown in each column of the administrator's page are dependent upon what you did during your last visit to Google Analytics.

- If you have just logged in and not selected a view, then the administrator's page opens to the first account listed on the **All Accounts** page. No property or view is selected.

- If you were in **Reporting** or **Customization**, then the page opens to the relevant account, property, and view.

With this in mind, let's create a new account with an associated property.

Create a new account and associated property

Your new account will have the following characteristics:

      Account name: Account 2

      Property name: My personal blog

      View name: Leave as default - All Web Site Data

      Website: www.chapter7.net

You begin by pulling down the "Account names" menu as shown below.

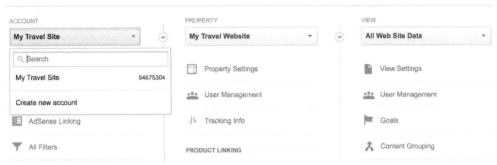

Select **Create new account** from the menu choices. This will take you to the "Account Creation" page. The steps you follow to create a new account and property are the same as those you followed to set up your travel agency website account and property. See if you can complete this process on your own. When you are done and subsequently return to your start page (by pressing the **Home** icon on the top of the page), you should see the figure shown opposite. Remember, if nothing appears below "Account 2" you can click on the folder icon to reveal the property and view.

If **All Web Site Data** is not displayed, click on the file folder icon next to **My personal blog.**

If you are having trouble creating this new account and property, follow the directions below after you select **Create new account** from the **Account** pull-down menu.

1. You'll see the page where you let Google Analytics know the parameters for data collection. On the top of the page, the **Website** box is highlighted. Leave this box checked.

2. Scroll down to **Setting up your account**.

3. In the box beneath **Setting up your account,** type in the name that you want to use to identify your Google Analytics account. This box is labeled "Account Name." Name your account "Account 2."

4. Scroll down to **Setting up your property**. You'll recall that, a web property is the total set of pages on which your tracking code is installed. Every property has a unique ID that you will receive later in the registration process. Name your property "My personal blog".

5. Beneath the property name is a text box labeled "Website URL." This is the full URL path by which you access the home page of your site. For this exercise type in "www.chapter7.net".

6. Choose "Other" for **Industry**.

7. Select the appropriate country and time zone from the next pair of pull-down menus.

8. Leave the four boxes on the bottom of the page checked.

9. Click **Get Tracking ID**.

10. **Accept** the terms of service.

If you've successfully followed these steps, you should see the figure shown on the middle of page 33 when you click on the **Home** link .

Add a second property to the account

The procedure for adding an additional property to an account is very similar to that just followed for adding a new account. Let's add a second property to the "Account 2" account. We'll call this property "My personal website". As before, click on **Admin** to go to the administrator's page. Make certain that "Account 2" is displayed in the account column (the left-hand column). If it is not displayed, then use the pull-down menu to select it.

Now, pull down the property menu and select **Create new property**, as shown below.

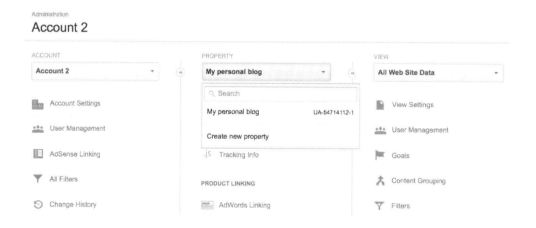

See if you can create a new property named "My personal website" at URL www.account2a.net. If you are successful you should see the figure shown opposite. Remember that you can see the view(s) associated with each property by clicking on the file folder icon next to the view name.

If you are having difficulty, follow the directions below after you have selected **Create new property**.

1. On the top of the page, the **Website** box is highlighted. Leave this as it is.

2. Scroll down to **Setting up your property**. Your website name is: "My personal website."

3. The website URL is: "www.account2a.net."

4. Choose "Other" for **Industry**.

5. Select the appropriate country and time zone from the next pair of pull-down menus.

6. Click **Get Tracking ID**.

7. On the tracking code page, click on the **Home** icon on the top left-hand side of the page to return to your starting home page.

If you followed these steps successfully, you should see the figure shown opposite which lists the two properties in your new account.

Rename an existing view

One view, "All Web Site Data", already exists for the property "My personal website" in "Account 2". Based on the prior example, try to rename this view to "View 1: Unfiltered".

If you are having difficulty, follow these steps:

1. Click on **Admin** to go to the administrator's page.

2. Use the pull-down menus to make certain that the account is "Account 2", the property is "My personal website", and the view is "All Web Site Data", as shown below.

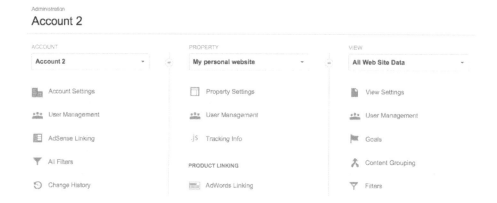

3. Click on **View Settings** in the right-most **View** column.

4. On the next page, in the **View Name** box, delete "All Web Site Data" and type "View 1: Unfiltered" as shown below.

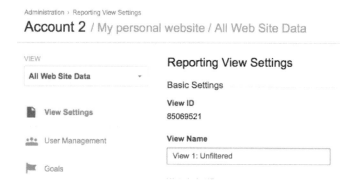

5. Scroll to the bottom of the page and press **Save.** A message on the top of the page should indicate that the renaming process was a "Success."

6. Click on the **Home** icon on the top left side of the page to return to the main home page where you should see the account, property, and view shown opposite

After the prior step, "My personal website" has one view. We now want to duplicate this view. The new view should be named "View 2: Filtered". See if you can use the **View Settings** on the **Admin** page link to accomplish this. If you are having difficulty, follow these steps:

1. From whatever page you are on, click on **Admin** to go to the administrator's page.

2. Use the pull-down menus to make certain that the account is "Account 2", the property is "My personal website", and the view is "View 1: Unfiltered", as shown below.

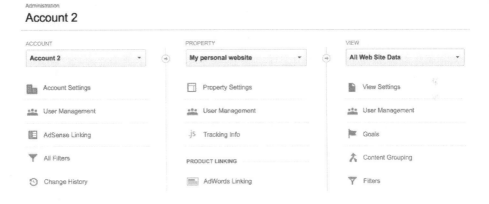

3. Click on **View Settings** in the right-most **View** column.

4. A new page will be displayed. On the top of the page and press **Copy view.**

5. On the top of the next page, delete the contents of the **Name** text box and then name the view "View 2: Filtered." Then press **Copy view.** A message on the top of the page should indicate that the duplication process was a "Success."

6. Click on the **Home** icon on the top left side of the page to return to the home page. If all has gone well you should see the figure opposite.

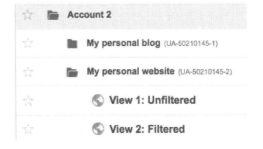

Two views now exist for the property "My personal website" in "Account 2". Based on the prior example, try to delete the view labeled "View 2: Filtered". If you are having difficulty, follow these steps.

1. From whatever page you are on, click on **Admin** to go to the administrator's page.

2. Use the pull-down menus to make certain that the account is "Account 2", the property is "My personal website", and the view is "View 2: Filtered", as shown below.

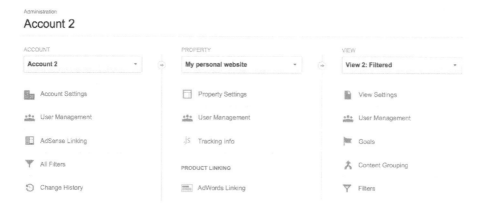

3. Click on **View Settings** in the right-most **View** column.

4. When the next page is displayed press **Delete view.**

5. On the next page confirm that you want to delete this view.

6. Click on the **Home** icon on the top left side of the next page to return to your home page. If all has gone well, you should see the display shown opposite.

Create a new view

Let's create an entirely new view, that will have the following characteristics: the account is "Account 2", the property is "My personal website", and the view name is "New View". See if you can use the **View Settings** link on the **Admin** page to accomplish this. If you are having difficulty, follow these steps:

1. From whatever page you are on, click on **Admin** to go to the administrator's page.

2. Use the pull-down menus to make certain that the account is "Account 2", the property is "My personal website", and the view is "View 1: Unfiltered".

3. Use the pull-down menu in the **View** column to display **Create new view**, as shown below. Click on this link.

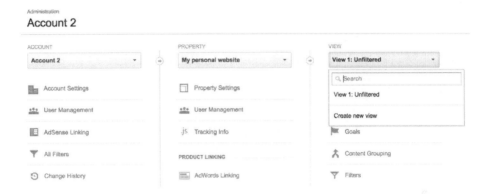

4. On the next page, leave **Website** highlighted.

5. Beneath **Setting up your view** is a text box labeled "Reporting View Name." Type "New View" into this box.

6. Click **Create view** on the bottom of the page. You will then be informed that the process has been a "Success." You should then see the new view name listed in the **View** column.

7. Click on the **Home** icon on the top left side of the page to return to the start page. If all has gone well you should see the view listed in the appropriate property.

Delete an existing property

You delete a property similarly to the way you delete a view. See if you can apply what you learned earlier about deleting a view to deleting the "My personal blog" property. If you are having trouble, just follow the steps below.

1. From whatever page you are on, click on **Admin**.

2. Use the pull-down menus to make certain that the account is "Account 2" and the Property is "My personal blog". There is only one view associated with this property: "All Website Data".

3. Click on **Property Settings** in the middle **Property** column.

4. When the next page appears, press **Delete property.**

5. On the next page, confirm that you want to delete this property.

6. You'll then see the page shown below. Note that the display has defaulted to our remaining property.

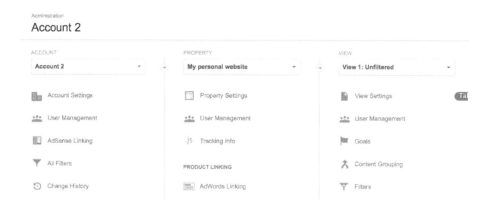

Delete an existing account

Finally, let's work through the steps required to delete an account. Don't actually delete the account, however, as it will be needed later in the book.

You delete an account the same way you delete a view. If we wanted to delete the "Account2" account, we would do the following:

1. From whatever page you are on, click on **Admin** to go to the administrator's page.

2. Use the pull-down menus to make certain that the Account is "Account 2," as shown below.

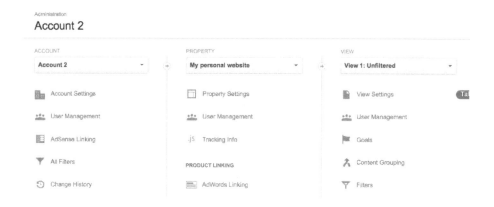

3. In the Account column, click on the top link, **Account Settings**.

4. When the next page is displayed, press **Delete account.**

5. On the next page we would confirm that you want to delete this account. **DO NOT COMPLETE THIS STEP.**

6. Click on the **Home** icon to return to your home page.

8

Practice With Accounts, Properties and Views

The exercises in this chapter address accounts, properties, and views. All of the information and procedures you'll need to respond to these exercises are presented in Chapters 6 and 7.

True/false and multiple choice

This first set of exercises explores your understanding of account, property, and view relationships and characteristics. You can check your answers on page 587.

1. CompanyCo owns four different websites that operate independently, that is, each website is for a different division, but are all part of the same company. You are assigned to monitor all four accounts but want to keep each division's data hidden from the other divisions. Which of the following is the **best** way to set up the account structure for these sites?

   a. Create four different accounts, one for each website.

   b. Create one account with four different properties, one for each division.

   c. Create four different views under one property (one for each website) so that the data for all four sites is combined in your reports.

2. John has a Google ID which he uses for his Gmail account. *True or False:* John can use this same ID to create new Google Analytics accounts.

3. *True or False:* There is a maximum of 15 views per property.

4. Jenny creates a single Google Analytics account in which there are two properties. Which of the following represents the most likely tracking code implementation?

   a. Property One: UA-41714766-1
      Property Two: UA-41714766-2

   b. Property One: UA-41714766-1
      Property Two: UA-41865468-1

5. *True or False:* A property and all of its accumulated data can be transferred from one account to another.

6. *True or False:* All properties must possess ecommerce capabilities.

7. *True or False:* The same property should not be assigned to more than one account.

8. Filters are applied to:

   a. Accounts

   b. Properties

   c. Views

   d. All of the above

9. *True or False:* Once views with filters have been created, there is no need to maintain the "raw, unfiltered" data view - this view can be deleted.

10. *True or False:* Which of the following can be deleted via the **Settings** link on the main administrator's page? Check all that apply.

    a. Accounts

    b. Properties

    c. Views

11. *True or False:* Views cannot be copied or duplicated.

12. *True or False:* Google Analytics allows a 60 day window for views to be created once a property is assigned a tracking code. After this window closes, no new views can be added to a property.

Hands-on

This second set of exercises explores your ability to create, modify, and delete accounts, properties and views. When you are done, or if you are stuck on a particular exercise, the procedures required to answer each exercise can be found on page 587.

1. Create a new Google Analytics account and property using the following information:

   Account name: Chapter8

   Property name: Exercises

   View name: Leave as default - All Web Site Data

   Website: www.chapter8.org

2. Add a second property to the Chapter8 account. Name this property "Property2".

3. Within Property2, change the name of "All Web Site Data" to "View1".

4. Notify Google Analytics that View1 is an ecommerce property.

5. Duplicate "View1". Name the duplicate file "View2".

6. Add an entirely new view to Property2. Name this view "View3".

7. Delete View3 from Property2.

8. Add a new view to Property2. Name this view "View4".

9. Delete Property2.

10. Delete the Chapter8 account.

Permissions

As the administrator of your account(s), you have complete and unrestricted access to all account functions. You can create and delete accounts, properties, and views and can determine what data is made available within various reports and views. You can also manage the format in which data appears.

In large companies, it is often necessary to share access to a Google Analytics account, property or view with others at the company. However, it is dangerous to allow everyone with access to manipulate account settings and property/view data. As a result, Google Analytics allows you to assign an individual the appropriately restricted level of access and interaction. Every individual you want to add must have a Google ID such as a Google email address.

Your first decision is to determine at what level you want to grant access. You can grant someone access at the account, property or view level. As you think about access levels, keep in mind that Google Analytics uses hierarchies to determine ultimate level of access. An individual given access at the account level, for example, has the potential for access to all properties and views within that account. Similarly, an individual with property level access will have potential access to all views within that property. Finally, an individual with view access will have access only to that individual view. As a general rule, you want to assign the lowest level of access that will allow the desired level of viewing and interaction.

There are three levels of interaction, which from highest to lowest are:

- **Edit**: Individuals with this level of access can perform administrative and report-related functions (e.g., add/edit/delete accounts, properties, views, filters, goals, etc., but not manage users) and see report data. These individuals also have the ability to engage in all the behaviors listed under Collaborate and Read & Analyze.

- **Collaborate**: Individuals with this level of access can create personal assets and share them. (*Assets* are tools that you create and use in Google Analytics to help you customize data analysis.) Individuals can also collaborate on shared assets, for example, edit a dashboard or annotation. These individuals also have the ability to engage in all the behaviors listed under Read & Analyze.

- **Read & Analyze**: Individuals with this level of access can see report and configuration data; can manipulate data within reports (e.g., filter a table, add a secondary dimension, create a segment); can create personal assets and share them; and can see shared assets. Individuals with this lowest level of access cannot collaborate on shared assets or perform any data editing.

Independent of level of access, you must also decide whether or not an individual will be allowed to **Manage Other Users**. An individual with this access can add or delete others at different levels of access and can assign permission to edit, collaborate, or read and analyze.

Assigning permissions

Once you have logged into Google Analytics, you assign permissions via the administrator's page, which you access by clicking **Admin** on the top of any page. Make certain that you have the desired account, property and view showing in the pull-down menus.

As shown below, all three columns on this page display an option for assigning permissions. Select **User Management** (the second link in each column) in the Account column if you want to assign permission at the account level. Select **User Management** in the Property column if you want to assign permission at the property level. Select **User Management** in the View column if you want to assign permission for just one specific view.

All **User Management** additions, changes and deletions follow the same procedure regardless of the level selected.

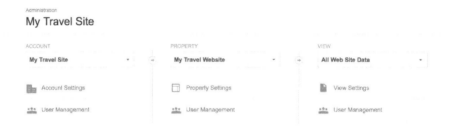

Creating permissions at the account level

Let's add a new user at the account level for our travel site. We want to make certain that "My Travel Site" is displayed in the far left hand-side Account column.

Clicking on **User Management** at the account level (that is, the second link in the far left-hand column on the administrator's page) takes us to the user management interface shown on the top of the next page. Notice that my email address appears in the first position as I am the initial administrator of the account. As such, I also have permission to manage users and have full access to all data-related functions.

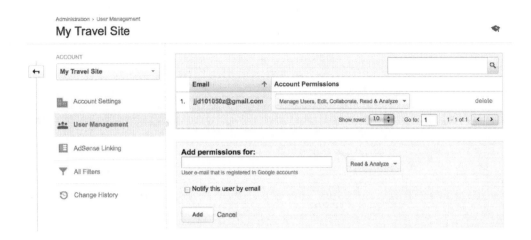

Pulling down the **Account Permissions** menu (see below) confirms that I have permission to do everything with this account.

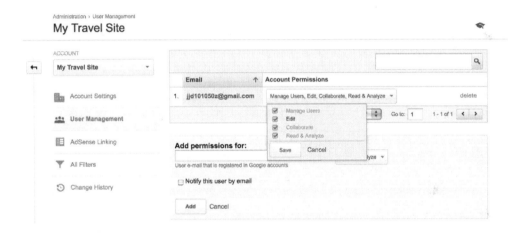

Now we'll start to add a new user to the account by filling in the **Add permissions for:** field with the email address of the new user, which in this case is "joeljay1050@gmail.com." Next, we'll use the pull-down menu next to the new user's email address to set the permission level (see the top of page 48). This new user will have permission at the Edit level, which includes Collaborate and Read & Analyze. Keep in mind that since we are setting permissions at the account level, this new individual will have Edit permissions for all properties and views within this account. Finally, we will not give this individual permission to Manage Users, so that box is left unchecked.

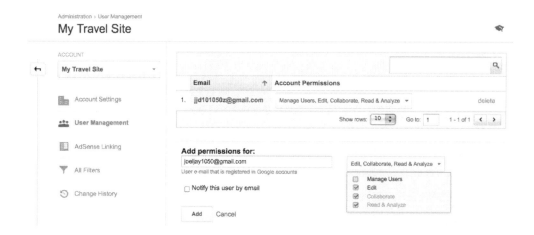

After all the information is checked, we click to inform the new user via email of access being granted and then we confirm by clicking **Add**, as shown below. We then receive a "Success" notification and see that the new user is now listed along with all others who have been granted permission (see below).

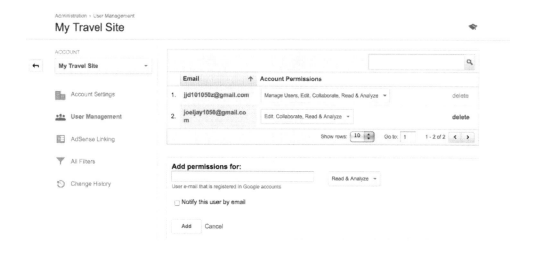

We can now click on the **Home** link (on the top of the page) to return to the Analytics start page.

The permissions hierarchy

We can follow the exact same steps to add a new user with permission at the property level. We'll add user permissionschapter9@gmail.com. The outcome is shown on the next page. Note how all the appropriate permissions are displayed similar to the prior, except now we are on the property level as opposed to the account level.

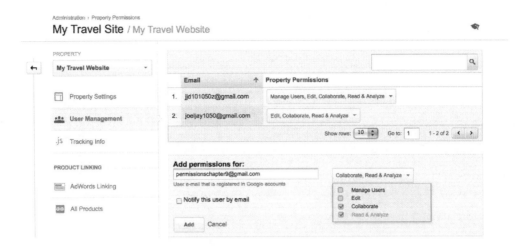

When we select **User Management** from the Account options (on the administrator's page) we see a different page, as shown below.

Notice how this user has no permission at the account level (as indicated by **None** being displayed in the Account Permissions pull-down menu). Clicking on **Permissions assigned at property or view level** brings up the screen shown on the top of page 50, which details the permissions relevant to this individual.

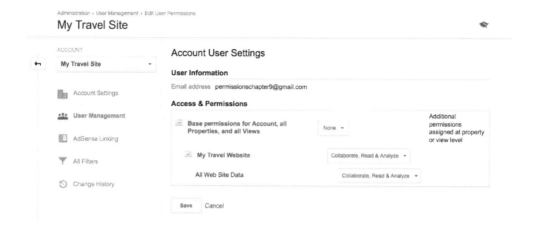

Modifying permissions

Finally, it is important to note that not only can a user be deleted (by pressing the relevant **Delete** button) but also that permissions can be further refined at any time through the pull-down menu next to the user's name, as shown below:

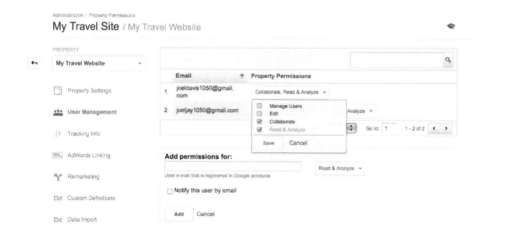

The selected check boxes can be changed to modify the level of permission. We can change permission from **Collaborate** to **Read & Analyze** by deselecting the check mark in the **Collaborate** box and then checking the box next to **Read & Analyze**.

10

Practice With Permissions

This chapter's three sets of exercises address permissions. All of the information and procedures you'll need to respond to these exercises are presented in Chapter 9.

True/false and multiple choice

This first set of exercises explores your understanding of permissions. You can check your answers on page 588.

1. Pearl is given user permission at the View level. What other level(s), if any, would she be able to access? Check all that apply.

   a. Property

   b. Account

2. You are the original administrator of your company's account. You give Ashley permission to Manage Other Users on this account. *True or False:* Ashley can delete you and remove your access to the account.

3. Your account has three properties. *True or False:* You can give Robert access to Collaborate on just one of the properties.

4. You want to give Barbara account level access so that she can perform all administrative and report-related functions. The level of access you would give her would be:

   a. Read & Analyze

   b. Collaborate

   c. Edit

5. *True or False:* Any individual who has Edit permission at the account level can add or delete users.

6. *True or False:* A Google ID (such as a Google email address) is required before one can be given permission to access a Google Analytics account.

7. *True or False:* Once you delete an individual from user permissions, that person can never again be given permission to access any account, property or view data.

8. *True or False:* An optional part of the user registration process is to have Google notify the individual by email that access has been granted.

Application

This set of exercises asks you apply your understanding of permissions. When you are done, or if you are stuck on a particular scenario, recommended responses can be found on page 588.

For each of the situations described below, decide the best level of permission. Explain your decision.

1. Tom is an intern who reports to you. Tom's primary job function is to monitor and report on the company's website traffic. Tom's email address is tomk@ gmail.com.

2. Your boss is named Kate Jones (KateJo@gmail.com). Kate wants to be actively involved in all aspects of how Google Analytics is used by the company and she wants to be as "hands-on" and involved as possible. Kate is also concerned about what will happen if you leave the company and she wants to be prepared to handle all possible contingencies, including adding and deleting users.

3. Amanda (amd339K@gmail.com) is a team leader specifically responsible for the company's ecommerce efforts. Amanda has a good background in Google Analytics and she is very good at creating innovative reports and new views that provide deep insights into data implications.

4. Ken (klopr@gmail.com) has good skills at data interpretation but is considered somewhat of a "loose cannon." He often acts first and thinks about the consequences later.

Hands-on

This last set of exercises asks you to apply your learning to the actual granting of permissions. Prior to doing these exercises you will need to create a new account and property with the following characteristics:

Account name: Chapter10

Property name: Permissions

View name: Leave as default - All Web Site Data

Website: www.chapter9.org

If you run into problems, see pages 46 to 50.

1. Give Denise (permissionschapter9@gmail.com) permission to Manage Other Users at the account level.

2. Delete Denise from permissions.

3. Give Tom (permissionschapter9@gmail.com) permission to Edit at the account level. Make certain to have Google notify Tom by email that permission has been granted.

4. Change Tom's (permissionschapter9@gmail.com) permission to Read & Analyze at the view level. Once you accomplish this, delete him from the permission roster.

Google Analytics Demystified

Section III:
Predefined and Custom Filters

Google Analytics filters allow you to specify the types of data included in the different views associated with a particular property. Filters accomplish this by restricting the data available within the view to which they are applied. A view with no filter presents all data collected for a property while a view with one or more filters presents only a subset of the data. In this case, the specific characteristics of the data are defined by the characteristics of the filter(s) applied. Filters provide a powerful way to reduce the effort required to examine important segments of data and, as a consequence, they make an important contribution to strategic decision-making.

-    Chapters 11 and 12 discuss predefined filters, a small but powerful set of filters that Google Analytics has made available to reduce the effort in filter creation.

-    Chapters 13 and 14 discuss and provide practice with regular expressions, the syntax used to move you beyond predefined filters to the creation of more flexible, extensive, and complex filters.

-    Chapters 15 and 16 discuss and provide practice with custom filters, the most powerful type of filter.

Google Analytics Demystified

Views With Predefined Filters

Every time you create a new property, Google Analytics creates an unedited (unfiltered) view of the data. Unless you rename it, this view is called **All Web Site Data**. By now, you should know how to rename and perform additional manipulations to this and other views as well as how to add additional views to a property.

The views you've dealt with so far have been unfiltered which means that all of the data collected by Google Analytics is present in the view. There are circumstances, however, where you will only want to view important subsets of the total data file. Here, you can create any number of additional views to assist in strategic decision-making and site evaluation/revision. Pages 28 to 30, for example, provide a description of the four views every website should have. Beyond these views, you might set up one view that only reports visitors from organic search and another view that only reports data from individuals referred to your site through your Wordpress blog.

The use and effect of filters in the creation of views is illustrated below. Imagine that you currently have one view: an unrestricted (i.e., unfiltered) view that includes all website visitors. Now you want to easily see the behaviors of site visitors who come to the site via a social platform such as YouTube or Facebook. You name this view "Social". Google Analytics monitors all of your website visitors and places their data in the un-restricted view. However, you can also apply a "Social Referral" filter to all the data coming into Google Analytics so that the "Social" view will only contain data generated by the individuals of interest, i.e., those that arrive via a social platform.

All website visitors from different referral sources

Appear in "Unrestricted" view

Social Referral Filter

Only website visitors from a social referral

Appear in "Social" view

The filter options are near limitless, so it is recommended that any filtered view of your data have a clear strategic grounding.

You restrict the data displayed in a view by applying one or more filters, which can either be predefined or custom. It is important to remember that any filter you apply to a view begins on the day the filter was applied and continues until the filter is removed. Google Analytics does not apply filters to historical data, nor does it remove filter effects should the filter be removed.

This chapter and the next focus on predefined filters. This is followed by a discussion of regular expressions and custom filters in Chapters 13 to 16.

What are predefined filters?

Predefined filters are Google's attempt to simplify your life. A predefined filter consists of three parts:

- The decision whether to *include* or *exclude* target data.

- The *source* of the included/excluded data. Sources can be traffic from a specific ISP domain, a specific IP address, a specific hostname, or a specific subdirectory.

- How the *source* of the data is to be *identified*. Here, the options are: equal to, begins with, ends with, and contains.

These characteristics work together to permit you to create a view that precisely presents a restricted data set, for example:

- You find that your Google Analytics data make little sense, in great part because the data include all of the behaviors of those in your company who visit the website through their computers while at work. You can create a view which collects data on all website visitors *except* those who come to the site through the company's IP address.

- Imagine that you create a YouTube channel as a means of (hopefully) driving traffic to your website. While you want the data generated by those referred by YouTube to be included in the total data set, you also want to examine the behaviors of these individuals independently. You can accomplish this by creating a view that includes only those individuals who come from a domain containing "youtube.com".

- You have a subdirectory on your site named "/historical archives" for which you want to examine traffic and other behaviors independent of other site data. You can accomplish this by creating two views, one which only includes data relevant to visits to this subdirectory and one which includes all collected data but excludes data from those who did not visit this specific subdirectory.

Creating a filtered view of your data using predefined filters is a straight forward process that should be begun only after you identify a strategic rationale for creating the view.

Let's work though each of the prior examples to see how predefined views are created. We'll use the **Account2** property and **My personal website** which you created earlier as the basis of these examples. In order to make things easier, delete any remaining views from this account and property except "View 1: Unfiltered".

Eliminate data whose source is the company IP address

This case illustrates a situation where you find that your Google Analytics data make little sense, in great part because the data include the behaviors of those in your company who visit the website though their computers while at work. As a result, we want to filter out traffic from our company IP address from all views except the master file, which is now labeled **View1: Unfiltered.** This is a two step process where we first create the new view and then apply the filter to the view.

We begin by creating a new view, which we'll label **View 2: Company IP Excluded**. Similar to the examples discussed earlier, we create a new view through these steps:

1. Sign into Google Analytics with the email associated with your travel website. Once you have access, click on **Admin** to go to the administrator's page.

2. Use the pull-down menus to make certain that the account is "Account 2", the property is "My personal website", and the view is "View 1: Unfiltered" (as shown below). Next, use the pull-down the menu in the View column to select **Create new view**.

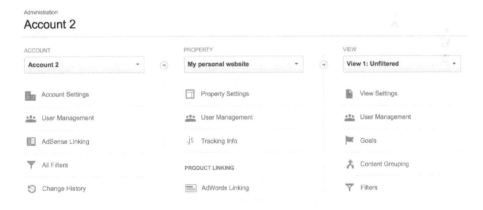

3. On the next page, leave **Website** highlighted.

4. In the text box labeled **Reporting View Name**, type in "View 2: Company IP Excluded", as shown on the top of page 60.

Administration › New Reporting View

Account 2 / My personal website

New Reporting View

Creating a new reporting view will provide you with unfiltered access to all data collected by the Tracking ID.

If you would like this reporting view to be constrained to a very specific subset of tracked data, you will need to create and apply one or more view filters to this data.

What data should this view track?

Website   Mobile app

Setting up your view

Reporting View Name

View 2: Company IP Excluded

5. Use the pull-down menus on the bottom of the page to indicate country and time zone.

6. Press **Create view.** You should be informed that the view creation was a "Success."

7. Click on the **Home** icon on the top left side of the page to return to your home page. If all has gone well you should see the figure opposite.

☆ 📁 Account 2

☆ 📁 My personal website (UA-54714112-2)

☆ 🌐 View 1: Unfiltered

☆ 🌐 View 2: Company IP Excluded

Next, we need to add a predefined filter to this view to inform Google Analytics that when reporting data in this view, it should ignore all individuals who arrive at our site through the company IP address. We accomplish this as follows.

1. From whatever page you are on, click on **Admin** to go to the administrator's page.

2. Use the pull-down menus to make certain that the account is "Account2", the property is "My personal website", and the view is "View 2: Company IP Excluded".

3. Click on **Filters** in the right-most **VIEW** column.

4. On the next page, click on **+New Filter**.

5. On the top of the next page select **Create new Filter**.

6. Let's name this filter "Company IP Excluded". Type this name into the text box labeled **Filter Name**.

7. We'll use a predefined filter. Click on this option.

8. Use the three drop down menus to select: **Exclude, traffic from the IP addresses, that begin with.** Type "46 249 223" in the first three boxes in the **IP address** box. (One set of digits per box. Leave the last box blank.) These three numbers represent the beginning of the IP address assigned to our company. (We're assuming here that our company is the exclusive user of this IP address.)

9. When you are done, and your screen looks like this, then press **Save**.

If you were successful, the confirmation page shown below will appear. This page should list the filter you just created.

Whenever you select this view, you will see data generated by all those who came to your site **except** for those visiting the site through the company's network as specified by the IP address.

Filtering for YouTube referrals

Now let's set up a filtered view that reports the behaviors only of those users who arrive at the site via a YouTube referral, keeping in mind that we also want to simultaneously filter out individuals arriving through our company IP address. As such, we need to apply two filters to this view.

Similar to the previous example, our first task is to create a new view, which we'll label "YouTube Referrals/Company IP Excluded." The next steps are:

1. From whatever page you are on, click on **Admin** to go to the administrator's page.

2. Use the pull-down menus to make certain that the Account is "Account 2", the Property is "My personal website", and the View is "View 1: Unfiltered". Next, as you did in the last example, use the pull-down the menu in the View column and then select **Create new view**.

3. On the next page, leave **Website** highlighted.

4. In the text box labeled **Reporting View Name**, type in "YouTube Referral/ Company IP Excluded", as shown below.

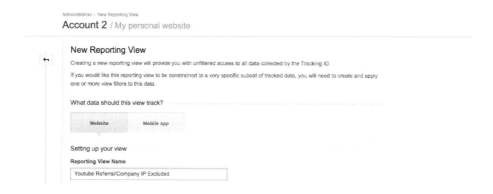

5. Use the pull-down menus on the bottom of the page to indicate country and time zone.

6. Press **Create view.** You should be informed that view creation was successful.

7. The next page displayed is your administrator's page. Your new view should be displayed in the View column, as shown on the top of the next page.

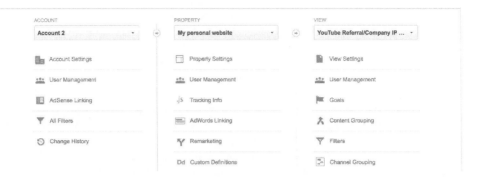

Now we need to add two predefined filters to this view to inform Google Analytics that when reporting data in this view, the data display should *include* only those individuals who arrive at our site through a YouTube referral but simultaneously *exclude* from this display any who are connected to the internet via our company IP address.

Since we have already created a company IP filter, we can apply that filter to this view rather than creating this filter anew from scratch. This process is as follows:

1. Access the Administrator's Page to make certain that the **YouTube Referral/ Company IP Excluded** view is displayed, as shown above.

2. In the View column, click on **Filters**.

3. On the next page, click on **+New Filter**.

4. On the next page, click on **Apply Existing Filter**.

5. On the next page, in the box labeled **Available Filters,** highlight **Company IP Excluded**. Press **Add** to place this filter in the **Selected Filters** column. Press **Save**. You'll then see the Company IP filter added to this view, as shown below.

A second predefined filter can now be added to this view to *include* only those individuals who were sent to our site via youtube.com. The steps to follow are:

1. Click on **Admin** to go to the administrator's page.

2. Use the pull-down menus to make certain that the account is "Account2," the property is "My personal website," and the view is "YouTube Referral/Company IP Excluded."

3. Click on **Filters** in the right-most **VIEW** column.

4. On the next page, click on **+New Filter**.

5. On the top of the next page, choose **Create New Filter**.

6. We'll use a predefined filter. Click on this option. Then use the text box to name this filter "YouTube Only".

7. Use the three drop-down menus to select: **Include only, traffic from the ISP domain, that contain**. Type "youtube.com" in the text box and check **No** to **Case Sensitive** (see below).

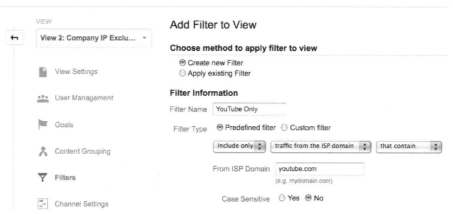

8. When you are done and your screen looks like the one above, press **Save**. Your confirmation page should resemble that shown below.

By default, view filters are applied to the data in the order in which the filters were added. In the prior example, the view's filter would first eliminate those individuals coming to the site through the company IP address and then, for those remaining, select (include) only those who were referred by YouTube. In this particular case, order does not matter but you should always be sensitive to order effects. We'll address this in more detail when we discuss custom filters.

Imagine that you have a subdirectory on your site named "/Historic archives" for which you want to examine traffic and other behaviors independent of other site data. You can accomplish this by creating a view that only includes visitor behaviors associated with this subdirectory. Let's create the view which includes only the data generated by individuals who visit this subdirectory of your site while again filtering out all individuals who came to the site via the company IP address.

Similar to the prior example, our first task is to create a new view, which we'll label "Music Archives/Company IP Excluded." The next steps are:

1. From whatever page you are on, click on **Admin** to go to the administrator's page.

2. Use the pull-down menus to make certain that the Account is "Account 2", the Property is "My personal website", and the View is "View 1: Unfiltered". Next, similar to what you did in the last example, pull-down the menu in the View column and then select **Create new view**.

3. On the next page, leave **Website** highlighted.

4. In the text box labeled **Reporting View Name**, type in "Historic Archives/Company IP Excluded", as shown below:

5. Use the pull-down menus to indicate the correct country and time zone.

6. Press **Create view.**

7. The next page displayed is your administrator's page. Your new view should be displayed in the View column, as shown on the top of page 66.

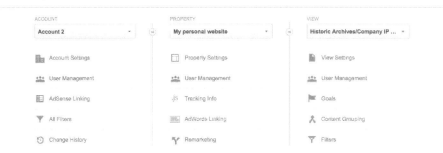

Next we need to add two predefined filters to this view to inform Google Analytics that when reporting data in this view, the report should *include* only those individuals who visited the targeted subdirectory but simultaneously *exclude* from this report any who are connected to the internet via our company IP address.

Since we have already created a company IP filter, we can apply that filter to this view rather than creating this filter anew from scratch. The process is as follows:

1. Access the Administrator's Page to make certain that the **Historic Archives/ Company IP Excluded** view is displayed, as shown above.

2. In the View column, click on **Filters**.

3. On the next page, click on **+New Filter**.

4. On the next page, click on **Apply Existing Filter**.

5. On the next page, in the box labeled **Available Filters,** highlight **Company IP Excluded**. Press **Add** to place this filter in the **Selected Filters** column. Press **Save**. You'll then see the Company IP filter added to this view, as shown below.

A second predefined filter can now be added to this view to *include* only those individuals who visited the "/Historic archives/" subdirectory. The steps to follow are:

1. From whatever page you are on, click on **Admin** to go to the administrator's page.

2. Use the pull-down menus to make certain that the account is "Account2", the property is "My personal website", and the view is "Historic Archives/Company IP Excluded".

3. Click on **Filters** in the right-most **VIEW** column.

4. On the next page, click on **+New Filter**.

5. On the top of the next page, choose **Create New Filter**.

6. Let's name this filter "Historic Archives".

7. We'll use a predefined filter. Click on this option.

8. Use the three drop down menus to select: **Include only, traffic to the subdirectories, that are equal to**. Type "/Historic archives/" in the text box and check **No** to **Case Sensitive** (see below).

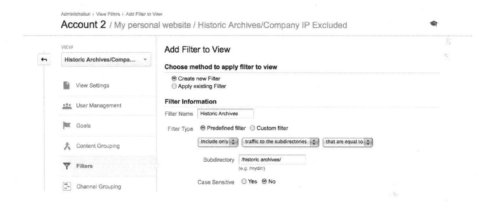

9. When you are done and your screen looks like the one above, press **Save**. Your confirmation page should resemble that shown below.

12

Practice With Predefined Filters

This chapter includes two sets of exercises to help you apply and extend your knowledge of predefined filters.

True/false and multiple choice

This first set makes certain that you understand key concepts. When you are done, or if you are stuck, the procedures required to answer each exercise can be found beginning on page 589.

1. What type of view presents the entirety of data collected by Google Analytics ?

   a. unaltered

   b. unfiltered

   c. untouched

   d. unrevised

2. Assume that you are interested in looking at individuals referred to your site from Wordpress.com. Which approach described below would allow you create a view that contained only these individuals?

   a. You can create a view with a predefined filter that includes only individuals coming from traffic from the ISP domain that begins with "Wordpress. com".

   b. You can create a view with a predefined filter that excludes all those individuals who did not come from traffic from the ISP domain that begins with "Wordpress. com".

   c. Both of the above filters would accomplish this goal.

3. *True or False:* Filters can be applied at both the property and view level of data collection.

4. *True or False:* Only one filter can be applied to any particular view at a time.

5. *True or False:* A filtered view will always contain data for fewer individuals versus an unfiltered view.

6. *True or False:* In the absence of any further manipulation, filters are applied to a view in the order in which they are created.

7. *True or False:* Once filters are applied to a view, their order of application cannot be changed.

8. You begin data collection on your site on 1/1/2014. On 3/1/2014 you create a view with a predefined filter. Which of the following is true of this new view?

   a. Google Analytics will apply this filter to all data beginning with data collected on 1/1/2014.

   b. Google Analytics will apply this filter only to data collected on and after 3/1/2014.

9. You begin data collection on your site on 1/1/2014 with a view that filters for You-Tube referrals. On 3/1/2014 you remove the filter. Which of the following is true?

   a. Google Analytics will remove the filter from all data in the view, going back to data collected from 1/1/2014 onward.

   b. Google Analytics will remove the filter's effects only from data collected on and after 3/1/2014.

10. You want to exclude all individuals who are referred to your site from Pinterest.com. Which of the following would you select to create the filter?

    a. traffic from ISP domain

    b. traffic from the IP addresses

    c. traffic to the subdirectories

    d. traffic to the hostname

11. You want to filter for individuals who were referred to your site via Wordpress.com. You know that you need to "include only traffic from the ISP domain". With this in mind, which of the following is the best way to filter for these individuals?

    a. that contain WORD

    b. that begin with WORD

    c. that contain WORDPRESS.COM

    d. that end with PRESS.COM

You will need to create a new property and view for this exercise. Name the new property "Chapter12". You can use your own judgment to complete the remaining portion of the property creation form. The new view associated with this property will, by default, be named "All Web Site Data". Use this new property and view to respond to the following exercises.

Exercises 1 through 6 address issues explicitly addressed in the prior chapter. Exercises 7 and 8 encourage you to explore on your own. When you are done, or if you are stuck, the procedures required to answer each exercise can be found beginning on page 589.

1. Create a new filter named "Exercise 1". This filter should eliminate the data gathered from individuals who use the company network. The company IP addresses range from 208.87.149.x to 208.87.149.y (where x and y are any number between 1 and 255).

2. Imagine that your company IP address has changed and now includes only the following IP address: 208.87.149.1. Revise the "Exercise 1" filter to reflect this change.

3. Create a new filter named "Exercise 3". This filter should include only those individuals who were referred to your site via a wordpress.com hostname.

4. Create a new filter labeled "No View Bicycle" that excludes all individuals who did visit the subdirectory "**/bicycles/**".

5. Imagine that you have three subdirectories: **/art**, **/artists** and **/works of art**. These are the only subdirectories that contain the word "art". Create a view named "Exercise 5" that would report data for individuals who visited any of these subdirectories.

6. Imagine that you have three subdirectories: **/art**, **/artists**, and **/artwork**. You also have two subdirectories named **/modern art** and **/abstract art**. These are all of the subdirectories that contain the word "art." Create a view named "Exercise 6" that would report data for individuals who visited any of just the first three subdirectories.

7. Move the "No View Bicycle" filter so that it is the first filter applied to the view.

8. Remove the "Exercise 3" filter from the list of filters.

Application

This final exercise asks you to think about strategic uses of predefined filters. If you are using the travel site provided with this book, then apply this exercise to that site. If you have your own website to which you want to apply Google Analytics, then apply this exercise to your own site.

The three images shown at the end of this exercise present all of your options for filter creation via the three pull-down menus.

Think about your strategic information needs. What types of filtered views provide information that can help you to better understand site user characteristics and behaviors? Think of three different views where the application of one or more filters to the view provides important insights. For each view, provide a description of the characteristics of the filter(s) applied to the view and include a brief discussion of your rationale for why the filter is important.

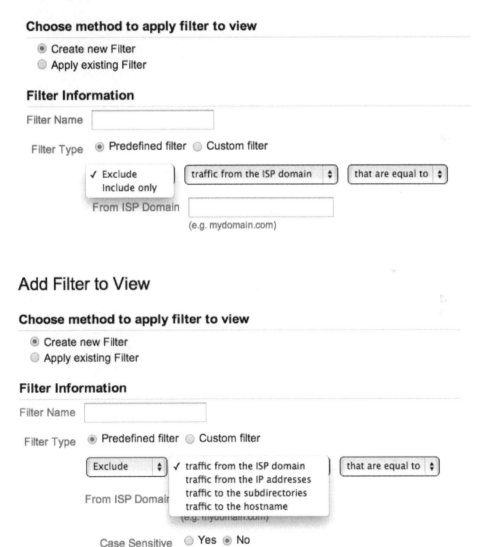

Add Filter to View

Choose method to apply filter to view

- ⦿ Create new Filter
- ◯ Apply existing Filter

Filter Information

Filter Name   [_____]

Filter Type   ⦿ Predefined filter   ◯ Custom filter

[Exclude ⬍]   [traffic from the ISP domain ⬍]   ✓ that are equal to
                                              that begin with

From ISP Domain   [_____]   that end with
                                                     that contain
(e.g. mydomain.com)

Case Sensitive   ◯ Yes   ⦿ No

13
Regular Expressions

Chapter 11 described predefined filters, an easy and powerful way to filter data within a property's view. Custom filters are even more flexible and powerful, but this flexibility and power comes with a cost: increased complexity.

Custom filters are more complex because they typically rely on the use of *regular expressions* (also known as regex) to communicate the filter's desired characteristics. A regular expression is a pattern of letters and/or numbers and/or special characters which are applied to one or more pieces of data collected on your behalf by Google Analytics. If the pattern matches, the regular expression returns a positive result.

The logic behind regular expressions is similar to that of a Google or Bing search. At its most basic level, you type in a word or phrase and the search engine returns "hits" that contain that word or phrase. A search for "yoghurt", for example, brings up the following, all of which contain the word "yoghurt":

Yogurt - Wikipedia, the free encyclopedia
en.wikipedia.org/wiki/Yogurt ▾
Yogurt or **yoghurt** or yoghourt (/ˈjoʊɡərt/ or /ˈjɒɡərt/; from Turkish: yoğurt; other spellings listed below) is a fermented milk product (soy milk, nut milks such as ...
Lactobacillus delbrueckii - Frozen yogurt - Streptococcus thermophilus - Raita

Yoghurt - Simple English Wikipedia, the free encyclopedia
simple.wikipedia.org/wiki/**Yoghurt** ▾
Yogurt, or **yoghurt**, is a dairy product made by bacterial fermentation of milk. The lactose in the milk becomes lactic acid when it is fermented. Lactic acid acts on ...

News for **yoghurt**

Bill Granger recipe: Spiced salmon and spinach toasts with garlic **yoghurt**
The Independent - 5 days ago
Bursting with greens, protein and healthy oils, this will wipe away any traces of cocktails and leave your body a temple.

Regex expressions work in the same way, except there is more flexibility (and somewhat greater complexity) in how the search is defined. Within the context of Google Analytics, you use regex expressions not to search the internet, but rather to search and examine your data. Data that matches the regex expression are considered "hits" and are either included or excluded from a property's view depending upon your instructions.

This chapter focuses on the regex expressions you're most likely to use. The next chapter shows you how to apply these expressions when creating custom filters for Google Analytics views.

The regex expression "OR"

Most search engines allows you to use the word "or" as part of your search request. Thus, rather than doing multiple sequential searches (for example: guitar then violin, then viola), you do just one search using the "or" connector: guitar or violin or viola. The results of this latter search contain all the hits of either guitar, violin or viola.

Regex doesn't use the word "or" but rather the pipe symbol: | . Thus, a regex search for "guitar", "violin" or "viola" would be: **guitar|violin|viola**. Note that there are no blank spaces.

Let's try this out. Visit the website Regex Tester at:

http://regexpal.com/

You'll see two boxes, where the smaller top box says "Write your regex here …" and the larger bottom box says "Type your data here …". Begin by typing the following into the bottom box:

oboe
oboes
clarinet
harp
harps
mandolin
trumpet
harpist
harpsichord

Now we want to write a regex expression that will "hit" only the words "harp" or "oboe".

Keep in mind that when using this site, a "hit" only occurs when the **entire** word is highlighted in the lower box.

In the top box we type the regex expression: **harp|oboe** which means "consider a hit positive when you find any sequence of letters which in its *entirety* is either 'harp' or 'oboe'." When this is done, notice how harp and oboe, our two targets, are *fully* highlighted in the lower box. Importantly, these are the only words that are fully highlighted. Our "or" regex expression worked.

The prior example also illustrates how the execution of any regex statement is quite literal. Since we have told it to look for "harp" or "oboe" then "harps", "harpist" and "harpsichord" are rightfully excluded from the list of hits. We can tell they are not considered a "hit" because they are not fully highlighted. Finally, there is no limit to the number of "or" commands that can appear in a single regex expression. If we change the prior regex to: **harp|oboe|trumpet** at Regex Tester, then all three terms would be fully highlighted.

Regex optional characters

Imagine that we still want to process items in the list provided in the previous section:

oboe
oboes
clarinet
harp
harps
mandolin
trumpet
harpist
harpsichord

However, now we not only want to "hit" oboe and harp but in addition we want to "hit" oboes and harps.

The less than ideal way to accomplish this would be to use a string of "or" statements, for example: **oboe|oboes|harp|harps**. While this would accomplish our goal, such long strings of "or" statements become cumbersome and their length increases the potential for error. A shorter and more efficient way to identify these four words would be to use the quantifier indicated by a question mark: **?**

A **?** in a regular expression is translated to mean "the character or group of characters immediately preceding the **?** are optional - they may occur zero or one time in order for a hit to occur."

-    The **?** can apply to just a single character. The regex expression **colou?r** will find both "color" (the u is found 0 times) and colour (where the u is found 1 time).

-    The **?** can apply to a group of characters contained within a set of parentheses where the **?** follows the closing parenthesis. **Dec(ember)?** matches both Dec and December. Similarly, you can use multiple question marks as in **Oct(ober)? 10(th)?** which matches Oct 10, October 10, Oct 10th, and October 10th.

Now let's apply this to our list. We begin with the "or" statement used in the prior section: **oboe|harp**. We then add the **s?** to the end of each word, which translates to mean "find the character string 'oboe' which may or may not end in an 's' or find the character string 'harp' which may or may not end in an 's'." Try this statement (**oboes?|harps?**) at Regex Tester to see that it fully hits (highlights) only the four target words of interest: oboe, oboes, harp, and harps.

Regex wildcard characters

Imagine that we want to identify individuals who use specific search terms via our website's search engine. We could use an "or" statement, but this would require that we know in advance all of the possible terms a person could use and then string these terms together in one incredibly long regex "Or" statement. There is a better way.

The **.*** combination of symbols in regex is translated to mean "find anything or nothing that appears in this position in any piece of data in the database that we are searching." Let's try this at Regex Tester

http://regexpal.com/

where we are interested in individuals who searched for something related to harps. Once again, you'll see two boxes, where the smaller top box says "Write your regex here ..." and the larger bottom box says "Type your data here ...". Begin by typing the following into the bottom box (making certain that the top box is empty):

autoharp
autoharps
harpsichord
harpsichords
harpist
harpists
harp
harps
vibraharp

Now we want to write a regex expression that "hits" all of these listed terms as they are all relevant to harps. So, in the top box we type the regex expression **harp.*** which means "consider a hit positive when you find any string of letters that starts with 'harp' no matter what, if anything, is on the end of the word." When this is done, notice how all six words beginning with "harp" but with different endings, are fully highlighted in the lower box. Pretty good, but not perfect. We need to expand our regex expression to include "consider a hit positive when you find any string of letters that contains 'harp' no matter what, if anything, is on the beginning or end of the word." We accomplish this by also adding the wildcard command **.*** to the beginning of our search term "harp", changing the regex statement in the top box to **.*harp.***. Change your regex statement at Regex Tester. Notice how all the words in the list are now fully highlighted, indicating that we have "hit" all of the target terms.

Imagine that we are an ecommerce site that sells a wide range of merchandise. Two products, bicycles and tricycles, are an important part of our business. As a result, we want to create a view in which we can look at those who have visited our site and who have used our site search engine to search for these products. We'll once again use Regex Tester to work through the logic of how this can be accomplished. Type the following list in the bottom box at Regex Tester. These are the search terms that we want to capture. (Note that there are some intentional misspellings as these might also appear as search terms.) Make certain that the top box is empty.

bicycle
bicycles
bike
bikes
biking
motorbike
motorbikes
biker
tricycle
tricycles
bicyclist
bicyclists
bicycl
cycl
bikr
tricycl

First we have to look at the characteristics of the target terms. It appears that the words, even the misspelled ones, fall into two groups: those that refer to cycles and those that refer to bikes. As a result, we could create a regex statement that uses wildcards and "or" to locate target terms. The regex statement would be **.*cycle.*|.*bike.***. This would be interpreted to mean "consider a hit positive when you find any string of letters that contains 'cycle' no matter what, if anything, is on the beginning or end of the word **or** consider a hit positive when you find any string of letters that contains 'bike', no matter what, if anything, is on the beginning or end of the word." Type the regex statement **.*cycle.*|.*bike.*** in the top box at Regex Tester and see which words are fully highlighted.

The **.*cycle.*|.*bike.*** statement found those words which had "cycle" or "bike" fully spelled out, but it missed important terms without this full spelling, for example, bicyclist and biking. Our regex statement was too restrictive. We can make the statement less restrictive by reducing the required number of matches in the search terms, for example, we can change the original regex statement to **.*cycl.*|.*bik.*** by dropping the final "e" on the end of each word. This revised regex statement would be interpreted to mean "consider a hit positive when you find any string of letters that contains 'cycl', no matter what, if anything, is on the beginning or end of the word **or** consider a hit positive when you find any string of letters that contains 'bik', no matter what, if anything, is on the beginning or end of the word." Type the regex statement **.*cycl.*|.*bik.*** in the top box at Regex Tester and see which words are fully highlighted. Note that now all target terms, including the misspelled ones, have been successfully found.

Groups of items

Think about the mathematical expression 10*(7+5). In the same way that this mathematical statement means 10*7 plus 10*5, the use of parentheses in regular expressions makes certain that the characters outside of the parentheses are applied equally and consistently to the characters inside the parentheses. When coupled with the | symbol, parentheses provide significant control over what terms are considered a positive match.

Consider the following list of words which might be used as part of our site search:

grandfather
grandmother
grandson
granddaughter
mother
father

We could use the **.*** instruction if we wanted to match all words beginning with "grand". This regex statement would be **grand.*** .But what if we only wanted to match the first two words? In this case, we would use parentheses like this: **grand(mother|father)**. This statement would be interpreted to mean "consider a hit positive when you find any string of letters that begins with grand and ends in either mother or father." Similarly, if we wanted to match alternative (mis)spellings of "pharmacy" we would use the regex expression **(ph|f|fh|)armacy** which would match "pharmacy", "farmacy" and "fharmacy".

Finally, note that we can use an empty | in our list of matching options to indicate that the target string alone should be considered a hit. Imagine, for example, that we want to match "bicycle", "tricycle" and "cycle" but not "unicycle" or "motorcycle". The regex statement **.*cycle** would not work as this would match all of the terms. The statement **(bi|tri)cycle** would not work because it would hit "bicycle" and "tricycle" but not "cycle". The solution is **(bi|tri|)cycle** where we add a third empty "Or" option after "tri". This regex statement would be interpreted as: "a hit is considered to be 'bi' plus 'cycle' (i.e., bicycle), or a hit is considered to be 'tri' plus 'cycle' (i.e., tricycle), or a hit is considered to be nothing plus 'cycle' (i.e., cycle)." Just the three target terms are selected.

Literals: Escape characters

We've seen that regex statements use some common symbols (such as the period and asterisk) as instructions. The period in the **.*** command, for example, does not mean "end of sentence" but rather provides direction for how the data is to be examined. There are times, however, when you want a period or other symbol in a regex statement to actually be read literally, that is, in its everyday meaning. This might occur, for example, when want a regex statement to evaluate a URL that contains periods.

Imagine that we have a subdirectory on our site named www.mysite.com/content. Within this directory there are a number of subdirectories, for example:

www.mysite.com/content/history
www.mysite.com/content/science
www.mysite.com/content/music
www.mysite.com/content/programming

We want to identify all individuals who viewed any content, not caring about the specific subject matter of the content. We can begin with this regex statement

www.mysite.com/content/.*

where the end of the statement is intended to mean "find anything or nothing that comes at this point in the URL." Unfortunately, we can't consider this regex statement correct (nor would it work as we intended) because the periods earlier in the URL (between www and mysite, and between mysite and com) would be interpreted as a regex instruction and not part of the URL. Fortunately, there is an easy way to fix this. Whenever you want regex to interpret a restricted letter or symbol literally and not as a command, precede that character with a backward slash: \ . Thus, if we want to find all instances of content viewing at this URL, the regex instruction would need to have a \ before each period:

www\.mysite\.com/content/.*

We can test this regex statement at Regex Tester. First, type the prior regex statement into the top box. Then type the following list in the bottom box:

www.mysite.com/control
www.mysite.com/content/history
www.mysite.com/content/math
www.mysite.com/history
www.mysite.com/math

Notice how our proposed regex statement matches only the URLs of interest.

Additional regex commands

The regex commands which we've discussed so far should serve nearly all your needs. While there are a significant number of additional commands, those which might be useful in more specialized circumstances are shown on page 80.

[ ]	A box enables a *single character* to be matched against a character list or range.
[^]	A compliment box enables a single character not within a character list or range to be matched.
^	The caret anchor matches the beginning of the line.
$	The dollar anchor matches the end of the line.

The application of these commands to string search and evaluation is shown below.

[hc]at	*hat* and *cat* are positive matches
[^b]at	any three letter word ending in "at" except *bat* is a positive match
^[hc]at	*hat* and *cat* are positive matches but only at the beginning of a line
[hc]at$	*hat* and *cat* are positive matches but only at the end of a line

The **[ ]** symbol explained above is often used with the **|** and **( )**. Imagine, for example, that we want to identify any referral from Google or Yahoo. We could use the regex expression: **([Gg]oogle|[Yy]ahoo)** would match: Google, google, Yahoo, and yahoo.

Defining a range of numbers

Beyond the search for matches involving letters, regex can also be used to define a range of numbers. These numbers can be amounts purchased, number of site visits, item codes or any other numeric identifier.

Imagine, for example, that each of the bicycles your company sells has an item code of between 59 and 78, and that you want to create a view which includes only those people who purchased a bicycle. You can use regex to conduct an examination of every purchased item's code and then include only those individuals with a code between 59 and 78.

Unfortunately, doing this by hand is cumbersome and often leads to error. Fortunately, there are online calculators which will do this for you. Regex_For_Range is one such calculator, which creates a regular expression to match a numeric range. The range generator is located at:

`http://utilitymill.com/utility/Regex_For_Range/42`

Let's see how this works for our bicycle item codes. Visit Regex_For_Range and in the **Minimum Value** box type the lowest number in the range, in this case 59. Next, in the **Maximum Value** box type the highest item code, 78. Leave **Match Whole Word** checked and press **Go!** The regex expression will appear in the bottom box, as shown on the next page.

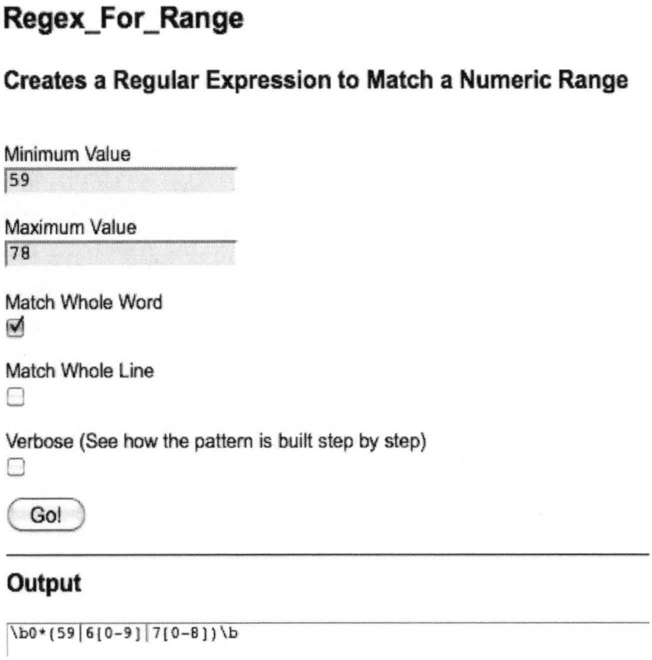

Regex_For_Range

Creates a Regular Expression to Match a Numeric Range

Minimum Value
`59`

Maximum Value
`78`

Match Whole Word
☑

Match Whole Line
☐

Verbose (See how the pattern is built step by step)
☐

(Go!)

Output

`\b0*(59|6[0-9]|7[0-8])\b`

Note, the **Output** shown above. When using the regex output from Regex_For_Range in Google Analytics, you can eliminate the first four characters, \b0*, before the first parentheses and the final \b. Thus, for the example above we, would use the regex expression **(59|6[0-9]|7[0-8])**.

We can confirm that this code accomplishes our goals by testing it at Regex Tester. Once again, you'll see two boxes, where the smaller top box says "Write your regex here ..." and the larger bottom box says "Type your data here ...". Begin by pasting the regex range expression in the top box. Then type some numbers between 0 and 100 (without decimals) in the lower box. Notice how all the numbers in the range of 59 to 78 are highlighted (indicating a positive hit), while the remaining numbers are not. Now add the numbers 59, 159 and 590 to the lower box. Finally, note that while 59 is highlighted (indicating a positive hit), 159 and 590 are not highlighted even though they contain the number 59.

14
Practice With Regular Expressions

No new account or property is required for these exercises. When you are done, or if you are stuck, the procedures required to answer each exercise can be found on page 592.

Use this list of words for numbers 1 through 6.

art
artist
smart
cart
apart
mart
dart
darts
artists
chart
artistry
artful
cup
teacup
cupcake
cupcakes
cups

1. Write a regex statement that will exactly match "art" or "cup" but nothing else.

2. Write a regex statement that will exactly match any word that begins with "art" but nothing else.

3. Write a regex statement that will exactly match any word that contains "art" but nothing else.

4. Write a regex statement that will match words that contain "art" and ends in "s" but nothing else.

5. Write a regex statement that will match "cup" or any term containing "art" but nothing else.

6. Write a regex statement that will match all words on the list.

Use the following list to answer questions 7 to 10.

mankind
man*kind
population
population*
history
historical
*historical
history250
history248
history557
history263
history448
history571
med249
59
78
159

7. Write a regex statement that will match "man*kind" but nothing else.

8. Write a regex statement that will match only those words containing an asterisk but nothing else. Do not use the regex **|** symbol in your response.

9. Write a regex statement that will match numbers 59, 78, and 159 and nothing else.

10 Write a regex statement that matches all words ending with a number between 248 and 263 but nothing else.

11. Write a regex statement that will match only the following URLs:

google.com.uk
google.com.de
google.co.uk
google.co.de

12. Write a regex statement that will find any website content that ends in either .pdf, .doc or .xcl. No other page endings, such as .html, should be considered a hit.

13. Write a regex statement that will locate the search terms: Vodaphone, Vodafone, and Vodapfone, but no other terms.

15

Views With Custom Filters

Chapter 11 demonstrated the contribution predefined filters can make to data views and subsequent strategic decision-making. A predefined filter grounded in a strategic information need can provide the specific insights required for website revision and improvement. The restricted and predefined parameters of these filters make them very easy to use while maintaining significant power.

Custom filters provide greater flexibility and range of parameters versus predefined filters. However, along with this greater power comes a bit more difficulty in use. When using custom filters, you need to do all the configuration work. Thus, while the use of custom filters can be challenging, mastering their implementation provides significant advanced control over the data that appear in your views.

The greater range of options for custom filters is reflected in the custom filter form, shown below. Note how the number of options has expanded beyond just **Include** and **Exclude** configurations.

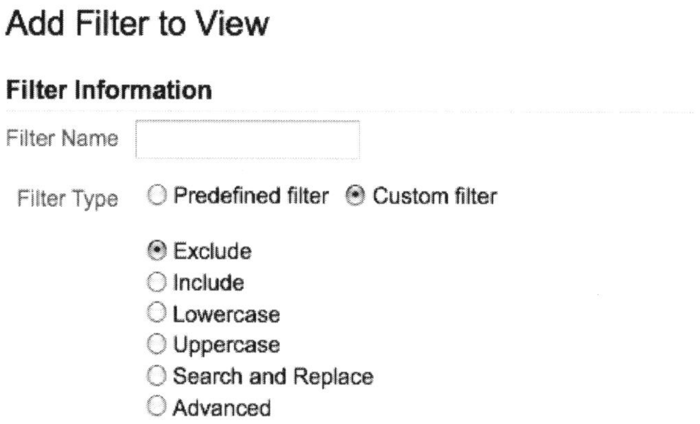

Add Filter to View

Filter Information

Filter Name [   ]

Filter Type ○ Predefined filter ⦿ Custom filter

⦿ Exclude
○ Include
○ Lowercase
○ Uppercase
○ Search and Replace
○ Advanced

Let's take a closer look at each of the custom filter options.

Exclude and Include

The logic underlying include and exclude custom filters is the same as that for predefined filters. You use include and exclude parameters when you want to examine data views that reflect one or more characteristics or behaviors of the tracked visitor. As we saw in Chapter 11, predefined filters allow you to include or exclude based on one of four characteristics:

- traffic from the ISP domain

- traffic from the IP addresses

- traffic to the subdirectories

- traffic to the hostname

Custom filters greatly expand this list. For a complete listing and definitions of all include and exclude characteristics available for use in custom filters see *Data Filters for Views: Custom Filter Fields* at:

https://support.google.com/analytics/answer/1034380?hl=en

You begin the creation of custom filters in exactly the same way as predefined filters.

1. Click on **Admin** to go to the administrator's page.

2. Use the pull-down menus to make certain that your desired **Account**, **Property** and **View** are displayed. Remember, similar to predefined filters, the filters you create will be added to whatever view is displayed. So, if you do not want to apply a new custom filter to the current view, then either select a different view or create a new view before proceeding.

3. Click on **Filters** in the right-most **VIEW** column.

4. On the next page, click on **+New Filter**.

5. Select **Create New Filter**.

6. Select **Custom Filter**.

Let's try some examples using include and exclude.

Case 1

Imagine that we have set up our website so that some content is free, while other premium content is available only for a fee. We want to look more closely at those individuals who pay for premium content in order to try to increase the proportion of site visitors who pay for access. We can create a view that includes only these individuals.

This view reflects an ecommerce transaction for which we have assigned the internal item code "99". To create a view with an associated filter that includes only the behaviors and characteristics of individuals with this ecommerce item code, we would (on the filter creation page):

- name the filter "Bought Content"

- check **Include**

- select "Ecommerce Item Code" from the **Filter Field** box

- type "99" in the **Filter Pattern** box.

We respond "No" to **Case sensitive** and the custom filter is complete, as shown below.

Pressing the **Save** button saves your new filter and displays the confirmation page shown below. The filter has been added to the current view.

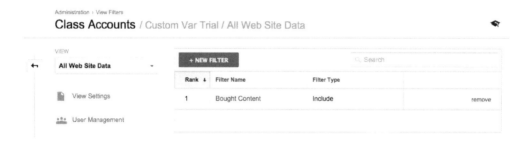

Case 2

Let's extend Case 1.

Imagine that you have seven tiers rather than one tier of content, and that you want to create a view that includes anyone who purchased any tier of content. Assume that you have assigned the numbers 36 through 42 to each of the tiers. As before, these numbers represent ecommerce item codes. To create a view with a filter that includes the behaviors and characteristics of these individuals, we would:

- name the filter "Ecommerce Codes"

- check **Include**

- select "Ecommerce Item Code" from the **Filter Field** box

- type the range of ecommerce codes in the **Filter Pattern** box.

But, in order to accomplish this last step we need to use regex to define the range of codes. This can easily be accomplished at Regex_For_Range at:

`http://utilitymill.com/utility/Regex_For_Range/42`

When we type in our minimum and maximum range values the regex code **(3[6-9]|4[0-2])** is returned. (Remember, at Regex_For_Range we eliminate the leading four characters and the final **/b** when using the generated regex.) This code should be copied and then pasted in the **Filter Pattern** box.

We respond "No" to **Case sensitive** and the custom filter is complete, as shown below.

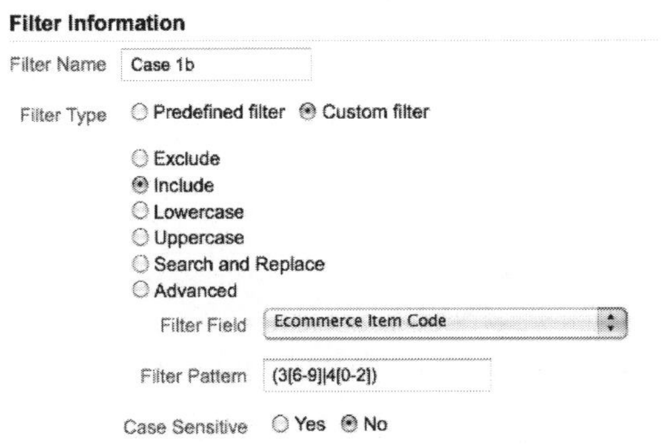

Filter Information

Filter Name | Case 1b

Filter Type | ○ Predefined filter ● Custom filter

○ Exclude
● Include
○ Lowercase
○ Uppercase
○ Search and Replace
○ Advanced

Filter Field | Ecommerce Item Code

Filter Pattern | (3[6-9]|4[0-2])

Case Sensitive | ○ Yes ● No

Pressing the **Save** button saves your filter and then displays the filter creation confirmation. The filter has been added to the current view.

Case 3

Imagine that California is an important region for our sales efforts and, as a result, it is crucial that we understand the behaviors and characteristics of Californians who visit our website. We can create a view with an associated filter that includes only these individuals. On the filter creation page we would:

- name the filter "Californians"

- check **Include**

- select "Region" from the **Filter Field** box

- type "California" in the **Filter Pattern** box.

We respond "No" to **Case sensitive** and the custom filter is complete, as shown below.

Pressing the **Save** button saves your new view and should then display the filter creation confirmation. The filter has been added to the current view.

Case 4

Let's take Case 3 one step further. Imagine that instead of only being interested in Californians in the view, we are instead interested in looking at Californians and New Yorkers together in the **same** view. Thus, the view will consist of individuals who live in **either** California **or** New York. You might think that this could be accomplished by setting up two filters for the view, one filter which selects (includes) individuals who live in California and a second filter which selects individuals who live in New York. This won't work, however, because of the sequential way in which Google Analytics applies multiple filters to a single view.

Imagine that you take the dual filter approach in which the California filter is applied first, followed by the New York filter. The chart below shows the last seven people who visited the website and where they live.

Person	Residence
1	California
2	New York
3	Maine
4	California
5	New York
6	Idaho
7	California

Applying the California filter first would eliminate persons 2, 3, 5, 6 as follows:

Person	Residence
1	California
~~2~~	~~New York~~
~~3~~	~~Maine~~
4	California
~~5~~	~~New York~~
~~6~~	~~Idaho~~
7	California

Unfortunately, this includes the two people from New York, whom we want to remain in the view. Reversing the order of the filters also doesn't work. As shown below, applying the New York filter first eliminates Californians 1, 4, and 7.

Person	Residence
~~1~~	~~California~~
2	New York
~~3~~	~~Maine~~
~~4~~	~~California~~
5	New York
~~6~~	~~Idaho~~
~~7~~	~~California~~

The solution to the problem lies in telling Google Analytics that you are want it to select either California or New York on the first (and only) pass through the data. As discussed in Chapter 13, this is accomplished by using the regex "or" symbol **|** as shown below.

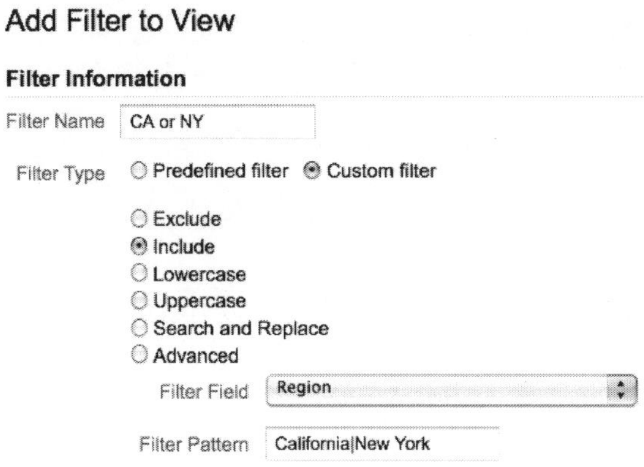

Add Filter to View

Filter Information

Filter Name   CA or NY

Filter Type   ○ Predefined filter   ⊙ Custom filter

- ○ Exclude
- ⊙ Include
- ○ Lowercase
- ○ Uppercase
- ○ Search and Replace
- ○ Advanced

Filter Field   Region

Filter Pattern   California|New York

Pressing the **Save** button saves this new view's filter.

Case 5

We've discussed the importance of filtering out the data generated by company employees before drawing insights from data collected by Google Analytics. We saw a simple example of how to do this using predefined filters. This situation is different, however, as our company uses only a restricted range of IP addresses and, as a result, we want to filter out only the IP addresses used by the company. The company IP address range is 63.212.171.1 to 63.212.171.23.

To create a view that excludes the behaviors and characteristics of individuals accessing the web site through company IP addresses we would:

- name the filter "Company IP filtered"

- check "Exclude"

- select "IP Address" from the **Filter Field** box

- type the range of IP addresses in the **Filter Pattern** box.

In order to accomplish this last step, we need to use regex to define the range of IP addresses. Generating the regex to represent the range of IP addresses can be accomplished at the generator provided by Analytics Market at:

`http://www.analyticsmarket.com/freetools/ipregex`

When we type in the minimum and maximum values for our IP range, the generator returns this regex statement:

^63\.212\.171\.([1-9]|1[0-9]|2[0-3])$.

This code should be copied and then pasted in the **Filter Pattern** box.[2]

We respond "No" to **Case sensitive** and the custom filter is complete, as shown below.

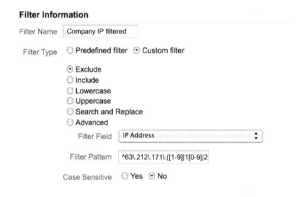

---

[2] Note that we are not using Regex Pal to generate this range. This is because we are generating IP addresses rather than just a range of numbers and so literal regex characters must be added to identify the period placed between the IP address blocks.

Case 6

Earlier we discussed how we would form a regex statement to identify individuals who used a variety of terms in our internal search engine to search for bicycles and related items. Google Analytics' custom filters can help us identify those who used these terms on an external search engine (such as Google or Bing) prior to arriving at our site.

To create a view that includes the behaviors and characteristics of individuals who were referred to our site via the use of targeted search engine terms, we would:

- name the filter "Search term related to bike or cycle"

- check **Include**

- select "Search Term" from the **Filter Field** box

- type **.*cycl.*|.*bik.*** in the **Filter Pattern** box.

We respond "No" to **Case sensitive** and the custom filter is complete, as shown below:

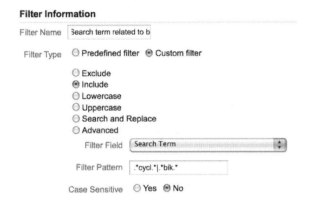

Lowercase and uppercase

Different individuals often take different approaches when typing a website page's URL. When I first set up one of my websites, each of the following was used to reach the purchase page:

http://www.Classmatandread.net/462Site/purchase.html

http://www.classmatandread.net/462Site/Purchase.html

http://www.classmatandread.net/462site/purchase.html

http://www.classmatandread.net/462site/Purchase.html

http://www.classmatandread.Net/462site/Purchase.html

All of these URLs work the same way and direct site users to the same page. However, because Google Analytics is case sensitive (and treats the same item differently when it is in upper versus lower case) each different approach resulted in a different reported page view, significantly complicating data review and analysis.

There is no strategic reason to create different pageviews since the underlying intent of all consumers is the same: to reach the purchase page. Fortunately, you can apply a custom filter to your data to transform URLs to either all upper case or all lowercase resulting in one single, consistent URL in your reports.

The approach to creating this filter is the same as the prior custom filters. Once you tell Google Analytics that you want to create a new filter, provide a name, and indicate custom filter, you would:

- name the filter, in this case "All Lowercase"

- check **Lowercase** or **Upper Case** to reflect your preference

- select "Request URL" in the **Filter Field** box

We respond "No" to **Case sensitive** and the custom filter is complete, as shown below:

Finally, note that this transformation is available for a wide range of data, as reflected in the options shown in the **Filter Field** pull-down menu.

Search and replace

The search and replace function allows you to substitute one term for another. This function works the same way in Google Analytics as it does in your word processing program. For example, when writing a document you can decide to replace all instances of "U.S." with "United States". The logic is identical for search and replace custom filters.

While search and replace filters have a wide range of applications, they are typically used to replace internal codes with explanatory labels or to merge different URLs into a single URL. Let's take a closer look at these two applications of search and replace.

Case 1

Almost all ecommerce sites assign department numbers to products, for example:

http://www.bestguitarstrings.com/546/aquila-strings

http://www.bestguitarstrings.com/546/arunez-strings

http://www.bestguitarstrings.com/446/elixr-strings

While these codes are useful internally, they require those viewing the company's Google Analytics reports to have memorized or look up the codes. It would facilitate data analysis and application if the Google Analytics reports automatically translated the department numeric code within each URL into a textual descriptor. This can be accomplished as follows:

- Name the filter "Dept1"

- Check "Search and Replace"

- Select "Request URL" in the **Filter Field** box

- Type "546" in the **Search String** field as this is the piece of data that is to be replaced

- Type "classical" in the **Replace String** field as this is the new label

We respond "No" to **Case sensitive** and the custom filter is complete, as shown below.

Since there are two department numbers that we want to replace, we would add a second search and replace custom filter to this view. This filter would replace "446" with "bass". When both filters are applied URLs of the form:

http://www.bestguitarstrings.com/546/aquila-strings

http://www.bestguitarstrings.com/446/elixr-strings

would now appear in Google Analytics reports as:

http://www.bestguitarstrings.com/classical/aquila-strings

http://www.bestguitarstrings.com/bass/elixr-strings

Case 2

Another common use case for the Search and Replace filter is to turn multiple URLs into one single URL. Imagine that you have multiple pieces of content on your website, where each piece of content is referred to by a unique URL, as follows:

example.com/content/cooking/cooking+in+june

example.com/content/cooking/may+treats

example.com/content/cooking/fab+fish+bbq

example.com/content/cooking/bravura+brownies+and+cakes

In addition to examining these URLs individually, you might also find it useful to create a summary URL that reports site visitors' interaction with **any** cooking-related content. The search and replace function can accomplish this by standardizing the end of the specified content-related URLs. As a result, if each of the prior URLs had one pageview each, the standardization of these URLs will result in four pageviews reported for the standardized URL:

example.com/content/cooking/

This would be accomplished as follows:

- Name the filter "Cooking Content"

- Check **Search and Replace**

- Select "Request URL" in the **Filter Field** box

- Type "example\.com/content/.*" in the **Search String** field. The .* at the end of the search string tells Google to find anything (or nothing) that appears in this position.

- Type "example\.com/content/" in the **Replace String** field as this is the new label

We respond "No" to **Case sensitive** and the custom filter is complete, as shown below.

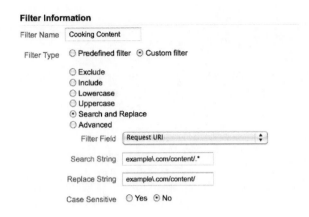

16

Practice With Custom Filters

There are two sets of exercises to help you apply and extend your knowledge of custom filters.

True/False and multiple choice

This first set makes certain that you understand key concepts. Feel free to open and refer to a custom filter creation page in your Google Analytics account when you are answering these questions. When you are done, or if you are stuck, the answers can be found beginning on page 593.

1. Which of the following can be used to create an include/exclude custom filter? Select all that apply.

    a. Page title

    b. Page length

    c. Ecommerce item code

    d. City

    e. County

    f. Social network

2. You want to screen for individuals who purchased any item with an item code between 41 and 53. Which regex statement(s) below would allow you to isolate these individuals? Check all that would be used.

    a. **[41-53]**

    b. **[41-49|50-53]**

    c. **(4[1-9]|5[0-3])**

3. *True or False:* Only one custom filter can be applied to any particular view at a time.

4. *True or False:* A particular view cannot contain both predefined and custom filters.

5. *True or False:* Once custom filters are applied to a view, their order of application can never be changed.

6. Assume that you are interested in looking at individuals referred to your site from either Wordpress.com or from Pinterest.com. You know that you need to select "include > referral". Which approach described below would allow you create a view that best filter for these individuals?

   a. Create two filters: one that screens for referrals from Wordpress.com and a second that screens for referrals from Pinterest.com. Even though Pinterest accounts for more referrals, the order of application does not matter.

   b. Create two filters: one that screens for referrals from Wordpress.com and a second that screens for referrals from Pinterest.com. Since Pinterest has a greater number of referrals, apply the Pinterest filter prior to the Wordpress filter.

   c. Create one filter using the regex "or" command of the form:
      wordpress.com|pinterest.com

   d. Create one filter using the regex "or" command of the form:
      .*[wordpress\.com|pinterest\.com].*

   e. Create one filter using the regex "or" command of the form:
      .*[wordpress.com|pinterest.com].*

7. *True or False:* Custom filters can be applied at both the property and view level of data collection.

8. You begin data collection on your site on 1/1/2014. On 3/1/2014 you create a view with a *custom* filter. Which of the following is true of this new view?

   a. Google Analytics will apply this filter to all data beginning with data collected on 1/1/2014.

   b. Google Analytics will apply this filter only to data collected on and after 3/1/2014.

9. *True or False:* Once a custom filter is added to a view, it can never be deleted from that view.

10. You begin data collection on your site on 1/1/2014 with a view that used a custom filter for YouTube referrals. On 3/1/2014 you remove the filter. *True or False:* Google Analytics will remove the filter from all data in the view, going back to data collected from 1/1/2014 onward.

You will need to create a new property and view for this exercise. To begin, name the new property "Chapter16." You can use your own judgment to complete the remaining portion of the property creation form. The new view associated with this property will be named by default "All Web Site Data". Use this new property and view to respond to the following exercises.

When you are done, or if you are stuck, the procedures required to answer each exercise can be found beginning on page x593.

1. Create a custom filter named "Mobile-Sam". This filter should include only those individuals who visit your site using a Samsung mobile devise.

2. Assume that you are an ecommerce site and that history books are given an item number between 238 and 302. Create a custom filter named "History" which contains only those sessions in which a history book was purchased.

3. Create a custom filter that excludes individuals whose sessions originate in either Atlanta or Chicago. Name this filter: "Exercise 3".

4. Create a custom filter named "Exercise 4" that includes only those individuals who entered your website via one of two test home pages:

   www.storefront.com/tpage.htm

   or

   www.storefront.com/tpage1.htm

5. Create a custom filter named "Shirts" that includes individuals where either a shirt, nightshirt, or sweatshirt was purchased. Any item is acceptable. No other item containing "shirt" (for example, t-shirt, undershirt) is of interest.

6. Assume that you want to track the search terms that people use to find your site. Create a custom filer named "Plane" that will capture individuals who use any term in the first column while ignoring those who use any of the terms in the second column.

airplane	**planet**
plane	**deplane**
triplane	**planed**
biplane	**planet**
airplanes	**aeroplane**
triplanes	

Section IV:
Data Characteristics

All Google Analytics reports are organized around the principles of dimensions and metrics. The two chapters in this section help you understand the characteristics of dimensions and metrics.

- Chapter 17 defines and explains dimensions and metrics and their use in Google Analytics reports.

- Chapter 18 provides exercises for you to apply your understanding of these concepts to Google Analytics data.

Google Analytics Demystified

Metrics and Dimensions

Google Analytics organizes and reports data in terms of dimensions, values, and metrics. It is important to understand what each of these terms represents prior to looking at any Google Analytics reports.

Google Analytics defines a dimension as "a descriptive attribute or characteristic of an object that can be given different values." Metrics are defined as the "individual elements of a dimension that can be measured as a sum or a ratio." Given that these definitions are a bit obtuse, it might help you to understand dimensions and metrics if we first discuss these concepts outside the context of Google Analytics.

Examples of a dimension and a metric

Think about students at a university. One dimension that describes students is "Academic Status." This dimension has five different values: Freshman, Sophomore, Junior, Senior, Graduate Student. We use metrics to describe a specific characteristic or aspect of a dimension's values, as shown in the table below where we describe the average grade point average of each type of student (as defined by the dimension's values) living in a particular dorm.

Dimension: Academic Status of Students in Dorm X

Values	Grade Point Average
Freshman	2.3
Sophomore	2.6
Junior	2.7
Senior	3.0
Graduate	3.7

The table illustrates how to distinguish dimensions, values and metrics. A dimension can be thought of as the overall category and is typically the table descriptor or label for the first column of information. In this case, the dimension is "Academic Status." Values are divisions of the dimension and typically occur in the first column of a table. The values in this table are Freshman, Sophomore, etc. Metrics are the actual numbers that appear in a labeled column of the table, typically beginning in the second column. The label "Grade Point Average" indicates that this is the metric being reported.

We are not limited to the selection of a single metric to describe a dimension's values. Let's keep our dimension and its values constant with the previous example, but change the metric. Imagine that we wanted to obtain insights into the eating habits of the students living in our fictitious dorm. We could select a range of relevant metrics to provide these insights. We could, for example, take a look at the last week and the total number of meals consumed and report:

- the percentage of meals cooked at home (that is, in the dorm),

- the percentage of meal purchased at a fast food restaurant, and

- the average cost of a meal.

All three of these metrics are reported in the table below, where the trend is for students to cook at home more, eat less fast food, and spend more per meal as they increase in academic status.

Dimension: Academic Status of Students in Dorm X

Values	Metrics		
	Percent Meals Cooked at Home	Percent Meals at Fast Food Rest.	Ave. Cost/Meal
Freshman	22.3%	43.2%	$3.23
Sophomore	24.6	40.1	3.78
Junior	34.7	31.9	4.33
Senior	43.0	23.3	4.75
Graduate	63.7	11.9	6.01

Finally, the table illustrates how the use of multiple related metrics to describe a single dimension provides greater insights than that provided by each metric alone. This is the advantage of selecting multiple related metrics to describe the values within a single dimension.

With this in mind, let's now look at how dimensions, values and metrics are presented in Google Analytics.

Dimensions and metrics in Google Analytics

The table shown on the top of the next page focuses on the types of individuals responsible for sessions on my website. The dimension is **User Type**, the dimension's values are the user classifications, in this case **New** and **Returning**, and the metrics are the data that appear in each of the columns. We can see, for example, that new users are responsible for significantly more sessions (1,223 sessions or 82.97% of all sessions) versus returning users (251 sessions or 17.03% of all sessions). Also note that since **User Type** must either be **New** or **Returning**, the combined percentages of these two dimension values equals 100%.

User Type	Acquisition			Behavior		
	Sessions ↓	% New Sessions	New Users	Bounce Rate	Pages / Session	Avg. Session Duration
	1,474 % of Total: 100.00% (1,474)	**82.97%** Site Avg: 82.97% (0.00%)	**1,223** % of Total: 100.00% (1,223)	**33.58%** Site Avg: 33.58% (0.00%)	**2.49** Site Avg: 2.49 (0.00%)	**00:00:47** Site Avg: 00:00:47 (0.00%)
1. New Visitor	**1,223** (82.97%)	100.00%	1,223(100.00%)	31.73%	2.41	00:00:31
2. Returning Visitor	**251** (17.03%)	0.00%	0 (0.00%)	42.63%	2.92	00:02:02

Similar to our student example, we are not limited to examining just one metric for any particular dimension. Google Analytics allows a broad range of options for metric selection. The table below, for example, maintains the **User Type** dimension, but changes the metrics to more detailed site related behaviors, in this case adding **Pages Per Session** and **Average Session Duration**.

User Type	Sessions ↓	Pages / Session	Avg. Session Duration	Bounce Rate
	1,474 % of Total: 100.00% (1,474)	**2.49** Site Avg: 2.49 (0.00%)	**00:00:47** Site Avg: 00:00:47 (0.00%)	**33.58%** Site Avg: 33.58% (0.00%)
1. New Visitor	**1,223** (82.97%)	2.41	00:00:31	31.73%
2. Returning Visitor	**251** (17.03%)	2.92	00:02:02	42.63%

Simultaneous examination of two dimensions

By default, Google Analytics' tables initially report a single dimension with multiple relevant metrics. These tables provide valuable insights. Insights can be even deeper, however, when two dimensions are examined simultaneously.[3]

Let's begin with the **New and Returning User** chart displayed earlier and shown again on the top of page 104.

---

[3] In this chapter we only discuss the value of examining two dimensions at the same time. We discuss how to generate these two dimensional tables later in the book in the context of data exploration.

User Type ?	Acquisition			Behavior		
	Sessions ? ↓	% New Sessions ?	New Users ?	Bounce Rate ?	Pages / Session ?	Avg. Session Duration ?
	1,474 % of Total: 100.00% (1,474)	**82.97%** Site Avg: 82.97% (0.00%)	**1,223** % of Total: 100.00% (1,223)	**33.58%** Site Avg: 33.58% (0.00%)	**2.49** Site Avg: 2.49 (0.00%)	**00:00:47** Site Avg: 00:00:47 (0.00%)
1. New Visitor	**1,223** (82.97%)	100.00%	1,223 (100.00%)	31.73%	2.41	00:00:31
2. Returning Visitor	**251** (17.03%)	0.00%	0 (0.00%)	42.63%	2.92	00:02:02

This chart provides important insights into the relative proportion of new and returning users and their site behaviors, but the table cannot answer additional relevant questions, for example: How are new and returning users accessing my site? This latter question can be answered, however, by adding a second dimension - **Source** - to the prior table.

We'll look at new and returning users separately. The table shown below lists only **New Visitors** in the first column (representing one value of the dimension **User Type**) and lists source used to access my site in the second column. (**Source** is the second dimension and its values are shown in this column). The data in the table indicate that the vast majority of new users access my site directly (763 sessions or 62.39%), with Facebook and Wordpress accounting for the majority of remaining sessions.

- Facebook accounts for 157 sessions or 12.84%.

- Wordpress accounts for 60 sessions or 4.91%

User Type ?	Source ? ⊚	Acquisition		
		Sessions ? ↓	% New Sessions ?	New Users ?
		1,223 % of Total: 82.97% (1,474)	**100.00%** Site Avg: 82.97% (20.52%)	**1,223** % of Total: 100.00% (1,223)
1. New Visitor	(direct)	**763** (62.39%)	100.00%	763 (62.39%)
2. New Visitor	Facebook	**157** (12.84%)	100.00%	157 (12.84%)
3. New Visitor	Wordpress	**60** (4.91%)	100.00%	60 (4.91%)
4. New Visitor	Press	**54** (4.42%)	100.00%	54 (4.42%)

Now let's look at **Returning Visitors** to see if the pattern of site access is similar or different from that of new visitors. The data is shown in the table below.

User Type	Source	Acquisition		
		Sessions ↓	% New Sessions	New Users
		251 % of Total: 17.03% (1,474)	0.00% Site Avg: 82.97% (-100.00%)	0 % of Total: 0.00% (1,223)
1. Returning Visitor	(direct)	79 (31.47%)	0.00%	0 (0.00%)
2. Returning Visitor	TransTest	24 (9.56%)	0.00%	0 (0.00%)
3. Returning Visitor	Internal	23 (9.16%)	0.00%	0 (0.00%)
4. Returning Visitor	Facebook	16 (6.37%)	0.00%	0 (0.00%)
5. Returning Visitor	google	16 (6.37%)	0.00%	0 (0.00%)
6. Returning Visitor	Wordpress	16 (6.37%)	0.00%	0 (0.00%)

In fact, the pattern of site access for returning visitors is both similar and different to new visitors. Similar to new visitors, direct access is still the most common way to access the site, but the relative percentage of this type of access is much lower for returning visitors versus new visitors. Facebook and Wordpress also account for site access, but these, too, are at lower levels for returning users versus new users. The specific values of the second dimension (**Source**) of the two lists are also not identical. The overall conclusion is that while direct access is the dominant form of site access for both new and returning users, beyond this, new and returning site users appear to have different preferences for site access.

This insight would not have been possible had we not examined the two dimensions simultaneously.

Full list of Google Analytics dimensions and metrics

Google Analytics provides access to nearly 300 dimensions and metrics. A full listing of what is available can be found by using the expandable menus listed at:

https://developers.google.com/analytics/devguides/reporting/core/dimsmets

18

Practice with Metrics and Dimensions

This chapter contains two sets of exercises designed to help you apply and extend your knowledge of dimensions and metrics.

Application (I)

This first exercise asks you to identify dimensions and metrics. For each item below, indicate whether the item represents a dimension or a metric. When you are done, or if you are stuck, the answers can be found beginning on page 597.

1. Pages viewed per session

2. Landing page

3. Referral source

4. Session length

5. Operating system

6. Sessions to transaction

7. Exit page

8. City of origin

9. Language spoken

10. Social source referral

11. Brand of mobile device

Each of the following numbered exercises below presents a table or related multiple tables. For each exercise:

- identify at least one dimension in the table(s);

- draw three insights from the table(s); and

- propose three strategic questions that are raised by your insights. Each question should address a future action or information need.

When you are done, or if you are stuck, the answers to each exercise can be found beginning on page 597.

1. (one table to examine)

Country / Territory	Acquisition			Behavior		
	Sessions ↓	% New Sessions	New Users	Bounce Rate	Pages / Session	Avg. Session Duration
	590 % of Total: 100.00% (590)	**83.90%** Site Avg: 83.22% (0.81%)	**495** % of Total: 100.81% (491)	**35.25%** Site Avg: 35.25% (0.00%)	**2.51** Site Avg: 2.51 (0.00%)	**00:00:47** Site Avg: 00:00:47 (0.00%)
1. Germany	202 (34.24%)	90.59%	183 (36.97%)	31.68%	2.13	00:00:11
2. United States	133 (22.54%)	66.92%	89 (17.98%)	35.34%	3.03	00:02:44
3. Hungary	96 (16.27%)	86.46%	83 (16.77%)	32.29%	4.02	00:00:11
4. Austria	69 (11.69%)	79.71%	55 (11.11%)	49.28%	1.35	00:00:15
5. Ireland	47 (7.97%)	89.36%	42 (8.48%)	34.04%	1.87	00:00:07
6. United Kingdom	42 (7.12%)	100.00%	42 (8.48%)	35.71%	1.88	00:00:26
7. Italy	1 (0.17%)	100.00%	1 (0.20%)	100.00%	1.00	00:00:00

2. (one table to examine)

Browser	Acquisition			Behavior		
	Sessions ↓	% New Sessions	New Users	Bounce Rate	Pages / Session	Avg. Session Duration
	590 % of Total: 100.00% (590)	**83.90%** Site Avg: 83.22% (0.81%)	**495** % of Total: 100.81% (491)	**35.25%** Site Avg: 35.25% (0.00%)	**2.51** Site Avg: 2.51 (0.00%)	**00:00:47** Site Avg: 00:00:47 (0.00%)
1. Chrome	501 (84.92%)	90.82%	455 (91.92%)	33.73%	2.39	00:00:16
2. Firefox	47 (7.97%)	59.57%	28 (5.66%)	42.55%	4.11	00:06:25
3. Safari	39 (6.61%)	23.08%	9 (1.82%)	46.15%	2.05	00:00:42
4. Internet Explorer	2 (0.34%)	100.00%	2 (0.40%)	0.00%	5.00	00:00:16

3. (two tables to examine)

Source	Sessions	Revenue	Transactions	Average Order Value	Ecommerce Conversion Rate
	590 % of Total: 100.00% (590)	$1,631,500.00 % of Total: 100.00% ($1,631,500.00)	171 % of Total: 100.00% (171)	$9,540.94 Site Avg: $9,540.94 (0.00%)	28.98% Site Avg: 28.98% (0.00%)
1. (direct)	303 (51.36%)	$822,100.00 (50.39%)	86 (50.29%)	$9,559.30	28.38%
2. Facebook	84 (14.24%)	$304,500.00 (18.66%)	35 (20.47%)	$8,700.00	41.67%
3. Wordpress	68 (11.53%)	$310,300.00 (19.02%)	29 (16.96%)	$10,700.00	42.65%
4. google	40 (6.78%)	$11,000.00 (0.67%)	1 (0.58%)	$11,000.00	2.50%
5. Youtube	25 (4.24%)	$106,300.00 (6.52%)	11 (6.43%)	$9,663.64	44.00%
6. Press	19 (3.22%)	$27,300.00 (1.67%)	3 (1.75%)	$9,100.00	15.79%
7. TransTest	16 (2.71%)	$31,000.00 (1.90%)	4 (2.34%)	$7,750.00	25.00%

Source	Browser	Sessions	Revenue	Transactions	Average Order Value	Ecommerce Conversion Rate
		590 % of Total: 100.00% (590)	$1,631,500.00 % of Total: 100.00% ($1,631,500.00)	171 % of Total: 100.00% (171)	$9,540.94 Site Avg: $9,540.94 (0.00%)	28.98% Site Avg: 28.98% (0.00%)
1. (direct)	Chrome	267 (45.25%)	$805,100.00 (49.35%)	84 (49.12%)	$9,584.52	31.46%
2. (direct)	Firefox	30 (5.08%)	$0.00 (0.00%)	0 (0.00%)	$0.00	0.00%
3. (direct)	Internet Explorer	2 (0.34%)	$0.00 (0.00%)	0 (0.00%)	$0.00	0.00%
4. (direct)	Safari	4 (0.68%)	$17,000.00 (1.04%)	2 (1.17%)	$8,500.00	50.00%

4. (two tables to examine)

User Type	Acquisition			Behavior		
	Sessions	% New Sessions	New Users	Bounce Rate	Pages / Session	Avg. Session Duration
	590 % of Total: 100.00% (590)	83.90% Site Avg: 83.22% (0.81%)	495 % of Total: 100.81% (491)	35.25% Site Avg: 35.25% (0.00%)	2.51 Site Avg: 2.51 (0.00%)	00:00:47 Site Avg: 00:00:47 (0.00%)
1. New Visitor	495 (83.90%)	100.00%	495 (100.00%)	31.92%	2.55	00:00:30
2. Returning Visitor	95 (16.10%)	0.00%	0 (0.00%)	52.63%	2.31	00:02:13

User Type	Sessions ↓	Revenue	Transactions	Average Order Value	Ecommerce Conversion Rate
	590 % of Total: 100.00% (590)	$1,631,500.00 % of Total: 100.00% ($1,631,500.00)	171 % of Total: 100.00% (171)	$9,540.94 Site Avg: $9,540.94 (0.00%)	28.98% Site Avg: 28.98% (0.00%)
1. New Visitor	495 (83.90%)	$1,488,200.00 (91.22%)	159 (92.98%)	$9,359.75	32.12%
2. Returning Visitor	95 (16.10%)	$143,300.00 (8.78%)	12 (7.02%)	$11,941.67	12.63%

Google Analytics Demystified

Section V:
The Audience Menu

Google Analytics provides extensive data with regard to the characteristics of individuals who visit your website or blog. You can learn their demographics and interests, the technology they use to begin and continue engagement, where they are located, their frequency/recency of sessions, and how they move through your site page by page. The chapters in this section help you to understand the full range of audience specific data and the application of this data to strategic decision-making.

- Google Analytics provides audience data through overviews or focused reports. Chapters 19, 21 and 22 introduce you to the Audience Overview report. Chapters 20 and 23 provide practice exercises to help you apply and extend what you have learned.

- Chapter 24 presents a detailed discussion of the full set of data provided through the Audience Menu. Chapter 25 contains exercises to help you confirm that you are comfortable working with this information.

Together, the chapters in this section show you different ways to access, manipulate and strategically apply audience data.

Google Analytics Demystified

19

Audience Menu: Top Graph

As discussed previously, after you log into Google Analytics you will see your home page, the page which lists all of your accounts, properties, and views. On this page, if they are not already open, click on the account and property that contains the data you want to see. Finally, click on the appropriate view. In the example shown opposite, we would click on **All Web Site Data**.

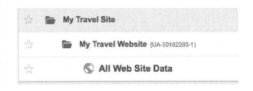

Checking the date range

The **Audience Overview** page is the first page shown after you click on your desired view. *Before going any further in examining this or any other data, always be certain that the date range is appropriate*, that is, that it spans the entire range of data collection in which you are interested. By default, Google Analytics only reports data for the prior 30 days.

The date range can be found in the upper right-hand corner of any data reporting page, as shown below.

If you want to change this date range, click on the downward facing arrow next to the ending date, and then use the calendar or date boxes to select the beginning and end of the desired date range (see below). Make certain that the pull-down menu beneath the initial date range says **Custom**.

Click **Apply** when done and all data displayed in the current session will be drawn from the date range you specified.

The top graph

By default, the top graph shows the number of site sessions by day for the selected date range, which in this case is January 1, 2014 to May 4, 2014 (see below). The line graph in this example shows that there are two distinct time periods underlying site sessions, with sessions spiking in early March.

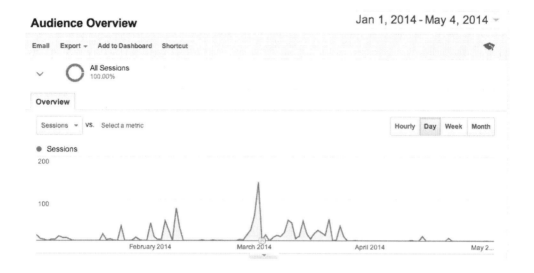

Sessions and other key metrics related to the Audience Menu are defined in this chapter's addendum.

Placing your cursor over any point on the line graph displays detailed information for that date, as reflected in the chart shown on the top of the next page. Here, we learn that 140 sessions occurred on March 2, 2014.

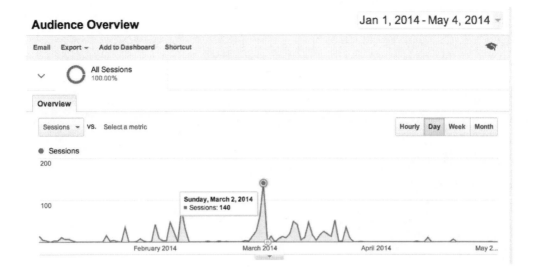

The menu options on the top right-hand side of the graph provide you with data grouping options. You can ask for data to be reported hourly (for restricted date periods), by the day (as in the prior chart), week or month. Just click on the desired time grouping period. The chart below presents the same data as the chart above, only this time grouped by week.

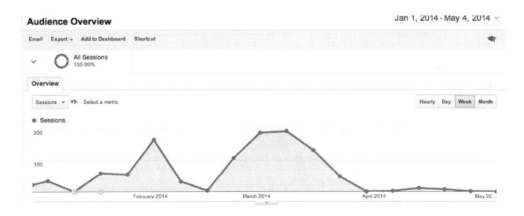

Changing the data displayed in the line graph

The display of site sessions is not the only metric that can be displayed in the line graph. Beneath **Overview** on the top left-hand side of the graph is a pull-down menu, currently (by default) labeled **Sessions**. You can select to chart any of the available metrics (see the top of page 116).

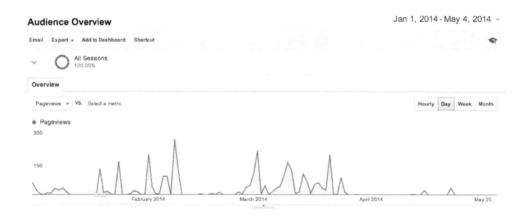

These metrics can be charted by your desired time period. The chart below, for example, displays **Pageviews** by **Day**.

Annotating the line graph

You can annotate any chart, that is, leave a note for yourself and others viewing the chart. Your annotation might be used, for example, to explain a rapid rise or fall in data trends or the start and end of an email campaign.

To annotate a chart, first click on the small downward facing arrow on the bottom center of the chart. Next, click (in the chart) to locate the date you want to annotate and then click on **+Create new annotation** located on the bottom right-hand side of the chart. It is easiest to accomplish this by charting your data using the **Day** option. Our target date is March 3, 2014. When this is done, you should see a screen resembling the that shown on the top of page 117.

Check the date in the date text box. If the incorrect date is showing, just click on the text box and then either type in or use the pull-down calendar to select the date for the annotation. Now, click whether you want the annotation to be shared or private and then type your annotation into the text box. Click **Save** when you are done. You'll now see a small annotation symbol on the target date (see below). You can close the annotation box by clicking on the upward facing arrow beneath the line graph.

At any point thereafter, clicking on the annotation symbol displays the corresponding annotation, as shown on the top of page 118.

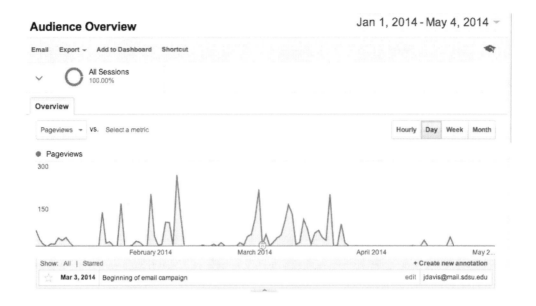

Finally, notice the information provided on the lower right-hand side of the annotation. My email address appears because I created the annotation. In addition, the **Edit** link allows me to edit any attribute of the annotation or even delete the entire annotation.

Simultaneously charting two metrics

You are not restricted to charting only one metric at a time. As described earlier, you use the pull-down menu on the top left-hand side of the line graph to select your primary metric. Next to this menu is the option to **Select a (second) metric**. Clicking on this link brings up a second pull-down menu which lists all the remaining metrics for the **Audience** data set (see below).

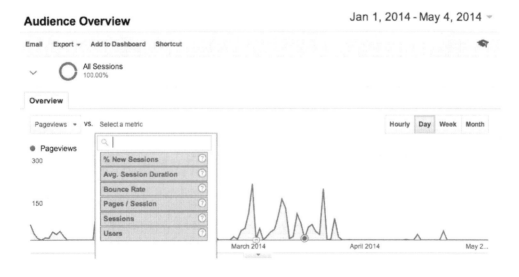

Google Analytics Demystified

Selecting a metric from this second pull-down menu adds the data for this second metric to your chart. The chart below, for example, simultaneously charts **Pageviews** and **Average Session Duration**. Note that each metric is presented in a different shade, and that the scales for each metric are on opposite sides of the chart. The scale for **Pageviews** is on the left-hand side of the chart, while the scale for the second variable, **Average Session Duration**, is located on the right-hand side of the chart.

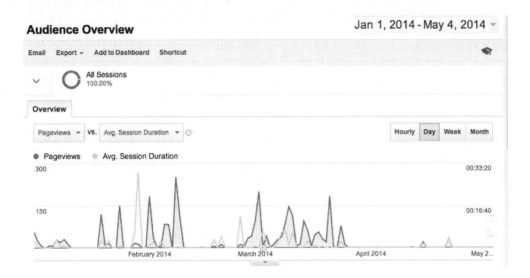

As before, putting your cursor over any specific date now brings up the data for both metrics for that date, as shown below.

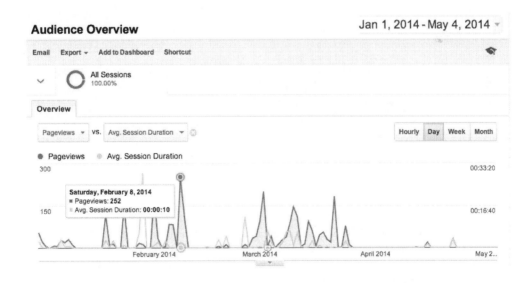

Finally, clicking on the small "x" next to your second metric eliminates that metric from the display.

Comparing metrics for two date ranges

We can compare a metric across two different time periods. The procedure for accomplishing this begins with the date range shown on the top of any data reporting page. First select your target date range by using either the calendar or date boxes to indicate start and end dates. Make certain that you have highlighted the appropriate start/end date box when selecting starting and ending dates. The display below shows that I've selected the period April 3, 2014 to May 3, 2014. The starting date box is highlighted.

Beneath the target date range boxes is a box labeled **Compare to**. Select this box and change the pull-down menu to its right to **Custom** and the calendar will change to display two date ranges, noting by color which dates have already been selected for the two time periods (see below). Note that Google Analytics will by default select a comparison time frame equal in length to the first (target) time frame.

If you are satisfied with the two date ranges, then click **Apply**. If this does not suit your needs, then you can always change your comparison date range.

- To set the comparison start date click in the left-hand date box beneath **Compare to** and then use the calendar to set the start date. (Note: the date box may not highlight when you click in it.) Once you select the date via the calendar, the date in the start box will change to the selected date.

- To set the comparison end date, click in the right-hand date box beneath **Compare to** and then use the calendar to set the end date. (Note: the date box may not highlight when you click in it.) Once you select the date via the calendar, the date in the end box will change to the selected date.

- Click **Apply**.

We'll select April 3, 2014 to May 3, 2014 for our first range and February 1, 2014 to March 31, 2014 as our second date range. When done, and the screen looks like that shown below, we click **Apply**. Note that the date ranges are not equivalent in length.

The line chart has now changed, where the metric **Sessions** is displayed for the two selected time periods, as shown below.

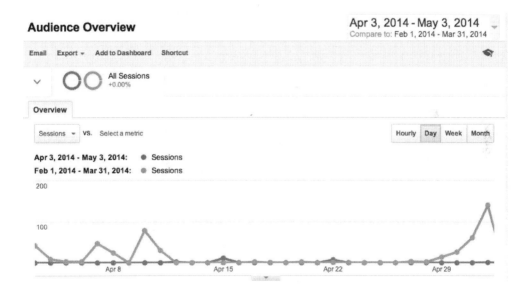

Chapter Addendum: Definitions of Key Metrics

Google Analytics provides a core set of metrics with regard to users, sessions, and pageviews. These metrics are defined as follows.

Users

The User metric reports the number of unique individuals who have had at least one session within the selected date range. This metric includes both new and returning individuals.

Sessions

Google notes that "The concept of a session in Google Analytics is important to understand because many features, reports, and metrics depend on how Analytics calculates sessions." Google Analytics defines a session as "a group of interactions that take place on your website within a given time frame. For example a single session can contain multiple pageviews, events, social interactions, custom variables, and ecommerce transactions."[4]

Time and activity both contribute to when Google Analytics considers a session to begin and end. There are three circumstances which define session stop time. Sessions end:

- After 30 minutes of inactivity

- At midnight

- If a user arrives via one campaign, leaves, and then comes back via a different campaign.

The impact of these events is illustrated in the following description of Mary's behaviors, where an "x" in the "New Session" column indicates that the behavior results in a new session being counted. Thus, over a three day period, Mary was responsible for six site sessions due to periods of activity and inactivity.

---

[4] *How Sessions Are Calculated in Analytics* at
https://support.google.com/analytics/answer/2731565?hl=en

Day	Time	Behavior	New Session
Monday	9:00	Mary visits for the first time	x
	9:25	Mary's infant starts to cry. Mary's computer stays on the website as Mary leaves to tend to her daughter.	
	9:56	*It's been more than 30 minutes since Mary viewed a page. Google Analytics ends the current session.*	
	11:30	It took a long time to get Mary's daughter to stop crying. Mary comes back to her computer and to your website. She begins to view pages on the website.	x
	11:45	Mary leaves the your website to surf surf elsewhere.	
	19:30	Mary returns to your website.	x
	20:05	Bedtime for Mary	
Tuesday	6:00	Mary returns to the website by typing the URL directly into her browser.	x
	6:20	Mary leaves the website to surf elsewhere.	
	11:42	Mary sees your Adwords ad and returns to your website by clicking on the ad. *Since the campaign source has changed, Google Analytics considers this the start of a new session.*	x
Wednesday	00:01	*Given the time, Google Analytics considers this the start of a new session.*	x

Google Analytics allows you to set the time limit that controls when a session is considered to have ended. When considering what the revised limit should be, keep your strategic goals in mind. A website with significant content, long blog entries, etc. may required longer session periods while sites with less or very simple content may require shorter session periods.

Session settings are altered on the property level. To access this function, click on **Admin** from any page and then make certain that the desired account, property and view are displayed. In the property column, click on **Tracking Info** and then on the next menu click on **Session Settings.** The page shown below will be displayed.

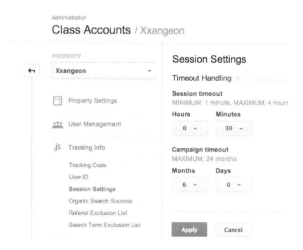

Provide the new timeout limits for either sessions or campaigns by using the pull-down menus and then press **Apply**.

Google Analytics will not apply new session or campaign timeout directions to historical data. As a result, it is best to create a new View (with annotation) if these parameters are changed, so that session characteristics are consistent across the entire time period being examined.

Percent new sessions

This is Google Analytic's estimate of the percent of first time (new) sessions during the selected time period. In the prior example Mary would have accounted for multiple sessions but only one new session when we consider the total week in which her visits took place.

Average session duration

Average session duration is calculated as the total duration of all sessions divided by the total number of sessions. Thus, if in a particular period all site users spent 5,000 minutes on your site distributed across 2,000 sessions, the average session duration would be 2.5 minutes (5000 ÷ 2000).

An individual's visit duration is calculated differently depending on whether or not there are *engagement hits* (such as playing a video) on the last page of a visit.

When there are no engagement hits, Google tracks the amount of time spent from the beginning of viewing the first page loaded upon entering the site to the beginning of viewing the last page seen before leaving the site, as illustrated in the following figure. Thus, in this example, the total session time would be 20 minutes (12:00 to 12:20).

NO PAGE ENGAGEMENT

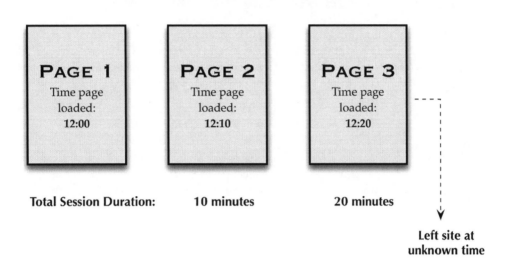

When there are multiple pages viewed with engagement hits, Google tracks the amount of time spent from the beginning of viewing the first page loaded upon entering the site to the start of engagement on the final page viewed, as shown below. In this case, total session time is 25 minutes, calculated by subtracting the time of the initial page load (12:00) from the time of the final engagement (12:25).

ENGAGEMENT ON
FINAL PAGE

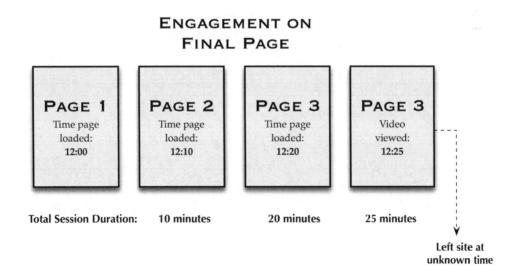

Google Analytics' calculation of session time requires a start and stop time. Thus, an individual must view at least two pages or have an initial page view with an engagement in order for this metric to be calculated. An individual without a second page view or engagement on the first page viewed is considered to have spent no time on site and so session length will be zero for that individual. Thus, it might be beneficial to build in some form of engagement (for example, a "read more" link), in order to get a more accurate reflection of session length. Building engagement into a page will also affect bounce rate, as described in the next section.

Finally, as session duration is an average, the calculation should be used directionally and with caution. Odd or skewed distributions can result in an overall average that does not represent your site visitor's typical session behavior. The metric can also be skewed if your site is designed for long engagement with just your entry page as the focus of behavior (as in a blog, for example).

Bounce rate

Bounce Rate is the percentage of single-page sessions, that is, sessions in which a site visitor leaves your site from the first page viewed without interacting with that or any other page. As with the other measures, Bounce Rate needs to be interpreted within the context of your site.

- A high bounce rate on a large, multipage site may indicate problems with landing page design or content. Here, individuals may be arriving at your site expecting but not finding specific content, or the landing page may be too confusing, cluttered or otherwise off-putting.

- A high bounce rate on a blog may be acceptable, however. Imagine, for example, that Denise comes to your blog and spends ten minutes reading your latest blog post. She's impressed and decides to return often. She leaves with a good attitude, but without any interaction with the page and without viewing any additional pages. Denise would be counted as a "bounce" and her time on site would be recorded as "0:00".

As noted previously, building engagement into your landing (or other pages) will reduce the bounce rate and will provide a more accurate estimate of those sessions without engagement or multiple page views.

Pages per session

Pages Per Session is the average number of pages viewed during a session on your site, keeping in mind that repeated views of a single page are counted in this calculation. Thus, if in a particular period there are 2000 total pageviews and 1,000 sessions, the average pages per session would be 2.0 (2000 ÷ 1000).

This calculation should be used directionally and with caution as it may not always represent your site visitor's *typical* behavior. Consider the following four site visitors:

	Number of Pageviews	Number of Sessions	Average Pages Per Per Session
Max	15	5	3.0
Ken	27	9	3.0
Sally	12	4	3.0
Candice	35	1	35.0
TOTAL	**89**	**19**	**4.7**

Google Analytics would calculate the pages per visit metric as 4.7 (89 pageviews divided by 19 visits), which is significantly higher than the *typical* pages per visit.

Pageviews

Pageviews is the total number of pages (which contain the Google Analytics tracking code) viewed during all sessions by all visitors. This measure is subject to inflation due to the way that duplicate page views are handled. If, for example, a visitor clicks reload after reaching a particular page, this is counted as an additional pageview and two pageviews would be recorded. Similarly, if a user navigates to a different page on the site and then returns to the original page, a second pageview is then recorded even though the original page had already been seen.

20

Practice With Audience Data (I)

This chapter's exercises address the analysis of audience metrics discussed in the prior chapter. As a result, all of the information and procedures you'll need to respond to these exercises are presented in Chapter 19.

True/false and multiple choice

This first set of exercises explores your understanding of audience data. You can check your answers beginning on page 601.

1. *True or False:* While you can set the starting date of a date range to anything you like, the ending date must always be the current date.

2. *True or False:* Only one date range can be examined at a time.

3. Which of the following are standard periods by which Google Analytics presents session and other metric data? Check all that apply.

   a. Hourly

   b. Daily

   c. Biweekly

   d. Weekly

   e. Monthly

   f. Semi-annually

   g. Annually

4. *True or False:* Only *session* data can be reported in the **Audience Overview** top of page line graph.

5. An individual comes to your site and spends six minutes reading the first page viewed, and then leaves the site without any engagement or other page views. *True or False:* The session duration for this individual would be zero.

6. *True or False:* It is considered "best practice" to annotate a chart whenever a campaign starts or ends.

7. Which of the following are metrics reported for audience data? Check all that apply.

    a. Sessions

    b. Average session duration

    c. Percent of sessions with multiple engagements

    d. Pages viewed per session

    e. Amount of content viewed per session

    f. Pageviews

    g. Content downloads

8. *True or False:* It is possible to create a line chart that simultaneously displays sessions and pageviews for a specified date range.

9. Which of the following situations would be considered a bounce?

    a. An individual spends less than 2 seconds viewing the landing page before viewing another page .

    b. An individual views only the landing page and then leaves without any additional engagement or pageviews.

    c. An individual views only the landing page, plays a video on that page, and then leaves without any additional engagement or pageviews

Application (I)

This exercise asks you to demonstrate your understanding of pageviews and sessions. Read the description of Dennis' surfing behaviors and then determine the total number of sessions, total session duration, and total number of pageviews he would have generated. The answer and explanation can be found beginning on page 601.

Day	Time	Behavior
Monday	09:00	Dennis visits for the first time. He begins to read the landing page.
	09:20	Dennis is done reading. He leaves the site without any additional pageviews or engagement.

	10:00	Dennis returns to the site and notices that the landing page has not changed.
	10.01	Dennis clicks to view a new page.
	10:02	Dennis clicks to view a new page.
	10:06	Dennis views a video on the same page.
	10:08	Dennis clicks to view a new page.
	10:11	Dennis leaves the page and the site without any further pageviews or engagement.
	23:59	Dennis visits the site. He begins to read the landing page.
Tuesday	00:01	Dennis leaves the landing page without any further pageviews or engagement.
	06:00	Dennis visits the site. He views the landing page.
	06.03	Dennis clicks to view a new page.
	06:05	Dennis clicks to view a new page.
	06:06	Dennis clicks to view a new page.
	06:11	Dennis leaves the site.

Application (II)

This exercise asks you to apply your understanding of audience data. Examine the three graphs shown on the next page. The graphs reflect the trend in user interactions with my travel agency website. We want to evaluate the effectiveness of an email campaign. Emails were sent on July 9, July 16, July 21, and July 28. As annotated in the top chart, the campaign had two goals: to increase the proportion of new sessions and to increase users' engagement with the site.

Our analysis can be found beginning on page 602.

Show:	All	Starred			+ Create new annotation
☆	Jul 9, 2013	Start of email campaign designed to (1) increase proportion of new sessions (2) increase engagement		edit	jdavis@mail.sdsu.edu
☆	Jul 16, 2013	Second email		edit	jdavis@mail.sdsu.edu
☆	Jul 20, 2013	SERVER CRASH!		edit	jdavis@mail.sdsu.edu
☆	Jul 21, 2013	Third email		edit	jdavis@mail.sdsu.edu
☆	Jul 28, 2013	Final email sent		edit	jdavis@mail.sdsu.edu

This final exercise asks you to manipulate your own audience data. Try to answer each of the following questions using the data for your travel website. Please answer them in order as the date range changes throughout the exercise. Refer to the prior chapter if you are unsure of any response.

1. Set your date range to reflect the entire time period in which your website has been active.

2. Display a line chart (by day) for the metric **Sessions**. On what day did you have the most sessions? How many sessions occurred on that day?

3. Display a line chart (by day) for the metric **% New Sessions**. On what day did you have the most **% New Sessions**? How many **% New Sessions** were there on that day?

4. Display a line chart (by day) that shows both **Sessions** and **% New Sessions** at the same time. Have the individual trends, as well as the relationship between these two metrics, remained constant over time?

5. Create a line chart (by day) that shows **Users**. Place an annotation on the date that you had the highest number of **Users.**

6. Change the prior line chart to display the data grouped by week.

7. Create two date ranges. One should be for the past two weeks, while the other should be for the two weeks prior (i.e., three to four weeks ago). Then create a line chart that plots **Average Session Duration**. How would you describe the similarities and differences in this metric when comparing the two time periods?

21

Audience Menu: Middle of Page Data

The metrics and charts in the center of the **Audience Overview** page (see below) provide summary information for key audience metrics within the selected time period. The data below relates to activity from January 1, 2014 to May 4, 2014.

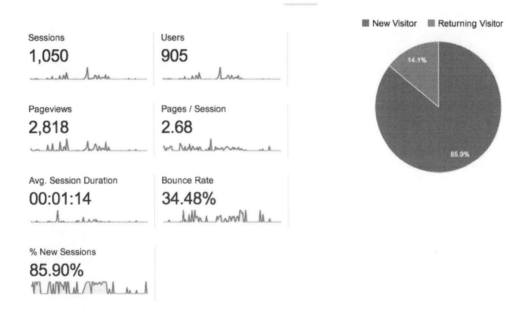

Each of these metrics was defined in Chapter 19. Note that clicking on any of the line graphs in this block brings detailed information on that metric up to the line graph shown on the top of the page (as discussed in Chapter 19). Clicking on the small line graph beneath **% New Sessions,** for example, changes the metric displayed in the top line graph to **% New Sessions.**

You'll recall from Chapter 19 that we can simultaneously examine two different time periods. When two time periods are selected, the data in this summary chart is changed to facilitate this comparison.

Imagine that we want to compare this set of metrics across two time periods: January 1, 2014 to February 28, 2014 and March 1, 2014 to May 4, 2014. The parameters used for creating this comparison are shown on the top of page 134.

The display then reports the comparative summary metrics for each time period, as shown below.

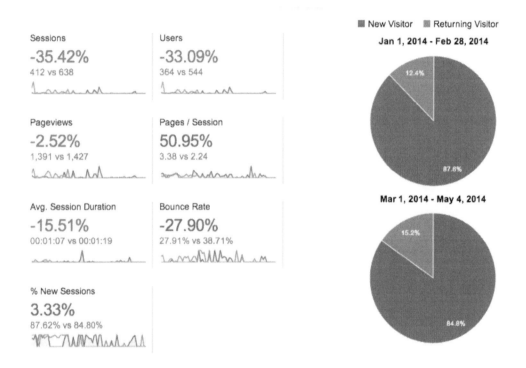

The percentages compare time period one to time period two, where a negative percentage indicates *lower* (or worse) numbers for period one versus period two and a positive percentage indicates *higher* (or better) numbers for period one versus period two. Thus, in this example, period one (January to February) had fewer sessions than period two (March to May). There were 412 versus 638 sessions. The positive percentage for average number of pages viewed per session indicates a higher average number of pages viewed per session in period one versus period two (3.38 versus 2.24 pages).

22

Audience Menu: Bottom of Page Data

The links and charts on the bottom of the **Audience Overview** page provide access to detailed audience descriptive dimensions and metrics, as shown below.

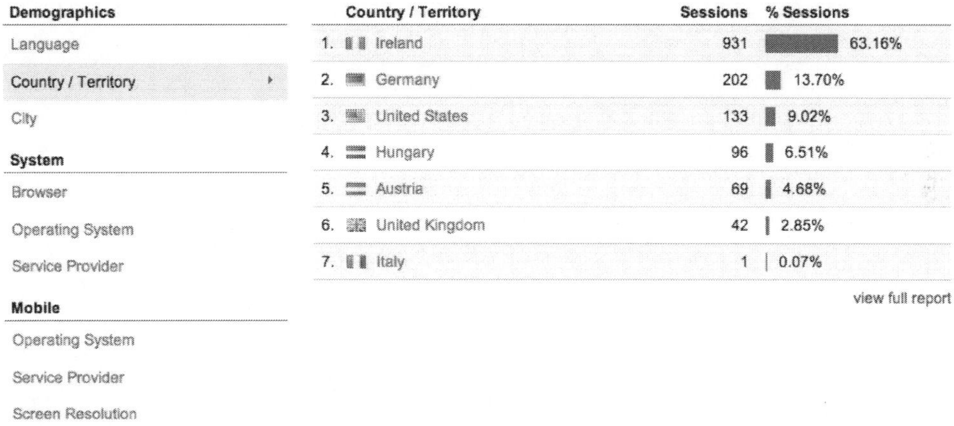

Demographics		Country / Territory		Sessions	% Sessions	
Language		1.	Ireland	931		63.16%
Country / Territory	▸	2.	Germany	202		13.70%
City		3.	United States	133		9.02%
System		4.	Hungary	96		6.51%
Browser		5.	Austria	69		4.68%
Operating System		6.	United Kingdom	42		2.85%
Service Provider		7.	Italy	1		0.07%
Mobile						view full report
Operating System						
Service Provider						
Screen Resolution						

Dimensions, organized into three large groups (Demographics, System, and Mobile), are shown on the left-hand side of the page. Each dimension is clickable, where a click brings up more detailed dimensions, values and metrics related to the selected dimension. The chart on the right-hand side of the page above, for example, tells me the countries in which my sessions originate and the percentage of sessions from each country. This chart was generated when I clicked on the **Country/Territory** link.

We have two options for exploring the data in more detail. First, we can click on active links within the table. Selecting any link within the table brings up a new page with a diverse range of information available for the selected dimension and value. Second, we can click on the **View Full Report** link beneath the table, which provides a detailed tabular report on the selected dimension.

Clicking a link in the table

Selecting a link in the **Audience Overview** bottom of page table takes you to a new page which provides greater detail on the selected dimension's value, in this case Ireland, which is the country in which the most site sessions occur. The map and table shown below are displayed when I click on Ireland in the summary table on the bottom of the **Audience Overview** page.

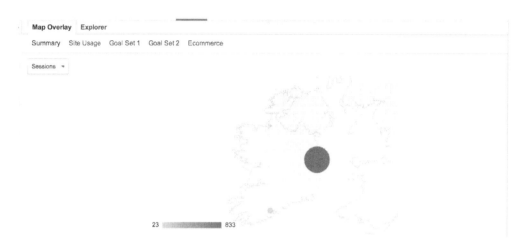

City	Acquisition			Behavior			Conversions eCommerce ▾		
	Sessions ↓	% New Sessions	New Users	Bounce Rate	Pages / Session	Avg. Session Duration	Transactions	Revenue	Ecommerce Conversion Rate
	931	82.71%	770	32.55%	2.45	00:00:45	295	$2,467,781.95	31.69%
	% of Total 63.16% (1,474)	Site Avg 82.97% (-0.32%)	% of Total 62.96% (1,223)	Site Avg 33.58% (-3.09%)	Site Avg 2.49 (-1.70%)	Site Avg 00:00:47 (-4.21%)	% of Total 64.96% (454)	% of Total 62.49% ($3,948,961.95)	Site Avg 30.80% (2.88%)
1. Dublin	833 (89.47%)	80.67%	672 (87.27%)	32.05%	2.47	00:00:49	258 (87.46%)	$2,050,081.95 (83.07%)	30.97%
2. Cork	47 (5.05%)	100.00%	47 (6.10%)	48.94%	1.02	00:00:01	23 (7.80%)	$253,800.00 (10.28%)	48.94%
3. (not set)	28 (3.01%)	100.00%	28 (3.64%)	17.86%	4.54	00:00:34	11 (3.73%)	$117,600.00 (4.77%)	39.29%
4. Sligo	23 (2.47%)	100.00%	23 (2.99%)	34.78%	2.13	00:00:09	3 (1.02%)	$46,300.00 (1.88%)	13.04%

We'll look at each data report separately.

The top map[5]

The location of the circles in the map informs me of the cities in which my sessions originate while the size of the circles indicates the *relative* number of sessions that come from each city. The larger the circle, the larger the city's number of sessions.

---

[5] The map is displayed whenever geography is the dimension of interest. Otherwise, line graphs are displayed.

The map is interactive. Rolling your cursor over any of the cities displays the relevant data for that city, in this case the data is related to sessions. Sessions are displayed in the cursor roll-over because this is the default metric shown in the pull-down menu in the upper left-hand corner.

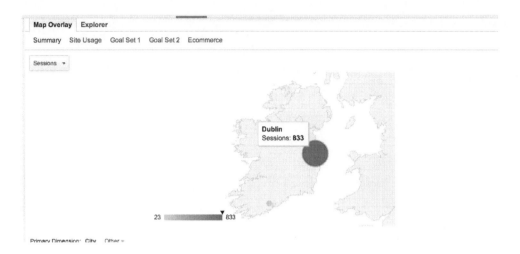

You are not restricted to the variables shown on the initial map, keeping in mind that all data will be restricted to the dimension value that brought you to this page, in this case Ireland. The figure shown below illustrates your options for alternative metric selection.

Selecting **Average Order Value** from the pull-down menu changes the map and displays this new information in the same format as the initial **Session**s map (see the top of page 138). Now, however, the circles and data have changed to report **Average Order Value.**

The bottom table

The table below is displayed beneath the map.

The first two sections of this table (labeled **Acquisition** and **Behavior**) report six of the metrics we've seen before on the **Audience Overview** page, except now the data is reported (organized) by city in tabular/numeric format.[6] Only Irish cities are shown because this page was generated when I selected "Ireland" from the table on the **Audience Overview** page. The last block of text relates to website conversions, in this case, ecommerce transactions. The data in this block is selectable through the pull-down menu next to **Conversions** on the top right-hand side of the chart.

-   **Transactions** reports the absolute number and percentage of all transactions for each value listed in the first column. In this case, Dublin accounts for 258 of 295 total Irish transactions (87.49%).

----

[6] Note that "not set" in line three of the table indicates that Google Analytics was unable to determine the exact city.

- **Revenue** reports the amount of sales generated and the overall percentage of sales. In this case, Dublin accounts for just over two million dollars in sales (or 83.07% of all sales).

- **Ecommerce Conversion Rate** reports the percentage of all sessions that resulted in a sale. In this case, 30.97% of all site sessions from Dublin resulted in a sale.

Charts in this format allow you to easily compare the performance of each metric to averages for the overall dimension. This is an important comparison because it provides insights into how specific metrics either exceed or lag behind the average, thereby identifying areas of website strength and weakness. The numeric table on page 138, for example, indicates that there is a significant difference in the bounce rate among visitors from different Irish cities. When using the overall Irish bounce percentage as the frame of reference, it is clear that the bounce rate in Cork is much higher than average. We would want to try to determine why this is the case in order to reduce this bounce percentage. Additionally, the ecommerce conversion rate in Sligo is considerably below the overall average. We would want to determine why this was occurring and plan a response that would increase this specific conversion rate.

Note that the number of dimensions reportable in this table varies depending upon the depth of detail collected by Google Analytics. The prior chart was generated directly from the Ireland link on the **Audience Overview** page. Note that on the very top of the table (in the left-hand corner) the **Primary Dimension** of **City** is highlighted and alone. This indicates that this is the only detail available for Ireland.

Clicking on the United States link from the table on the **Audience Overview** page brings up a different level of detail. Selecting this link first reports data by state, as illustrated below. (Note that Google Analytics defines states as "Regions.")

Now there are more options next to **Primary Dimension**. Data for the United States is available on the **City** and **Metro** level. All cities or metro areas can be shown in the same table (by clicking on either **City** or **Metro** as shown in the following two tables.)

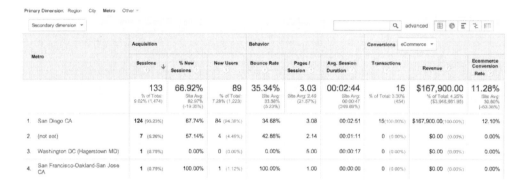

Finally, note that items shown in the first column are also interactive links. Clicking on any of these links will display additional relevant information, if available.

Changing dimensions and metrics in the bottom table

Acquisition, **Behavior** and **Conversions** are the default metrics displayed in the bottom of page table. You are not limited to these metrics, however.

Immediately beneath the tab labeled **Map Overlay** on the top of the map are alternative display options. **Summary** is already selected as the default (see below).

Clicking on **Site Usage** changes the dimensions and metrics presented in the bottom of page table (see below). Now all metrics relate to site usage behaviors.

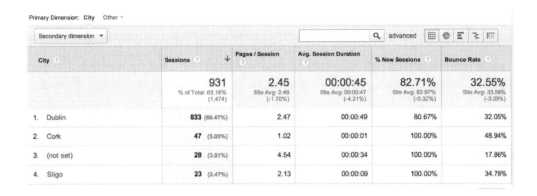

Similarly, selecting **Ecommerce** displays ecommerce metrics in the bottom of page table (see below).

Secondary dimensions

Most numeric tables allow you to add a secondary dimension to the basic analysis.

The secondary dimension option, when available, can be found in the upper left-hand corner of a numeric table. Secondary dimensions are accessed via a pull-down menu which by default is labeled **Secondary dimension** (see table above). Pulling down this menu brings up a range of additional dimensions and metrics which can be added to the primary analysis (see table on the top of page 142).

Let's try to determine how browser and type of access (mobile versus desktop) affect transactions and sales. We begin on the **Audience Overview** page, selecting **Browser** to bring up the listing of browsers used to access my site (see below).

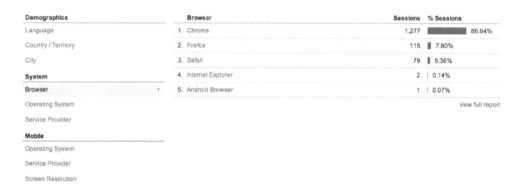

Clicking on the **view full report** (lower right in the table above) link brings up the table shown below. Something is odd about the reported metrics. While it is not surprising that one browser type may dominate, it is surprising that there were **no** transactions among those using Firefox, Internet Explorer or an Android browser (granted, the sample size for the latter two is small).

We can look more deeply at this data by selecting **Device Category** from the **Secondary Dimension** pull-down menu (see below).

When this is done, the table shown below is displayed. The metrics in this table provide important direction for site revision and future site success. With regard to Firefox, all sessions originated from desktops, but there were no transactions. Is there something on our site that is not working with Firefox, in particular, the purchase page? With regard to Safari and Android, these sessions originated on a mobile devise and again there were no transactions. To what extent is our site optimized for mobile, and what, in particular on our site, might not be working with mobile devices?

Alternative table formats

As we saw earlier, the table shown on the top of page 144 is the primary display once Ireland is selected as the dimension value of interest. Note that in the upper-right hand corner above the chart is a series of icons.

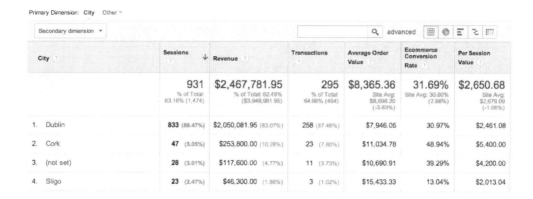

City ?	Sessions ↓ ?	Revenue ?	Transactions ?	Average Order Value ?	Ecommerce Conversion Rate ?	Per Session Value ?
	931 % of Total: 63.16% (1,474)	$2,467,781.95 % of Total: 62.49% ($3,948,981.95)	295 % of Total: 64.98% (454)	$8,365.36 Site Avg: $8,698.20 (-3.83%)	31.69% Site Avg: 30.80% (2.88%)	$2,650.68 Site Avg: $2,679.09 (-1.06%)
1. Dublin	833 (89.47%)	$2,050,081.95 (83.07%)	258 (87.46%)	$7,946.05	30.97%	$2,461.08
2. Cork	47 (5.05%)	$253,800.00 (10.28%)	23 (7.80%)	$11,034.78	48.94%	$5,400.00
3. (not set)	28 (3.01%)	$117,600.00 (4.77%)	11 (3.73%)	$10,690.91	39.29%	$4,200.00
4. Sligo	23 (2.47%)	$46,300.00 (1.86%)	3 (1.02%)	$15,433.33	13.04%	$2,013.04

Each of these icons (see below for a larger visual) allows you to alter both what data are displayed and the format in which the data are displayed.

The box icon on the far left represents the default view. Selection of this icon presents the data in tabular format, as shown in the table at the top of this page.

The next icon, the circle, allows you to turn any set of available metrics into a numeric table and pie chart, again keeping in mind that the data displayed are restricted to only that which is relevant to your selected dimension. My selection of this icon displays the table and pie chart shown below. Similar to prior data displays, the default view displays sessions. I've also selected the same metric for both the tabular and pie displays, allowing the pie chart to display the tabular data.

The data display can be changed by using the pull-down menus. The chart below, for example, illustrates what happens when both displays are set to **Transactions**.

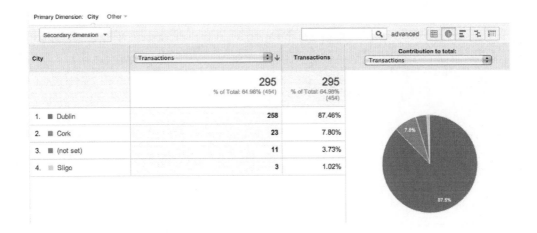

This chart would be interpreted as follows:

- There were 295 total transactions in Irish cities.

- 258 of these transactions originated in Dublin. This represents 87.46% of all Irish transactions.

The previous examples selected the same metric to be displayed in both the numeric table and pie chart. In this circumstance, the pie chart simply presents an alternative display to the numeric table. This does not have to be the case, however.

We can use this charting option to examine the relationship between two metrics by selecting different metrics for the numeric and pie chart. The chart shown below, for example, displays the number of sessions in the first column and revenue in both the second numeric column and the pie chart. We select these measures by using the pull-down menus.

While all of this data is available in the original numeric table, conducting an analysis that focuses on just two metrics makes it easier to identify and answer important strategic questions. Given the prior two displays, we might ask: What is the relationship between sessions and revenue, that is, are some cities over-performing or underperforming when their percent contribution to sessions is compared to their percent contribution to revenue? We can answer this important question by incorporating the relevant data from each of the prior two displays into a single table, as shown below.

Relationship of Sessions and Revenue in Irish Cities

City	% Sessions	% Revenue	Index[7]
Dublin	87.46%	83.07%	95
Cork	7.80	10.28	132
Sligo	1.02	1.88	184

This chart is informative. While Dublin accounts for the vast majority of both sessions and revenue, the relationship between these two measures (as reflected in the relatively lower index) is "off." Dublin's revenue is a bit less than you would expect given its percentage of sessions. The remaining two cities are over-performing, that is, they are generating more revenue than their percentage of sessions would predict. Thus, we are faced with two important yet different strategic questions:

- How do we increase the revenue per session in Dublin?

- How do we increase sessions in Cork and Sligo to capitalize on the relatively greater revenue generated per session?

The next icon, the bars, allows you to turn any set of available metrics into a bar chart, again keeping in mind that the data displayed is restricted to only that which is relevant to your selected dimension. Selection of this icon displays the table and bar chart for sessions shown on the top of the next page.

---

[7] An index compares the size of one group to another through division. The index for Dublin, for example, is calculated by dividing Dublin's revenue percentage by the session percentage and then multiplying the outcome by 100. An index of 100 is average. The more an index lies above or below 100, the greater the difference in size between the two measures.

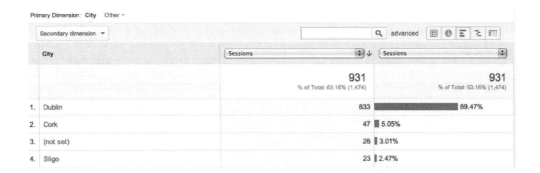

As with the earlier displays, you can report the data for one or two metrics through use of the pull-down menus.

The next icon, the over/under bars, allows you to turn any set of available metrics into a bar chart that compares each value's metric to the overall average, noting the percentage by which that metric is over or under the average. Selection of this icon displays the table and bar chart shown below.

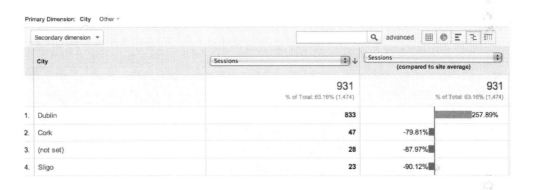

Finally, the icon on the far right allows you to cross-tabulate the data. Personally, I've found little use for this data display.

23
Practice With Audience Data (II)

This chapter presents several sets of exercises to help you apply and extend your knowledge of the type of metrics and reports available through **Audience Overview**.

True/false and multiple choice

This first set makes certain that you understand key concepts. Feel free to open and refer to the Audience Overview discussion or access the Audience Overview in your analytics account when you are answering these questions. When you are done, or if you are stuck, the answers can be found on page 603.

1. Which of the following metrics is not provided in the middle of the **Audience Overview** page?

    a. Sessions

    b. Users

    c. Average session duration

    d. % New Users

2. Imagine that you have decided to compare audience metrics for two time periods. *True or False:* The most recent of the two time periods must always be selected as the "compare to" period.

3. You click on the small line graph beneath the **% New Sessions** metric (see below).

    True or False: Clicking on this graph brings up a window to adjust the date range of the display.

4. *True or False:* The metrics displayed in the center of the **Audience Overview** page can only display one date range at a time.

*Questions 5 to 7 refer to the data available on the bottom of the **Audience Overview** page.*

5. Which of the following dimensions are available on the bottom of the **Audience Overview** page? Check all that apply.

   a. Language

   b. Browser

   c. Screen Resolution

   d. City

6. Clicking on the **Country/Territory** link will display a list of all countries in which sessions originated. *True or False:* This list will be ordered alphabetically.

7. You click on **Demographics > City** to bring up a display of all cities in which sessions originated. You click on "San Diego." Which of the following is true?

   a. The next screen displays metrics for all cities in California in which sessions originated.

   b. The next screen displays metrics for only San Diego.

*Questions 8 to 10 refer to the map shown when you click on the name of a specific country from **Demographics > Country/Territory** on the bottom of the **Audience Overview** page.*

8. *True or False:* **Sessions** are the default metric when the initial map is displayed.

9. *True or False:* The size of circles on the map visually communicates each location's population size.

10. Which of the following are alternative metrics that the map can display? Check all that apply.

    a. Ecommerce, such as transactions and revenue

    b. Site usage, such as bounce rate and average session duration

*Questions 11 to 13 refer to the table shown when you click on the name of a specific country from **Demographics > Country/Territory** on the bottom of the **Audience Overview** page.*

11. *True of False:* None of the metrics displayed in this numeric table can be changed or altered.

12. *True of False:* Secondary dimensions can be applied to this table.

13. There are two pull-down menus displayed when you select the pie or line chart option above the numeric table. *True or False:* These menus may be set to report/display different metrics.

Application

This exercise asks you to think strategically about the information provided through the **Audience Overview** page. Please use the charts provided to answer each of the following questions. When you are done, or if you are stuck, our responses can be found beginning on page 603.

1. Based on the data shown in the chart below, what conclusions can you draw about browser type and site engagement?

2. Based on the data shown in the chart below, what conclusions can you draw about browser type and ecommerce outcomes?

	Browser	Sessions	Revenue	Transactions	Average Order Value	Ecommerce Conversion Rate
		807 % of Total: 100.00% (807)	$1,442,900.00 % of Total: 100.00% ($1,442,900.00)	207 % of Total: 100.00% (207)	$6,970.53 Site Avg: $6,970.53 (0.00%)	25.65% Site Avg: 25.65% (0.00%)
☐	1. Chrome	736 (91.20%)	$1,442,900.00 (100.00%)	207 (100.00%)	$6,970.53	28.12%
☐	2. Firefox	54 (6.69%)	$0.00 (0.00%)	0 (0.00%)	$0.00	0.00%
☐	3. Safari	12 (1.49%)	$0.00 (0.00%)	0 (0.00%)	$0.00	0.00%
☐	4. Internet Explorer	5 (0.62%)	$0.00 (0.00%)	0 (0.00%)	$0.00	0.00%

3. Imagine that your ecommerce company had a "good December" and wanted to carry the momentum into and through January. Use the following charts to determine how well the company achieved this goal. The table is set up as follows:

4. The data shown in the following charts represent your top three cities. What conclusions can you draw about these cities?

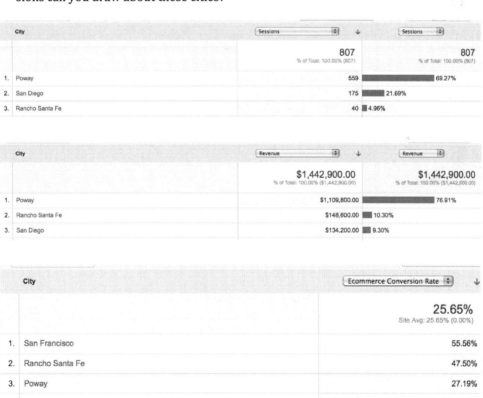

This exercise asks you to apply your understanding of all of the data provided on or through the **Audience Overview**. Please answer each of the following questions using your own Google Analytics account and the data collected for your travel website. If it has been more than a month since you started to collect data, make certain to set your date range to include the entire time span of data collection.

1. What is the overall trend in site **Sessions**? Have you seen consistent growth or decline or have sessions been sporadic?

2. On what date did you have the greatest number of sessions? How many sessions occurred?

3. Annotate the date with the greatest number of sessions. Annotate the date with the least number of sessions.

4. What is the overall trend in **% New Sessions**? Have you seen consistent growth or decline or have **% New Sessions** been sporadic?

5. On what date did you have the greatest number of **% New Sessions**? How many sessions occurred?

6. Create a bar chart that displays both **Bounce Rate** and **Pageviews** on the same graph. Does there appear to be any relationship between the two?

7. Are your site interactions (sessions) primarily driven by new sessions?

8. What percent of your site sessions originated outside of the United States? What is the percentage?

9. Over the time period being used, provide the metric to respond to each of the following information requests.

    a. What was the total number of sessions?

    b. What was the average bounce rate?

    c. What was the average session duration?

    d. What is the average number of pages/session?

10. What city is responsible for the greatest percentage of site sessions? What is the percentage?

11. What is the primary browser used to access your site? What is the percentage of sessions accounted for by that browser?

12. Focus on the browsers used to create sessions on your site. Is the bounce rate similar or different for the browsers used?

13. Focus on the different cities from which sessions originated. Is site usage similar or different across the cities responsible for the most sessions?

14. Select two additional metrics that provide insights into your website's audience. Why are these metrics important and what insights do they provide?

24
The Full Audience Menu

The left-hand side of every Google Analytics report page contains menu options that allow you to access data across a broad range of categories. The menu headers are: **Real-Time, Audience, Acquisition, Behavior** and **Conversions**. For now, let's finish looking at **Audience** data. (Note that "Behavior" menu options get a bit confusing because there are actually two of these. One appears as an option in this Audience Menu while the other heads its own major menu. The data reported via each option are quite different. We discuss the first option in this chapter. Chapters 26 to 32 discuss the full Behavior Menu and its options.)

Clicking on the **Audience** link opens a menu of additional audience dimensions (see below). Each of the dimensions, in turn, has one or more data reporting options and metrics.[8]

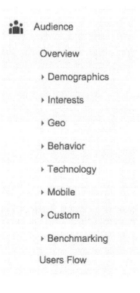

---

[8] One of the options shown in the Audience Menu is Benchmarking, which is activated after you check the "Share anonymously with Google and others" box in your Google Analytics account settings tab on the Administrator's page. Benchmarking allows you to review and compare your results to metrics by channel, location, or device for 1,600 industries and 1,250 markets. While this data is interesting, we feel that the limitations of the underlying data lead us to recommend that this data only be used directionally and only in those circumstances where you are certain that the benchmark data represents websites which have goals and objectives identical to yours.

Under certain circumstances, Google Analytics will provide estimates of your website users' demographics and interests. You can obtain this data by clicking on the relevant link beneath either the **Audience > Demographics** or **Audience > Interest** links, where the dimensions display the following values and metrics:

- Demographics
    Overview (overview of traffic by age and gender)
    Age (traffic by age ranges)
    Gender (traffic by gender)

- Interests
    Overview (overview of traffic by affinity and other categories)
    Affinity Categories (behavior by affinity categories)
    In-Market Categories (behavior by in-market categories)
    Other Categories (behavior by other interest categories)

These reports can help you understand the characteristics of the individuals who initiate site sessions, and as a result, can contribute to strategic planning. You can, for example, examine your analytics data by these demographic or interest characteristics to better understand the differences in age or interests between converting and non-converting users.

Similar to other data collected by Google Analytics, cookies play a key role in data collection for demographic and interest metrics.

- Google uses multiple, complimentary approaches to estimating demographic information. When someone visits a website that has partnered with the Google Display Network, Google uses cookies to store a number in their browser to remember his or her visits. This number uniquely identifies a web browser on a specific computer, not a specific person. Browsers may be associated with a demographic category (such as gender or age range) based on the sites that were visited. In addition, some sites, such as social networking sites, provide Google with the demographic information that people volunteered to share. Google may also use demographics derived from Google profiles.

---

[9] Data in this section is adapted from the following Google sources: *Reach people of specific age and gender* (https://www.google.com/analytics/web/?hl=en#report/visitors-demographics-overview/a41714766w71256007p74402499/), *Reach people interested in your products or services* (https://support.google.com/adwords/answer/2497941?hl=en&utm_id=ad), *Overview of Demographics & Interests reports* (https://support.google.com/analytics/answer/2799357?hl=en), and pages linked from *About the audience reports* (https://support.google.com/analytics/answer/1012034?hl=en&ref_topic=1007027).

Think about Sara, who loves to garden. Many of the gardening sites and blogs on the Google Display Network that Sara visits have a majority of female visitors. Based on this, Sarah's browser would be added to the "female" demographic category. Thus, if Sara uses this browser to visit your site, then Google will count her visit as generated by a female.

-   Google predicts an individual's interests from his or her web browsing behaviors. When someone visits a Google partner website, Google uses the content of the page or website as well as data from third-party companies to associate interests with a visitor's anonymous cookie ID, taking into account how often that individual visits sites of different categories. In addition, Google may use information that people provide to these partner websites about interests.

    Google places visitors in an interest category for 30 days, but this can change depending on the sites they visit. Imagine, for example, how a gardening enthusiast would most likely visit gardening-related sites over long periods of time. If that person then moves on to another interest (such as cooking) and is no longer reading as many pages about gardening but is reading a lot of pages related to cooking, Google will update the person's profile to remove gardening and include cooking. If, however, the gardening enthusiast continues to visit gardening websites for a long period of time, he or she will likely be included in that interest category for a longer period of time.

Things to keep in mind[10]

Google analytics demographic and interest information should always be used directionally rather than definitively. This is the case for four reasons:

-   Google may not actually know the real age and interests of the vast majority of your site users.

    You can see the accuracy of Google's classifications by using the browser you use most often online and then taking a look at your own Google Ads settings at:

    `https://www.google.com/settings/ads`

    Is your description accurate? The profile and interests associated with the Safari browser on my personal computer have me classified as a 55 to 64 year old woman who is interested in bicycles, rap music and fitness, all of which (needless to say) don't apply. The profile and interests associated with the Firefox browser on my personal computer classify me as a 35 to 44 year old male interested in East Asian and electronic music (all of which, again, are inaccurate descriptors).

---

[10] *Demographics and Interest Reports in Google Analytics* (http://www.seerinteractive.com/blog/demographics-and-interest-reports-in-google-analytics).

- Data thresholds are applied to demographic and interest reports, which means that not all of the user data may be available, so you may be viewing partial and perhaps nonrepresentative data.

- Your website users may have opted out of having data collected in their Google Ads Settings. There may also be other ways of opting out of having this data collected that could also impact what is reported by Google Analytics. Again, you may only have partial data, which should be used with caution.

- Data from users who are not logged into their Google account when browsing might not be recorded.

How accurate are the data?

Given that not all data are displayed and that a great deal of the data is estimated, it is important to understand data accuracy prior to its application to strategic planning. Overall, it appears that demographic and interest data accuracy increases along with sample size, so be very careful about using this data when it reflects a relatively low number of sessions.[11]

Implementing demographic and interest data collection

You will need to change three things on your site in order to collect and access this data. It is necessary to:

- Modify your tracking code to support display advertising.

- Update your privacy policy to adhere to Google's privacy policy with regard to display advertising and data collection.

- Enable Demographics reports in the Analytics interface.

Specific guidance for implementing demographics and interest data collection and reporting can be found at:

`https://support.google.com/analytics/answer/2819948?hl=en&ref_topic=2799375`

`https://support.google.com/analytics/answer/2444872?hl=en&utm_id=ad`

---

[11] For more detailed discussion of data accuracy see: *Google Analytics Demographic Reports: How accurate are the Genders and Ages?* (http://aladata.co.uk/google-analytics-demographic-reports-accurate-genders-ages/); *How accurate are Google Analytics age and demographics reports?* (http://pr0v.com/accurate-google-analytics-age-gender-demographics/); *How accurate are Google Analytics demographics reports?* (http://www.humix.be/en/blog/how-accurate-are-google-analytics-demographics-reports).

Clicking on the **Audience > Geo** link brings up options to view either language or location information. These links lead to the same information as that generated through the **Audience Overview** page and, as a result, you should already know how to interpret and manipulate this data. Keep the following in mind when interpreting this data:

- Language spoken is inferred from the user's browser locale.

- Location is derived from mapping IP addresses to geographic locations. City location may not be accurate for visits from mobile devices.

Finally, it is possible that you will see "(not set)" in these reports. In this context "(not set)" means that Google Analytics could not determine where someone was located.

Behavior

Clicking on the **Audience > Behavior** link brings up three options: **New Vs. Returning, Frequency and Recency**, and **Engagement.**

New Vs. Returning

The **Audience Overview** page we looked at earlier presented summary information for Sessions, Users and % New Sessions. The **Audience > Behavior > New Vs. Returning** option provides another perspective on these metrics.

When this option is selected from the left-hand menu, the first thing we see is the standard reporting table (see below), with metrics reported individually for new and returning visitors.

This table always has the potential to provide important strategic insights. In my case, there is some depressing news for my travel agency website. First, almost all of my sessions are generated by new visitors. Repeat business is almost nonexistent. Second, the behaviors of new visitors versus returning visitors are quite different. Unfortunately for our travel agency, returning visitors have a higher bounce rate and are much less likely to make a purchase (as reflected in the Ecommerce Conversion Rate column). Clearly, something needs to be done to address this situation. The business cannot be successful without returning visitors. Why aren't people coming back? When they come back, why aren't they staying and buying? Both of these questions need an immediate answer.

In situations such as this, it is often beneficial to use the charting options on the top of the table to focus on one or two specific metrics. The first chart below uses the over/under chart option and the pull-down menus to focus on the relative size of new to returning website visitors. This chart makes it easy to see that almost all of my traffic is from new visitors. The second chart below simultaneously displays both sessions and ecommerce conversion rate for new versus returning visitors. As with the first chart, this approach makes the differences between the two groups much easier to see.

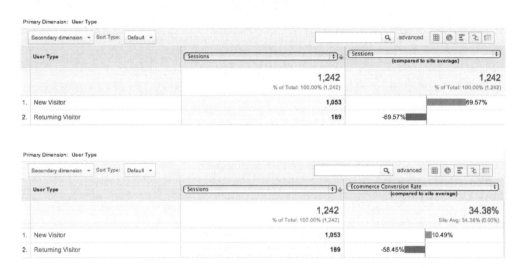

Frequency and Recency

This report lets you see the extent to which your site is able to maintain user interest over time using sessions as the classifying metric. **Audience > Behavior > Frequency** reports the number of single and multiple sessions taking place within a specified time frame. **Audience > Behavior > Recency** tells you how many days, if any, have elapsed between the first and subsequent sessions.

Clicking on the **Audience > Behavior >Frequency** and **Audience > Behavior > Recency** options first displays a distribution of sessions (**Count of Sessions**) within your specified time period, as shown on the top of page 160. A **Count of Sessions** equal to one (in the first column) indicates a single session, that is, a session without a return to the site. Here you can see that the news for my website continues to be quite depressing. As expected from the prior data, the overwhelming majority of site visitors had only a single session: 1,053 out of a total 1,242 sessions were a single session. Among the remainder, very few sessions were two or more by the same individual.

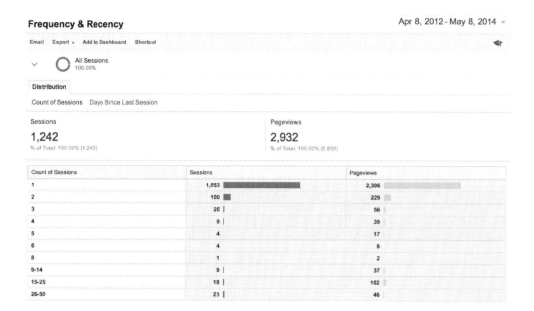

Clicking on **Days Since Last Session** on the top of the chart changes the data view to that shown below. A **Days Since Last Session** equal to zero indicates a new user. A **Days Since Last Session** equal to one indicates that a user visited and then returned on the next day. Here we can see that site users make up their minds very quickly - they either never come back after their first session or they initiate another session very quickly. Few site visitors initiate a session after a time lag (from first visit) of two or more days.

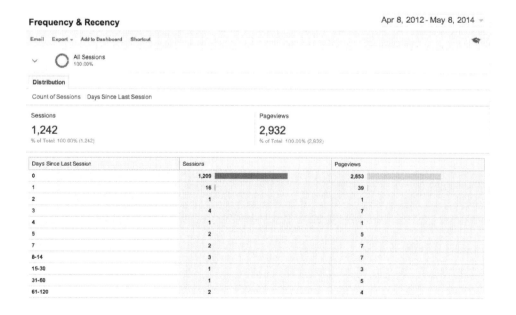

Engagement

The last **Behavior** metric is **Engagement**, which reports how much time people spend on your site (reported as Session Duration) and how many pages they view (reported as Page Depth).

The chart of **Session Duration** for my site is shown below. The news for my site keeps getting worse. The overwhelming majority of site visitors spend less than 10 seconds on my site.

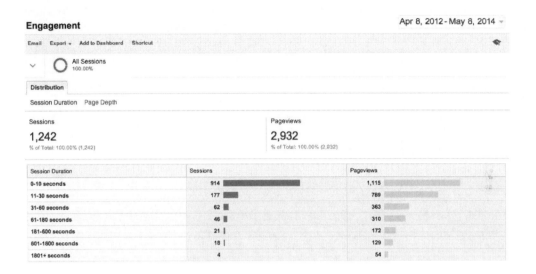

The news from the **Page Depth** report (below) is no better. The overwhelming majority of site visitors leave after viewing just a single page.

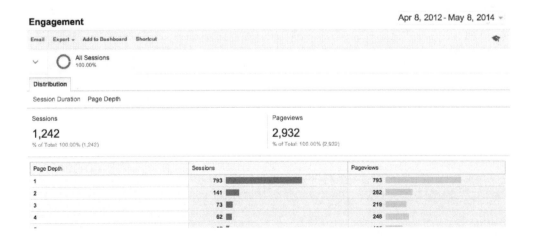

The **Audience > Technology** link provides the opportunity to view two technology-related aspects of user behavior: **Browser & OS** and **Network**. Note that links to this information also appear on the **Audience Overview** page.

Browser and OS Report

The **Audience > Technology > Browser & OS** report lets you see the different browsers people use to reach your site, along with information about the systems that run those browsers. Google notes that "this information is helpful when you are making design decisions about your site. For example, if the bulk of your visitors are using screen resolutions of 1024 x 768 and above, you can design for the additional viewing area. With information about which browsers visitors use and whether they maintain recent versions of Flash, you can scope your testing to cover the most likely population."

Selecting the **Audience > Technology > Browser & OS** report first brings up information on the various browsers used to initiate sessions on your site (see below). Chrome is the overwhelming favorite for my site.

Note that links to additional, related information (Operating System, Screen Resolution, Screen Colors, Flash version) run across the top of the table. Clicking on any of these links brings up a table with the relevant information. Selecting Screen Resolution, for example, displays the table shown on the top of page 163.

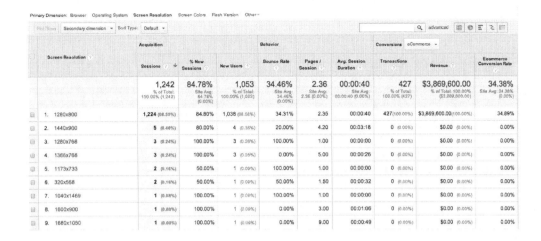

Screen Resolution	Acquisition			Behavior			Conversions eCommerce		
	Sessions	% New Sessions	New Users	Bounce Rate	Pages / Session	Avg. Session Duration	Transactions	Revenue	Ecommerce Conversion Rate
	1,242 % of Total: 100.00% (1,242)	84.78% Site Avg: 84.78% (0.00%)	1,053 % of Total: 100.00% (1,053)	34.46% Site Avg: 34.46% (0.00%)	2.36 Site Avg: 2.36 (0.00%)	00:00:40 Site Avg: 00:00:40 (0.00%)	427 % of Total 100.00% (427)	$3,869,600.00 % of Total: 100.00% ($3,869,600.00)	34.38% Site Avg: 34.38% (0.00%)
1. 1280x800	1,224 (98.55%)	84.80%	1,038 (98.56%)	34.31%	2.35	00:00:40	427 (100.00%)	$3,869,600.00 (100.00%)	34.89%
2. 1440x900	5 (0.40%)	80.00%	4 (0.38%)	20.00%	4.20	00:03:18	0 (0.00%)	$0.00 (0.00%)	0.00%
3. 1280x768	3 (0.24%)	100.00%	3 (0.28%)	100.00%	1.00	00:00:00	0 (0.00%)	$0.00 (0.00%)	0.00%
4. 1366x768	3 (0.24%)	100.00%	3 (0.28%)	0.00%	5.00	00:00:26	0 (0.00%)	$0.00 (0.00%)	0.00%
5. 1173x733	2 (0.16%)	50.00%	1 (0.09%)	100.00%	1.00	00:00:00	0 (0.00%)	$0.00 (0.00%)	0.00%
6. 320x568	2 (0.16%)	50.00%	1 (0.09%)	50.00%	1.50	00:00:32	0 (0.00%)	$0.00 (0.00%)	0.00%
7. 1040x1469	1 (0.08%)	100.00%	1 (0.09%)	100.00%	1.00	00:00:00	0 (0.00%)	$0.00 (0.00%)	0.00%
8. 1600x900	1 (0.08%)	100.00%	1 (0.09%)	0.00%	3.00	00:01:06	0 (0.00%)	$0.00 (0.00%)	0.00%
9. 1680x1050	1 (0.08%)	100.00%	1 (0.09%)	0.00%	9.00	00:00:49	0 (0.00%)	$0.00 (0.00%)	0.00%

Network Report

The **Audience > Technology > Network** report lets you see which service providers account for the most sessions and the domain to which they are connected. Google notes that "having insight into which service providers your visitors use can help you design your site's content. For example, if your site offers video content and you see that visitors are evenly distributed among providers that offer a variety of connection speeds, you can offer them a choice of video quality (720p and 360p). If the bulk of your visitors use providers that offer high connection speeds, you can offer high-definition video, along with higher resolution graphics and a higher quality audio-compression format."

Selecting **Audience > Technology > Network** provides the names of the networks individuals used to initiate sessions on your site. The table below shows some of the networks used to access my site.

Service Provider	Acquisition			Behavior			Conversions eCommerce		
	Sessions	% New Sessions	New Users	Bounce Rate	Pages / Session	Avg. Session Duration	Transactions	Revenue	Ecommerce Conversion Rate
	1,242 % of Total: 100.00% (1,242)	84.78% Site Avg: 84.78% (0.00%)	1,053 % of Total: 100.00% (1,053)	34.46% Site Avg: 34.46% (0.00%)	2.36 Site Avg: 2.36 (0.00%)	00:00:40 Site Avg: 00:00:40 (0.00%)	427 % of Total: 100.00% (427)	$3,869,600.00 % of Total 100.00% ($3,869,600.00)	34.38% Site Avg: 34.38% (0.00%)
1. subscriber block 2	262 (21.10%)	91.60%	240 (22.79%)	35.88%	1.88	00:00:37	106 (24.82%)	$963,700.00 (24.90%)	40.46%
2. kabel deutschland breitband customer 20	199 (16.02%)	90.95%	181 (17.19%)	31.16%	2.15	00:00:11	86 (20.14%)	$800,600.00 (20.69%)	43.22%
3. hutchison 3g ireland ltd.	133 (10.71%)	87.22%	116 (11.02%)	34.59%	2.11	00:00:29	60 (14.05%)	$498,800.00 (12.89%)	45.11%
4. subscriber block 1	122 (9.82%)	73.77%	90 (8.55%)	36.89%	2.59	00:00:31	37 (8.67%)	$340,300.00 (8.79%)	30.33%
5. hutchison 3g ireland limited	113 (9.10%)	75.22%	85 (8.07%)	18.58%	3.12	00:00:45	39 (9.13%)	$285,500.00 (7.38%)	34.51%

Selecting **Hostname** from the top of the table changes the display to report the hostname(s) or domain(s) that visitors used to reach your site. Google notes that "Typically this is your site's domain. For example, if you host your blog on mysite.example.com, then your hostname report will contain mysite.example.com. In some cases, your website might be hosted on other domains, such as when you create a mirror (copy) of your site to host on a domain in another country (e.g. mysite.example.uk). In addition, if someone copies a page from your website directly without modifying any of the source code (including the tracking code) and places that page on their own website, your reports will reflect traffic to that page from that hostname as well. You can use view filters to ensure that only traffic from allowed hosts reaches your reports."[12]

Mobile[13]

The **Audience > Mobile** menu provides two types of reports: **Overview** and **Devices**. The **Audience > Mobile > Overview** report classifies sessions on the basis of the type of device used to access your site. The **Audience > Mobile > Devices** report provides significant detail *about* the mobile devices that were used by people engaged in site sessions.

The **Audience > Mobile > Overview** report is organized around three device category dimensions, defined as follows:

- **Desktop** contains towers, laptops, netbooks and game consoles such as Playstation 3 and the Nintendo Wii/Wii U.

- **Mobile Phones** covers smart phones and hand held game consoles such as the Nintendo 3DS and Playstation Vita.

- **Tablets** includes standard iPads, Google Nexus, Galaxy Tabs, and also e-readers such as the Kindle Fire.

The table below is displayed when I select the **Audience > Mobile > Overview** report. As you can see, almost all my site sessions are initiated via desktop. Almost no sessions are through mobile and no sessions at all are via tablets (as this value is missing from the report).

---

[12] *Hostname* (https://support.google.com/analytics/answer/1032966?hl=en)

[13] *Audience: Mobile* (https://support.google.com/analytics/answer/1011360?hl=en) and *What You Can Learn From Google Analytics Mobile Reports* (http://searchenginewatch.com/article/2308358/What-You-Can-Learn-From-Google-Analytics-Mobile-Reports)

The **Audience > Mobile > Mobile Devices** report is shown below. By default, the initial set of data displays the names of the mobile devices used to access your site. In this case, two mobile devices were used for site sessions. But, more data is available.

When you look across the top of the report, you can see that you can also view information related to: Mobile Device Branding, Service Provider, Mobile Input Selector (e.g., touchscreen, joystick, stylus), and Operating System. The table below, for example, shows the display generated from the **Service Provider** link.

Google points out that "understanding mobile traffic to your site can give you an indication of whether you need to design your site to accommodate both mobile and computer traffic, or whether the traffic justifies a *separate* mobile site. For example, while mobile visits may represent only a few percent of your overall visitors, you might find that they convert at a higher rate and that the average value of mobile transactions is higher. In this case, a site devoted exclusively to mobile platforms (streamlined content, simpler navigation) might further encourage transactions via smart phones."

Custom variables

Google notes that custom variables will be "depreciated" in the final migration to Universal Analytics. As a result, we won't address these metrics.

The last option within Audience reports is **Users Flow**, which provides a graphical representation of the paths users took through your site. **Users Flow** identifies how sessions begin, move through different pages, and then ultimately end.

Let's start with a basic chart where we use **Country/Territory** as the organizing dimension. When we select this dimension from the pull-down menu, the chart shown below appears. Note that during this time period all of our sessions were initiated in the United States, so is the only dimension value shown in the first column.

The chart is composed of different size boxes and grey bands. The boxes contain page names from your web site. The size of the individual boxes indicates the relative number of sessions occurring on any individual page. The larger the box, the greater the number of sessions. The grey bands show connections between the values of your organizing dimension and pages of your site or between two site pages. The larger the grey band the greater the connection between two items. You can see the exact size of the relationship by placing your cursor over any grey band, as shown on the top of page 167.

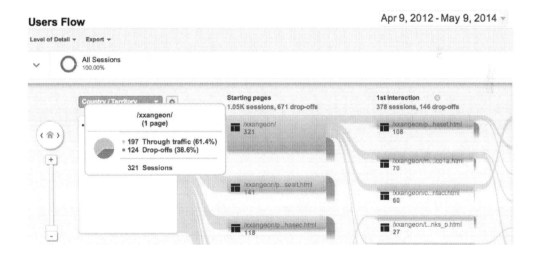

Users Flow   Apr 9, 2012 - May 9, 2014

Level of Detail ▾   Export ▾

⌄   ◯ All Sessions
        100.00%

Country / Territory ▾ ⚙

Starting pages
1.05K sessions, 671 drop-offs

1st Interaction ☺
378 sessions, 146 drop-offs

‹ 🏠 ›

United States to /xxangeon/

321 Sessions
30.6% of total traffic

/xxangeon/
321

/xxangeon/p...hasef.html
108

/xxangeon/m...jco1a.html
70

/xxangeon/p...sealt.html

The middle column of the above chart shows the starting page of site sessions and indicates that the most common starting page is my site home page. This is good news. However, the information provided at the top of the column provides some important but disturbing news. Note that at the top of **Starting Page** column, it reports that there were 1,005 sessions with 671 drop-offs. This means that of all those sessions started on my site (on any page) about two-thirds "dropped off" or left without any further pageviews. Losing this large percentage of sessions at the outset is very bad news. What we would need to determine is: To what extent is the drop-off rate representative of all pages or does it reflect the poor performance of just one or two pages?

We can look at the drop-off rate for the primary starting pages by rolling our cursor over the page box. The next two charts indicate what happens when we do this for the two most common starting pages.

Users Flow   Apr 9, 2012 - May 9, 2014

Level of Detail ▾   Export ▾

⌄   ◯ All Sessions
        100.00%

Country / Territory ▾

Starting pages
1.05K sessions, 671 drop-offs

1st Interaction ☺
378 sessions, 146 drop-offs

‹ 🏠 ›

/xxangeon/
(1 page)

▪ 197 Through traffic (61.4%)
▪ 124 Drop-offs (38.6%)

321 Sessions

/xxangeon/
321

/xxangeon/p...hasef.html
108

/xxangeon/m...jco1a.html
70

/xxangeon/p...sealt.html
141

/xxangeon/c...ntact.html
60

/xxangeon/p...hasec.html
118

/xxangeon/t...nks_p.html
27

Fortunately, the drop-off problem appears to be confined to our "purchasealt.html" page. While the drop-off rate for the home page is 38.6% (not great, but better than the overall rate of 67%) the drop-off rate for the "purchasealt.html" page is nearly 100%. There is clearly a problem when a session starts on this page.

The prior charts presented the default view for user flow: The organizing dimension is presented in the left-hand column, starting pages for visits to your site are in the middle column, and 1st interactions with your site (beyond the landing page) are in the right-hand column. But, what about interactions that take place after the first? Notice the circle icon to the left of the first column. Clicking on the arrows in the icon moves the chart to the left or right, thereby displaying additional interactions, as shown on the following chart.

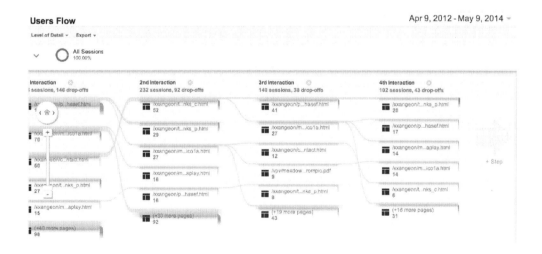

Restricting the Data View

Since users flow charts tend to be data heavy and visually overwhelming, there are times when you want to focus on just a subset of the data. I might, for example, just want to examine the behaviors of those who came to my site via Facebook or from a particular city. Let's use the latter as our example.

We begin by choosing **City** as our organizing dimension from the pull-down menu (see chart below). This results in the chart shown on the top of page 170, where city names are shown (in the first column) as the values of our selected dimension.

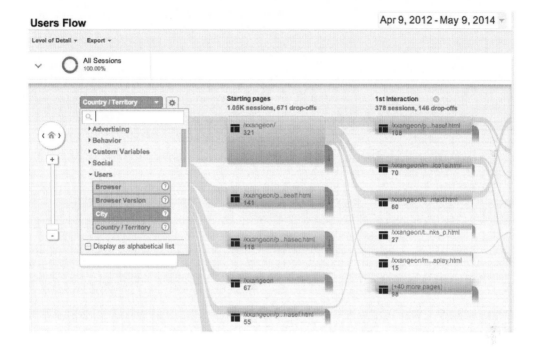

Let's imagine that I want to reduce the complexity of the chart by focusing on just those sessions that originated in San Diego. There are two ways to accomplish this.

First, clicking on the box labeled "San Diego" brings up a menu with three options (see below).

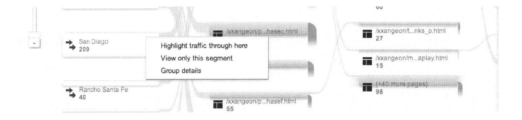

Selecting the **Highlight traffic through here** option keeps all of the reported data from the original chart, but now, all traffic *not* through San Diego is faded out, and all traffic that *is* through San Diego is highlighted. This is illustrated in the chart shown on the top of the next page. Clicking once again on "San Diego" and selecting **Clear Highlighting** from the pop-up menu brings the chart back to its original form.

Alternatively, I can eliminate all data not of interest. Once again, I begin by clicking on San Diego, only this time I select **View only this segment.** When this option is chosen the chart changes to display only sessions initiated in San Diego (see below).

✓ The two pop-up menu options ("Highlight traffic through here" and "View only this segment") can be applied to any page shown in a box. As a result, you can perform detailed analyses of session paths focusing on any page listed as the start page or subsequent interaction.

Grouping Data

There may be times when you want to examine a subset of the data in one chart, but this subset consists of two or three elements rather than just one. You might, for example, want to look at user flow for two cities in different parts of California. The **Users Flow** options allow this to be done easily and quickly. Let's illustrate this by focusing on the desire to simultaneously look at two California cities: San Diego and San Francisco.

We begin with the standard Users Flow chart organized by city, as shown below. We are interested in just two cities: San Diego and San Francisco.

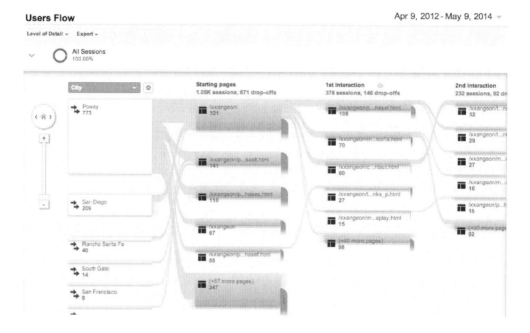

Next, we indicate that we want to form a grouping of these two cities for display. We do this by clicking on the small gear symbol to the left of City (see below).

When this is done the popup window shown below appears.

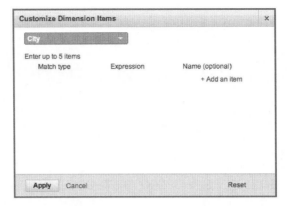

We want to group two cities. To begin, we click on **+Add an item** and on the new line displayed we leave **Match type** set to the default **Equals** and we type San Diego into the **Expression** box. We then do the same for San Francisco. When we are done, the information provided in the window is as shown below.

Finally, when we are sure that the information is correct, we press **Apply** and the display changes to include just the two cities of interest, as shown on page 174.

Level of Detail ∨   Export ∨

∨   ◯ All Sessions
         100.00%

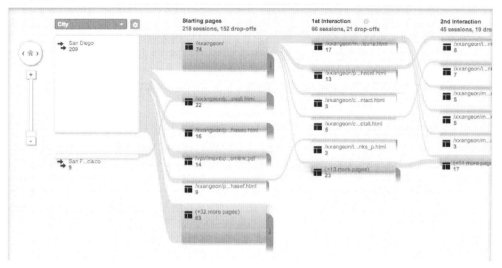

25

Practice With Audience Data (III)

This chapter presents several sets of exercises to help you apply and extend your knowledge of the type of metrics and reports available through the full **Audience** menu.

This first set makes certain that you understand key concepts. Feel free to open and refer to any of the prior chapters in this section or access the **Audience** menu in your analytics account. When you are done, or if you are stuck, the answers can be found on page 605.

1. *True or False:* All Google Analytics users have automatic access to demographic and interest metrics.

2. *True or False:* Google Analytics associates demographic and interest metrics with individual browsers rather than individual people.

3. *True or False:* Google Analytics can help you identify differences in user characteristics and engagement when new visitors are compared to returning visitors.

4. Google Analytics **Audience** metrics provide a range of insights. Which of the following specific metrics are provided? Check all that apply.

    a. Count of sessions

    b. % new sessions

    c. Days since last session

    d. Number of sessions per week

    e. Average session duration

    f. Average pages per session

    g. Average number of click interactions

5. The **Audience > Mobile > Devices** report is organized around three categories. *True or False:* These categories are: desktop, mobile phones and tablets.

6. *True or False:* The **Audience > Users Flow** report provides interaction data for only the first two pages viewed during a site session.

7. Which of the following can be used as the organizing dimension for a Users Flow report? Check all that apply.

    a. Social network

    b. Landing page

    c. Browser

    d. Country/Territory

    e. Census region

8. A grey band connects two web pages on the **Audience > Users Flow** report. *True or False:* The size of the band indicates the strength of connection between two pages.

9. *True or False:* Rolling your cursor over a specific page on the **Audience > Users Flow** report provides data on the percentage of individuals moving through the page and the percentage of people who drop-off or leave the site on that page.

Application

This exercise asks you to think strategically about the information available through the **Audience** menu options. Please use the provided charts to answer each of the following questions. When you are done, or if you are stuck, our responses can be found on page 605.

1. The two tables below contain information on site sessions and ecommerce outcomes organized by country. What conclusions can you draw with regard to similarities and differences between these two countries?

Primary Dimension: Country / Territory   City   Continent   Sub Continent Region

Country / Territory	Sessions	Pages / Session	Avg. Session Duration	% New Sessions	Bounce Rate
	820 % of Total: 100.00% (820)	2.27 Site Avg: 2.27 (0.00%)	00:00:39 Site Avg: 00:00:39 (0.00%)	85.49% Site Avg: 85.49% (0.00%)	33.66% Site Avg: 33.66% (0.00%)
1. Ireland	793 (96.71%)	2.31	00:00:40	85.12%	32.91%
2. Germany	27 (3.29%)	1.04	00:00:01	96.30%	55.56%

Country / Territory	Sessions	Revenue	Transactions	Average Order Value	Ecommerce Conversion Rate	Per Session Value
	820 %of Total: 100.00% (820)	$2,535,681.95 % of Total: 100.00% ($2,535,681.95)	306 % of Total: 100.00% (306)	$8,286.54 Site Avg: $8,286.54 (0.00%)	37.32% Site Avg: 37.32% (0.00%)	$3,092.30 Site Avg: $3,092.30 (0.00%)
1. Ireland	793 (96.71%)	$2,467,781.95 (97.32%)	295 (96.41%)	$8,365.36	37.20%	$3,111.96
2. Germany	27 (3.29%)	$67,900.00 (2.68%)	11 (3.59%)	$6,172.73	40.74%	$2,514.81

2. The following tables contain information related to new and returning visitors. Based on this data, what conclusions can you draw with regard to similarities and differences between these two groups?

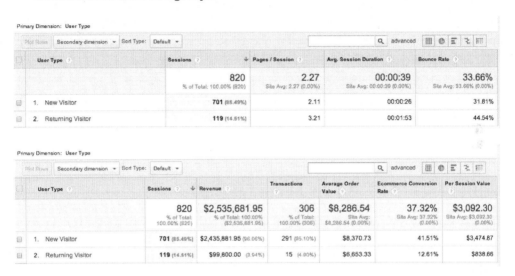

User Type	Sessions	Pages / Session	Avg. Session Duration	Bounce Rate
	820 % of Total: 100.00% (820)	2.27 Site Avg: 2.27 (0.00%)	00:00:39 Site Avg: 00:00:39 (0.00%)	33.66% Site Avg: 33.66% (0.00%)
1. New Visitor	701 (85.49%)	2.11	00:00:26	31.81%
2. Returning Visitor	119 (14.51%)	3.21	00:01:53	44.54%

User Type	Sessions	Revenue	Transactions	Average Order Value	Ecommerce Conversion Rate	Per Session Value
	820 % of Total: 100.00% (820)	$2,535,681.95 % of Total: 100.00% ($2,535,681.95)	306 % of Total: 100.00% (306)	$8,286.54 Site Avg: $8,286.54 (0.00%)	37.32% Site Avg: 37.32% (0.00%)	$3,092.30 Site Avg: $3,092.30 (0.00%)
1. New Visitor	701 (85.49%)	$2,435,881.95 (96.06%)	291 (95.10%)	$8,370.73	41.51%	$3,474.87
2. Returning Visitor	119 (14.51%)	$99,800.00 (3.94%)	15 (4.90%)	$6,653.33	12.61%	$838.66

3. Imagine that your goal is to increase session engagement and that you initiate new site changes in an attempt to accomplish this. The baseline period is July 1, 2013 to July 15, 2013. Changes were initiated on July 16, so you choose the period of July 16, 2013 to July 31, 2013 as the target period in which you will look for improvement. The following two tables present information for the two periods. What can you conclude regarding the effectiveness of your changes?

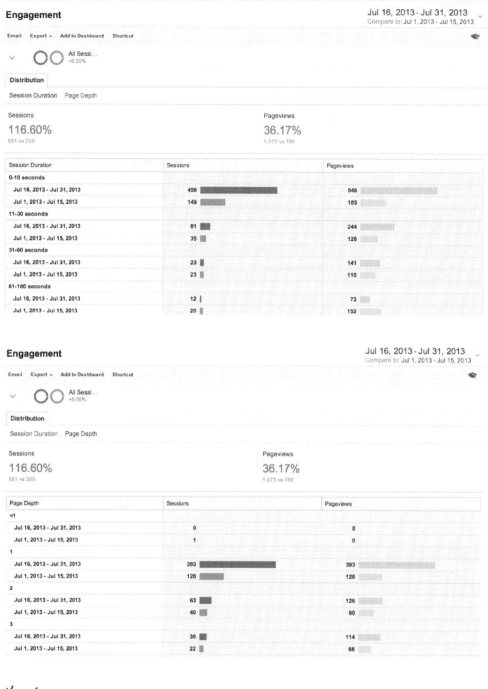

Engagement

Email   Export ▾   Add to Dashboard   Shortcut

All Sessi...
+0.00%

Distribution

Session Duration   Page Depth

Sessions	Pageviews
116.60%	**36.17%**
581 vs 269	1,073 vs 788

Session Duration	Sessions	Pageviews
0-10 seconds		
Jul 16, 2013 - Jul 31, 2013	456	546
Jul 1, 2013 - Jul 15, 2013	149	185
11-30 seconds		
Jul 16, 2013 - Jul 31, 2013	61	244
Jul 1, 2013 - Jul 15, 2013	35	126
31-60 seconds		
Jul 16, 2013 - Jul 31, 2013	23	141
Jul 1, 2013 - Jul 15, 2013	23	110
61-180 seconds		
Jul 16, 2013 - Jul 31, 2013	12	73
Jul 1, 2013 - Jul 15, 2013	20	152

Engagement

Email   Export ▾   Add to Dashboard   Shortcut

All Sessi...
+0.00%

Distribution

Session Duration   Page Depth

Sessions	Pageviews
116.60%	**36.17%**
581 vs 269	1,073 vs 788

Page Depth	Sessions	Pageviews
<1		
Jul 16, 2013 - Jul 31, 2013	0	0
Jul 1, 2013 - Jul 15, 2013	1	0
1		
Jul 16, 2013 - Jul 31, 2013	393	393
Jul 1, 2013 - Jul 15, 2013	126	126
2		
Jul 16, 2013 - Jul 31, 2013	63	126
Jul 1, 2013 - Jul 15, 2013	40	80
3		
Jul 16, 2013 - Jul 31, 2013	38	114
Jul 1, 2013 - Jul 15, 2013	22	66

Hands-on

This exercise asks you to apply your understanding of the data provided through the **Audience** menu's options. Please answer each of the following questions using your own Google Analytics account and the data collected for your travel website. If it has been more than a month since you started to collect data, make certain to set your date range to include the entire time span of data collection.

1. Think about all site sessions. How many different languages are reported? If more than one is reported, what is the primary language reported?

2. Think about all site sessions. How many different countries are reported? If more than one is reported, what is the primary country from which sessions originated?

3. From which state have the most sessions originated? If more than one state is reported, are there differences in session and ecommerce behaviors across states?

4. From which cities have the most sessions originated? If more than one city is reported, are there differences in session and ecommerce behaviors across cities?

5. If you have more than two cities listed: Are there differences in these two cities in terms of browsers used to initiate a session?

6. What are the primary browsers used to initiate a session on your site? Are there differences in session and ecommerce behaviors across browser types?

7. What percent of site visitors are new and returning? From a business perspective, looking at differences in session and ecommerce behaviors across visitor type, are you satisfied with the current situation? Why or why not?

8. Think about session frequency, recency, and engagement. What site strengths and weaknesses are revealed in each of these metrics?

9. What technology is used to initiate site sessions? What is the dominant form of technology? Are there differences in session and ecommerce behaviors across different forms of technology?

10. From which page do the majority of site sessions begin? Is this page effective or ineffective in moving individuals through to a page in which a first interaction occurs?

11. Overall, what percentage of your sessions drop-off between the starting pages and first interactions?

12. When looking at first interactions, which page accounts for the most sessions? Are some starting pages more effective than others in driving users to this first interaction page?

Google Analytics Demystified

Section VI:
The Behavior Menu

Google Analytics provides extensive data with regard to the characteristics of individuals who visit your website or blog. You can learn their demographics and interests, the technology they use to begin and continue engagement, where they are located, their frequency/recency of visits, and how they move through your site page by page. The chapters in this section help you understand the full range of data provided and the application of this data to strategic decision-making.

- Google Analytics provides audience data through overviews or focused reports. Chapters 26, 28 and 29 introduce you to the Audience Overview report. Chapters 27 and 30 provide practice exercises to help you apply and extend what you have learned.

- Chapter 31 presents a detailed discussion of the full set of data provided through the Audience Menu. Chapter 32 contains exercises to help you confirm that you are comfortable working with this information.

Together, the chapters in this section show you different ways to access, manipulate, and strategically apply audience data.

Google Analytics Demystified

26

The Behavior Menu: Overview

Google Analytics provides multiple perspectives on how users interact with different pages on your site. The **Users Flow** chart, discussed earlier, shows the pages users interact with and the order in which these interactions take place. Beyond this approach to the data, Google Analytics also provides you with detailed information on how site users interact with each page of your site as well as with your site as a whole. This information is available through the **Behavior** menu (see below).

This chapter focuses on the **Behavior > Overview** report. The next chapter addresses **Behavior > Site Content. Behavior > Site Speed** is discussed in Chapter 29. **Behavior > In-Page Analytics** are discussed in Chapter 31.[14] We'll return to this menu later in the book when we discuss **Events** (Section X) and **Experiments** (Section XV).

---

[14] **Behavior > Behavior Flow** works nearly identically and is interpreted similarly to **Users Flow** discussed in earlier, but here, the focus is on content rather than users. As a result, we won't explicitly discuss this option. We also do not address **AdSense** and **Site Search,** which may be used by only a few purchasers of this book.

Data presented on the **Behavior > Overview** page is formatted in the same way as the **Audience > Overview** page, except that now the data focuses on users' interactions with site pages rather than on the characteristics of users themselves.

Top of Page

By default, the chart on the top of the page shows the trend in **Pageviews** over your selected time period. As with the **Audience Overview**, you can modify the time period by which the data is grouped and presented. The chart below, for example, shows my website's trend in pageviews between January 1, 2014 and May 4, 2014, as indicated by the date frame in the upper right-hand corner.

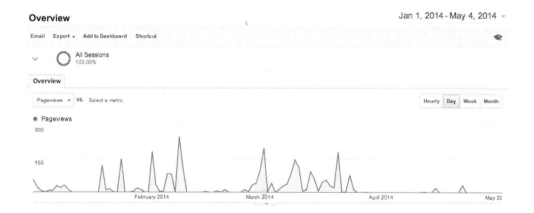

You are not limited to charting pageviews. The pull-down menu on the top left-hand side of the chart allows you to chart other page interaction metrics, as shown on the top of the next page. Each of these new metrics is defined in the addendum to this chapter.

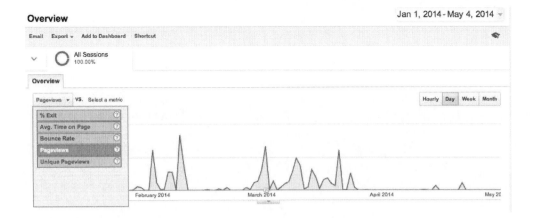

The chart below, for example, shows the **Average Time on Page**.

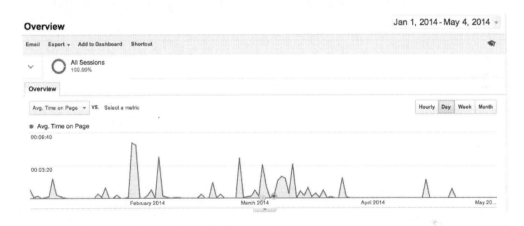

Similar to the **Audience Overview** chart, you can examine two metrics simultaneously. Imagine, for example, that you wanted to know how the trend in site users is related to users' average time on page. You can either generate and compare the metrics in individual charts (as in the prior two examples) or you can display both metrics on the same chart. This latter approach is accomplished by selecting **Pageviews** from the drop-down menu and **Ave. Time on Page** from the **Select a Metric** menu. This generates the chart shown on the top of page 186.

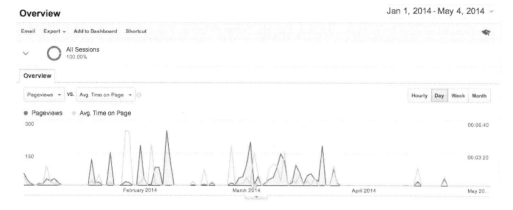

Finally, note that any annotations made to charts when using other menu options also appear on this chart. Of course, you can also add new annotations to this chart by following the same procedure you used to add annotations to the **Audience Overview** chart discussed earlier.

Middle of the Page

The metrics and charts in the center of the **Behavior > Overview** page provide summary information for key website page and content interaction metrics within the selected time period (see below). The metrics are the same as those available through the pull-down menus in the top of page chart.

Pageviews	Unique Pageviews	Avg. Time on Page	Bounce Rate	% Exit
2,818	2,024	00:00:44	34.57%	37.15%

Similar to the **Audience Overview** display, clicking on any of the line graphs in this block brings detailed information on that metric up to the line graph shown on the top of the page. Clicking on the small line graph beneath **Unique Pageviews**, for example, changes the metric displayed in the top line graph to **Unique Pageviews**.

Bottom of the Page

The bottom of the **Behavior > Overview** option display allows you to examine data in terms of page characteristics (Page and Page Title), site search, and event categories (see the left-hand side of the table shown on the top of page 187). This example table displays pageviews ranked by page title. The two most viewed pages are my home page and purchase page.

Site Content		Page Title	Pageviews	% Pageviews
Page		1. xqanqeon - Home Page Welcome	144	27.96%
Page Title	▸	2. xqanqeon - Buy a tour	124	24.08%
Site Search		3. xqanqeon - More Information	83	16.12%
Search Term		4. xqanqeon - Contact	41	7.96%
Events		5. xqanqeon - Purchase Thanks - 2 Day Tour	26	5.05%
Event Category		6. xqanqeonE - More Information	26	5.05%
		7. xqanqeon - Videos	24	4.66%
		8. xqanqeon - Contact Confirmation	23	4.47%
		9. xqanqeon - Purchase Thanks - 10 Day Tour	12	2.33%
		10. (not set)	6	1.17%

view full report

Clicking on the view **full report link** beneath the table always brings up a more detailed display on the selected metric or dimension.

Chapter Addendum: Behavior Terms Defined

The following are definitions of key dimensions and metrics used to describe user interactions with your website pages.

Pageviews

Pageviews reports the total number of pages (which contain the Google Analytics tracking code) viewed during all sessions by all users. Note that this measure is subject to inflation due to the way that duplicate page views are handled. If, for example, a user clicks reload after reaching a particular page, this is counted as an additional pageview and two pageviews would be recorded. Similarly, if a user navigates to a different page on your site and then returns to the original page, a second pageview is then recorded even though the original page had already been seen.

Unique Pageviews

Unique pageviews represent the number of visits during which a page was viewed at least once, for example:

- If a visitor views the same web page seven times during the same visit, then it will count as seven pageviews but only one unique pageview.

- If the same visitor exits your site, but comes back later after the session expires and views the same web page two more times, the metric will be increased to nine pageviews and two unique pageviews.

Average Time on Page

As the name implies, this metric reports the average amount of time visitors spent viewing a specified page or set of pages (for example, all pages on your website).

Bounce Rate

Bounce Rate is the percentage of single-page visits, that is, visits in which a site user leaves your site from the first page viewed without interacting with that or any other page.

Google Analytics reports both Bounce Rate and % Exit (defined next). While these metrics are very similar, they provide you with different information. A bounce occurs when a user comes to your website and only looks at a single page before leaving the site. When a visitor bounces, he does not visit any other pages on your site, nor does he interact with anything on the single page viewed. The exit rate does not take into consideration how many pages the visitor looked at. It only looks at exits compared to the total visits.

% Exit reports how many people leave your site from a particular page or from the site overall. Google Analytics calculates % Exit for each page of your site by dividing the total number of exits from a page by the total number of pageviews for that particular page.

The % Exit metric is important because it tells you how many people are leaving from each page. If your visitors are leaving the site from a "Thank You" page or after completing a sale, this may be desirable. If they are leaving from other pages, this may reflect a lack of desired information or frustration with that page or their prior experience on the site. Either way, this would lead you to conduct a more detailed analysis to determine the underlying causes.

27

The Behavior Menu: Site Content

This chapter focuses on the information provided through the **Site Content** submenu in the **Behavior** main menu (see below).

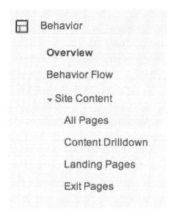

All Pages

Clicking on **Behavior > Site Content > All Pages** brings up two different views for data exploration.

Top of Page

The default display for the **Behavior > Site Content > All Pages** option brings up a chart similar to that shown on the top of the next page. The power of this chart comes from the **Navigation Summary,** which can be selected from above the chart on the left-hand side. The Navigation Summary allows you to see the behaviors associated with any page on your site, specifically, what happens when site users start on that page, where they go next, and how they exit. The insights provided by the Navigation Summary are an excellent complement to the insights provided by the **Users** and **Behavior Flow** reports.

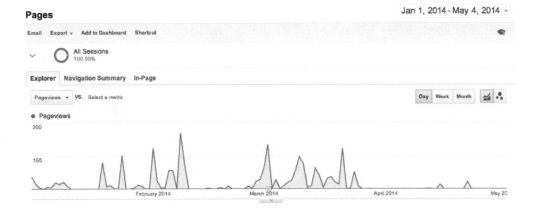

Clicking on **Navigation Summary** brings up the display shown below.

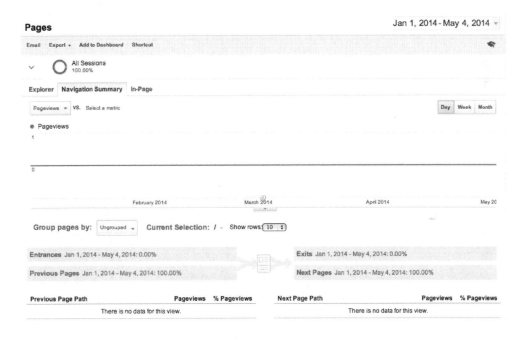

To begin using this option, select the page on which you want to focus using the pull-down menu next to **Current Selection**, in the top, middle of the display (see above).

When you pull-down this menu, a list of all your website pages (which contain GATC) are displayed, as shown below.

Select the page in which you are interested. When I select my site's contact page the display changes to that shown below. Note that the URL of my contact page is now shown next to "Current Selection."

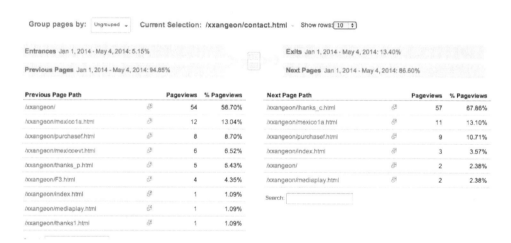

Let's focus on the four grey boxes on the top of the display beneath the URL of my contact page.

- The two grey boxes on the left-hand side tell you how the page is reached. These arrows report the percentage of site users who reach the page directly (**Entrances**) and the percentage who come to the page via another page (**Previous Pages**). In this case, nearly all users viewing the contact page (94.85%) reached the page via another page; few came directly to this page.

- The two grey boxes on the right-hand side tell you want happens when people leave this page. **Exits** reports the percentage of users who leave the site entirely while **Next Pages** reports the percentage who remain on the site and view another page. In this case, most users (86.6%) stay on the site after viewing my contact page.

Beneath the arrows are two columns, one labeled **Previous Page Path** and the other labeled **Next Page Path**. These columns provide the detail on pages viewed prior to and after the target page. Keep in mind that the base for this percentage is all pageviews prior to or after the target page. Thus, these relative numbers will change as the target page is changed.

What can we learn from each column of data?

- The information shown in the left-hand column (beneath **Previous Page Path**) indicates that most users (58.70%) who access the contact page go directly there from my homepage. This is troubling, since they go to the contact page without any site interaction. What is there about the home page that is driving this? The remainder of paths to the contact page come from a diverse range of prior pages.

- The information shown in the right-hand column (beneath **Next Page Path**) indicates that my "thank you for sending an email page" (thanks_c.html) is the most frequently viewed page after viewing my contact page. This is to be expected, as this page is automatically shown after a contact email is sent. The percentage, however, is troubling. Only 67.86% of those viewing the contact page actually send an email and see the thank you page. This means that about one-third of those intending to send a contact email left the page without doing so. We need to determine why and then, perhaps, redesign the contact page to encourage contact through form completion.

Bottom of Page

The data presented on the bottom of the **Behavior > Site Content > All Pages** report provides data in a format similar to tables you've already seen (see top of page 194). Here, however, the columns focus on user-page interaction rather than the user characteristics reported in the **Audience** menu. The meaning of each column header was provided in the addendum to the prior chapter.

Of particular importance on this table are the metrics that report **Average Time on Page** and **% Exit**. The former metric provides valuable insights into the level of engagement with a particular page, while the latter metric helps you see the locations from which individuals are leaving the site. When taken together, both metrics help you identify the specific site pages that need revision.

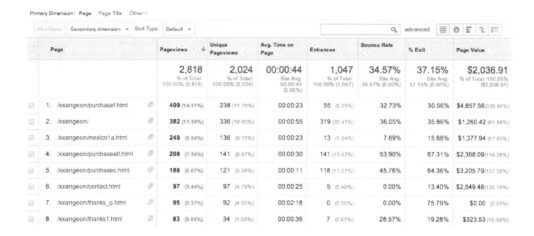

Page	Pageviews ↓	Unique Pageviews	Avg. Time on Page	Entrances	Bounce Rate	% Exit	Page Value
	2,818	2,024	00:00:44	1,047	34.57%	37.15%	$2,036.91
	% of Total: 100.00% (2,818)	% of Total: 100.00% (2,024)	Site Avg 00:00:44 (0.00%)	% of Total: 100.00% (1,047)	Site Avg: 34.57% (0.00%)	Site Avg: 37.15% (0.00%)	% of Total: 100.00% ($2,036.91)
1. /xxangeon/purchasef.html	409 (14.51%)	238 (11.76%)	00:00:23	55 (5.25%)	32.73%	30.56%	$4,857.56 (238.48%)
2. /xxangeon/	382 (13.58%)	336 (16.60%)	00:00:55	319 (30.47%)	36.05%	35.86%	$1,260.42 (61.88%)
3. /xxangeon/mexico1a.html	249 (8.84%)	136 (6.72%)	00:00:23	13 (1.24%)	7.69%	15.66%	$1,377.94 (67.65%)
4. /xxangeon/purchasealt.html	208 (7.38%)	141 (6.97%)	00:00:30	141 (13.47%)	53.90%	67.31%	$2,368.09 (116.26%)
5. /xxangeon/purchasec.html	188 (6.67%)	121 (5.98%)	00:00:11	118 (11.27%)	45.76%	64.36%	$3,205.79 (157.38%)
6. /xxangeon/contact.html	97 (3.44%)	97 (4.79%)	00:00:25	5 (0.48%)	0.00%	13.40%	$2,549.48 (125.16%)
7. /xxangeon/thanks_p.html	95 (3.37%)	92 (4.55%)	00:02:18	0 (0.00%)	0.00%	75.79%	$0.00 (0.00%)
8. /xxangeon/thanks1.html	83 (2.95%)	34 (1.68%)	00:00:36	7 (0.67%)	28.57%	19.28%	$323.53 (15.88%)

By default, pages are ordered by the absolute number of pageviews. Similar to the **Audience** tables you learned about earlier, you can use the charting options on the top of the table to create pie, bar, and percent differential charts. In addition, clicking on any individual page will bring up a chart displaying data for just that page.

The chart above lists pages by their URL address. If you can't remember which pages are associated with which URLs, then just click on the **Page Title** option located just above Secondary dimension in the Primary Dimension line. This will change the display to pages ordered by title rather than URL.

Finally, you can focus on a single page by clicking on its URL or title. This is useful when you want to create page specific tables or add a secondary dimension to the report.

Content drilldown

The **Behavior > Site Content > Content Drilldown** report allows you to examine user interaction with your website pages by "drilling down" into the folder structure you've set up on your site. You move from the highest level directories to the level of terminal pages.

Selecting the **Behavior > Site Content > Content Drilldown** option generates a table similar to that shown on the top of the next page. The column headers provide information on page interaction averaged for all of the pages within a particular directory (listed in the far left-hand column). Given that almost all of my website pages are within the **/xxangeon** directory, it is not surprising that the vast majority of page interactions occur within this directory.

Page path level 1	Pageviews	↓ Unique Pageviews	Avg. Time on Page	Bounce Rate	% Exit
	2,818 % of Total: 100.00% (2,818)	2,024 % of Total: 100.00% (2,024)	00:00:44 Site Avg: 00:00:44 (0.00%)	34.57% Site Avg: 34.57% (0.00%)	37.15% Site Avg: 37.15% (0.00%)
1. ☐ /xxangeon/	2,696 (95.67%)	1,944 (96.09%)	00:00:38	33.96%	37.46%
2. ☐ /vpv/	73 (2.59%)	48 (2.37%)	00:03:17	50.00%	26.03%
3. ☐ /zmscmizzle/	13 (0.46%)	4 (0.20%)	00:01:55	100.00%	15.38%
4. ☐ /cv/	7 (0.25%)	5 (0.25%)	00:00:04	25.00%	57.14%

Clicking on a specific directory allows you to "drilldown" for more detail on page interactions within that directory. Clicking on the **/xxangeon/** directory produces the table
shown below. The page with the most pageviews in this directory is my purchase page
(purchasef.html), as shown below.

Page path level 2	Pageviews	↓ Unique Pageviews	Avg. Time on Page	Bounce Rate	% Exit
	2,696 % of Total: 95.67% (2,818)	1,944 % of Total: 96.05% (2,024)	00:00:38 Site Avg: 00:00:44 (-13.50%)	33.96% Site Avg: 34.57% (-1.76%)	37.46% Site Avg: 37.15% (0.83%)
1. ☐ /purchasef.html	409 (15.17%)	238 (12.24%)	00:00:23	32.73%	30.56%
2. ☐ /	382 (14.17%)	336 (17.28%)	00:00:55	36.05%	35.86%
3. ☐ /mexico1a.html	249 (9.24%)	136 (7.00%)	00:00:23	7.69%	15.66%
4. ☐ /purchasealt.html	208 (7.72%)	141 (7.25%)	00:00:30	53.90%	67.31%
5. ☐ /purchasec.html	188 (6.97%)	121 (6.22%)	00:00:11	45.76%	64.36%

This process of clicking on a higher order classification to view lower order pages can be
repeated until a terminal page or action within the directory is reached.

Landing pages

The **Behavior > Site Content > Landing Pages** menu option provides insights into how
users enter your site and where they go afterwards. Similar to the **All Pages** report, two
data view options are presented, one on the top of the page and the other in tabular
form on the bottom of the page.

Top of page

The power of this chart comes from the **Entrance Paths** option shown above the line
chart next to the Explorer tab (see below).

Clicking on this option brings up the display shown below.

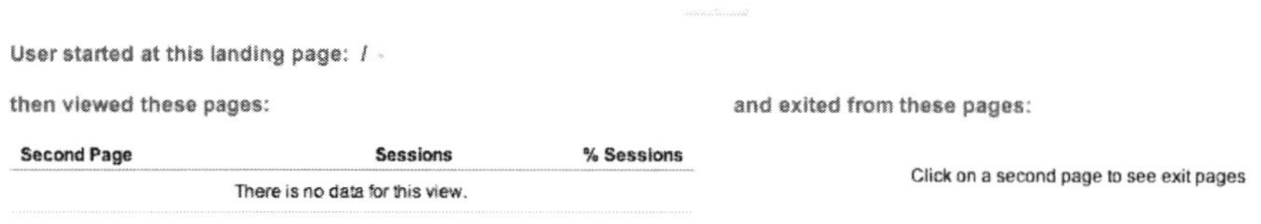

User started at this landing page: / -

then viewed these pages: and exited from these pages:

Second Page	Sessions	% Sessions
There is no data for this view.		

Click on a second page to see exit pages

The **Entrance Paths** option allows you to see the paths a user takes after landing on (i.e., entering) your site via a specified page. Similar to the prior charting options, the insights provided by the **Entrance Paths** report are an excellent complement to the insights provided by the **Users** and **Behavior Flow** reports, as well as the **All Content** reports.

To begin, using the pull-down menu next to **User started at this landing page,** select the landing page on which you want to focus (see below). We'll select the main entry page to the site, **/xxangeon**. However, before leaving this display, it is important for you to note the relative ranking of different landing pages as this will inform you of the extent to which users are following your "ideal" entrance and subsequent paths through your site.

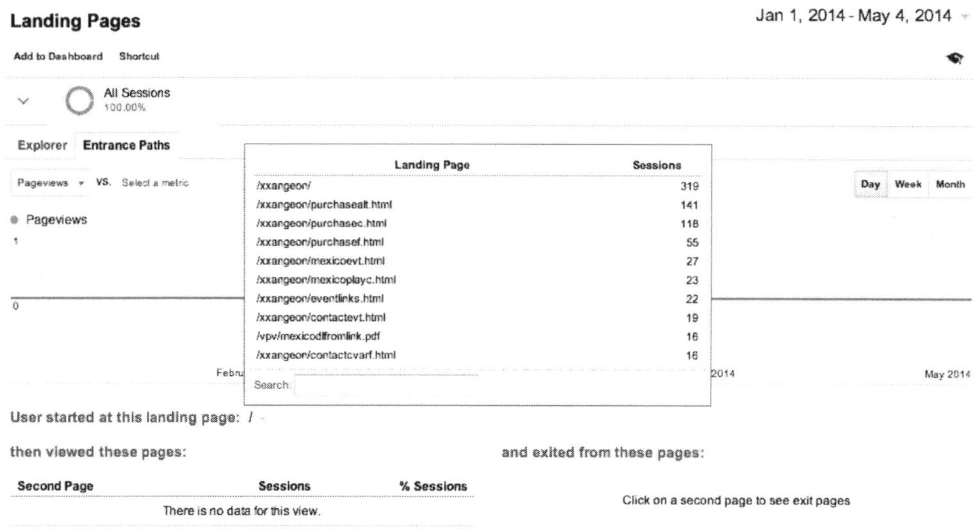

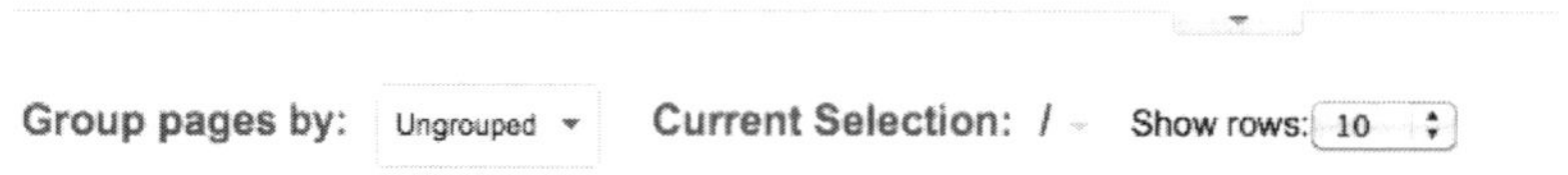

Landing Pages   Jan 1, 2014 - May 4, 2014

Add to Dashboard   Shortcut

All Sessions
100.00%

Explorer   **Entrance Paths**

Pageviews ▾ VS. Select a metric

● Pageviews

Landing Page	Sessions
/xxangeon/	319
/xxangeon/purchasealt.html	141
/xxangeon/purchasec.html	118
/xxangeon/purchasef.html	55
/xxangeon/mexicoevt.html	27
/xxangeon/mexicoplayc.html	23
/xxangeon/eventlinks.html	22
/xxangeon/contactevt.html	19
/vpv/mexicodlfromlink.pdf	16
/xxangeon/contactcvarf.html	16

Day Week Month

Search:

User started at this landing page: / -

then viewed these pages: and exited from these pages:

Second Page	Sessions	% Sessions
There is no data for this view.		

Click on a second page to see exit pages

Group pages by: Ungrouped ▾   **Current Selection:** / -   Show rows: 10 ▾

After I select my target landing page, the display changes to that shown on the top of page 197.

User started at this landing page: /xxangeon/ ~

then viewed these pages:

Second Page	Sessions	% Sessions
/xxangeon/purchasef.html	66	32.35%
/xxangeon/mexico1a.htm l	56	27.45%
/xxangeon/contact.html	52	25.49%
/xxangeon/	15	7.35%
/xxangeon/mediaplay.ht ml	9	4.41%
/xxangeon/contactalt.htm l	3	1.47%
/xxangeon/F2.html	1	0.49%
/xxangeon/mexicoplayc. html	1	0.49%
/xxangeon/purchasec.ht ml	1	0.49%

and exited from these pages:

Click on a second page to see exit pages

In this example, the column labeled **Second Page** indicates where site users went after entering the site through the site's home page. Interestingly, users tend to go directly to the purchase page (purchasef.html) or the Mexico information page (mexico1a.html). Is this direct path to the purchase page one which we want to encourage or redesign the site to discourage?

We can begin to answer this question by clicking on the purchase page in the **Second Page** column. The new display (see below) shows what happens to site visitors who enter on the home page and then immediately click through to the purchase page.

User started at this landing page: /xxangeon/ ~

then viewed these pages:

Second Page	Sessions	% Sessions
/xxangeon/purchasef.htm l	66	32.35%
/xxangeon/mexico1a.htm l	56	27.45%
/xxangeon/contact.html	52	25.49%
/xxangeon/	15	7.35%
/xxangeon/mediaplay.ht ml	9	4.41%
/xxangeon/contactalt.htm l	3	1.47%
/xxangeon/F2.html	1	0.49%
/xxangeon/mexicoplayc. html	1	0.49%
/xxangeon/purchasec.ht ml	1	0.49%

and exited from these pages:

Exit Page	Sessions	% Sessions
/xxangeon/thanks_p.html	24	36.36%
/xxangeon/purchasef.htm l	20	30.30%
/xxangeon/mediaplay.ht ml	9	13.64%
/xxangeon/thanks_c.html	5	7.58%
/xxangeon/	3	4.55%
/xxangeon/contact.html	2	3.03%
/xxangeon/mexico1a.htm l	1	1.52%
/xxangeon/mexicocm.ht ml	1	1.52%
/xxangeon/mexicogi.html	1	1.52%

Search:

After making a purchase users are sent to a "thank you for your purchase" page (/thanks_p.html). The second column shows that this is the most common exit page after viewing the purchase page. This is to be expected. But there is bad news. The percentage of users who view the purchase page (in the first column) and then leave from this page (as shown in the second column) is 30.3%. Thus, about one-third of users view the purchase page and then leave the site without any further engagement (including contact or purchase). We would certainly want to examine the characteristics of the purchase page to determine why such a large percentage of users are leaving from this page.

Bottom of Page

The data presented on the bottom of the **Behavior > Site Content > Landing Pages** report provides data in a format similar to tables you've already seen (see below). Here, however, the columns focus on user-page interaction rather than the user characteristics reported in the **Audience** menu. The meaning of each column header was provided in the addendum to Chapter 26.

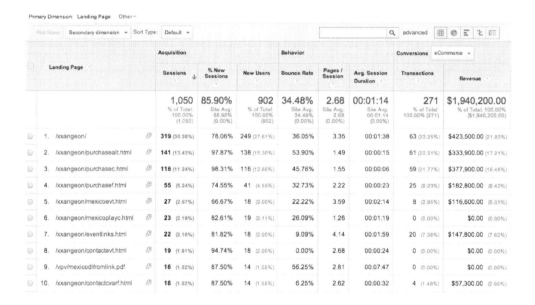

	Landing Page	Acquisition			Behavior			Conversions eCommerce	
		Sessions	% New Sessions	New Users	Bounce Rate	Pages / Session	Avg. Session Duration	Transactions	Revenue
		1,050 % of Total 100.00% (1,050)	**85.90%** Site Avg 85.90% (0.00%)	**902** % of Total 100.00% (902)	**34.48%** Site Avg 34.48% (0.00%)	**2.68** Site Avg 2.68 (0.00%)	**00:01:14** Site Avg 00:01:14 (0.00%)	**271** % of Total 100.00% (271)	**$1,940,200.00** % of Total: 100.00% ($1,940,200.00)
1.	/xxangeon/	**319** (30.38%)	78.06%	249 (27.61%)	36.05%	3.35	00:01:38	63 (23.25%)	$423,500.00 (21.83%)
2.	/xxangeon/purchasealt.html	**141** (13.43%)	97.87%	138 (15.30%)	53.90%	1.49	00:00:15	61 (22.51%)	$333,900.00 (17.21%)
3.	/xxangeon/purchasec.html	**118** (11.24%)	98.31%	116 (12.86%)	45.76%	1.55	00:00:06	59 (21.77%)	$377,900.00 (19.48%)
4.	/xxangeon/purchasef.html	**55** (5.24%)	74.55%	41 (4.55%)	32.73%	2.22	00:00:23	25 (9.23%)	$182,800.00 (9.42%)
5.	/xxangeon/mexicoevt.html	**27** (2.57%)	66.67%	18 (2.00%)	22.22%	3.59	00:02:14	8 (2.95%)	$116,600.00 (6.01%)
6.	/xxangeon/mexicoplayc.html	**23** (2.19%)	82.61%	19 (2.11%)	26.09%	1.26	00:01:19	0 (0.00%)	$0.00 (0.00%)
7.	/xxangeon/eventlinks.html	**22** (2.10%)	81.82%	18 (2.00%)	9.09%	4.14	00:01:59	20 (7.38%)	$147,800.00 (7.62%)
8.	/xxangeon/contactevt.html	**19** (1.81%)	94.74%	18 (2.00%)	0.00%	2.68	00:00:24	0 (0.00%)	$0.00 (0.00%)
9.	/vpv/mexicodifromlink.pdf	**16** (1.52%)	87.50%	14 (1.55%)	56.25%	2.81	00:07:47	0 (0.00%)	$0.00 (0.00%)
10.	/xxangeon/contactcvarf.html	**16** (1.52%)	87.50%	14 (1.55%)	6.25%	2.62	00:00:32	4 (1.48%)	$57,300.00 (2.95%)

Pages are ordered by the absolute number of times a particular page serves as an entry page to your site. Similar to other tables, you can use the charting options on the top of the table to create pie, bar, and percent differential charts. In addition, clicking on any individual page will bring up a chart displaying just that page. As with other charts, this is useful when you want to add a secondary dimension to the examination of that page.

Exit pages

The **Behavior > Site Content > Exit Page** menu option provides insights into how users leave your site. Similar to other reports, two data view options are presented, one on the top of the page and the other in tabular form on the bottom of the page.

The chart on the top of the page is fairly useless and can be ignored. The chart on the bottom of the page is identical to the Entrance Page report, except here pages are ordered in terms of the number of site users leaving your site after viewing a particular page.

28

Practice with Site Content

This chapter presents several sets of exercises to help you apply and extend your knowledge of the type of metrics and reports available through the **Behavior > Site Content** menu options.

True/false and multiple choice

This first set makes certain that you understand key concepts. Feel free to open and refer to Chapter 27 or access the **Behavior > Site Content** menu in your analytics account. When you are done, or if you are stuck, the answers can be found on page 606.

Questions 1 and 2 relate to the line char ton the top of the
***Behavior > Site Content > All Pages** display.*

1. You want to change this display so you can track the path through the site beginning with the page with the greatest number of views. From the top of the chart you would select:

    a. Explorer

    b. Navigation Summary

    c. In-Page Analytics

    d. Export

    e. Shortcut

2. Which of the following metrics can be displayed on the line chart? (Select all that apply.)

    a. Pageviews

    b. Average time on site

    c. Average time on page

    d. % Exit

    e. Transactions per page

Questions 3 and 4 relate to the display provided after
*the **Navigation Summary** is selected from above*
*the **Behavior > Site Content > All Pages** line chart*

3. To see a list of pages ordered in terms of views, you would use the pull-down menu next to:

    a. Group pages by

    b. Current selection

    c. Show rows

4. Which of the following can be determined after a page is selected from the **Current Selection** pull-down menu? (Select all that apply.)

    a. The percentage of site users entering on that page

    b. The percentage of users leaving the site directly from the selected page

    c. The specific pages viewed before the selected page

    d. The relative standing of the selected page in terms of average viewing time

    e. The percentage of users viewing media such as a video on the selected page

Questions 5 and 6 relate to the
***Behavior > Site Content > Content Drilldown** display shown below.*

Group pages by: Ungrouped ▾ Current Selection: /462site/purchasef.html ▾ Show rows: 10 ⬍

Entrances May 31, 2013 - Oct 6, 2013: 56.05% **Exits** May 31, 2013 - Oct 6, 2013: 79.03%

Previous Pages May 31, 2013 - Oct 6, 2013: 43.95% **Next Pages** May 31, 2013 - Oct 6, 2013: 20.97%

5. What percent of site users entered the site on the selected page?

    a. 56.05
    b. 43.95
    c. 79.03
    d. 20.97

6. What percent of site users left the site immediately after viewing the selected page?

    a. 56.05
    b. 43.95
    c. 79.03
    d. 20.97

7. *True or False:* The directory level is the starting point for **Behavior > Site Content > Content Drilldown** metrics.

8. *True or False:* **Behavior > Site Content > Content Drilldown** allows you to see engagement metrics on the individual page level.

9. **Behavior > Site Content > Content Drilldown** provides which of the following metrics? (Select all that apply.)

   a. Unique pageviews

   b. Average time on page

   d. Average number of user interactions per page

   e. Total number of sessions per page

Application

This exercise asks you to think strategically about the information provided through the *Behavior > Site Content* menu options. Please use the charts provided to answer each of the following questions. It is recommended that the charts be examined in the sequence in which they are presented. When you are done, or if you are stuck, our responses can be found on page 606.

The tables shown on page 202 display data for a travel site organized identically to yours. The charts were generated by using the **Navigation Summary** on the top of the *Behavior > Site Content >* **All Pages** report. The key pages in this site are:

/xqanqeon	Home page
/mediaplay.html	See a video
/contact.html	Contact us
/information.html	More information
/purchase.html	Tour listing page (select a tour for purchase)
/thanks_p15M.html	Finalize/complete purchase
/search.html	Site search

Since this is an ecommerce site, finalizing a purchase is an important goal.

What conclusions can you draw about the path that site users take to purchase? How effective is the purchase page once users arrive? What changes, if any, would you recommend to improve the chances of finalizing a sale?

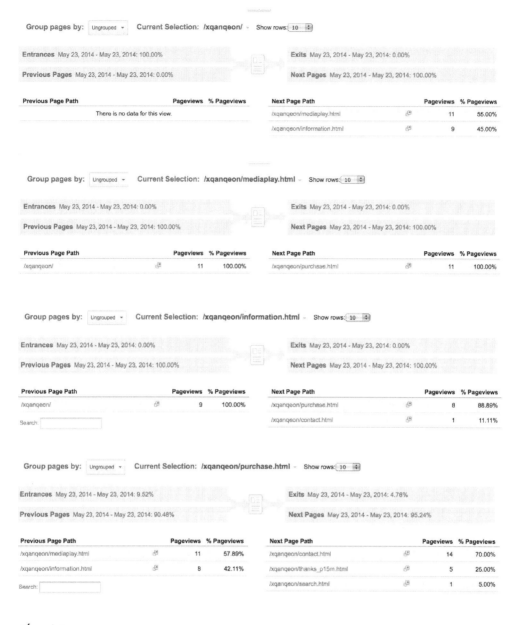

Hands-on

This exercise asks you to apply your understanding of the data provided through the **Behavior > Site Content** menu options. Please answer each of the following questions using your own Google Analytics account and the data collected for your travel website. If it has been more than a month since you started to collect data, make certain to set your date range to include the entire time span of data collection.

1. On what date did you have the greatest number of pageviews? Is this the same date as the greatest number of unique pageviews?

2. Which specific page has the highest average time spent on page? Which page has the lowest average time spent on page?

3. Which specific page has the highest bounce rate? Which page has the lowest bounce rate?

4. Which page on your site has the most pageviews?

5. With regard to the page identified in the prior question: What percent of users begin on this page? What percent of users leave your site from this page? Among users who did not leave the site after seeing this page, what page is most likely to be seen next?

6. Which page on your site is the most common entry (landing) page?

7. With regard to the page identified in the prior question: What percent of users begin on this page? What percent of users leave your site from this page? Among users who did not leave the site after seeing this page, what page is most likely to be seen next?

8. Which page on your site is the most common exit page? What percent of users exit from this page?

9. The contact page on your site is "contact.html". Once the form is submitted, the user is taken to a "thank you for contact page" at "thanks_c.html". Keeping these two pages in mind, what percent of those viewing the contact page actually submit the form?

29
The Behavior Menu: Site Speed

Metrics related to how quickly your site overall and specific pages are loading can be found in the **Site Speed** menu beneath the **Behavior** main menu (see below).[15] This information is particularly important when you want to maximize the chances of a positive user experience with your website or blog.

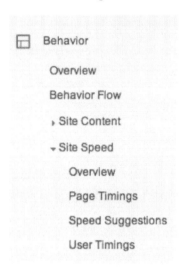

As indicated in the menu options above, **Site Speed** provides data on three aspects of site load speed and latency. These are:

- *Page-load time for a subset of site pageviews.* As with metrics we have already discussed, you can view the data across different dimensions to see how quickly your pages loaded from a variety of perspectives (e.g., in different browsers, in different countries). This data can be seen via the *Overview* and *Page Timings* menu options. No additional configuration of your website or blog is required to collect this data.

- *Execution speed or load time of any discrete hit, event, or user interaction that you want to track* (for example, how quickly images load or response time to button clicks). Data for these metrics is available in the **User Timings** report. Google

---

[15] Primary sources for this chapter are: *About Site Speed* at
https://support.google.com/analytics/answer/1205784?hl=en and *Interpret Site Speed* at
https://support.google.com/analytics/answer/2383341?hl=en

notes that the collection of this data "Requires additional set up that must be completed by a qualified developer."

-   *How quickly the browser parses the document and makes it available for user interaction.* No additional configuration is required to collect this data. Data for these metrics are available in the **Page Timings** report.

Site Speed metrics can help you determine how well your site and specific pages perform with regard to how quickly users are able to see and interact with content. You can identify areas that need improvement and then track the extent to which those improvements reduce load times. Finally, when you determine that improvements are necessary, Google provides suggestions through the Speed Suggestions menu option.

Overview

The **Behavior > Site Speed > Overview** option displays summary information for metrics related to site speed and latency. Each of these metrics, as well as others related to site and page speed, are defined in this chapter's addendum.

Top of Page

The chart shown on the top of the **Behavior > Site Speed > Overview** page presents (by default) a line graph of **Average Page Load Time**. When all is working well on your site, the line and peaks should be relatively flat, indicating consistency in this metric. Spikes in the line graph may be an indication of specific site problem(s), and a page-by-page analysis of load times may be warranted. A drop in the line graph indicates improvement in average site load times and should appear whenever you are successful in modifying pages to reduce load time.

The need to monitor this metric on a daily basis is illustrated in the line graph shown below. We noted a significant rise in **Average Page Load Time** on March 12 and took steps to remedy the problem before it became worse.

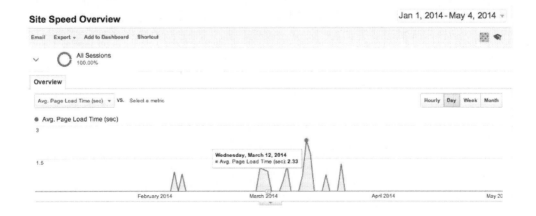

Similar to other line charts, you have the option of changing the displayed metric. The range of speed-related metrics can be found by using the pull-down menu beneath the **Overview** tab, as shown below.

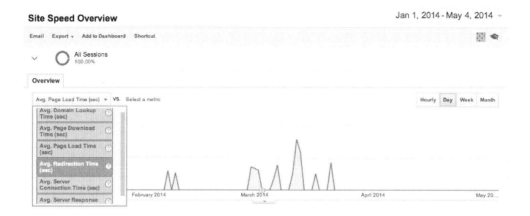

Finally, similar to other line graphs, you can chart two metrics at the same time or you can chart the same metric in two different time periods.

Middle of Page

The data shown in the middle of **Behavior > Site Speed > Overview** display reports website averages for the set of speed metrics (see below). Since all of these metrics relate to site speed, lower numbers are better, indicating faster load and connection speeds. The average metrics for my site appear to be quite acceptable.

Keep in mind, however, that these are averages and, as such, are influenced by extreme measures. A high overall average page load time, for example, may be deceptive if its high average is influenced by the extremely high load time of just one or two pages. As a result, while low numbers in these metrics are a good sign, higher numbers should be interpreted cautiously and should lead to a more detailed examination of individual page performance, as discussed later in this chapter.

The bottom of the page chart (see below) allows you to examine average page load times by browser, country/territory or page.

Site Speed	Browser	Avg. Page Load Time (sec)
Browser	1. Chrome	1.10
Country / Territory		view full report
Page		

Examination by browser and country/territory (and its subdivisions of city) allows you to isolate any site problems related to these two areas. High load times for a particular browser may indicate that the site needs to be better optimized for that browser. High load times for a particular country may also indicate that optimization should be explored when sending site content to IP addresses located in that country. Clicking on **view full report** for these metrics takes you to more detailed tables.

While browser and country insights are important, perhaps the most important link is **Page,** which allows you to see the load times and other speed data for individual pages. Since clicking on **view full report** for this metric takes you to the same display as that obtained through the **Page Timings** menu option, we'll discuss **Page Timings** in the next section.

Page Timings

Selecting the **Behavior > Site Speed > Page Timings** menu option brings up two displays. First, on the top of the page, the same **Average Page Load Time** chart as presented in the **Behavior > Overview** page is displayed. As with the earlier chart, the metric(s) and time frame for the display can be customized to meet your strategic information needs.

The chart on the bottom of the **Behavior > Site Speed > Page Timings** display shows page load times for individual site pages. (Note that if you are taken to the over/under line chart, you can click on the table icon above the chart to display the data as a table. The table icon, which resembles a grid, is on the upper right-hand side of the table (the first in the row of three icons.) The resulting table, organized by page URL, is shown on the top of page 208.

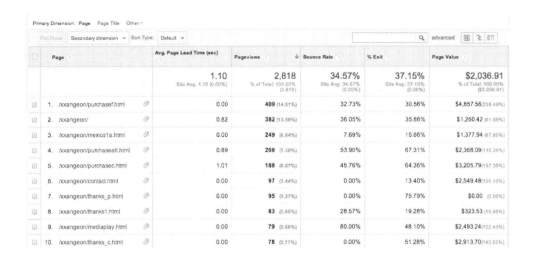

Page	Avg. Page Load Time (sec)	Pageviews	↓ Bounce Rate	% Exit	Page Value
	1.10 Site Avg: 1.10 (0.00%)	2,818 % of Total: 100.00% (2,818)	34.57% Site Avg: 34.57% (0.00%)	37.15% Site Avg: 37.15% (0.00%)	$2,036.91 % of Total: 100.00% ($2,036.91)
1. /xxangeon/purchasef.html	0.00	409 (14.51%)	32.73%	30.56%	$4,857.56 (238.49%)
2. /xxangeon/	0.82	382 (13.56%)	36.05%	35.86%	$1,260.42 (61.88%)
3. /xxangeon/mexico1a.html	0.00	249 (8.84%)	7.69%	15.66%	$1,377.94 (67.65%)
4. /xxangeon/purchasealt.html	0.89	208 (7.38%)	53.90%	67.31%	$2,368.09 (116.26%)
5. /xxangeon/purchasec.html	1.01	188 (6.67%)	45.76%	64.36%	$3,205.79 (157.38%)
6. /xxangeon/contact.html	0.00	97 (3.44%)	0.00%	13.40%	$2,549.48 (125.16%)
7. /xxangeon/thanks_p.html	0.00	95 (3.37%)	0.00%	75.79%	$0.00 (0.00%)
8. /xxangeon/thanks1.html	0.00	83 (2.95%)	28.57%	19.28%	$323.53 (15.88%)
9. /xxangeon/mediaplay.html	0.00	79 (2.80%)	80.00%	48.10%	$2,493.24 (122.40%)
10. /xxangeon/thanks_c.html	0.00	78 (2.77%)	0.00%	51.28%	$2,913.70 (143.05%)

Selecting the **Page Title** option from above the chart (on the left-hand side in the Primary Dimension row) makes the table easier to interpret by listing pages by name rather than URL, as shown below.

Page Title	Avg. Page Load Time (sec)	Pageviews	↓ Bounce Rate	% Exit	Page Value
	1.10 Site Avg: 1.10 (0.00%)	2,818 % of Total: 100.00% (2,818)	34.57% Site Avg: 34.57% (0.00%)	37.15% Site Avg: 37.15% (0.00%)	$2,036.91 % of Total: 100.00% ($2,036.91)
1. xxangeon	0.82	1,327 (47.09%)	31.81%	29.84%	$1,717.20 (84.30%)
2. 462site Dryekkixx	0.94	820 (29.10%)	44.88%	47.68%	$3,917.93 (192.35%)
3. Contact	0.89	311 (11.04%)	34.88%	45.98%	$1,050.00 (51.55%)
4. (not set)	0.00	291 (10.33%)	22.15%	25.77%	$750.42 (36.84%)
5. xxangeonx	1.88	46 (1.63%)	25.00%	71.74%	$0.00 (0.00%)
6. Scroll Test Page	0.00	14 (0.50%)	0.00%	50.00%	$0.00 (0.00%)
7. Three To Purchase Pg Links	0.00	5 (0.18%)	66.67%	40.00%	$600.00 (29.46%)
8. Pinterest_Scenes	0.00	4 (0.14%)	0.00%	0.00%	$0.00 (0.00%)

At this point, we are only interested in the first two columns: **Average Page Load Time** and **Pageviews**. Pageviews is important because we don't want to draw conclusions about pages for which there are so few views that the reported load times become unreliable. As a general rule of thumb, we recommend at least 30 pageviews occur before you pay much attention to the Average Page Load Time.

You want to use this chart to identify pages with relatively long load times. This can easily be done by clicking on the **Average Page Load Time** column header. Doing so orders all of your pages in terms of load time from high to low. The table on the top of page 209 presents all of our pages by URL where the pages with the longest average load times are presented first. These are the pages which may require attention.

Google Analytics Demystified

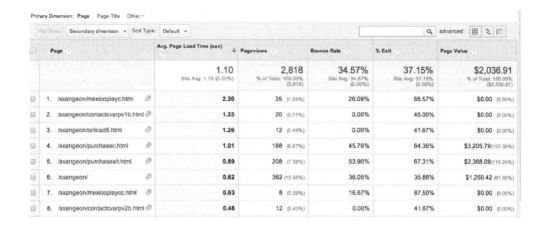

In my case, all of my pages seem to load quickly except one (listed in the first position), which is still fast but a bit longer than the others. I may want to take a look at this page to see how this load time can potentially be reduced. Google Analytics' **Speed Suggestions** might help.

For context, industry guidelines recommend that pages load in three seconds or less. Industry research found that 75% of users said that they would not return to a website that took longer than 4 seconds to load and nearly half of all users expect webpages to load in 2 seconds or less.

Speed Suggestions

Selecting the **Behavior > Site Speed > Speed Suggestions** option displays a list of your site's pages ordered by pageviews. Similar to Average Page Load Time, this display is easier to apply to strategic decision-making if you click on the **Average Page Load Time** column header. This will order your pages from highest to lowest in terms of average load time. As we saw in the previous table, most of our pages are doing quite well. There is only one page loading in two seconds or more (see below).

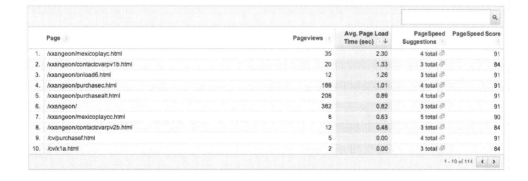

The table's last column presents a **Page Speed Score**. This score indicates how much room for improvement a particular page has, with scores nearer to 100 indicating less room for improvement than scores closer to zero. Our one relatively slower page has a score of 91, which indicates that some slight improvement can be accomplished. Clicking on the link for this page in the **Page Speed Suggestions** column brings up the following display. You'll notice that the Page Speed Score for Desktop is the same as that shown on the previous table.

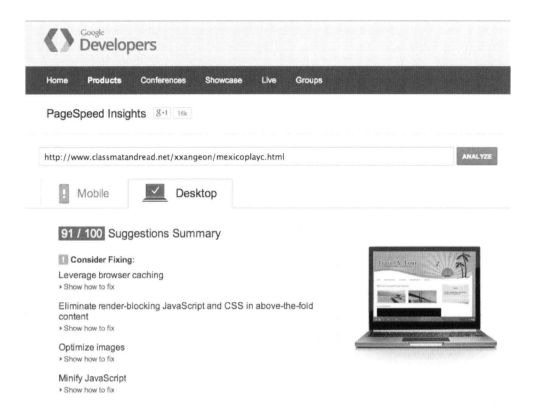

Clicking on any **Show how to fix** link brings up specific suggestions (as shown below) for the **Optimize Images** suggestion.

Referring back to the main suggestions page, you'll notice a tab for Mobile and a tab for Desktop. The preceding data and discussion applied to site engagement via desktop devices. But, what about when the site is accessed via a mobile device?

We can address this question by going back to the initial table displayed when **Speed Suggestions** is selected. This table orders pages by the number of pageviews, from highest to lowest, as shown below. As can be seen, all have quite high PageSpeed scores.

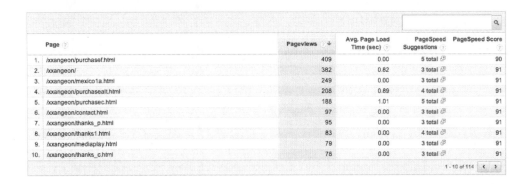

	Page	Pageviews	Avg. Page Load Time (sec)	PageSpeed Suggestions	PageSpeed Score
1.	/xxangeon/purchasef.html	409	0.00	5 total	90
2.	/xxangeon/	382	0.82	3 total	91
3.	/xxangeon/mexico1a.html	249	0.00	3 total	91
4.	/xxangeon/purchasealt.html	208	0.89	4 total	91
5.	/xxangeon/purchasec.html	188	1.01	5 total	91
6.	/xxangeon/contact.html	97	0.00	3 total	91
7.	/xxangeon/thanks_p.html	95	0.00	3 total	91
8.	/xxangeon/thanks1.html	83	0.00	4 total	91
9.	/xxangeon/mediaplay.html	79	0.00	3 total	91
10.	/xxangeon/thanks_c.html	78	0.00	3 total	91

1 - 10 of 114

For each of our high pageview pages, we also want to confirm that the page is working well via mobile devices. We can check this by first clicking on the page's link in the **PageSpeed Suggestions** column and then on the **Mobile** tab in the subsequent suggestions page. When this is done, a display evaluating our mobile performance is displayed.

We receive two mobile scores: one for speed and one for user experience.

The **mobile speed** score is shown below. While the mobile score for this page is a bit below its desktop speed score, the score is still high in an absolute sense and implementing some of mobile speed suggestions should help improve load time speed when the site is accessed via a mobile device.

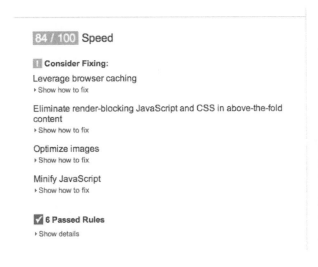

84 / 100 Speed

Consider Fixing:

Leverage browser caching
▸ Show how to fix

Eliminate render-blocking JavaScript and CSS in above-the-fold content
▸ Show how to fix

Optimize images
▸ Show how to fix

Minify JavaScript
▸ Show how to fix

☑ **6 Passed Rules**
▸ Show details

There do appear to be significant problems when our site is evaluated in terms of the **mobile user experience** it provides (see below). Our score is 51 out of 100, which indicates a great deal of room for improvement. We would want to give serious consideration to Google's suggestions for improving the mobile user experience.

Chapter Addendum: Site Speed Terms Defined[16]

Average Page Load Time

Average Page Load time is the average amount of time (in seconds) that it takes for pages in the analytical sample to load. This metric applies to both overall site performance and specific pages. The amount of time calculated for a specific page begins with the initiation of a pageview request (e.g., a click on a page link) and ends when the page is completely loaded in the browser window. The load times for specific pages can be improved via Google Analytics' Speed Suggestions.

Average Page Download Time

This is the average amount of time for a page, or all pages in the site sample, to download. This metric is influenced by user connection dynamics (which are out of your control) and the amount of source code on a page (which is within your control). Generally, the greater the amount of source code, the slower the download time. Two easy things to reduce source code are to eliminate in-line styles via CSS and to place all Javascript in external files.

Average Domain Look-up Time

This metric reports the average amount of time (in seconds) taken in the DNS look-up for a specific page or the average of all site pages included in the sample. If you are finding that DNS look-up is taking an unusual amount of time, then try to DNS diagnostics tools at:

http://mxtoolbox.com/DNSLookup.aspx

Problems in this area, however, are generally beyond your control.

Average Redirection Time

This metric reports the average amount of time (in seconds) spent in redirects before fetching a particular page or for the site as a whole. If there are no redirects, this metric's value is typically expected to be zero. If you are using redirects on your site, then you will want to minimize the amount of time it takes to accomplish this. At minimum, you

---

16 Definitions are provided by Google Analytics *Interpret Site Speed* at:
https://support.google.com/analytics/answer/2383341?hl=en&ref_topic=1282106. Implications adapted from *Speed Matters; Improve usability with Google Analytics Site Speed Reports* at:
http://www.iacquire.com/blog/speed-matters-improve-usability-with-google-analytics-site-speed-reports

should eliminate any multiple or daisy-chain redirects. You can also use the Rex Swain's HTTP viewer to identify any problems.

The viewer is located at:

`http://www.rexswain.com/httpview.html`

Average Server Connection Time

This the average amount of time (in seconds) spent in establishing a TCP connection for a particular page or for the site as a whole. Slow connection times may be the result of server or hosting problems, and conversations with these individuals may be warranted when server connection times are slow.

Average Server Response Time

The is the average amount of time (in seconds) a site's server takes to respond to a user request, including the network time from the user's location to the server. As with the prior metrics, this metric applies to both overall site performance and specific pages. Vender notes that "A couple of things might be involved here. Your web server can be poorly configured to handle even a basic amount of user connections and processes. If you have an amateur configure your server settings it's very likely that RAM and process allocations are NOT optimized. Get a seasoned web server administrator to configure your web server. Another possibility is that you're running a database-driven site and NOT taking advantage of caching. For example, if you are running a WordPress site and don't use a caching plugin, then you're making your server work way too hard. No matter what CMS you are using, if you have pages that query your database for content BUT that content relatively remains static over a period of time, you should be caching that content so your server only needs to generate that content once over multiple requests."

30

Practice With Site Speed

This chapter presents three sets of exercises to help you apply and extend your knowledge of the type of metrics and reports available through the **Behavior > Site Speed** menu options.

True/false and multiple choice

This set of questions makes certain that you understand key concepts. Feel free to open and refer to Chapter 29 or access the **Behavior > Site Speed** menu in your analytics account. When you are done, or if you are stuck, the answers can be found on page 607.

1. *True or False:* Site speed metrics such as page load time reflect the entirety (100%) of all pageviews.

2. *True or False:* Site speed metrics cannot be viewed with secondary dimensions.

3. Site Speed reports provide which of the following metrics? (Select all that apply.)

   a. Average page load time

   b. Average page download time

   c. Average link selection time

   d. Average server response time

   e. Average content distribution time

4. *True or False:* Site Speed reports allow you to order site pages from longest to shortest in terms of average load time.

5. *True or False:* It is recommended that a page have at least 50 pageviews prior to the analysis and application of site speed metrics.

6. *True or False:* Industry guidelines recommend that pages load in a maximum of three seconds.

7. *True or False:* A User Experience Score for a particular page is only available for pages viewed via a mobile device.

8. The PageSpeed Score for a specific page represents:

   a. the amount of room for improvement, with higher numbers indicating less room for improvement

   b. the amount of room for improvement, with lower numbers indicating less room for improvement

   c. the average load time in seconds

   d. the average load time in milliseconds

9. *True or False:* Google provides suggestions for the improvement of both desktop and mobile site speed.

Application

These two exercises ask you to apply your understanding of site speed concepts. When you are done, or if you are stuck, the procedures needed to respond to each question can be found beginning on page 607.

1. The following two charts provide speed-related metrics for all pages with an average page load time of .72 seconds or more. Each page listed is one of the site's purchase pages with the exception of **/462site,** which is the site home page. What conclusions can you draw from the two tables? What next steps would you take?

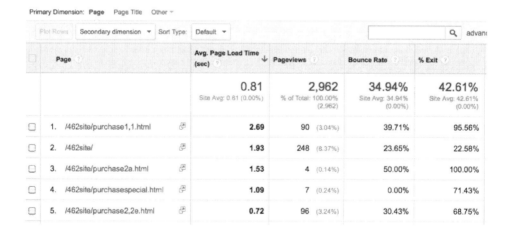

Primary Dimension: **Page**   Page Title   Other ▾

	Page	Avg. Page Load Time (sec) ↓	Pageviews	Bounce Rate	% Exit
		0.81 Site Avg: 0.81 (0.00%)	2,962 % of Total: 100.00% (2,962)	34.94% Site Avg: 34.94% (0.00%)	42.61% Site Avg: 42.61% (0.00%)
☐ 1.	/462site/purchase1,1.html	2.69	90 (3.04%)	39.71%	95.56%
☐ 2.	/462site/	1.93	248 (8.37%)	23.65%	22.58%
☐ 3.	/462site/purchase2a.html	1.53	4 (0.14%)	50.00%	100.00%
☐ 4.	/462site/purchasespecial.html	1.09	7 (0.24%)	0.00%	71.43%
☐ 5.	/462site/purchase2,2e.html	0.72	96 (3.24%)	30.43%	68.75%

	Page ?	Pageviews ?	Avg. Page Load Time (sec) ? ↓	PageSpeed Suggestions ?	PageSpeed Score ?
1.	/462site/purchase1,1.html	90	2.69	4 total ℗	91
2.	/462site/	248	1.93	3 total ℗	91
3.	/462site/purchase2a.html	4	1.53	4 total ℗	91
4.	/462site/purchasespecial.html	7	1.09	5 total ℗	88
5.	/462site/purchase2,2e.html	96	0.72	5 total ℗	85

2. You hire a consultant to improve site efficiency and site speed metrics. The consultant begins to institute changes on March 21 and continues through June 30. You compare speed metrics in this period to the prior period (December 9 to March 30), as shown below.

Mar 21, 2014 - Jun 30, 2014
Compare to: Dec 9, 2013 - Mar 20, 2014

What conclusions can you draw about the consultant's impact on the website's speed related metrics?

Avg. Page Load Time (sec)
15.90%
1.26 vs 1.09

Avg. Redirection Time (sec)
203.98%
0.54 vs 0.18

Avg. Domain Lookup Time (sec)
0.00%
0.00 vs 0.00

Avg. Server Connection Time (sec)
-100.00%
0.00 vs 0.03

Avg. Server Response Time (sec)
-5.45%
0.12 vs 0.12

Avg. Page Download Time (sec)
115.33%
0.02 vs 0.01

Hands-on

This exercise focuses on **Average Page Load Time**. If it has been more than a month since you started to collect data, make certain to set your date range to include the entire time span of data collection.

1. Has the Average Page Load Time been consistent since the launch of your website?

2. Has the Average Page Download Time been consistent since the launch of your website?

3. Is the overall site Average Page Load Time a good indicator of the performance of all site pages?

4. Is Average Page Load Time consistent or different across browsers?

5. Select the page on your site with the most pageviews? Does the Average Page Load time for this page differ across different browsers?

6. Select the page with the highest (worst) Average Page Load Time. How can you explore why this might be happening?

7. Based on Average Page Load Time, how many of your site's pages should be examined for ways to improve this metric?

31

The Behavior Menu: In-Page Analytics

The **Behavior > In-Page Analytics** menu option allow you to explore the extent to which users interact with links and other engagement items on your website pages.

The In-Page Analytics display

Selecting **Behavior > In-Page Analytics** from the main menu should bring up the In-Page Analytics display. If you receive an error message ("Problem loading In-Page Analytics"), simply click on **Load in Full View** to see the display.

Beyond this message, there is also a slight chance that Google Analytics will not immediately display your home page in spite of what you believe are the correct underlying settings. My site's home page is:

http://www.googleanalyticsdemystified.com/xqanqeon

But, there are times when **Behavior > In-Page Analytics** takes me to just the primary URL, as shown below.

Typing the subdirectory name into the browser without changing any of the other URL components brings up the desired **Behavior > In-Page Analytics** display. When I type the name of the subdirectory into the appropriate place, my browser looks like this:

Then the **Behavior > In-Page Analytics** report is provided, as shown below. From this page, you can move through In-Page Analytics in the same way that you move through your site. Clicking any link will load a new display for the linked page.

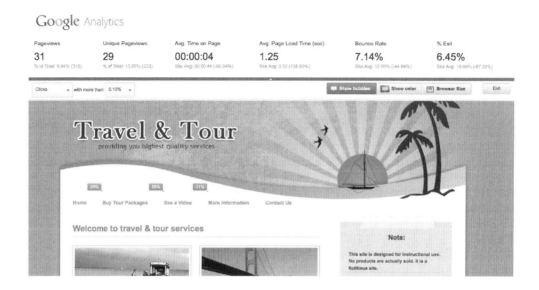

The In-Page Analytics display

There are three parts to the **Behavior > In-Page Analytics** display.

Top of page summary

The top of the page summary provides page-related metrics for the page being displayed. These metrics are pulled from a number of different reports, as shown below.

Google Analytics

Pageviews	Unique Pageviews	Avg. Time on Page	Avg. Page Load Time (sec)	Bounce Rate	% Exit
31	29	00:00:04	1.25	7.14%	6.45%
% of Total: 9.84% (315)	% of Total: 13.00% (223)	Site Avg: 00:00:44 (-90.04%)	Site Avg: 0.52 (138.89%)	Site Avg: 12.90% (-44.64%)	Site Avg: 19.88% (-67.22%)

Bottom of page display

The bottom of the page displays your selected webpage and the click rate for links and other engagement items on this page. The screen shown on the top of page 221, for example, indicates that of the five links on the top of my home page, only three are used at all at a rate of 28% to 38%. The click through rate is the boxed percentage above each link.

Note that hovering your cursor over any percentage or link displays more detailed information, as shown below.

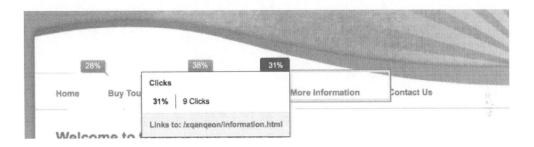

Finally, longer pages, which require scrolling to see links on the bottom of the page will display "% Clicks Below" on the bottom of the page. The percentage displayed reflects the cumulative percentage of clicks on links below the part of the page displayed. This metric can help you understand the difference that page location can make to the link click-through rate.

The Control Bar

The Control Bar appears between the top of page metric summary and the detailed web page display. The links and pull-down menus in this bar (see below) allow you to change and customize which metrics are displayed and the form in which they are displayed. These options are discussed next, keeping in mind that the default settings typically allow you to understand key information needed for decision-making.

The left-hand side of the Control Bar contains two pull-down menus. The menu labeled "Clicks" (by default) allows you to select the specific metric to see in the display (see left-hand figure below). Here you can see the standard metrics available (the four on the top of the pull-down menu) as well as metrics specific to your site. The menu labeled ".10%" (by default) allows you to set a display threshold (see right-hand figure below). Using these two menus together allows you to better satisfy your information needs, for example, displaying only those links that are clicked by more than 10% of that page's users.

Three display options are shown on the right-hand side of the Control Bar, as shown below.

- The **Show Bubbles** option is selected by default. Activation of this option displays the click (or other metric) in a box above each link meeting the selection/threshold criteria. Deselecting this option removes the percentages from the display.

- The **Show Color** option is deselected by default. Selecting this option color codes the displayed percentages to visually highlight differences. The legend used to interpret the colors appears at the top left of the web page. This option can be used alone or in conjunction with Show Bubbles.

- **Browser Size** lets you see the portion of your page that is visible without scrolling. Once you select this option, a slider will appear. The percentage on the slider represents the portion of the displayed page that is visible without scrolling. If, for example, you set the slider to 70%, then the portion of the page that is visible to 70% of traffic (without scrolling) is highlighted while the rest of the page is identified by a color overlay.

When you select the **Browser Size** option, a new set of options appears in the center of the control bar (see below). Each option provides a different base for data presentation.

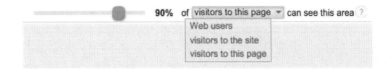

-   **Visitors to this page** estimates the percentage of the page that is visible when the calculation reflects the experiences of just those visiting the page. This option takes into account both the date range of your report and any segments you have applied.

-   **Web users** estimates the page's viewable area based on the overall experiences from across the Web. Selecting this option after setting the slider bar to 70%, for example, would display the percentage of the page that is visible to 70% of all traffic on the Web without scrolling. This option does not take into account either the date range of your report or any segments you have applied.

-   **Visitors to the site** estimates the page's viewable area based on the overall experiences of those visiting your site. Selecting this option after setting the slider bar to 70%, for example, would display the percentage of the page visible to 70% of all site users without scrolling. This option takes into account the date range of your report, but not any segments you have applied.

To the far right of the slider is a box labeled **Show Percentages**. Checking this box provides more detail on page viewability without scrolling. This option allows you to move your cursor to any point on the page. Once you are in the desired position, a box will appear to inform you of the estimated percentage of viewers who can see that point on the page without scrolling.

Finally, **Page Layout** (which is accessible via the gear icon on the right-hand side of the page) let's you identify the alignment for the primary content on the displayed page so the Browser Size feature is best aligned with that content.

Pros and cons of In-Page Analytics

Nick Lewis and Krystian Szastok have presented a concise and useful point of view with regard to the pros and cons of Google's In-Page Analytics. Their perspective follows:[17]

> The biggest pro of In-Page Analytics is the ability to see where people click on the page and follow navigation paths through your site. In-Page offers an intuitive visual map that gives instant access to detailed navigation data and in a way

---

[17] Excerpted from *Pros and Cons of In-Page Analytics* at http://moz.com/ugc/the-pros-and-cons-of-inpage-analytics

that can make necessary on-page optimization and even web design changes more immediately obvious than trying to mentally map dry data onto the page yourself.

The 'clicks below' feature, which shows a collective percentage of clicks on links below the part of the page you're looking at, is particularly useful in tracking vertical drop off in interest. It can be quite revealing as to how much of a difference page location can make to the attention a link gets.

Great as In-Page Analytics can be, it's not all roses, and the Devil's in the detail. Where it displays a percentage to represent the proportion of visitors to a page who clicked a certain link, it does so by the target url, rather than the actual link. So for example, if your logo links to your homepage and you also have a home button, it will show the same percentage across both of them rather than telling you whether people clicked the logo or the home button most. [Enhanced In-Page Analytics will fix this, as discussed in the next section.] Similarly, there is no way of tracking clicks to on-page anchors, meaning that if you have a lot of content on a page, and have used anchors for usability, you can't tell which particular part is prompting people to click.

Enhanced link attribution

Standard In-Page Analytics has two limitations. First, it treats all links with the same destination identically. Thus, if you have both a text and an image link going to the same URL, the click-through rate reported for each link will be the same regardless of the actual number of clicks associated with each link. Second, Standard In-Page Analytics cannot track buttons, menus, and actions driven by javascript.

Fortunately, enhanced link attribution removes both of these limitations.

Enhanced link attribution is activated in a two step process.

- First, you will need to add a line of code to your GATC. The bottom of your tracking code now looks like this:

    ```
    ga('create', 'UA-XXXX-X');
    ga('send', 'pageview');
    ```

    You tell Google Analytics that you want to enable enhanced link attribution by adding one line of code to each page on which you want enhanced link attribution, as shown below.

    ```
    ga('create', 'UA-XXXX-X');
    ga('require', 'linkid', 'linkid.js');
    ga('send', 'pageview');
    ```

- Second, you must change your setting in the Administrative panel. Go to this panel (by clicking Admin from the top of any page) and make certain that the desired account, property, and view are displayed. Then, in the Property column click on the **Property Settings** menu option. On the next page select **Use enhanced link attribution** and click **Apply**.

Google notes two considerations with the use of enhanced link attribution.[18]

First, "enhanced link attribution offers more-detailed reports, and disambiguates clicks to the same destination page that come from more than one element on the page. However, the additional detail comes at the cost of some speed in generating the report, so only turn it on if you need it. You can always turn it off again if you no longer need it."

Second, you may see a percentage range rather than exact percentages. Google Analytics provides this explanation:

Analytics tries to identify exactly which elements on the page users clicked. If an element has a unique ID, then Analytics is able to identify the number of clicks on that element. If an element does not have a unique ID, then Analytics looks up to three levels higher in the DOM structure for a unique ID (i.e., the element's parent's parent). If Analytics is still unable to find a unique ID, then you see a range.

In addition to elements not having unique IDs, there are other reasons why Analytics may not be able to identify whether users clicked elements on the page. For example, in cases where users clicked the back button, refreshed the page, or simply navigated directly to another page on the site, there are no clicks to attribute to page elements, so Analytics displays a range.

Take, for example, these navigations from Page A to Page B:

- Page A -> Page B, 100 navigations attributed to clicks on Element ID-1
- Page A -> Page B, 200 navigations attributed to clicks on Element ID-2
- Page A -> Page B, 50 navigations that can't be attributed to any Element ID

In this case:

- Element ID-1: 100-150 clicks
- Element ID-2: 200-250 clicks
- Elements with no ID: 0-50 clicks

---

[18] *Enhanced Link Attribution* at https://support.google.com/analytics/answer/2558867?hl=en

32

Practice With In-Page Analytics

This chapter presents three sets of exercises to help you apply and extend your knowledge of **Behavior > In-Page Analytics**.

True/false and multiple choice

This first set of questions makes certain that you understand key concepts. Feel free to open and refer to Chapter 31 or access **Behavior > In-Page Analytics** in your analytics account. When you are done, or if you are stuck, the answers can be found on page 609.

1. *True or False:* **Behavior > In-Page Analytics** provides data for only the site's home page.

2. *True or False:* **Behavior > In-Page Analytics** provides data for only those pages with 200 or more pageviews.

3. On the top of the **Behavior > In-Page Analytics** display are summary metrics. *True or False:* You can customize the metrics shown in this display.

4. *True or False:* By default, the **Behavior > In-Page Analytics** display shows the click-through rate for all links with clicks greater than .1%.

5. Which of the following can be selected as the metric to be shown on the **Behavior > In-Page Analytics** display? (Select all that apply.)

    a. Clicks

    b. Pageviews

    c. Transactions

    d. Browser

    e. Location

6. *True or False:* The **Show Bubbles** option allows you to show/not show boxes with click-through rate percentages on the **In-Page Analytics** display.

7. *True or False:* You can use the **Show Color** option to color code different levels of percentages on the In-Page Analytics display.

8. Which of the following shows you the difference in clicks when the nonscroll area of a page is compared to the area that must be scrolled to be seen?

    a. Clicks above

    b. Scrolling clicks

    c. Clicks below

9. Assume that you have two links on a page that take a user to the same URL. What needs to be done in order to have **Behavior > In-Page Analytics** track the click-through rates of these links independently? (Select all that apply.)

    a. Enable enhanced attribution in Administration

    b. Make certain that each link's wording is different

    c. Have the links appear in different colors

    d. Make certain that the word length of each link is different

    e. Place the links on different parts of the page

    f. Add extra line of code to your Google Analytics Tracking Code

Application

These two exercises ask you to think strategically about the information provided by In-Page Analytics. Our responses appears on page 609.

1. Examine the display shown below. This is the home page of a travel site like yours. What inferences can you draw about users' mindset when they visit this page? What next steps would you take to reduce any page weaknesses?

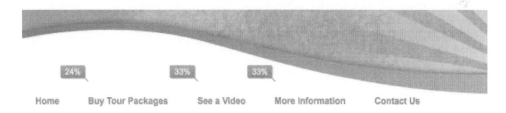

2. Examine the display shown on page 228. This is the home page of a travel site like yours. Assume that the results shown are after the home page was redesigned to foster greater levels of engagement. Based on this data, what is your evaluation of the redesign? What steps would you recommend be taken next?

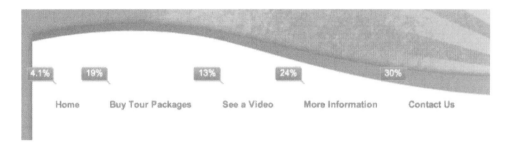

Avg. Time on Page	Avg. Page Load Time (sec)	Bounce Rate
00:00:48	0.00	40.00%
Site Avg: 00:00:23 (113.63%)	Site Avg: 0.00 (0.00%)	Site Avg: 64.71% (-38.18%)

4.1%	19%	13%	24%	30%
Home	Buy Tour Packages	See a Video	More Information	Contact Us

Hands-on

These two exercises ask you to apply your understanding of the data provided through In-Page Analytics. Please answer each of the following questions using your own Google Analytics account and the data collected for your travel website. If it has been more than a month since you started to collect data, make certain to set your date range to include the entire time span of data collection. Answers will reflect your own unique data set.

1. What is the click-through rate for each of the top of page links on your travel site's home page? What do these percentages tell you about users' mindset as they enter your site through this page?

2. There are two pages that can only be accessed by typing the full URL directly into your browser. These pages are: **information1a.html** and **information1b.html**. In my case, the full URLs are:

   ```
   http://www.googleanalyticsdemystified/xqanqeon/
   information1a.html
   ```

   ```
   http://www.googleanalyticsdemystified/xqanqeon/
   information1b.html
   ```

   The full URLs to these documents on your site will have the same ending (beginning with **/information1a.html** or **/information1b.html**) preceded by your site's primary URL.

   Let's make certain that you understand how these URLs work. Type the first URL above into your browser and press return. The **information1a.html** page from my site should display. Now close and reopen your browser and then retype the same URL into your browser, but do not press return. Highlight and then replace everything up to **/information1a.html** with the full URL to your site. If the **information1a.html** page displays, then you've identified the correct URL (make a note of this as you will need it shortly). If you receive a "page not found error," then the URL you are using is not correct. Correct and retest until you are successful.

The two links shown in the body of both the **information1a.html** and **information1b. html** pages go to the same place - your website's home page.

First, using different browsers, visit **information1a.html**. Click on the top link ("Link one to home page") between five and ten times and click on the lower link ("Link two to home page") fifteen or more times. Wait a day and then use In-Page Analytics to examine this page. You should see how the percentage reported for each link is the same, even though you know the actual click-through rates are different. Remember that since this and the other information page are not linked to any site pages, you'll need to type the full URL of the page in your browser in front of the # shown when your home page displays in In-Page Analytics. Review pages 219 to 220 if you are unsure how to accomplish this.

Now, add enhanced link attribution to **information1b.html**. Make certain to add the additional HTML code as well as to make the appropriate change in the administrative panel. (Review pages 224 to 225 for guidance.) Once again, click on the top link between five and ten times and click on the lower link fifteen or more times. Wait a day and then use In-Page Analytics to examine this page. You should see that the percentage reported for each link is now different.

Section VII: Segments

Our approach to data examination in the **Audience** and **Behavior** menus has focused on the information provided for all website users who pass through any active filters. This approach assumes that we've selected the total sample as the analytical sample. As a consequence, we've deferred addressing many questions. For example:

- How can I best understand the behaviors of those who make a purchase on the first day they visit my site?

- How valuable are our downloadable materials and do they contribute to conversion? Do the conversion or transaction behaviors of those who download materials differ from the behaviors of those who do not?

Questions such as these vary across websites with different content and goals. Regardless of the specific question, the answers typically lie in segmentation: an examination of small subgroups of the total user base.

The two chapters in this section provide insights into the segmentation process and the use of Google Analytics' segments to create small but important subgroups of individuals who will be the specific focus of our analytical efforts. Chapter 33 provides an introduction to segmentation and segment creation. Chapter 34 provides practice in creating and using these segments. With this overview in mind, we'll return to segments in upcoming chapters as we apply this approach to website goals, downloadable materials, campaigns, and events.

Google Analytics Demystified

33

Segmentation and Google Analytics Segments

Segmentation is the process of dividing a large, heterogeneous group of individuals into smaller, homogeneous groups. A simple segmentation could, for example, divide all website visitors into two groups: those who made a purchase and those who did not. We could then look at the behaviors and characteristics of both groups to see what factors beyond purchase differentiate and explain the behaviors of individuals in each group.

The previous example illustrates the two types of variables used in segmentation. *Classification variables* are the basis for segment formation and can be selected from any of the broad range of Google Analytics dimensions. Classification variable(s) can be a single dimension (such as transaction outcome) or they can entail a combination of dimensions. Additionally, once a dimension is chosen, you can use all or just some of the dimension's values for segment formation. The following, for example, segments website users on the basis of three dimensions: transaction outcome, type of user, and landing page. These classification variables result in the two groups shown below:

Segment 1: Individuals who made a transaction on their first visit, were new visitors, and entered via the home page

Segment 2: Individuals who did not make a transaction on their first visit, were new visitors, and entered via the home page

Once classification variables have been used to form segments, one or more *descriptive variables* are used to describe the users within each segment. In this example, we could select **relevant** descriptive variables from the metrics provided in the Audience and Behavior reports. The table shown on the top of the next page does just this.

Descriptive Metric	Segment 1 (Purchasers)	Segment 2 (Nonpurchasers)
Time spent on home page (sec)	:58	:11
Ave. home page load time (sec)	1.2	3.2
% Exit from home page	21%	65%
% Viewing media	65%	11%
% Viewing purchase page	100%	8%
Browser		
Chrome	45%	48%
Safari	22	42
Firefox	33%	10

Examining the selected descriptive metrics by segment provides important insights for future strategic discussion and decision-making. We can see that those who make a purchase versus nonpurchasers appear to be highly engaged with the home page, are unlikely to leave the site from this page, view media, and make it to the purchase page. The opposite is true for nonpurchasers. Moreover, the distribution of browser types is different for the two groups, as is home page load time. This data would lead us to explore several issues, among the most important: home page optimization for Safari; how to increase home page engagement/reduce exit rate; and how to increase media page usage.

When to Use Segmentation

There is no limit to the number of segments that can be formed using Google Analytics data. As a result, it is important that any use of segmentation be grounded in one of the following types of situations, where the segmentation helps you to better understand:

- data patterns and trends provided in the primary reports

- why website goals are/are not being achieved

- opportunities for website improvement, promotion, and targeting

Segment controls

So far, "all site sessions" have served as the sample for our analyses. Confirmation can be found on the top, left-hand side of any page, where "All Sessions 100%" is displayed next to the blue circle (see top of next page). This indicates that the report presents data on all site sessions for the selected date range.

Customize   Email   Export ▾   Add to Dashboard   Shortcut

⌄   ◯ All Sessions
              100.00%

But, this doesn't have to be the case. We can restrict our analysis to one or more segments, where a segment is defined by any single or combination of Google Analytics
dimensions and metrics.[19] You access segments via the **+Add Segment** option on the top
of almost any page (located beneath the blue circle **All Sessions** identifier). When you
click **+Add Segment**, the segments page displays, as shown below.

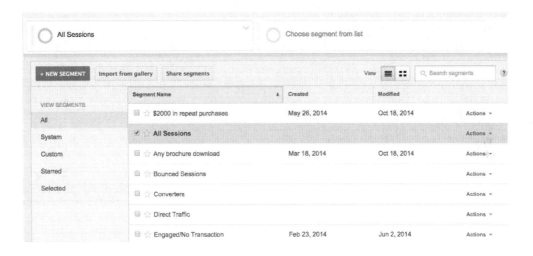

The top row of the display indicates the segments currently being used (in this case, "All
Sessions") and provides the opportunity to add a segment to your data view. This latter
option is labeled **Choose segment from list** (see the top right-hand side of the above
figure). Clicking on this option and then on any listed segment adds the segment to your
analysis. The display on the top of page 236, for example, illustrates what happens when
we add the segment "Any brochure download" to the data view.

---

[19] Both advanced segments and filters restrict the data presentation to a specified group of
sessions or users. Filters permanently restrict the types of individuals reported while segments
are temporary and can be eliminated at any time.

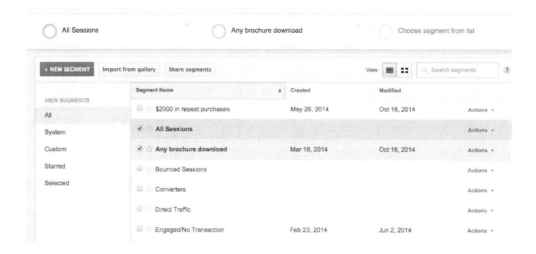

Any segment displayed on the top row can be deleted from the data view by selecting **Remove** from the pull down arrow options which appear in the upper right-hand corner (see below).

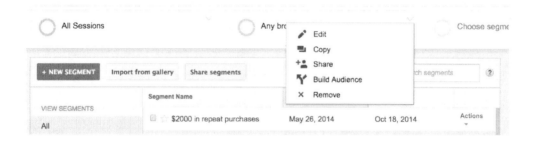

The next row shows segment creation and display options. There are three options on the left-hand side.

- You create a new segment by clicking the **+ NEW SEGMENT** link.

- **Import from gallery** allows you to obtain custom segments created by others.

- **Share segments** takes you to your administrator's page where you can perform sharing, deletion, and related activities.

There are two options on the right-hand side next to **View** (see the upper right-hand side of the figure on the top of this page). These options determine how custom segments are displayed. The two figures shown on page 237 illustrate what happens when the bar and grid options are selected.

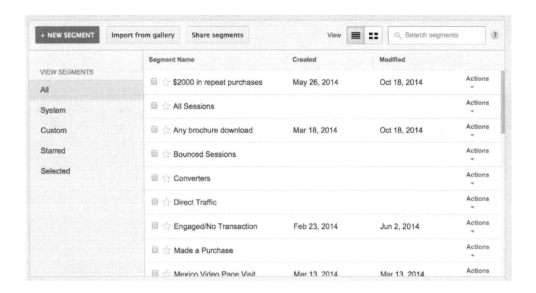

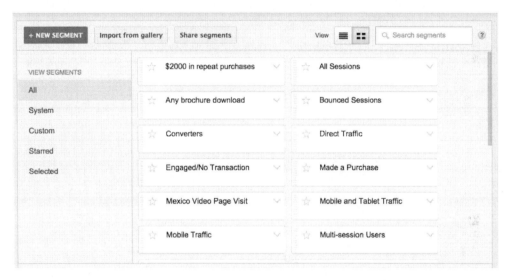

Segments are grouped in different ways, as shown in the left-hand column labeled **View Segments**. "All" displays every available segment. "System" displays those segments predefined and made available by Google Analytics. "Custom" displays segments created by you. "Starred" presents a list of your preferred custom segments. Finally, "Selected" lists those segments being applied to the current data view.

The two options on the bottom of the page complete the segment application process (see the figure on page 238). **Apply** applies the selected segments to the current data view while **Cancel** leaves things as they were before the segment page was opened.

Google Analytics provides a number of built-in segments, which can be seen when the **System** option is selected in the View Segments column. These segments allow you to immediately restrict your data presentation in order to better understand users and sessions defined by the most common types of characteristics and behaviors. The full list of System segments is shown below.

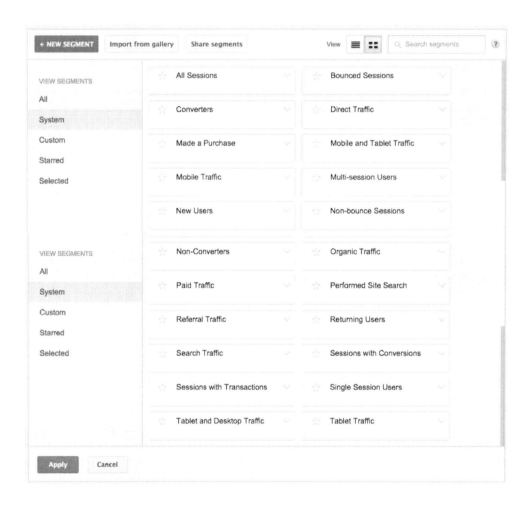

The listed names reflect the characteristics of the users or sessions within the segment. "Mobile Traffic," for example, will restrict the data view to only those sessions begun via a mobile device, while "Sessions with Transactions" restricts the data view to only those sessions in which a transaction took place.

Imagine that we want to examine this latter group of sessions. To examine just those sessions with transactions, we would deselect (remove) "All Sessions" and select "Sessions with Transactions." Clicking on **Apply** changes the data presented to only this group of sessions. The two figures below illustrate how selecting to view only this segment changes the data provided.

The figure below provides information on all sessions during the selected time frame.

In contrast, the figure below provides information on only those sessions in which a transaction took place. Notice, how all the data displays are labeled to indicate that only the segment of "Sessions with Transactions" is being reported.

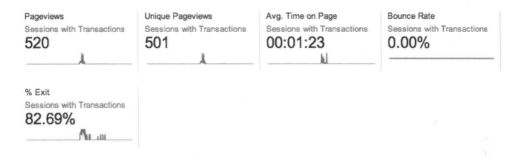

The reports shown above provided the data for one segment at a time, either "All Sessions" or "Sessions with Transaction". This is fine if we want to focus on only one segment. There are times, however, when we want to compare two segments. We might, for example, want to compare the characteristics of the "Sessions with Transaction" segment to "All Sessions". In this circumstance, we would select both segments at the same time. This would place the data for both segments in the same display, as shown on the top of page 240.

Keep two things in mind with regard to the segment data display. First, it not necessary to include "All Sessions" as one of your segments. The table below displays session information for three segments, none of which is "All Sessions". Here we are examining information related to sessions initiated via different sources: direct, referral and search.

Second, once segments are selected the metrics displayed will change to reflect your current data selection. The report above was generated from the **Audience > Overview** menu, while the report shown on the top of page 241 was generated from the **Conversions > Ecommerce > Overview** menu option. Notice how the segments remain constant, but the data changes.

Ecommerce Conversion Rate	Transactions	Revenue	Average Order Value
Direct Traffic	Direct Traffic	Direct Traffic	Direct Traffic
31.66%	272	$2,244,381.95	$8,251.40
Referral Traffic	Referral Traffic	Referral Traffic	Referral Traffic
2.88%	3	$42,000.00	$14,000.00
Search Traffic	Search Traffic	Search Traffic	Search Traffic
3.70%	2	$27,000.00	$13,500.00

Finally, keep in mind that you can always return to your complete data set by deselecting all segments and then selecting "All Sessions" from the System display.

Creating New Segments

Google Analytics' System segments allow you to explore many different types of questions and information needs. There are times, however, when your site goals or information needs require you to examine a segment of users or sessions which you define. The process to accomplish this is straight-forward.

First, click on the **+Add Segment** option which is located on the top of every report page. Then, when the segment option page appears, click on **+Create New Segment** on the top of the page. This will take you to the segment creation page, shown below.

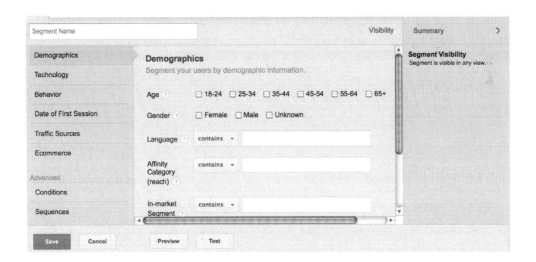

Our first tasks typically require us to name the segment (in the **Segment Name** text box) and to determine whether we want the segment to be available in all views or just the current view. We make this latter decision by clicking on **Visibility**, which appears on the top of the page on the same line as **Segment Name**. In this example, we'll leave the segment name until the end.

The options on the left-hand side of the page indicate the types of dimensions available for use in custom segment creation. Clicking on **Behavior**, for example, brings up the options shown below.

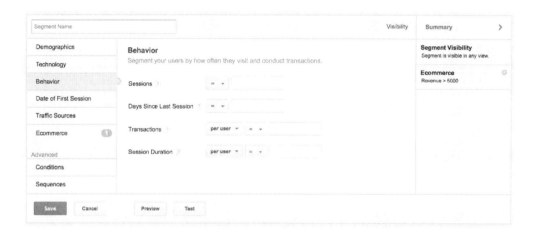

Let's now create a custom segment. The segment will contain only those users who spent more than $5,000 in a single (and only) session. This requires us to select from two different dimensions. First, we click on **Ecommerce** on the left-hand side of the page, and then complete the form using the pull-down menu options as shown below, where we fill in the field relevant to our segment, in this case revenue.

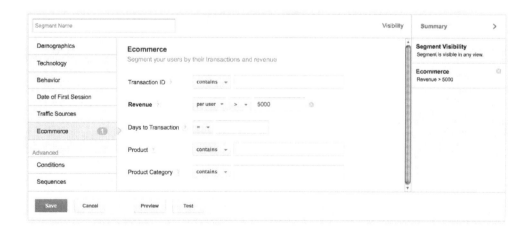

Next, we select **Behavior** from the left-hand menu options and specify that we want to include only those users with a single session. Since this is the last specification, we'll also name this segment (see below).

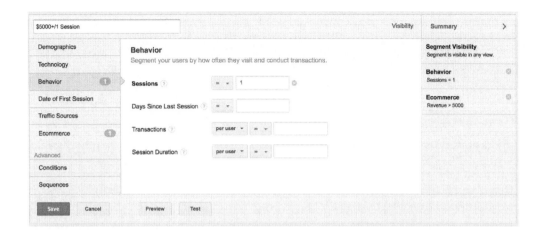

Notice, in the above figure, the segment parameter summary shown on the right-hand side of the page. This column will always display the current set of parameters applied to the segment. This display is particularly useful when (as in this case) you form a segment using different dimensions.

On the bottom of the page is a **Test** option. Selecting this option tells us whether the created segment contains any sessions or users. In our case, the created segment contains about 40% of all site users and about half of all site sessions, as indicated below.

When we are satisfied with our segment, we select **Save** (which appears on the bottom of the page). When we revisit the segments page, the new custom segment will appear in both the "All Segments" and "Custom Segments" lists. The "All Segments" list is shown below.

Now when we select this segment, our data view will contain only the users/sessions contained in this segment, as shown below.

Finally, there may be times when you want to create a segment with characteristics that go beyond those available through the **Demographics, Technology, Behavior, Date of First Session, Traffic Sources,** and **Ecommerce** menu options. Two options are available and are discussed in the next two sections.

Creating New Segments: Adding Conditions

The **Conditions** option is on the lower part of the left-hand menu. This option lets you create a segment according to single or multi-session conditions alone or in conjunction with other types of user or session characteristics. Selecting **Conditions** brings up the display shown below.

Your options for defining the **Conditions** to be used for segment definition are shown on the top, middle of the display just to the right of "Filter" where you decide whether to create the segment based on Sessions or Users (via the **Sessions** pull-down menu) and whether the characteristic will be used to Include or Exclude (via the **Include** pull-down menu). Beneath these options is a pull-down menu which, by default, displays **Ad Content**. This menu gives you access to Google Analytics dimensions and metrics, both those defined by Google, as well any goals or related metrics you have created on your own (see below).

Let's use **Conditions** in conjunction with other types of segment characteristics to create a new segment based on multiple criteria. This segment will consist of non-purchasing users, specifically:

-   users who signed up for website club membership, *and*

-   who downloaded materials, *and*

-   who spent 5 seconds or more on the site in a single (and only session),

-   **but did not** have a session with a transaction.[20]

We start by selecting **Conditions** from the left-hand side menu. On our website, registration for club membership is measured by Goal 20. Since this is a user characteristic, we set the top of form **Filter** options to "Users", and since we want those who converted (i.e., signed up for membership), we set the next filter to "Include". From the pull-down menu (currently labeled **Ad Content**), we select **Goal Conversions** from the blue menu options, and from the new list we select "Goal 20 completions". We then set the quantity to one (which indicates goal conversion). All of the previous actions result in the screen shown on the top of page 246. Clicking on **+Add Filter** allows us to add a second condition to this segment. Notice this first set of conditions now appears on the right-hand side of the display.

---

[20] Note that since you have not as yet created the goals and materials used in the creation of this segment, the items referred to will not appear in your lists of options.

The second segment characteristic relates to downloadable materials. These materials are all named so that they end in **.pdf** and are treated as if they were a normal pageview. To add this characteristic to our segment, we click on **+Add Filter** beneath the segment characteristic just created. Then, in the new display, from the pull-down menu which is currently labeled **Ad Content**, we select **Behavior** from the green (left-hand side) menu options and from the new list we select **Page**. We then use exact match regex to indicate that a match is any pageview ending in .pdf (see figure below). Notice that both the current and previous conditions are now displayed on the right-hand side of the display.

Clicking on **+Add Filter** allows us to add a third condition to this segment.

The third segment characteristic relates to time spent on site, in this case a single session of five seconds or more. To add this characteristic to our segment, we select **Behavior** from the left-hand side menu and indicate that we want session duration to be greater than or equal to five seconds per session and we want the total number of sessions to be only one. As shown on the top of page 247, we provide these characteristics on the lines labeled **Session Duration** and **Sessions**. We change the **Session Duration** pull-down menu from "users" to "session" as we are interested in session duration. Once done, notice how this new segment characteristic is added to the previous ones on the right-hand side of the page.

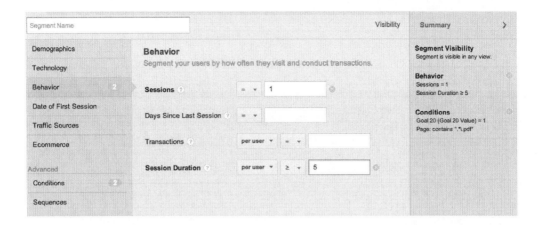

The fourth and final segment characteristic requires that no transaction be made. There are several ways to accomplish this, but we'll simply use one of the Ecommerce options to set session revenue to zero. This results in the screen shown below. Notice this new segment characteristic is added to the prior ones on the right-hand side of the page. Since this is the final segment characteristic, we give the segment a descriptive name, test and if all looks right press **Save**. This new segment then appears on our list of custom segments.

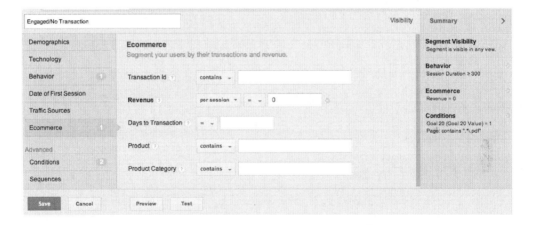

Creating New Segments: Sequences

The previous example showed how the **Conditions** option allows you to use the full range of Google Analytics dimensions and metrics to define a segment of site users/sessions and how to combine these conditions with standard segment characteristics. There are times, however, when you want to define a segment in terms of the *sequence* of behaviors displayed during a site visit rather than the cumulative filtering of characteristics. This is accomplished via the **Sequences** option.

Selecting the **Sequences** option brings up the screen shown below.

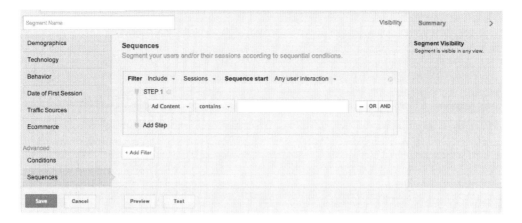

Imagine that we've designed our travel website to (ideally) lead a user to purchase. The path to purchase is believed to be:

> View Page F2.html -> View Page F3.html ->
> View options on Purchase Page (purchase.html) ->
> View "Thank You Page" after purchase is made (thanks.html)

The **Sequences** option allows us to create a segment that consists only of those individuals who took this exact path to purchase. We begin by selecting this option from the left-hand menu. Next, we select **Include** and **Users** from the **Filter** options. We allow the **Sequence start** to come at any time during a visit (thus leaving the final menu set to **Any user interaction**). Finally, we select **Page** from the green **Behavior** option (by using the pull-down menu which, by default, is labeled **Ad Content**). Finally we identify the first page in our funnel via a regex expression. All of these actions result in the display shown below.

Clicking on **Add Step** allows us to add the second step to the sequence. Here, the process is the same except that the page represented in this second step is F3.html. Doing this displays the figure shown below. Notice how the summary on the right-hand side updates to include this step.

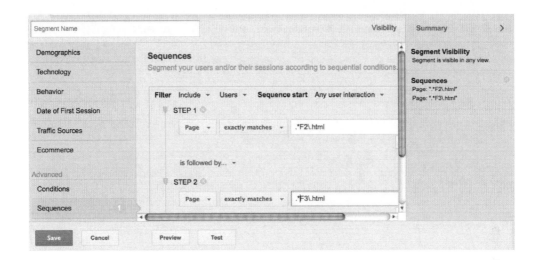

We follow this same procedure for adding the final two steps to our sequence. When both steps have been added, the **Summary** on the right-hand side of the page displays the full sequence, as shown below.

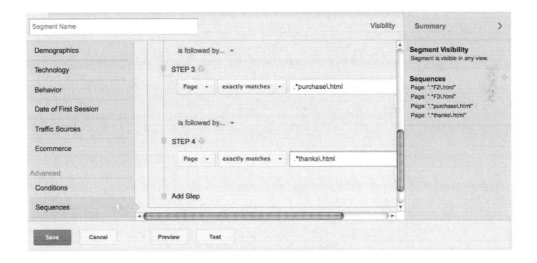

Finally, we give the segment a descriptive name, test and, if all looks well, press **Save**. This new segment then appears on our list of custom segments.

Beyond System and Custom segments, there is one additional way for you to define segments. You can view and import segments created by others.

You begin the view/import process by selecting **Import from gallery** on the top of the initial segment display page. When this is done, an overlay page will appear (see below) in which a listing of segments for all categories will be shown. You can narrow the display to specific types of segments by selecting and deselecting topics from the left-hand **Filter by category** menu.

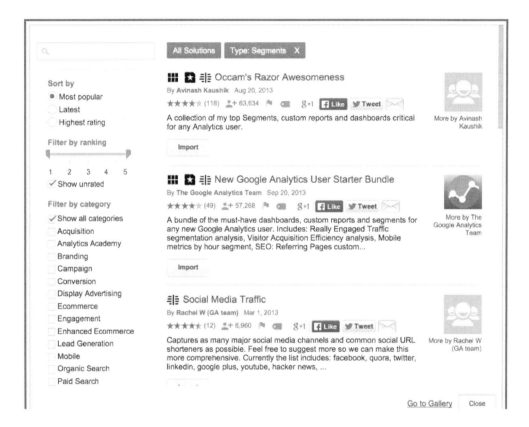

When you are thinking about importing segments, it is important to read the descriptions of the types of segments available, keeping in mind that you are looking for segments relevant to your specific website's characteristics, objectives, and goals. Also keep in mind that a segment that is close to what you need, but needs minor modification, can always be edited after import. Clicking on any title displays more detail on a new page (see top of page 251). You then select the **Import** option on the top of the page. When this is done, you will see a new page which displays of all items available for import. Since at this point we are only interested in custom segments, we select all of the listed segments and deselect all other items. Finally, we select how we want to use these new segments: either in all views or only the currently active view.

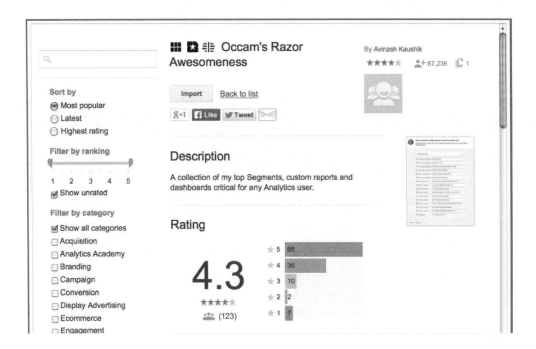

Clicking **Create** takes us to the administrative display where all segments associated with the current view are displayed. We can then modify the list and edit custom and imported segments through the choices in the **Actions** column on the main segment display page.

Segment size

Whenever you apply a segment to a set of Google Analytics data, the segment's size is shown on the top of the page beneath the segment name. The figure opposite shows the application of two segments: one segment reflects site sessions initiated by new site users, while the second segment reflects sessions initiated by returning users. Since all sessions must fit into one of these two segments, the sum of the two segments is 100%. Note that these are the

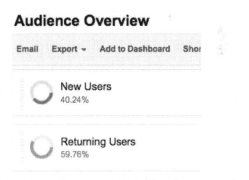

same percentages as shown in the new/returning visitor numeric table, shown on the top of page 252. The percentages agree because both the above summary and the data table below reflect sessions.

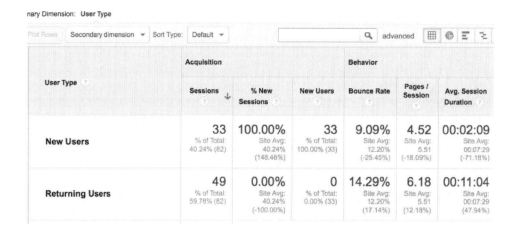

| | Acquisition | | | Behavior | | |
User Type	Sessions ↓	% New Sessions	New Users	Bounce Rate	Pages / Session	Avg. Session Duration
New Users	33 % of Total: 40.24% (82)	100.00% Site Avg: 40.24% (148.46%)	33 % of Total: 100.00% (33)	9.09% Site Avg: 12.20% (-25.45%)	4.52 Site Avg: 5.51 (-18.09%)	00:02:09 Site Avg: 00:07:29 (-71.18%)
Returning Users	49 % of Total: 59.76% (82)	0.00% Site Avg: 40.24% (-100.00%)	0 % of Total: 0.00% (33)	14.29% Site Avg: 12.20% (17.14%)	6.18 Site Avg: 5.51 (12.18%)	00:11:04 Site Avg: 00:07:29 (47.94%)

When we move to apply these segments to a different type of metric, the relative size of the two segments changes, for example, when we apply these two segments to pages (rather than sessions). The segment summary is shown opposite, while the pages numeric table is shown below. As expected, the two data views agree and the sum of the two segments also equals 100%. However, the percentages reported for each segment have changed because the underlying metric has changed.

Pages

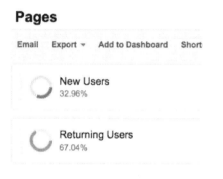

Email   Export ▾   Add to Dashboard   Short

New Users
32.96%

Returning Users
67.04%

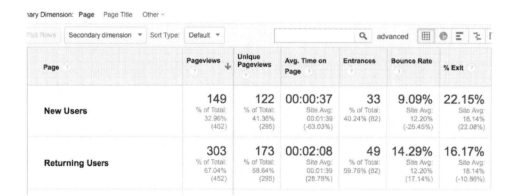

Page	Pageviews ↓	Unique Pageviews	Avg. Time on Page	Entrances	Bounce Rate	% Exit
New Users	149 % of Total: 32.96% (452)	122 % of Total: 41.36% (295)	00:00:37 Site Avg: 00:01:39 (-63.03%)	33 % of Total: 40.24% (82)	9.09% Site Avg: 12.20% (-25.45%)	22.15% Site Avg: 18.14% (22.08%)
Returning Users	303 % of Total: 67.04% (452)	173 % of Total: 58.64% (295)	00:02:08 Site Avg: 00:01:39 (28.78%)	49 % of Total: 59.76% (82)	14.29% Site Avg: 12.20% (17.14%)	16.17% Site Avg: 18.14% (-10.86%)

The takeaway from this is straightforward: ***Whenever you are using the percentages reported for one or more segments, make certain that you interpret this percentage in terms of the appropriate underlying metric.***

34

Practice With Segments

This chapter presents three sets of exercises to help you apply and extend your knowledge of segments.

True/false and multiple choice

This first set of questions makes certain that you understand key concepts. Feel free to open and refer to the previous chapter or access the segments display in your analytics account. When you are done, or if you are stuck, the answers can be found on page 610.

1. *True or False:* Segments are formed on the basis of *classification* variables.

2. *True or False:* A segment can only be formed using one metric at a time.

3. *True or False:* A segment can only be formed on the basis of five or less descriptive variables.

4. *True or False:* You can access segments by clicking on the upward facing arrow next to the blue circle on the top of any report page.

5. Which of the following allows you to see segments created for your use by Google Analytics? (Select all the apply.)

    a. All

    b. System

    c. Custom

6. *True or False:* Segments can be formed on the basis of ...

    a. Only sessions

    b. Only users

    c. Both sessions and users

7. *True or False:* When you create a custom segment, it is automatically made available to all views within the current property.

8. Which of the following are available to use in the creation of a custom segment? (Select all that apply.)

   a. Demographics

   b. Technology

   c. Ecommerce

   d. Date of First Session

9. *True or False:* During the custom segment creation process, the REVIEW option allows you see the percentage of users and/or sessions to which the segment applies.

10. You decide to create a custom segment using the **Conditions** option. *True or False:* A maximum of three dimensions or metrics can be applied to the segment.

11. You decide to create a custom segment using the **Conditions** option. The first criteria uses **Sessions**. *True or False:* All subsequent criteria used in this segment must also use **Sessions**.

12. *True or False:* Once a segment is imported it can never be modified.

13. *True or False:* Best practices recommend that you import only those segments that are relevant to your site's goals and objectives.

14. Which of the following type(s) of segment can be edited and deleted? (Select all that apply.)

   a. Imported

   b. System

   c. Custom

15. You create three custom segments and examine session-related metrics in terms of these segments. You then move on to examine content related metrics, such as pageviews. *True or False:* The percentages reported for each segment's size will not change as you move from session to user metrics.

Application

This exercise asks you to apply your understanding of custom segments. Before beginning, please create a new View in which all custom segments will be created. You should delete this View when done with this exercise. You can choose the name of each segment. When you are done, or if you are stuck, the procedures needed to respond to each request can be found beginning on page 610.

1. Create a custom segment consisting of users who used either Chrome or Safari to initiate a session on your site.

2. Imagine that you revised your website on July 8, 2014. Create a custom segment to identify all users who visited your site on or after this date **and** who had a single session duration of 5 minutes or more.

3. Create a custom segment which consists of users who spent $5,000 or more in one session **and** who took 3 or more days to make the transaction.

4. Create a custom segment consisting of individuals who meet all of the following requirements: (a) landed on the home page where the page's title is "Welcome", (b) purchased two or more items, and (c) were referred to the site by any Wordpress URL.

5. Locate and import three existing custom segments.

Hands-on

Think about your travel website. Identify three strategic information needs that custom segments can help you answer. Then do the following for each segment:

-   Describe the characteristics of the segment and the information need the segment addresses.

-   Explain why the information need is important.

-   Create the segment in Google Analytics and apply the segment to data analysis.

-   Discuss key findings and the extent to which the segment helped answer your information need.

-   Based on the preceding step, describe next steps.

Google Analytics Demystified

Section VIII:
Goals

So far we've looked at how to use and interpret a wide array of metrics. There are opportunities, however, to supplement these standard metrics with metrics that we create and which are uniquely relevant to our website's or blog's specific goals and objectives. The chapters in this and the following two sections illustrate how to accomplish this. Section IX focuses on creating metrics that track downloadable materials, while Section X focuses on events, where we create metrics that, for example, monitor video use and content consumption.

This section focuses on website goal metrics. The six chapters in this section demonstrate how to create and apply custom Google Analytics goal metrics to specific strategic needs.

- Chapter 35 introduces you to three types of goals: destination, duration, and views. The chapter provides examples of when and how to apply these types of goals to assess the extent to which website objectives are being achieved. Chapter 36 provides practice in the creation of these types of goals.

- Chapters 36 to 38 provide instruction for how to read and interpret goal-related metrics.

- Chapter 39 shows how to apply goals to the creation of custom segments.

- Chapter 40 provides practice in the analysis and application of goal metrics to strategic decision-making.

Google Analytics Demystified

Destination, Duration, and View Goals

Google Analytics provides an easy and powerful way for you to collect information related to your website's specific goals and objectives. Your ability to make better strategic decisions may, for example, require you to identify and better understand site users who:

- view certain pages or

- pass through the website in a certain way or

- spend a minimum amount of time on the site or

- interact with a predefined number of pages.

The extent to which these and other goals have been achieved can be determined through the creation and analysis of custom goals.

Google Analytics allows you to create four different types of goals. These are:

- *Destination:* A destination goal is achieved when a website user loads (lands upon) a specific page, for example, a "Thank You" page after completing a purchase or contact form.

- *Duration:* A duration goal is achieved when a website user spends a pre-specified amount of time on the site, for example, five minutes or more.

- *Pages/Screens Per Visit:* This goal is achieved when a website user views a pre-specified number of pages or screens, for example, when three or more pages have been loaded.

- *Event:* This goal is achieved when a website user's behavior matches a pre-specified behavior, for example, viewing a video or downloading a PDF file.

We'll look at the first three types of goals in this section. Events are discussed in Section X.

You create goals through the **Admin** link on the top of every Google Analytics page. Once you click on this link, you'll see the main Administrator's Page (see below). Make certain that the relevant **Account, Property**, and **View** are displayed. Then click on the **Goals** link in the **View** column. The link to goals is in this column because goals are created specific to a view. Thus, different views for the same property may have different goals.

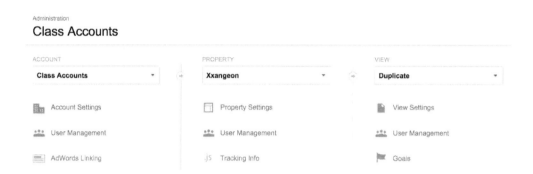

Your goals summary page will be displayed next (see below). Here all of the goals for the current view are displayed. At the moment, we have not yet set up any goals for this view, so this portion of the display is blank.

The critical elements on this screen are:

- **+ NEW GOAL:** A click on this link creates a new goal from scratch.[21]

---

[21] Next to **+NEW GOAL** is a link that allows you to import goals that have been created by others. Since Google Analytics best practice requires that goals should be created specific to your site's objectives and organization, we recommend that you use this option to gather ideas but not to directly import goals.

- **Goal:** The names of all goals created for the current view are listed in this column.

- **Past 7 day conversions:** The number of site users who satisfied the goal's parameters within the last week.

- **Recording:** Visuals in this column indicate whether the goal is currently turned "on" or "off". Google Analytics only monitors goals which are turned "on."

Finally, the note beneath the table reminds us that we can only have 20 goals per view. If we need to create more goals than this we do so with another view since once a goal is created it cannot be deleted even when it is turned "off."

Destination goals

We'll create three destination goals: one simple goal that uses just a single destination page, a more complex goal to which we assign a funnel, and a third destination goal that monitors all pageviews within a specific directory.

Simple Destination Goal

This goal is considered a "conversion"[22] when a user sees the "Thank You" page displayed after the contact form is completed. The ending URL of the "Thank You" page is **thanks_c. html**. As noted earlier, we begin the goal development process by clicking on **+NEW GOAL** which brings up the display shown below.

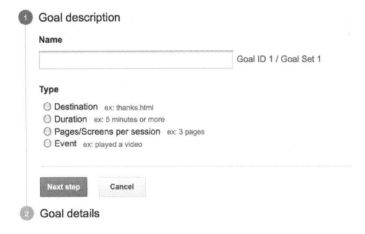

---

[22] Google Analytics uses the term "conversion" to indicate that a goal has been attained, an event has taken place, or a purchase has been made.

The first step in destination goal creation responds to the information requests on this **Goal description** screen. We give the goal a descriptive name (in this case we'll call the goal "Contact Page Sent") and we indicate that it is a destination goal by selecting the button labeled **Destination**. The screen now appears as shown below.

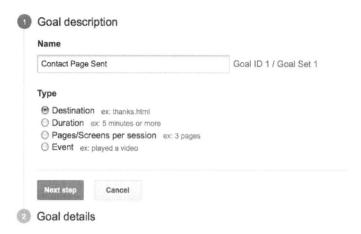

Clicking on **Next step** brings up the display shown below.

This second step collects specific goal characteristics. Since we decided that this was a **Destination** goal, we need to provide the destination page URL. This URL is typed into the top box labeled "Destination," making certain that we provide the directory name, but not the main site URL. The contact "Thank You" page for our website is **/xqanqeon/ thanks_c.html.**

For the moment, we'll leave **Value** and **Funnel** off, as they do not apply in this particular case. Finally, we'll use the **Verify this Goal** link to confirm that we are doing things properly. We should see the percentage of conversions, assuming any occurred, within the prior seven days. If you are receiving a 0% conversion message, use the **Content** menus to make certain that this outcome is correct, keeping in mind that a 0% conversion rate can be correct if no one has completed the goal or even visited your site in the past seven days. If everything seems correct, then click on the **Create Goal** link, and your goal will appear in the main goal table, as shown below.

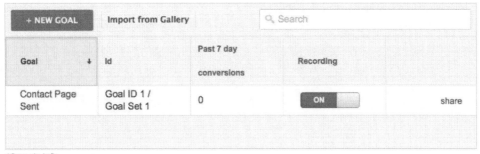

Note two things about this display. First, once created, your goal will automatically begin to collect data unless recording is manually turned "off." Second, you now have the ability to share this goal (via the **share** link) with other views.

Destination Goal With Funnel

Goal development with a funnel or destination starts similarly to the previous goal. We click on **+NEW GOAL** from the goal listing page, and then in Step 1 we name the goal and indicate that it is a destination goal. In this case, the destination is the "Thank You" page following a purchase. The name of the goal is "Purchase Thank You Page".

Step 2 begins similar to a simple destination goal where we type in the URL of the destination page. Our travel website actually contains six "thank you for purchase pages," one for each of the travel packages shown on the purchase page. The URL and names of the thank you pages are:

/xanqeon/thanks_2b.html
/xanqeon/thanks_10b.html
/xanqeon/thanks_15b.html
/xanqeon/thanks_2m.html
/xanqeon/thanks_10m.html
/xanqeon/thanks_15m.html

Since we are only interested in whether a purchase has been confirmed, we indicate (via regex) that our destination goal is any one of these pages, as follows:

.*thanks_[2|10|15].*

We indicate this by selecting **Regular Expression** from the pull-down menu just to the left of our destination URL (see figure on the bottom of this page).

Beneath the destination page URL there are options to add value and funnel information to this goal. It isn't appropriate to add value information in this case, however, because we will have actual purchase information.

Beyond goal value, you can decide to create a funnel leading to the goal destination page, where a funnel represents the path you expect users to take en route to the destination page. According to Google: "When you specify steps in a Funnel, Analytics can the track where visitors enter and exit the path on the way towards your goal. You may see, for example, a page or screen in a Funnel from which a lot of traffic exits before completing the goal - indicating a problem with that step. You might also see a lot of traffic skipping steps, indicating the path to conversion is too long or contains extraneous steps."

We begin the funnel creation process by clicking on the "On/Off" icon beneath **Funnel (Optional)**. Doing so brings up the additional information request shown on the bottom of the figure below.

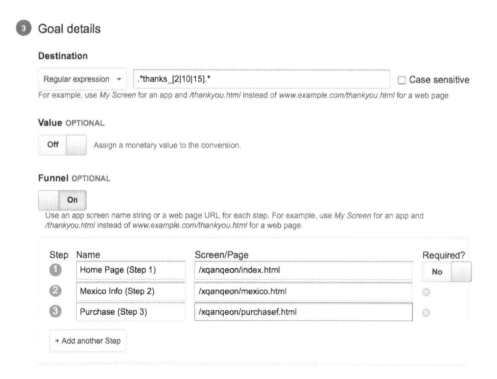

We're going to set up a funnel leading to the purchase "Thank You" page, whose URL was typed into destination box. The funnel reflects our best estimate of how a site user moves from the beginning to the end of the purchase process.

Our best judgment is that the purchase is a four step process, ending in the "Thank You" goal destination page. The three steps prior to this page (beginning with the first page viewed) are believed to be: **index.html** (the home page), **mexico.html** (the Mexico information page) and **purchasef.html** (the purchase page,). We'll need to type each of these into the funnel activation form, indicating that the first step is not required, that is, it is possible to enter and leave the funnel via pages other than this one. After each step is added, we click the **+Add another Step** icon to extend the funnel to a new page. When we're done, the page displays the figure shown below.

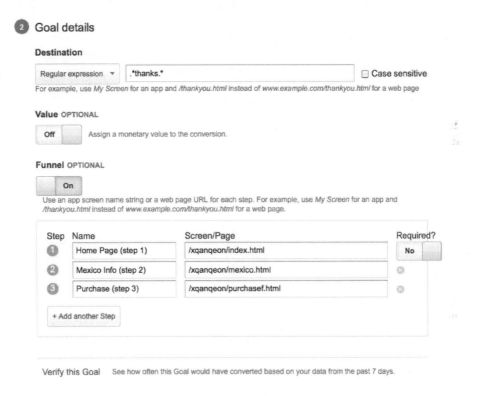

Note that only the pages which lead up to the destination are provided above. The final destination page ("Thank You") has already been identified. Once we verify the goal, clicking **Create Goal** (on the bottom of the page) adds the goal to our goal summary page, as shown on the top of page 266.

Goal	↓	Id	Past 7 day conversions	Recording	
+ NEW GOAL		Import from Gallery		🔍 Search	
Contact Page Sent		Goal ID 1 / Goal Set 1	0	ON	share
Purchase Thank You Page		Goal ID 2 / Goal Set 1	0	ON	share

Destination is any page within a specified directory

Imagine that we have a website with multiple pages organized by subject matter. We might, for example, have thirty pages of travel photos placed in the **/photo** subdirectory of our site. The URLs to these pages might be of the form:

http://mysite.com/photo/mexico_country.html
http://mysite.com/photo/mexico_north.html
http://mysite.com/photo/bahamas.html
http://mysite.com/photo/carribean.html

We want to know whether individuals are visiting the pages within this subdirectory. However, similar to our purchase thank you page, we are not interested in visits to specific pages as this can be determined from the standard data reporting menus. Instead, we are interested in the overall number of people visiting _any_ page within the **/photo** subdirectory. Goals and regex allow us to collect the appropriate data. As a result, the goal we are creating will be considered a conversion when a visitor reaches any page within the **/photo** subdirectory.

We begin the goal development process as we did in the preceding examples. We click on **+NEW GOAL**, name the goal (in this case "Visit to Photo Subdirectory"), and indicate that it is a destination goal. Clicking on **Next step** brings up the Step 2 page, **Goal details**.

Step 2 collects specific goal characteristics (as shown on the top of page 267). Since we decided that this was a **Destination** goal, we need to provide the destination URL. This is typed into the top box. We use regex to indicate that the destination is any page within the **/photo** subdirectory. The following syntax accomplishes this:

.*photo.*

Note that we've selected **Regular expression** from the pull-down menu. We'll leave **Value** and **Funnel** off, as they do not apply in this particular case. Thus, prior to verifying the goal, the page will look like that shown on the top of the next page.

2 Goal details

Destination

| Regular expression ▼ | .*photo.* | ☐ Case sensitive |

For example, use *My Screen* for an app and */thankyou.html* instead of *www.example.com/thankyou.html* for a web page

Value OPTIONAL

| Off | | Assign a monetary value to the conversion. |

Funnel OPTIONAL

| Off | |

Specify a path you expect traffic to take towards the destination. Use it to analyze the entrance and exit points that impact your Goal.

Verify this Goal   See how often this Goal would have converted based on your data from the past 7 days.

Finally, we'll use the **Verify this Goal** link to confirm that we are doing things properly. We should see the percentage of conversions, assuming any occurred, within the prior seven days. Clicking on the **Create Goal** link saves the goal and takes you back to the goal summary page, shown below.

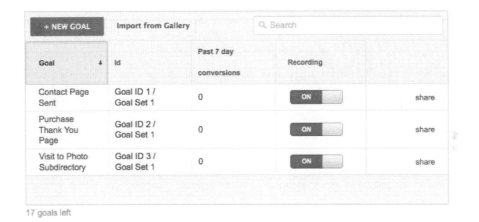

+ NEW GOAL	Import from Gallery		🔍 Search	
Goal ↓	**Id**	**Past 7 day conversions**	**Recording**	
Contact Page Sent	Goal ID 1 / Goal Set 1	0	ON	share
Purchase Thank You Page	Goal ID 2 / Goal Set 1	0	ON	share
Visit to Photo Subdirectory	Goal ID 3 / Goal Set 1	0	ON	share

17 goals left

Duration goals

A duration goal is considered a conversion when a site user has spent a predefined amount of time on your site. You begin to create this goal in the same way as a destination goal: you click on **+NEW GOAL**, name the goal (in this case "Time on site > 2 minutes"), indicate that it is a **Duration** goal, and then click **Next step**. After this, you'll see the display shown on the top of page 268.

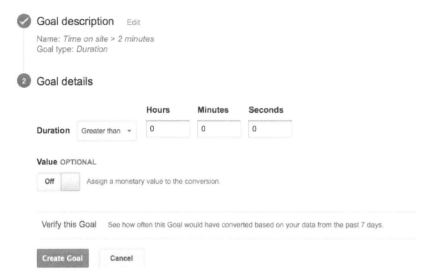

All that remains at this point is to set the minimum amount of time for goal conversion (in this case, two minutes), verify and then create the goal. The goal summary page will update to show the addition of this new goal.

Pages/Screens per session goals

A pages/screens per session goal is very similar to a duration goal, except this goal is considered a conversion when a site user has viewed a predetermined number of pages or screens during a single session. You begin to create this goal in the same way as a destination goal: you click on **+NEW GOAL**, name the goal (in this case "Pages > 4 per session), indicate that it is a **Pages/Screens per session** goal, and then click **Next step**. After this, you'll see the screen shown below.

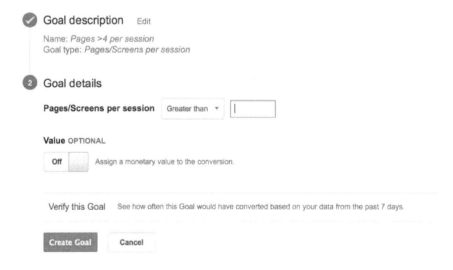

All that remains at this point is to set the minimum number of pages/screens per session for goal conversion (in this case, four), verify, and then create the goal. The goal summary page will update to show the addition of this new goal, as shown below.

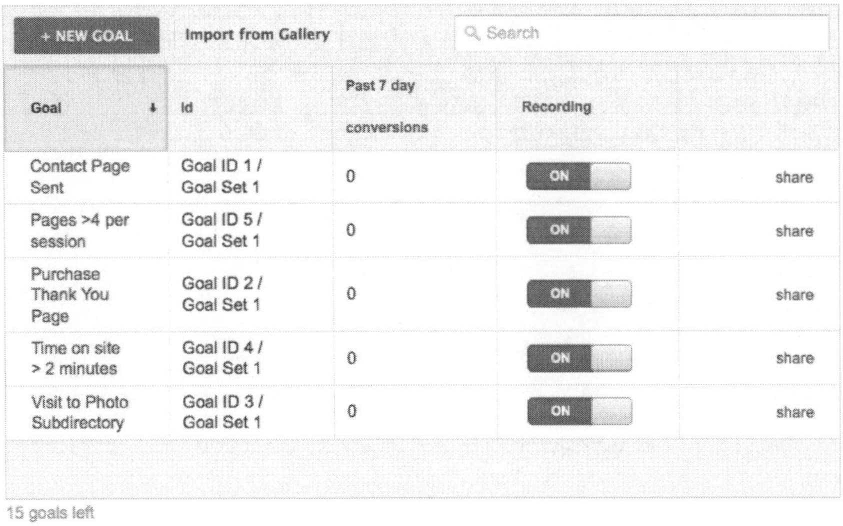

Goal ↓	Id	Past 7 day conversions	Recording	
Contact Page Sent	Goal ID 1 / Goal Set 1	0	ON	share
Pages >4 per session	Goal ID 5 / Goal Set 1	0	ON	share
Purchase Thank You Page	Goal ID 2 / Goal Set 1	0	ON	share
Time on site > 2 minutes	Goal ID 4 / Goal Set 1	0	ON	share
Visit to Photo Subdirectory	Goal ID 3 / Goal Set 1	0	ON	share

15 goals left

A Caution Regarding Duration and Page View Goals

Tim Ash makes a persuasive case for avoiding duration and pageview goals. Please read his perspective here:

http://blog.kissmetrics.com/pageviews-time-on-site/

Revising an existing goal

It is possible to revise the parameters of an existing goal. Simply go to the goal summary page and click on the name of the goal you wish to revise. But be very careful because Google Analytics will not apply your changes retroactively. As a result, changing the parameters of a goal will mix the conversions for the old parameter with conversions for the revised parameter. It is much a better practice to turn the old goal OFF and create a new goal in its place.

Goal value

So far, we haven't assigned a value to any of our goals. We didn't need to assign a value to the goal which included actual product purchase, and the other goals did not have a value which was nonaribtrary. How much, for example, is two minutes on site worth? This is not to say, however, that values should never be set for non-ecommerce goals.

Imagine that you have a site that is designed to attract new clients. Each new client, on average, generates $1,000 in revenue. Your site provides a content section which provides whitepapers and you know from experience that 15% of those downloading a whitepaper will eventually become a client. In situations such as these, you can create a goal which would be achieved when any whitepaper is downloaded. The value of this goal could be calculated as follows:

Goal Value = Percentage Converting * Average Revenue Generated

Goal Value = .15 * $1,000

Goal Value = $150

Similar logic can be applied to a contact form goal. If you know that 2% of those completing a contact form eventually become clients, then a contact form completion goal can be valued at $2, calculated as:

Goal Value = Percentage Converting * Average Revenue Generated

Goal Value = .02 * $1,000

Goal Value = $2

36

Goal Reporting: The Conversions Menu

You'll recall that Google Analytics uses the term "conversion" to indicate that a goal has been achieved. Thus, not surprisingly, the metrics related to goal conversions are found beneath the **Conversions** menu, as shown below.

This chapter examines each of these options.

Overview

By default, the **Conversions > Goals > Overview** page reports two sets of goal-related metrics for the property and view being examined. Some of these metrics are summative, that is, the metrics report the performance of all goals grouped together, while others relate to individual goals. Consider the data reported near the top of the **Conversions > Goals > Overview** page shown on the top of page 272. The goals represent some of those I created for my travel website.

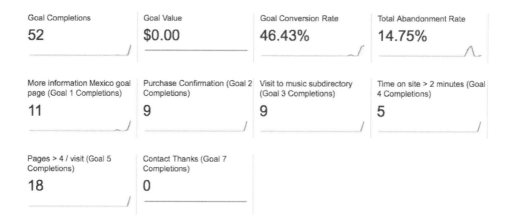

Goal Completions	Goal Value	Goal Conversion Rate	Total Abandonment Rate
52	$0.00	46.43%	14.75%

More information Mexico goal page (Goal 1 Completions)	Purchase Confirmation (Goal 2 Completions)	Visit to music subdirectory (Goal 3 Completions)	Time on site > 2 minutes (Goal 4 Completions)
11	9	9	5

Pages > 4 / visit (Goal 5 Completions)	Contact Thanks (Goal 7 Completions)
18	0

The top row presents summative metrics. The data indicate that in sum there were 52 total goal completions with an average goal conversion rate of 46.43%. This information is interesting, but relatively useless. Since these are summative measures, they can be skewed by goals that are performing either extremely well or extremely poorly. Furthermore, this metric assumes that all goals are of equal value, but is this is rarely the case. Similarly, the goal completion page table shown on the bottom of the **Conversions > Goals >Overview** page (see below) is relatively useless because it presents the terminal pages for all goals in one table. It is impossible to see which pages are the specific terminal pages for each specific goal.

Goals		Goal Completion Location	Goal Completions	% Goal Completions
Goal Completion Location	▶	1. /xxangeon/thanks1.html	13	25.00%
Source / Medium		2. /xxangeon/thanks_p.html	10	19.23%
		3. /xxangeon/mexico1a.html	9	17.31%
		4. /xxangeon/music/mandolin.html	6	11.54%
		5. /xxangeon/purchasef.html	4	7.69%
		6. /xxangeon/index.html	3	5.77%
		7. /xxangeon/music/guitar.html	3	5.77%
		8. /xxangeon/	2	3.85%
		9. /xxangeon/contact.html	1	1.92%
		10. /xxangeon/music/oboe.html	1	1.92%

Given the summative nature of the data being reported, the only truly useful information on the **Conversions > Goals > Overview** page is the conversion rate for each goal, which can be found in the row(s) beneath the summative metrics. In this case, the data is presented in the second and third rows of the table shown on the top of this page. These data report the number of completions (i.e., conversions) for each of the goals I've set up for my website. As such, you can use this data for a quick overview of each goal's number of completions.

The problem with these metrics is that we don't have any context for guiding their interpretation. Are eleven completions for Goal 1 good or bad? They are good if eleven represents a significant percentage of sessions; they are bad if eleven represents only a small portion of site sessions. The context for interpreting the absolute number of conversions is easy to find when we manipulate the data presented on the **Conversions > Goals > Overview** page.

The top of the **Conversions > Goals > Overview** report provides a pull-down menu labeled **Goal Option** with the default setting of **All Goals**. This option can be found directly below the **+Add Segment** option (see below).

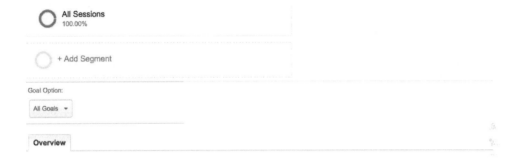

Selecting this menu displays all goals for the desired view, where goals turned "On" are displayed in blue, underlined, bold type (these are Goals 1 to 5 and 7 below). Goals turned "Off" are displayed in grey scale (as in Goal 6 below).

Selecting any of the active goals revises the overview page to display just the information on the selected goal, as shown below when we select Goal 1 from the pull-down menu.

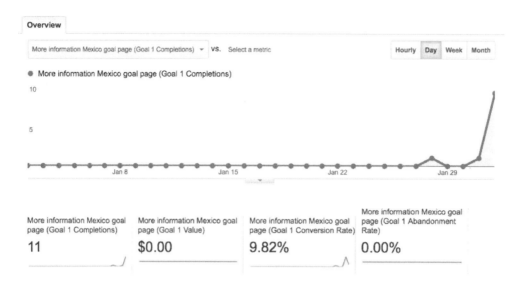

Now we have the context to interpret this goal's conversion rate. Overall slightly less than 10% of site users (exactly 9.82%) converted this goal. Note that both goal value and abandonment rate are both zero. Goal value is zero because we did not assign this goal a value when it was created. Abandonment rate is zero because it is a single page destination goal and therefore there is no place to "abandon" goal acquisition. Thus, as general practice, abandonment rate should be ignored for any goal lacking a prespecified funnel.

> Keep in mind, that the conversion rate is the result of dividing conversions by sessions for the time period indicated for the report. Thus, conversions will be artificially low if they are started sometime after the start of the reporting period. As a result, make certain that the time period corresponds with the start of goal creation.

The table on the bottom of the goal-specific **Conversions > Goals > Overview** page provides two types of data for the specific goal being examined. First, it tells you the terminal page when the goal was completed. This is useless data for destination goals, as the terminal page is identical to the destination page, as shown below:

Goals		More information Mexico goal page (Goal 1 Completions)	% More information Mexico goal page (Goal 1 Completions)
Goal Completion Location ▸ Source / Medium	Goal Completion Location		
	1. /xxangeon/thanks1.html	11	100.00%

For Duration and Pages/View goals, the data in this table report where on the site a user was when the goal was achieved. The data for our Duration goal (time on site greater than two minutes) is shown below.

Goals		Goal Completion Location	Time on site > 2 minutes (Goal 4 Completions)	% Time on site > 2 minutes (Goal 4 Completions)
Goal Completion Location	▸			
Source / Medium		1. /xxangeon/	2	40.00%
		2. /xxangeon/mexico1a.html	2	40.00%
		3. /xxangeon/thanks_p.html	1	20.00%

The actionability of this data is relatively low unless there is a desire for the visitor to be on a specific page when the goal was converted.

Goal URLs

The second option in the **Goals** menu (**Conversions > Goals > Goal URLs**) brings up a page that reports both the terminal URL and the number of conversions by terminal URL for all goals (see below). Since these metrics are summative, this data has very little value since all goals are grouped together in a single display.

Goal Completion Location	Goal Completions ↓	Goal Value
	52 % of Total: 100.00% (52)	**$0.00** % of Total: 0.00% ($0.00)
1. /xxangeon/thanks1.html	13 (25.00%)	$0.00 (0.00%)
2. /xxangeon/thanks_p.html	10 (19.23%)	$0.00 (0.00%)
3. /xxangeon/mexico1a.html	9 (17.31%)	$0.00 (0.00%)
4. /xxangeon/music/mandolin.html	6 (11.54%)	$0.00 (0.00%)
5. /xxangeon/purchasef.html	4 (7.69%)	$0.00 (0.00%)
6. /xxangeon/index.html	3 (5.77%)	$0.00 (0.00%)
7. /xxangeon/music/guitar.html	3 (5.77%)	$0.00 (0.00%)
8. /xxangeon/	2 (3.85%)	$0.00 (0.00%)
9. /xxangeon/contact.html	1 (1.92%)	$0.00 (0.00%)
10. /xxangeon/music/oboe.html	1 (1.92%)	$0.00 (0.00%)

Valuable data can be obtained for destination goals when, similar to the preceding example, the data view is set to report metrics for just a single goal. For example, the figure below displays data for our "Thank You" destination goal, the page displayed after someone downloads a Mexico information PDF.

This initial view simply summarizes data we saw on other tables. The value of this table is hidden in the **Secondary Dimension** pull-down menu (upper-left hand side of the display). Selecting this menu allows you to examine the goal conversion process in more detail. Of great value are the **Goal Conversion** options, which allow you to see one, two or three steps prior to goal conversion (see below).

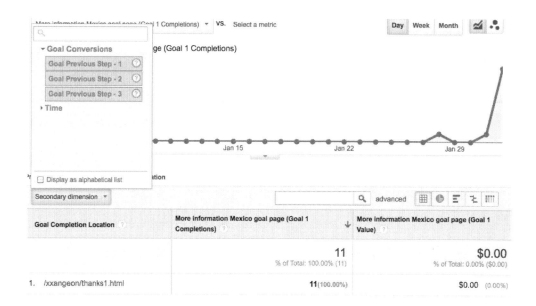

We've set up our site so that the Mexico information download can only be accomplished via our Mexico Information page (mexico1a.html). Selecting **Goal Previous Step 1** from the **Secondary dimension** menu displays a table that shows the page viewed immediately prior to conversion (see below).

The data are quite informative. Nine of the eleven conversions are as expected. These visitors move from the Mexico information page (mexico1a.html) to the "Thank You" for downloading page. However, the remaining two conversions reflect access to this page by typing the "Thank You" page URL directly into a browser. Given the relative size of this group, we would want to determine why individuals were taking this path to conversion and how to revise our site so that all individuals who convert this goal have downloaded the target PDF from the Mexico Information page.

Finally, we can obtain even more insights into the path to conversion by selecting **Goal Previous Step 2** and **Goal Previous Step 3** from the **Secondary dimension** menu.

Reverse goal path

The previous data option allowed you to focus on the first, second or third page viewed prior to goal conversion. This focus was achieved by showing only one of these prior steps in the table at one time.

The **Conversions > Goals > Reverse Goal Path** option presents all three steps in a single table. As with the preceding data, these data are best viewed when it is specific to one individual destination goal, as shown on the top of page 278 for the Mexico download "Thank You" page goal.

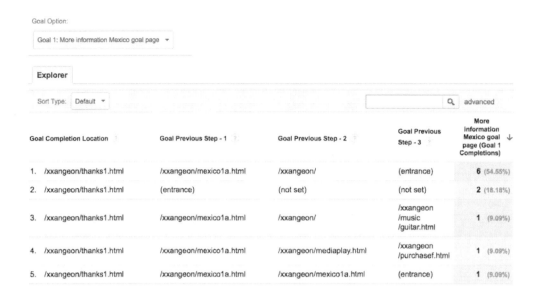

Notice how this additional level of detail makes the identification of underlying trends more difficult to see versus the table that presents just the step immediately prior to conversion. The data displayed in the Goal URLs table (discussed on page 277) indicate that mexico1a.html was the last page to be viewed prior to conversion for nine of twelve conversions. The same finding is available from this chart, however now it is not as easy to see because the second step prior to conversion differs. (You can confirm that the numbers are the same by adding all conversions in which mexico1a was the last page prior to conversion, that is, Goal Previous Step -1. These are lines 1, 3, 4, and 5.)

Funnel visualization

Funnel visualization (**Conversions > Goals > Funnel Visualization**) is only appropriate for those goals in which you created a funnel during the goal creation process.

Imagine that we create a purchase "Thank You" page, where we believe that the path to purchase and conversion would move through several steps (pages), as shown below :

View Page F2.html (Step One) -> View Page F3.html (Step Two) ->

View Page F4.html (Step Three) -> Make a Purchase ->

Convert on "Thank You Page"

Selecting the **Conversions > Goals > Funnel Visualization** option for our Purchase "Thank You" page destination goal displays the chart shown on page 279.

Purchase Confirmation

This Goal was completed in 10 sessions | 38.46% funnel conversion rate

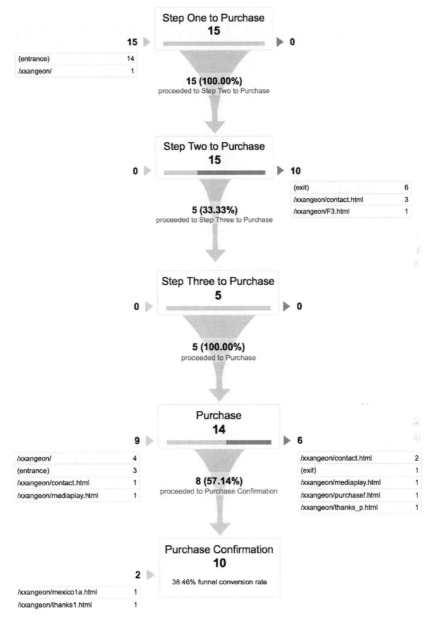

The first things to notice about the funnel are the funnel and step names. **Purchase Confirmation** in the chart refers to the name we gave this goal during goal creation. Similarly, the names of each step, "Step One to Purchase," "Step Two to Purchase," etc., are the names we gave to each step when specifying funnel characteristics during goal creation.

Each funnel step has an inwardly and outwardly facing arrow. The arrow pointing into the funnel tells you how many people entered the funnel at that stage and from where on the site they came. The arrow pointing outward indicates the number of people leaving the funnel at that point and where went. With this in mind, we would interpret the first three steps of the funnel as follows:

-   **Step One to Purchase:** Fifteen people entered the funnel on this page (which is F2.html). All entered the funnel from the site home page. The page seems to be working as intended as no individuals leave the funnel at this point.

-   **Step Two to Purchase:** No additional people entered the funnel, but ten people (67%) left the funnel after viewing this page. Clearly, rather than motivating people to proceed to purchase, this page is instead motivating most people to abandon the process. Even worse, the majority of these individuals are exiting the site altogether. Clearly, there is a problem with this page that needs to be addressed.

-   **Step Three to Purchase:** This page seems to be working as intended. All who move to this funnel step proceed on to the purchase page. As expected, no new visitors enter the funnel at this point.

-   **Purchase:** The data shown here indicate several problems with our assumptions and site content. First, nine individuals have arrived at the purchase page without moving through the funnel. We would want to compare the actual purchases of these individuals versus "funnel purchasers" to see if the funnel is doing more harm than good and, more fundamentally, whether the funnel is needed at all. Second, nearly half of all individuals arriving at this page leave without making a purchase. This is also cause for concern, and the characteristics of this page, would need to be examined with an eye toward revision.

-   **Purchase Confirmation**: It's problematic that only 38.46% of all visitors who enter the funnel at some point complete a purchase and are sent to the "Thank You" confirmation page. This is especially worrisome because this percentage is inflated by the two individuals who arrived at the end of the funnel without making a prior purchase.

Taken as a whole, visitors' behaviors along the funnel path indicate a pressing need for further examination, analysis, and website revision.

This is the final option in the **Conversions > Goals** menu. This funnel is interpreted similarly to the **Users Flow** funnel discussed in Chapter 24.

37
Goal Reporting: The Multi-Channel Menu

The **Multi-Channel Funnels** menu provides additional ways to gain insights into conversions (see below). For now, we'll focus on the **Time Lag** and **Path Length** options within the **Conversions > Multi-Channel Funnels** menu. We'll look at the remaining options later in the book, once you've added additional referral sources for your travel website.

Time Lag

The **Conversions > Multi-Channel Funnels > Time Lag** option shows you the amount of time that has elapsed between a user first entering your site and goal conversion. When you first click on this menu option, you're shown a summary for all goals collapsed into one grouping, as shown on the top of page 283 for users visiting my website during summer, 2013.

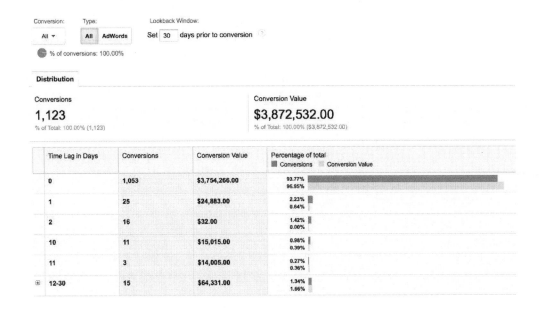

Similar to other summative conversion data, this report is less useful than reports that focus on an individual goal.

A focus on an individual goal can be accomplished by using the pull-down menu beneath **Conversion** on the top of the page. At the moment, the menu indicates that **All** goal conversions as well as ecommerce data are to be displayed (see below).

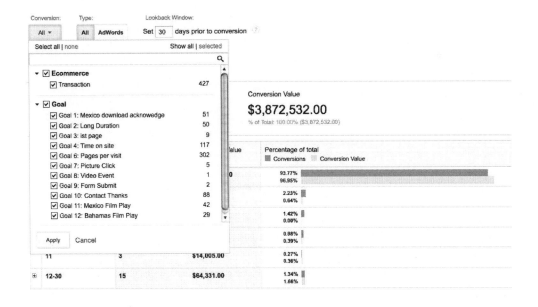

You unclick to remove individual goals from the display. Leaving just one goal checked allows you to focus the data report on only that goal.

I'm going to select my Transaction goal and examine all website sessions with a transaction within the prior 30 days. (This date range can be changed, but 30 days is generally recommended.) When this is done, the table shown below is displayed. As can be seen, the overwhelming percentage of purchases/conversions are made on the same day as the first site session. Among the few remaining transactions, most take twelve or more days.

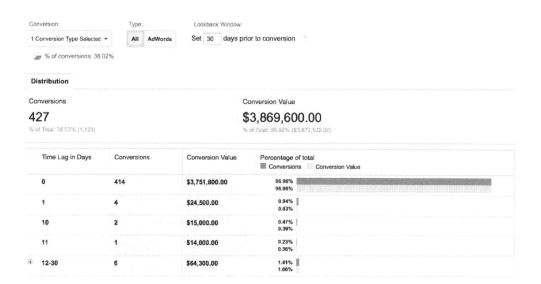

Time Lag in Days	Conversions	Conversion Value	Percentage of total Conversions	Conversion Value
0	414	$3,751,800.00	96.96% 96.96%	
1	4	$24,500.00	0.94% 0.63%	
10	2	$15,000.00	0.47% 0.39%	
11	1	$14,000.00	0.23% 0.36%	
12-30	6	$64,300.00	1.41% 1.66%	

Thus, it appears that we have two types of transactions: those that take place during an initial session and those that take place in a session after a significant delay, in this case twelve days or more. Using segments, we would want to take a more detailed look at both of these types of transactions.

Path Length

Conversions > Multi-Channel Funnels > Path Length allows us to focus on a specific goal in order to see how many steps preceded the conversion. For example, when I select my purchase goal, the table shown on the top of page 285 is displayed. Note that the path to purchase conversion is quite short, with most users seeing only one page prior to making a purchase. Thus, our notion of a long multi-stage path to purchase seems not to be the case. We could use the **Conversions > Goals** reports to determine the specific pages viewed prior to purchase to better understand the overall purchase process.

Distribution

Conversions	Conversion Value
427	**$3,869,600.00**
% of Total: 38.02% (1,123)	% of Total: 99.92% ($3,872,532.00)

Path Length in Interactions	Conversions	Conversion Value	Percentage of total ▪ Conversions ▪ Conversion Value
1	2	$27,000.00	0.47% / 0.70%
2	364	$3,266,100.00	85.25% / 84.40%
3	38	$366,900.00	8.90% / 9.48%
4	9	$81,800.00	2.11% / 2.11%
5	3	$19,500.00	0.70% / 0.50%
6	1	$15,000.00	0.23% / 0.39%
8	1	$0.00	0.23% / 0.00%
12+	9	$93,300.00	2.11% / 2.41%

38
Goal Reporting and the Real-Time Menu

The Google Analytics **Real-Time** menu allows you see what is happening on your website or blog at nearly the same time as actions occur. You can see what pages are being visited, how many users are viewing each page, where users are coming from (locations and traffic sources), and goal and event conversions. The **Real-Time** menu is accessed via the **Real-Time** menu option near the top left of every reporting screen (see below).

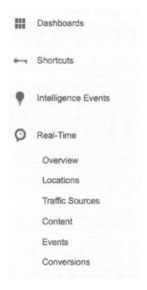

The figure shown on the top of page 287 is the **Real-Time > Overview** display that summarizes key metrics. Perhaps of greatest importance are the number of users currently on the site (in this example there are two, shown as both the numeric and the bars on the top right-hand side) and the pages currently being viewed (shown on the bottom right-hand side).

The figure below is the **Real-Time > Content** display that provides more detailed information on current content consumption.

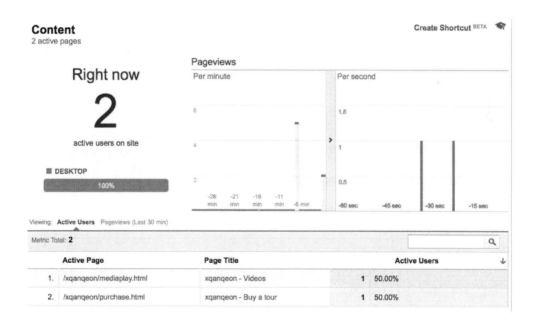

Unfortunately, you'll soon discover that once the novelty of real-time monitoring wears off, this data is only strategically useful for a limited range of situations, one of which is monitoring goal conversions.

Real time goal conversions

You can monitor destination goal conversions in real-time via the **Real-Time > Conversions** option.[23] Once this is selected, you'll see a list of all active destination goals and the number of users who have converted each goal. The figure below, for example, shows that each of two goals has been converted by a single active user. Note that selecting the option next to **Active Users** allows you to see goal conversions for the prior 30 minutes. This option is labeled **Goal Hits (Last 30 min)**.

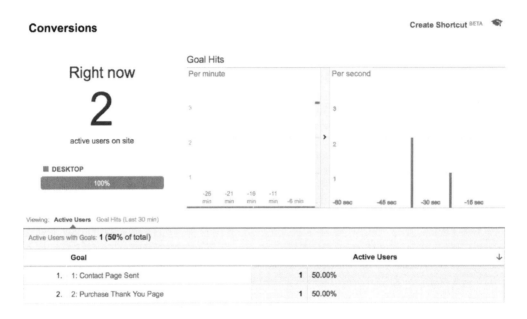

There are two strategic uses for monitoring goal conversion in real time. The first allows you to confirm that your goals are working as intended. The second provides insights into the effectiveness of your marketing campaigns.

Confirming that goals are working as intended

You'll recall that our travel site uses six different pages to confirm a purchase, where each page is specific to a tour selection. We want to monitor each page through the standard content menu. Additionally, we have created a goal that converts whenever *any* of these pages is viewed. This allows us to easily keep track of the total number of

---

[23] Only destination goals can be monitored in real time. Goals are available for monitoring immediately after they are created.

purchases. We can use real time to make certain that we have properly created this goal. First, we select **Real-Time > Conversions** and make certain that the goal of interest is displayed. In our case, the purchase "Thank you" page is the second goal listed (see below).

Next, we select the **Real-Time > Content** option. Leaving this display open, we visit our travel site in another browser window or another browser. We make a "purchase" and confirm that the correct thank you page is being displayed. In our case it is, as shown below.

Finally, we again select the **Real-Time > Conversions** option and make certain that the purchase goal has increased by one. This change indicates that our goal is recording as intended (see below).

Monitoring marketing activities

Imagine that you are running a time-sensitive campaign designed to increase membership sign-ups. You have two approaches you want to test: a 10% off offer and a 14 months for the price of 12 offer. A special web page has been designed for each offer. You have an email list of 15,000 target individuals to whom membership offers will be sent.

One option for executing this promotion simply divides the list in half, sending each half a different offer and monitoring the results in the usual way. However, real time offers an alternative.

First, we set up each membership sign-up page as a goal. One goal converts when someone signs up for 10% off and the second goal converts when someone signs up for 14 months for price of 12. One thousand of each offer are emailed to a randomly selected portion of the total list. You monitor conversions for each offer in real-time knowing that historically the majority of sign-ups will take place within two hours of the email blast. Your next step, at he end of two hours, depends upon the observed real-time trend:

- If neither offer meets the target sign-up goal then no further emails are sent out until new offer(s) are developed.

- If both offers meet the target sign-up goal and the offers are not significantly different from each other in terms of sign-ups, then the remaining list is divided in half, with each half receiving one of the offers.

- If only one offer meets the target sign-up goal or if both meet the goal and one is significantly better than the other, then the entire remainder of the list is emailed the stronger offer.

39
Goals and Custom Segments

Chapters 33 and 34 illustrated how powerful strategic insights could be obtained through the use of segments, where a segment was formed through the use of one or more Google Analytics provided metrics. As you'll see in this and forthcoming chapters, segments can also be formed on the basis of metrics that you generate specifically for your website. One of these metrics is goal conversion.

Any custom segment can be formed with goal conversion metrics. You can form the segment using only goal conversion metrics, or you can combine goal conversion metrics with other standard metrics. For example:

- a segment can contain only those individuals who converted on Goal 1 (or any other goal).

- a segment can contain only those individuals who converted on both Goal 1 and Goal 2.

- a segment can contain only those individuals who converted on Goal 1 but did not covert on Goal 2.

- a segment can contain only those individuals who converted on Goal 1 and who live outside the United States.

- a segment can contain only those individuals who converted on Goal 1 and who came to the site via a social referral and who made a purchase.

Creating a custom segment using goals

You create a custom segment using goal metrics in the same way you created other custom segments. You access segments via the **+Add Segment** option on the top of almost any page located beneath the blue circle **All Sessions** identifier. When you click **+Add Segment** the segments page displays. You then begin the segment creation process by clicking the **+ New Segment** link. The segment creation page will then display.

Goal metrics are incorporated into a segment's definition via the **Conditions** option, which is shown on the bottom left-hand side of the page. The selection of this option brings up the **Conditions** page, as shown on the top of page 293.

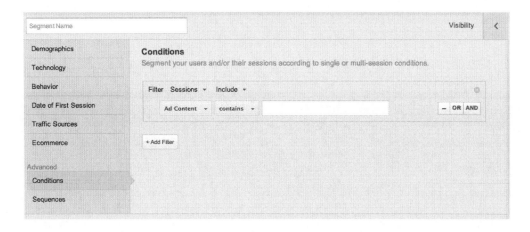

Pulling-down the menu currently labeled **Ad Content** displays both green and blue menu options. Near the bottom of the blue menu options is **Goal Conversions** (as shown below).

Opening this menu displays all of the goals that you created for your property and view (see the figure on the top of page 294 for a partial list of my website's goals).

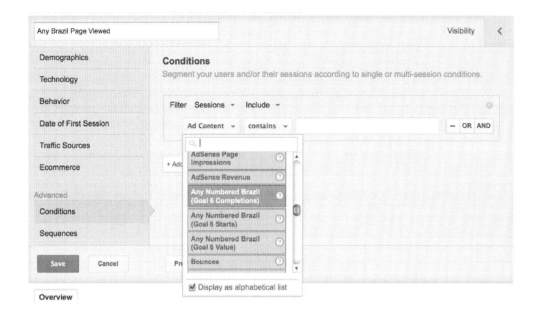

Let's illustrate the remainder of the process using this scenario:[24]

> Imagine that my travel website is running a special offer on vacations in Brazil. Three new pages were added to the site as a way to promote this offer. The pages' URLs end in **brazil1.html**, **brazil2.html**, and **brazil3.html**. *These are the only pages on the site that describe Brazil vacations.* When we add the pages to the site, we also create a goal that converts whenever any one of these three pages is visited. The name of the Goal is "Goal 6: Any Numbered Brazil." We want to use custom segments to determine if goal conversion has any impact on subsequent behaviors, that is, if engagement and purchase behaviors differ as a function of viewing one of these pages. Finally, we set an internal objective for this goal: we will be happy if 20% of site sessions ential viewing one of these pages.

We create the desired segment by selecting "Goal 6: Any Numbered Brazil" from the pull-down menu (see above figure). Selection of this goal changes the display to that shown on the top of page 295, where the goal name (Any Brazil Page Viewed) is now incorporated into the display.

---

[24] This scenario references goals and pages that are not part of your travel website.

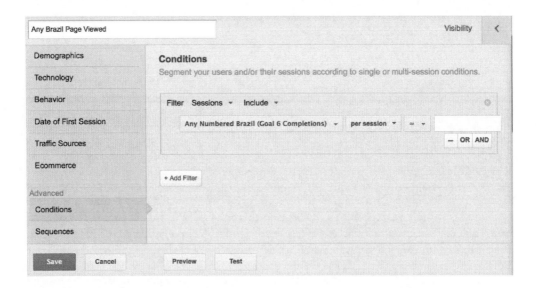

We complete the segment creation process by indicating that we want the segment to **include** users who convert one or more times per session (as shown below).

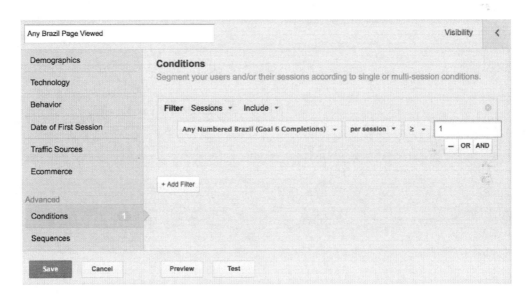

Finally, we test, save and apply this segment to our main display. In this case, applying this segment to session data indicates that this segment accounts for 25.86% of all sessions occuring during the chosen date range (see display on the top of page 296) .

It shows "Audience Overview" header with date and some segment info.

The header shows:
Audience Overview   May 12, 2014 - Jun 11, 2014

Email Export Add to Dashboard Shortcut

Any Brazil Page Viewed
25.86%

+ Add Segment

This segment is now available for use in data analysis, but taking one more step will increase our insights. We initially set up this goal to see if purchase-realated behaviors increased when site users visited one or more of the special Brazil pages. Since it is beneficial to provide context for interpreting the behaviors of this segment, we need to create a second segment consisting of those who did not convert this goal. Thus, we need a second segment to represent those who did not visit any of the special Brazil pages.

We create this segment of "nonconverters" in a manner almost identical to the prior segment. Once again, we select "Goal 6: Any Numbered Brazil". We name the segment "No Brazil Page Viewed", set the Filter to Sessions, only now we indicate that we want to Exclude individuals who converted, thus setting the numeric parameter to >= to 1 (see below).

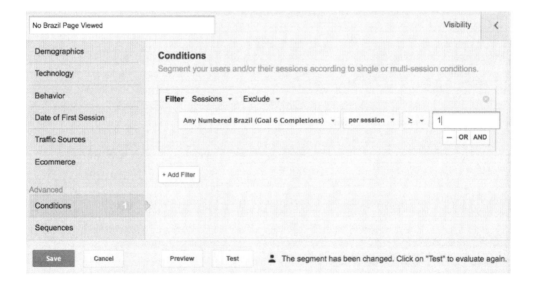

We then test, save and apply the segment. Now, while the absolute percentages may change depending upon the dimension, the two segments together will always add to 100%. This is illustrated on page 297, where the first figure (**Audience Overview**) shows segment size for sessions and the second figure (**Ecommerce Overview**) shows segment size for transactions.

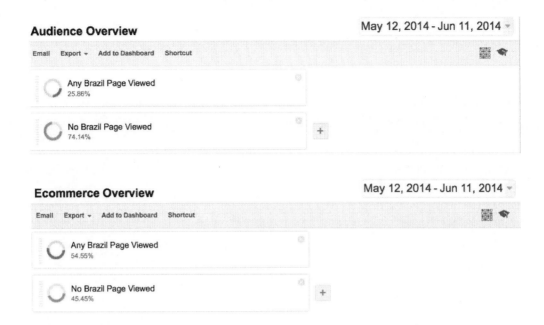

We can now use the two custom segments to determine any influence/effects of our special Brazil tour offer pages.

Let's start by examining vistation to these pages. The **Audience > Overview** summary (shown above) indicates that 25.86% of all site sessions involved the viewing of one or more of the Brazil pages. Since our goal was to have 20% of site sessions view the Brazil offer, this outcome is acceptable.

Next, we can see if site engagement differs across the two groups. Selecting **Behavior > Site Content > All Pages** brings up the table shown below. The percentage of pageviews accounted for by the "Conversion" segment (i.e., "Any Brazil Page Viewed") is in line with the segment's share of sessions (as seen in the **Audience > Overview** summary above). Moreover, page engagement metrics appear to be comparable for the two groups.

Finally, we can examine ecommerce metrics using the **Conversions > Ecommerce > Overview** menu. This results in two important data displays.

First, as shown below, we can see that over half of all transactions were made by those who visited these pages. Since, as noted earlier, only about 25% of all site sessions involved the special Brazil pages, this ratio leads us to believe that the offers on these pages were very motivating.

Second, in the data shown below, we can see that the purchase conversion rate for those who visited the special offer pages (40%) was significantly higher than that for those who did not visit these pages (11%). This outcome provides additional evidence that the offer was motivating. Given that the average order value for the two groups is nearly the same, it does not appear that we are overly discounting the offer.

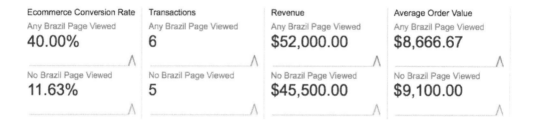

40

Practice With Goals

This chapter presents two sets of exercises to help you apply and extend your knowledge of goal reporting.

True/false and multiple choice

This first set of questions makes certain that you understand key concepts. Feel free to open and refer to the preceding chapters or access goal-related reports in your analytics account. When you are done, or if you are stuck, the answers can be found on page 613.

1. Which of the following are types of custom goals?

   a. Pages/Screens per session

   b. Duration

   c. Minutes/screen

   d. Destination

2. *True or False:* Goals are created on the <u>Property</u> level.

3. *True or False:* Goals can be turned "on" and "off" as needed.

4. *True or False:* Any view can have an unlimited number of goals.

5. *True or False:* You can get around the goals per view limit by deleting unneeded goals.

6. Which of the following are possible destination goal conversions? (Select all that apply.)

   a. When a single page such as index.html is viewed

   b. When one of two pages is viewed, for example, either th1.html or th2.html

   c. When any page within a specific directory is viewed

7. Google Analytics uses the term _____ to indicate that a goal has been achieved.

    a. hit

    b. conversion

    c. creation

    d. achievement

8. *True or False:* Every goal must have an assigned value.

9. *True or False:* A funnel to a destination goal can only be created when the goal is an ecommerce transaction.

10. You use the **Verify This Goal** option and see a 0% conversion rate. *True or False:* This should always be interpreted to mean that there is a problem with how the goal was created.

11. *True or False:* There is no limit to the number of steps you can place in a goal funnel.

12. *True or False:* When creating a goal funnel, you can allow users to enter at any stage of the funnel.

13. *True or False:* Goal values can only be assigned to ecommerce-related goals.

14. The **Conversions > Goals > Overview** page reports the number of conversions for _____ .

    a. all goals, both active and inactive

    b. only active goals

15. You are on the **Conversions > Goals > Overview** page. Which of the following pull-down menus allows you to focus on the metrics for one specific goal?

    a. All Sessions

    b. Export

    c. +Add Segment

    d. Goal Option

16. *True or False:* Google estimates goal value when no value is explicitly provided during the goal creation process.

17. The destination page and goal completion URL will be the same for which types of goals? (Select all that apply)

    a. Destination goals

    b. Duration goals

    c. View goals

18. Imagine that you are examining a specific goal via the **Conversions > Goals > Goal URLs** menu option. How many steps prior to conversion can be seen via the **Secondary Dimension > Goal Conversion** pull-down menu?

    a. None

    b. One

    c. Two

    d. Three

19. *True or False:* The **Conversions > Goals > Funnel Visualization** menu option allows you to see how well your proposed funnel actually describes a path to conversion.

20. *True or False:* Only destination goals can be used as the basis for custom segments.

21. Which of the following metrics can be monitored in real time? (Select all that apply)

    a. Content currently being viewed

    b. Destination goal conversions

    c. Duration goal conversions

    d. Referral sources

    e. User country

22. *True or False:* A goal must be operational for at least one data cycle (24 hours) before it can be monitored in real time.

Application

This exercise asks you to draw conclusions from custom segments and goal-related metrics. Our responses can be found beginning on page 613.

This exercise focuses on one particular travel site goal: *Goal 1 - Package Info.* The goal has a conversion when a complete tour information package is viewed. The two custom segments created specific to this goal are:

- **Goal 1:Failure** is a custom segment comprised of those without a conversion,

- **Goal 1: Success** is a custom segment comprised of those with a conversion.

Using the data presented in the following table provide a point of view on the success or failure of this goal and discuss potential next steps.

Hands-on (I)

This exercise asks you to apply your understanding of goals. Create a new view in which to create the goals. You can delete the view when done.

When you are finished, or if you are stuck, the procedures needed to respond to each request can be found beginning on page 614.

1. Create a destination goal for your website media page: **mediaplay.html**. There is no funnel or value for this goal. Name this goal "Exercise 1".

2. Imagine that your website has five different memberships, and you have a different confirmation page for each membership, as shown below.

    /membership_bronze.html
    /membership_silver.html
    /membership_gold.html
    /membership_premier.html
    /membership_trial.html

    Create a goal that will show a conversion whenever any of these pages is viewed. There is no funnel or value for this goal. Name this goal "Exercise 2".

3. You imagine that the path to the purchase page is:

> **index.html** (the home page)
> **mediaplay.html** (the media page)
> **purchase.html** (the purchase option page)

The purchase page is your destination. Create a goal that uses a funnel to explore this path to your destination. There is no value for this goal. Name this goal "Exercise 3".

4. Create a session duration goal of more than 5 minutes. There is no value for this goal. Name this goal "Exercise 4".

5. Create a pages/screens per session goal of more than 2 pages. There is no value for this goal. Name this goal "Exercise 5".

Hands-on (II)

This exercise asks you to create your own set of goals. You can name each goal whatever you think is appropriate and you can set each goal's parameters to reflect the goals you think are reasonable for your site.

To Begin

Create the four goals described below. Once the four goals are created, visit (and ask your friends to visit) your website keeping the goal parameters in mind. On some of your visits convert one or more goals; on other visits do not convert any goals. It is best to visit using Chrome, clearing your browser history after every several visits. Try to generate at least 30 visits so that you have enough goal-related metrics to complete this exercise.

1. Create a simple destination goal for the travel website page of your choice. There does not need to be a funnel or value for this goal.

2. Create a destination goal for the travel website page of your choice (different than that used in question one). This page should be the end result of a three step funnel. Create the funnel as part of the goal. There does not need to be a value for this goal.

3. Create a duration goal for the travel website. There does not need to be a funnel or value for this goal.

4. Create a Pages/Screens per session goal. There does not need to be a funnel or value for this goal.

Data Analysis

Once you have enough data generated for the previous four goals, address the following questions.

1. With regard to your simple destination goal:

    -   How many conversions took place?

    -   What percentage of all sessions resulted in a conversion?

    -   What page was most commonly viewed immediately prior to conversion?
    -
    -   What is the overall trend in conversion time lag?

    -   What is the overall trend in conversion path length?

    -   Assuming the goal set was an important one, to what extent are you satisfied/ dissatisfied with the goal conversion rate? Based on all of the data available, what changes, if any, would you make to improve the goal's conversion rate?

2. With regard to your destination goal funnel:

    -   How many conversions took place?

    -   What percentage of all sessions resulted in a conversion?

    -   What is the overall trend in conversion time lag?

    -   What is the overall trend in conversion path length?

    -   Assuming the goal set was an important one, to what extent are you satisfied/ dissatisfied with the goal conversion rate? Based on all of the data available, what changes, if any, would you make to improve the goal's conversion rate?

    -   Still assuming the goal set was an important one, to what extent are you satisfied/dissatisfied with the assumptions you made about the path to conversion? Based on all of the data available, what changes, if any, would you make to improve the goal's conversion rate?

3. With regard to your duration goal:

    -   How many conversions took place?

    -   What percentage of all sessions resulted in a conversion?

    -   What is the average number of pageviews associated with goal conversion?

- Assuming the goal set was an important one, to what extent are you satisfied/ dissatisfied with the goal conversion rate? Based on all of the data available, what changes, if any, would you make to improve the goal's conversion rate?

4. With regard to you Pages/Screens per session goal:

    - How many conversions took place?

    - What percentage of all sessions resulted in a conversion?

    - Is there a consistent trend in terms of the page viewed at the time of conversion?

    - Assuming the goal set was an important one, to what extent are you satisfied/ dissatisfied with the goal conversion rate? Based on all of the data available, what changes, if any, would you make to improve the goal's conversion rate?

Google Analytics Demystified

Section X:
Tracking Downloads

We've seen how Google Analytics provides insights into user characteristics and users' interactions with the different pages on your website. This information is available, for example, in the **Users Flow** report or in the **Site Content** section of the **Behavior** menu. But many websites offer a broader range of interaction such as video and downloadable content such as PDFs, Excel documents, ebooks, etc. Google Analytics can't track these events directly, but with some minor tweaks to your pages' HTML code, you can successfully track visitor interactions these types of content. This section helps you understand how to track downloads and strategically use these metrics to improve website performance.

- Chapter 41 shows you how to track user interactions with downloadable content and demonstrates how to send relevant data to Google Analytics.

- Chapter 42 provides practice in tracking and analyzing downloadable content.

- Chapter 43 provides examples of how to go beyond basic download metrics to increase the potential for website success.

- Chapter 44 provides practice in the use and analysis of download-related metrics.

The tracking of video interactions is discussed in the context of events in Chapter 54.

41

Tracking Downloads

Google Analytics allows you treat interactions with downloadable items as if they were regular pageviews. These items can be any form of content: PDFs, Excel files, Word documents, or video. The ability to track these downloads allows you to monitor your site content and to analyze these interactions using all of the same menus and techniques used to analyze actual pageviews.

At the moment, your travel website is set up to offer downloadable PDFs which are not yet trackable. You can see these by clicking on any of the links on your "More Information" page. We'll create the opportunities for tracking these downloads from your site in this and the next chapter. Before doing so, however, let's first see how trackable downloads are reported in Google Analytics. Then we'll see how to implement this activity.

How are downloads reported?

Tracked downloads are reported in exactly the same way as regular pageviews, and as a result, you determine the labels used to identify the download. Thus, it is important for you to organize and name your downloads in a way that makes them easy to find and understand in Google Analytics reports. At minimum, in terms of location, your downloadable content should be placed in a separate subdirectory.[25]

Let's look at a simple example.

Imagine that I have a subdirectory (also called a "folder") with two downloads. The subdirectory is named **/information/** and the two downloads provide tour information for Mexico and the Bahamas. The Mexico document is named **mexico_dl.pdf** and the Bahamas document is named **bahamas_dl.pdf**.

---

[25] We recommend the following readings if you are unfamiliar with how directories and subdirectories are used to organize website content: *Web Style Guide, Site Structure* (http://webstyleguide.com/wsg3/5-site-structure/3-site-file-structure.html), *How to Design a Website* (http://how-to-design-a-website.com/website-usability/website-directory-structure/), and *Folder Hierarchy Best Practices for Digital Asset Management* (http://www.damlearningcenter.com/resources/articles/best-practices-for-folder-organization/).

The table shown below illustrates the top level of my site's organization and is the table which appears when I select **Content Drilldown** in the **Behaviors > Site Content** menu. The first listing, **/xqanqeon/**, is the folder which contains all of my site content. Thus, it is not surprising that this folder has the greatest number of pageviews.

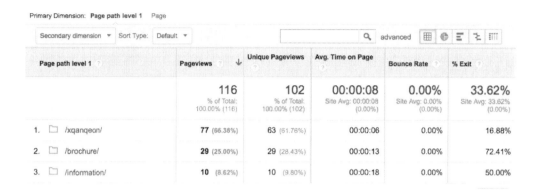

I also have two folders with downloadable elements. The **/brochure/** directory contains long PDFs, while the **/information/** folder contains short, one page fact sheets. We can see that users are more interested in longer versus shorter downloads, as the **/brochure/** directory has nearly three times as many downloads versus the **/information/** directory.

We are interested in the **/information/** folder as it contains the two downloadable PDFs of interest. We can see that, in total, there were ten downloads from this folder (as evidenced in the pageviews column) and that all of these downloads were initiated by different users. We determine this by dividing *pageviews* by *unique pageviews*. The closer this ratio is to 1.0, the greater the proportion of downloads by different users.

Clicking on the **/information/** link in the table above brings up detailed information on each of the two downloads contained within the folder (see the table below).

The metrics in this table inform us of two things with regard to downloads and subsequent behaviors.

- There are equal numbers of Mexico and Bahamas downloads, and all downloads were initiated by different site users.

- Site engagement differs dramatically between the two downloads. Those who downloaded the Mexico PDF stayed on the site and all viewed at least one more page (as evidenced in the **%Exit** of 0% from this page). Those who downloaded the Bahamas PDF had no further site engagement and immediately left the site (as evidenced in the **%Exit** of 100% from this page). Clearly, we would want to explore why those viewing the Bahamas PDFs are behaving in this manner, and then modify the site or the Bahamas PDF's characteristics to reduce or eliminate these behaviors.

Finally, we can always gain deeper insights into download behaviors through the use of secondary dimensions. The chart below, for example, indicates that all of the downloads took place by Irish site users.

Your site's structure and downloadable content

You are the one who ultimately determines the directory structure for your downloads and what the downloads will be named. With regard to structure, you can place all of the downloads in a single directory, choosing, for example, from labels such as:

/downloads/
/brochures/

or you can use a nested approach, choosing, for example, from labels such as:

/brochures/mexico/
/brochures/bahamas/

Remember that your specific strategic information needs should be the guide for how downloadable elements are organized on your site and subsequently labeled in Google Analytics reports.

Let's look at your travel site's organization. All of my (and your) website downloads have been placed in the **/brochure/** directory. There are three downloads for Mexico and three downloads for the Bahamas. The Mexican downloads are named:

mexico_dl_image.pdf

mexico_dl_text.pdf

mexico_dl_button.pdf

while the Bahamas downloads are named in a parallel manner:

bahamas_dl_image.pdf

bahamas_dl_text.pdf

bahamas_dl_button.pdf

It is important to note that each PDF has been named in a way that allows us to easily see the topic country, the fact that it is a download (as indicated by **_dl**) and the source of the download request (image, text, or button). This type of clear naming makes it much easier to interpret reports when your website offers many downloadable elements.[26]

For the moment, let's just focus on the Mexican PDFs. The full URLs to each of the Mexican PDFs on my site are:

`http://www.googleanalyticsdemystified.com/xqanqeon/brochure/mexico_dl_image.pdf`

`http://www.googleanalyticsdemystified.com/xqanqeon/brochure/mexico_dl_text.pdf`

`http://www.googleanalyticsdemystified.com/xqanqeon/brochure/mexico_dl_button.pdf`

The full URLs to these documents on your site will have the same ending (beginning with **/brochure)** preceded by your site's primary URL.

Let's make certain that you understand how these URLs work. Type the first URL above into your browser and press return. The **mexico_dl_image.pdf** should download from my site. Now close and reopen your browser and then retype the same URL into your browser, but do not press return. Highlight and then replace everything up to **/brochure** with the full URL to your site. If the **mexico_dl_image.pdf** document downloads, then you've identified the correct URL (make a note of this as you will need it shortly). If you receive a "page not found" or "document error," then the URL you are using is not correct. Correct and retest until you have a successful download.

---

[26] For simplicity, we use the terms "download," "downloadable element," and PDF interchangeably. However, as mentioned earlier, the tools and techniques discussed for PDFs apply for any downloadable piece of content: video, Excel files, images, etc.

If you use different browsers, you've seen how the same action is often treated differently. Downloads, for example, are handled differently in Firefox and Chrome. In light of this situation, our approach to tracking downloads is browser independent, and as a result, the appropriate data should be sent to Google Analytics regardless of the browser employed by the site user.

Our approach to tracking downloads requires that you do two things: First, you'll need to incorporate a very small customized javascript script on each page from which a download is available. Second, you'll need to make a small addition to the link or image that initiates the download. The following discusses each of these steps.

The javascript script

The javascript script must be placed in the HTML code on every page from which you want to track one or more downloads. This script does not need to be placed on pages without downloads and it only needs to appear once in a page's HTML code regardless of the number of download options appearing on the page. The script should be placed directly after the Google Analytics tracking code, as shown below (for my site), where the Google Analytics tracking code is in the smaller type and the new javascript script is in larger type:

```
<head>
<script>
(function(i,s,o,g,r,a,m){i['GoogleAnalyticsObject']=r;i[r]=i[r]||function(){
(i[r].q=i[r].q||[]).push(arguments)},i[r].l=1*new
Date();a=s.createElement(o),
m=s.getElementsByTagName(o)[0];a.async=1;a.src=g;m.parentNode.insertBefore(
a,m)  })
(window,document,'script','//www.google-analytics.com/analytics.js','ga');
ga('create', 'UA-50182280-1', 'googleanalyticsdemystified.com');
ga('send', 'pageview');
</script>
```

```
<script>
function download(file)
{
ga('send', 'pageview', file);
alert("Thanks for your download.");
(window.location="YOUR FULL URL HERE"+file);
}
</script>
```

We have already placed this script on your "More Information" page (`information.html`). You can verify this by opening the page in your HTML editor. Note that the script needs to be customized for your site before it is active, as described next.

Three instructions are embedded in the script after the javascript function is named.

- **ga('send', 'pageview', file)** sends the name of the downloaded file to Google Analytics. This line never needs to be changed.

- **alert("Thanks for your download.")** uses a pop-up window to acknowledge the download. The time lag between the appearance of this window and initiation of the download allows time for all browsers to send the name of the downloaded file to Google Analytics. You can customize the message by changing the text between the quotation marks. Make certain that any changes leave the beginning and ending quotation marks intact.

- **(window.location="YOUR FULL URL HERE"+file)** provides the browser with the full URL to the location of your download.

  This step requires you to replace **YOUR FULL URL HERE** between the quotation marks with the URL to your downloads, up to but not including the subdirectory in which they are housed. Hopefully, you identified this URL in the previous section. But, for review, the PDFs on my (and your) site are located in the **/brochure/** directory. On my site the full URL to one of the downloads is:

  `http://www.googleanalyticsdemystified.com/xqanqeon/brochure/mexico_dl_image.pdf`

  This step requires that we place within the javascript the URL up to but not including the folder containing the PDFs. In my case, the URL in the script appearing between the quotation marks (and which would replace "YOUR FULL URL HERE") would be:

  `http://www.googleanalyticsdemystified.com/xqanqeon`

  You need to replace the phrase **YOUR FULL URL HERE** with the full URL that leads to your downloads. Make certain to place this URL between the quotation marks (replacing the indicated phrase) and leave the rest of the line as is. Also, take care not to leave any spaces between the quotation marks and your URL.

When you have made the preceding changes, save the page without changing its name and then proceed to see how to modify the HTML code for the text, image, and button links.

Our approach tracks a download by altering the link which initiates the download. This alteration puts the javascript script into motion, sending data to Google Analytics and sending the requested PDF or other content to the site user. We'll begin with text links and then move on to two variations of image links.

An ordinary HTML text link to a Mexico information PDF would be:

<a href="information/mexico.pdf">Click to download more information on Mexico</a>

Here, the name of the downloadable document is **mexico.pdf** which is in the **information/** folder. The link text that appears on the web page is: **Click to download more information on Mexico.** You can see this link by viewing your "More Information" page in a web browser and you can verify this link structure by looking at your "More Information" page's HTML code.

We're going to change the basic form of this text link to the following format:

<a href="javascript:download('/information/mexico.pdf)">Click Here</a> to download more information on Mexico

You'll use this link format anywhere on your site you want to allow a trackable download to take place via a text link. Leave the link as is except for the three elements which need to be addressed whenever you use this format:

- *Mandatory:* Replace **/information/mexico.pdf** with the location and name of the content to be download when the link is clicked. Since the location and name of the content are the same on my site and yours, in this example, we would change this to: **/brochure/mexico_dl_text.pdf** to indicate the actual location and name of the file to be downloaded when the link is clicked upon. Note the PDF has been named to indicate its country of focus, that is a download, and that the download request was initiated via a text link.

- *Optional:* Replace **Click Here** with the text you want to appear as the active link. You can leave this as is if you desire.

- *Mandatory:* Replace **to download more information on Mexico** with whatever text appropriately completes the sentence. For this example, we will change this text to read: **to obtain a brochure on Mexican travel.**

To accomplish this customization on your site open your "More Information" page in your HTML editing program (if it is not already open). Find the current text link to the **mexico.pdf** which is:

<a href="information/mexico.pdf">Click to download more information on Mexico</a>

Replace the current link with the link below. This link contains all of the required modifications discussed earlier:

<a href="javascript:download('/brochure/mexico_dl_text.pdf')">Click Here</a> to obtain a brochure on Mexican travel

Tracking downloads via an image link (I)

We can initiate a download by having a user click on an image. We'll look at two ways to accomplish this. An ordinary HTML image link to a Mexico information PDF would be:

<a href="information/mexico.pdf"><img src="images/mexico.jpg"></a>

Here, the name of the downloadable document is **mexico.pdf** which is in the **information/** folder. The image named **mexico.jpg** resides in the **images/** directory. You can see this link by viewing your "More Information" page in a web browser and you can verify this link structure by looking at your "More Information" page's HTML code.

We're going to change the basic form of this text link to the following:

<a href="javascript:download('/information/mexico.pdf')">
<img src="images/mexico.jpg"></a>

You'll notice that this format is nearly identical to that used to create our text link. The only difference is that the text which appears on the web page has been replaced by an image.

You'll use this link format anywhere on your site you want to allow a trackable download to take place via an image click. Two elements need to be addressed whenever you use this format:

- *Mandatory:* Replace **/information/mexico.pdf** with the location and name of the content to be download when the link is clicked. Since the location and name of the content are the same on my site and yours, in this example, we would change this to: **/brochure/mexico_dl_image.pdf** to indicate the actual location and name of the file to be downloaded when the link is clicked upon. Note the PDF has been named to indicate its country of focus, that is a download, and that the download request was initiated via an image link.

- *Mandatory:* Replace the image name with the image that you want to use as the link. For this example, change this image to **images/mexico1.jpg**.

To accomplish this customization on your site open your "More Information" page in your HTML editing program (if it is not already open). Find the current image link to the **mexico.pdf** which is:

<a href="/information/mexico.pdf"><img src="images/mexico.jpg"></a>

Replace the current link with the link below. This link contains all of the required modifications discussed earlier:

```
<a href="javascript:download('/brochure/mexico_dl_image.pdf')">
<img src="images/mexico1.jpg"></a>
```

Tracking downloads via an image link (II)

Not all image links need to be pretty pictures. There are times when we want to use an image "button" to start the download. This procedure is exactly the same as the prior, except that we change the name of the image and PDF. The standard HTML code for this type of image link would be:

```
<a href="information/mexico.pdf"><img src="images/dl.jpg"></a>
```

Here, the name of the downloadable document is **mexico.pdf** which is in the **information/** folder. The image is named **dl.jpg** resides in the **images/** directory. You can see this link by viewing your "More Information" page in a web browser and you can verify this link structure by looking at your "More Information" page's HTML code.

We're going to change the basic form of this text link to the following:

```
<a href="javascript:download('/information/mexico.pdf')">
<img src="images/mexico.jpg"></a>
```

You'll notice that this format is identical to that used to create the prior image link.

You'll use this link format anywhere on your site you want to allow a download to take place via an image click. Two elements need to be addressed whenever you use this format:

- *Mandatory:* Replace **/information/mexico.pdf** with the location and name of the content to be download when the link is clicked. Since the location and name of the content are the same on my site and yours, in this example, we would change this to: **/brochure/mexico_dl_button.pdf** to indicate the actual location and name of the file to be downloaded when the link is clicked upon. Note the PDF has been named to indicate its country of focus, that is a download, and that the download request was initiated via a button link.

- *Mandatory:* Replace the image name with the image that you want to use as the link. For this example, change this image to **images/dl.jpg**.

To accomplish this customization on your site open your "More Information" page in your HTML editing program (if it is not already open). Find the current image link to the **mexico.pdf** which is:

```
<a href="/information/mexico.pdf"><img src="images/dl.jpg"></a>
```

Replace the current link with the link below. This link contains all of the required modifications discussed earlier:

```
<a href="javascript:download('/brochure/mexico_dl_button.pdf')">
<img src="images/dl.jpg"></a>
```

Save your file after the last change (using the same name) and upload the file to your server. This new "More Information" page will replace the original page.

Confirming that data is being sent to Google Analytics

We saw in Chapter 38 how the Google Analytics **Real-Time** menu can help us see if our goals are working as intended. The **Real-Time** menu can also be used to confirm that our efforts to track downloads are also working.[27]

Once you've upload the revised "More Information" page to your server, log into your Google Analytics account and select **Content** from the **Real-Time** menu options. Using Chrome, access your site's information page and click on the Mexico download text link. After the download is completed, click on the Mexico image link. Finally, after the download completes, click on the Mexico button link. If the links are working, you should see the name of each downloaded PDF in the **Real-Time > Content** display, as shown below where we have selected the **Pageviews (Last 30 min)** option. Keep in mind that depending upon your broadband speed the names may or may not appear at the same time and your order may be different than that shown below.

---

[27] We've tested this approach in Firefox, Chrome and Safari and it has worked in all three browsers, although Safari can at times still be problematic with this and other scripts we'll present later in this book. We recommend testing in Chrome or Firefox. The sporadic problems with Safari should have little impact as Safari's share of usage is estimated to be less than 4%.

42

Practice with Tracking Downloads

This chapter presents two sets of exercises to help you apply and extend your knowledge of download tracking.

This first set of questions makes certain that you understand key concepts. Feel free to open and refer to the prior chapter or access your analytics account. When you are done, or if you are stuck, the answers can be found beginning on page 617.

1. *True or False:* Google Analytics can monitor and report download metrics in the same way that it treats standard pageviews.

2. Which of the following can be tracked as a download by Google Analytics? (Select all that apply)

   a. PDFs

   b. Excel documents

   c. Video

   d. Images and pictures

3. You have decided to track the downloads for a file named **canada.html**. Which of the following metrics for this file are provided by Google Analytics? (Select all that apply)

   a. pageviews

   b. unique pageviews

   c. %Exit

4. *True or False:* In order for Google Analytics to track downloads, all downloads must be placed in a directory or folder named **/downloads**.

5. *True or False:* Google Analytics can only track downloads initiated via a text link.

6. Imagine that you have four downloads on a page of your website. *True or False:* The script needs to appear four times in the HTML code.

7. *True or False:* Before using the script, in the line **ga('send', 'pageview', file)**, the word "file" should be replaced with the name of the file being downloaded.

8. *True or False:* The message in the line **alert("Thanks for your download.")** can be changed without any harm to the script.

9. *True or False:* The entire line **alert("Thanks for your download.")** can be deleted from the script with no adverse effects.

10. *True or False:* Before using the script, the URL in quotes in the line **(window.location="http://www.googleanalyticsdemystified.com/xqanqeon"+file)** should be replaced by the URL for your site up to but not including the directory containing the download(s).

Hands-on

This exercise asks you to modify a webpage so that you can track your own downloads. If you run into problems, the recommended approach can be found on pages 313 to 318. The correct form of the links can be found on page 617.

You will need to modify your travel agency information web page to add three downloadable elements. You will add the following download options:

- a Bahamas brochure named **bahamas_dl_text.pdf,** which will be downloaded from a text link.

- a Bahamas brochure named **bahamas_dl_image.pdf,** which will be downloaded from an image link. The image to be used is named **bahamas1.jpg,** and is located in your site's image folder.

- a Bahamas brochure named **bahamas_dl_button.pdf** which will be downloaded from a button link. The image to be used is named **dl.jpg** and is located in your site's image folder.

It is not necessary for you to create the actual downloadable PDFs as all three are available in the **/brochure** folder.

In addition, if you followed the procedures in the prior chapter, then the customized javascript script should already be placed in the page's HTML code. Otherwise, you will have to customize the script per the prior chapter's directions.

Once you create the links for the three downloads, place each link in the appropriate place in the HTML code. Your text link should replace:

<a href="brochure/bahamas_dl_text.pdf">Click to download more information on Bahamas</a>

Your image link should replace:

<a href="brochure/bahamas_dl_image.pdf"><img src="images/bahamas.jpg"></a>

Your button link should replace:

<a href="brochure/bahamas__dl_button.pdf"><img src="images/dl.jpg"></a>

Upload the revised page and confirm that the documents are in fact being downloaded. Then, use the Google Analytics **Real-Time** menu to make certain that the downloads are being tracked and recorded.

43

Applications of Download Tracking

It takes considerable thought and time to create downloads that have perceived value among site users. Once these downloads are created, download tracking helps us evaluate how to best bring these downloads to users' attention and how to evaluate the impact of these downloads on subsequent user interactions and behaviors.

This chapter illustrates two applications of download tracking by addressing two strategic questions:

- Are all three methods of initiating a download (text, image, button) equally effective in motivating a download?

- Is there a difference across downloads in terms of purchase behavior?

But, these are not the only questions that can be asked. Depending upon your specific website goals, other questions might be:

- Is there a difference between downloads in terms of motivating a site revisit?

- Are some downloads more effective than others in stimulating contact, registration, or other related behaviors?

- Which download topics are of more/lesser interest to site users?

- To what extent are there differences between downloads in terms of increasing site engagement?

- To what extent do downloads stimulate referrals and trackbacks to the site?

Evaluating differences in download options

We always want to make certain that the format used to initiate a download is the most effective, especially given the time and effort that goes into content creation. As we saw in the previous chapters, we can initiate a download via text, image or button. Download tracking allows us to determine which of these approaches is the most effective.

Imagine that similar to the information page on our travel websites, we offer three download options on the same page. All three options provide more information on Mexico, but differ in the type of link used (text, image, button). We want to determine which download option best motivates a site user to request a download.

The first thing we do is locate and name each download to facilitate interpretation of the relevant Google Analytics reports. All three downloads are placed in the **/brochure/ mexico_dl/** folder and we name each download as follows:

mexico_image.pdf

mexico_link.pdf

mexico_button.pdf

We locate the pageviews for each type of link through **Content Drilldown** located in the **Behavior > Site Content** menu. Selecting this menu option brings up the top level directory display, as shown below, where on the second line we can see that 32 downloads have taken place in total from this folder.

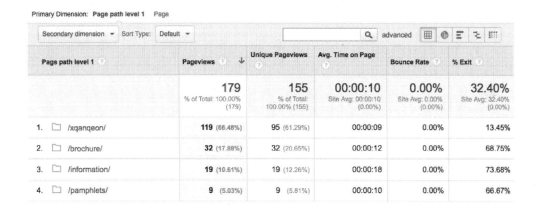

We click on **/brochure/** to bring up the display shown below. As noted above, the three PDFs (one for each link option) are located within the **mexico_dl folder** (shown on the first line of the display). The Pageviews column for this folder tells us that there have been 17 total downloads from this folder. The 1.0 ratio of pageviews to unique pageviews indicates that each user downloaded only one PDF.

Clicking on the **mexico_dl** folder brings up detailed information on each download option, as shown below. The Pageviews column shows a distinct user preference for the button link: about 70% of all downloads were via this link. This information would guide website revision, as we can potentially increase the number of downloads by changing our text and image links to buttons.

Primary Dimension: **Page path level 3** Page Other

Secondary dimension Sort Type: Default advanced

Page path level 3	Pageviews	Unique Pageviews	Avg. Time on Page	Bounce Rate
	17 % of Total: 9.50% (179)	17 % of Total: 10.97% (155)	00:00:09 Site Avg: 00:00:10 (-13.26%)	0.00% Site Avg: 0.00% (0.00%)
1. /mexico_button.pdf	12 (70.59%)	12 (70.59%)	00:00:10	0.00%
2. /mexico_link.pdf	3 (17.65%)	3 (17.65%)	00:00:05	0.00%
3. /mexico_image.pdf	2 (11.76%)	2 (11.76%)	00:00:11	0.00%

Evaluating download influence on purchase behavior

Downloads are often used to influence subsequent site behaviors, for example, increasing engagement or motivating a registration, contact or purchase. Let's look at the latter circumstance to see how download tracking can help us determine the extent to which downloads differ in terms of motivating a purchase and purchase amount.

We begin as we did in the prior exercise by locating and naming each download to facilitate interpretation of the relevant Google Analytics reports. All three downloads are placed in the **/brochure/brazil_dl/** folder, and we name each download as follows:

brazil1.pdf

brazil2.pdf

brazil3.pdf

Each download has different content.

We can examine the relationship between download content and subsequent purchase behaviors by isolating individuals who saw only one of the brochures. Groups are formed via custom segments to reflect the one download viewed. Since we have three downloads, three custom segments will be formed, one for each download.[28]

---

[28] This is the cleanest test of download impact. But, if sample size were sufficient, we could examine not only those who saw only one download, but also those who saw some combination of downloads. The procedure would be the same, except that more groups would be formed

The custom segment creation process begins the same as when other metrics are used for group definition. You access custom segments via the **+Add Segment** option on the top of almost any page, located beneath the blue circle **All Sessions** identifier. When you click **+Add Segment**, the segments page displays. You then begin the segment creation process by clicking the **+New Segment** link. The segment creation page will then display.

Custom segments formed on the basis of downloads use a specific pageview as the include/exclude condition. As with all custom segments based on a specific condition, we begin group definition via the **Conditions** option, which is shown on the bottom left-hand side of the page. The selection of this option brings up the **Conditions** page, shown below.

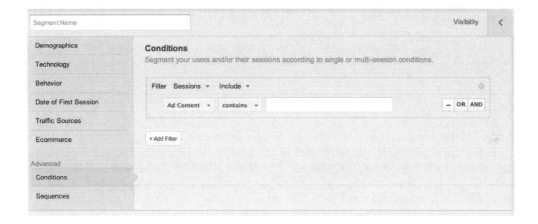

Pulling-down the menu currently labeled **Ad Content** displays both green and blue menu options. We select the green **Page** option within the **Behavior** classification, shown below.

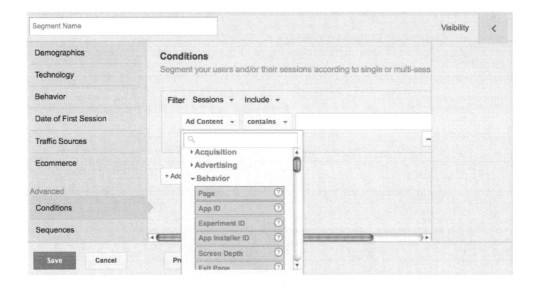

Selecting this option changes the display to that shown below.

We define our first group on this page. On the **Filter** line that appears, we leave **Sessions** as the unit of analysis, we leave **Include** as the type of selection, and we type in the page of interest in the text box (using regex to indicate the page is **brazil1.pdf**), changing the pull-down menu from **contains** to **matches regex**. This will include in the segment all users who saw **brazil1.pdf**. However, we also want to exclude from this group users who may have seen either page **brazil2.pdf** or **brazil3.pdf**. To accomplish this, we add a second filter to this group. This filter excludes any session from this group which contained a view of **brazil2.pdf** or **brazil3.pdf**. Once all this is done, we test the group, as shown below.

Given positive verification, the custom segment is saved and activated. The process is repeated for custom segments two and three, as illustrated in the following two figures.

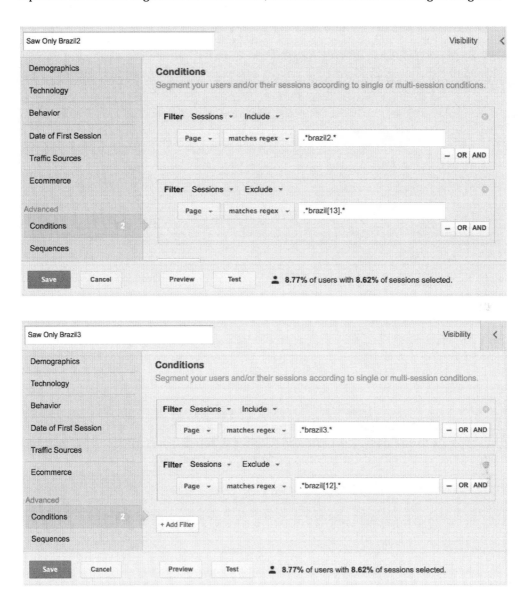

We can now use the three custom segments to explore reactions to and impact of the three different downloads.

Reactions to the three different downloads can be seen in the pageview data, obtained via the **Behavior > Site Content > All Pages** menu option. This table (see below) provides two important insights. First, site users appear to be much more likely to download the **brazil3.pdf.** Clearly, this PDF's topic is of greater interest. Second, the **brazil3.pdf** is much more likely to keep a user on the site. Only 21.74% of those who downloaded the **brazil3.pdf** left the site after the download versus nearly half (45.45%) of those who downloaded the **brazil1.pdf.** All in all, the **brazil3.pdf.** seems to have much better potential for fostering site engagement.

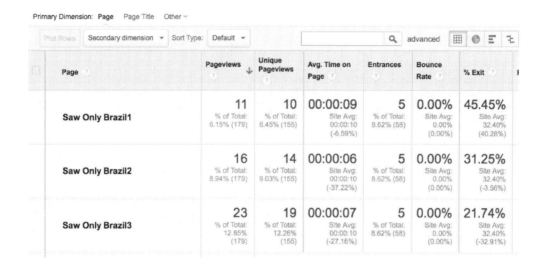

The strength of the **brazil3.pdf** can be seen in the ecommerce data, obtained through the **Conversions > Ecommerce > Overview** menu option (see top of page 329). This data parallels that of the pageview data and reinforces the conclusions that the strongest download is **brazil3.pdf** and the weakest download is **brazil1.pdf.**

When we look at the **Ecommerce Conversion Rate** (which reflects the percentage of sessions that resulted in a transaction, see page 329) we can clearly see the overwhelming superiority of the **brazil3.pdf** download. Significantly more of those who saw this PDF purchased a tour at a much higher average order value. Based on this data, we would most likely eliminate **brazil1.pdf** and **brazil2.pdf** as download options and attempt to create more downloadable content similar to **brazil3.pdf.**

Ecommerce Conversion Rate	Transactions	Revenue	Average Order Value
Saw Only Brazil1	Saw Only Brazil1	Saw Only Brazil1	Saw Only Brazil1
0.00%	0	$0.00	$0.00
Saw Only Brazil2	Saw Only Brazil2	Saw Only Brazil2	Saw Only Brazil2
40.00%	2	$7,000.00	$3,500.00
Saw Only Brazil3	Saw Only Brazil3	Saw Only Brazil3	Saw Only Brazil3
80.00%	4	$45,000.00	$11,250.00

44

Practice with Download Tracking Metrics

If you've completed the examples and exercises from Chapters 41 and 42, then your "More Information" page should have six working links: text/image/button links for a Mexico PDF and text/image/button links for a Bahamas PDF. This chapter asks you to generate and analyze metrics through the use of these links.

Getting ready for data collection

We recommend that you create a new view for your travel agency website prior to data collection. You can name this view whatever you like. Creating this new view will allow you to better focus on data that has been recently collected, the majority of which will likely be in response to this chapter's activities.

Generating data

You will need data to analyze. Data can be generated through either or both of these activities:

- Visit your website many times using your Chrome browser, making certain that you clear your browser history after every few visits to create a mix of new and returning site users. Use the download links on your "More Information" page to download one or more PDFs per visit. On some visits view additional website pages after the download completes. On some visits leave immediately after the download has taken place. On some visits make a purchase. On other visits leave without a purchase.

- Provide your friends with a link to your website and ask them to visit your "More Information" page several times over the course of two to three days. Encourage them to use the download links to download one or more PDFs per visit. Explain that on some visits they can view additional pages after the download completes and that on other visits they can leave immediately after the download has taken place. Explain that on some visits they can make a purchase, while on other visits they leave without a purchase.

Use your Google Analytics account to monitor the total number of downloads via the **Behavior > Site Content > Content Drilldown** menu option. The number of pageviews for the **/brochure/** directory indicates the combined number of Mexico and Bahamas downloads, respectively. When you have at least 40 pageviews in this directory, you can move on to the next steps: custom segments and analysis.

Creating custom segments

Three custom segments will help you answer several of the questions posed for data analysis. Create one segment which includes any sessions in which one or more of *only* the Mexican PDFs were downloaded (call this segment "Any Mexican PDF") and create a second segment which includes any sessions in which one or more of *only* Bahamas PDFs were downloaded (call this segment "Any Bahamas PDF"). In addition to these two segments, create a segment which contains sessions in which no PDF was downloaded.

Three additional custom segments will also be useful. Create one segment that includes only those sessions in which only the **mexico_dl_text.pdf** was downloaded; create a second segment that includes only those sessions in which only the **mexico_dl_image.pdf** was downloaded; and finally create a third segment that includes only those sessions in which only the **mexico_dl_button.pdf** was downloaded.[29]

Data analysis

Please provide a point of view, supported by Google Analytics data, that responds to each of the following questions.

> *Questions 1 through 8 focus on any overall differences in site behaviors when we compare Mexico and Bahamas PDF downloads. Some of these questions can be answered by using the first three segments described above.*

1. Overall, which country accounts for the most downloads?

2. What does the relationship between pageviews and unique pageviews tell you about whether site users are more or less likely to download just a single document?

3. Overall, are there differences in *site engagement* between those who downloaded Mexican PDFs, those who downloaded Bahamas PDFs, and those who did not download any document? Do you believe that the downloads have a positive or negative impact on site engagement?

---

[29] See pages 324 to 329 if you don't recall how to create these segments.

4. Overall, are there differences in *purchase behaviors* between those who downloaded Mexican PDFs, those who downloaded Bahamas PDFs, and those who did not download any document? Do you believe that the downloads have a positive or negative impact on purchase behaviors?

5. When you focus on site engagement, how well does the overall summary metric for Mexican downloads reflect the behaviors of the three individual PDFs?

6. When you focus on purchase behaviors, how well does the overall summary metric for Mexican downloads reflect the behaviors of the three individual PDFs?

7. When you focus on site engagement, how well does the overall summary metric for Bahamas downloads reflect the behaviors of the three individual PDFs?

8. When you focus on purchase behaviors, how well does the overall summary metric for Bahamas downloads reflect the behaviors of the three individual PDFs?

Questions 9 through 11 focus on the overall difference on site behaviors when we compare the three Mexico PDFs. The latter three segments created on page 331 will help you answer some of these questions.

9. Which of the three Mexico downloads is the most popular? The least popular?

10. Which of the three Mexico downloads was the most effective in stimulating site engagement? Which was the least effective?

11. Which of the three Mexico downloads was the most effective in fostering positive purchase behaviors? Which was the least effective?

Section X:
Events

Our discussion of download tracking in Section IX illustrated how Google Analytics can track user-site interactions in more detail than page level reporting. Fortunately, Google Analytics allows us to move beyond tracking this single interaction to monitor almost any type of user-site interaction. Event tracking is the means used to accomplish this. Event tracking allows us to determine, for example:

- whether or not a video embedded on our site was played, and if played, whether the video was watched all the way to the end.

- how much of a specific page was actually read.

- which elements of a form are roadblocks to completion.

- which pages/blog entries are responsible for the greatest amount of social sharing.

The ten chapters in this section explore events and demonstrate how critical strategic insights can be obtained from using this feature of Google Analytics.

45

Introduction to Events

Google Analytics explains events as "user interactions with content that can be tracked independently from a web page or a screen load. Downloads, mobile ad clicks, gadgets, Flash elements, AJAX embedded elements and video plays are all examples of actions you might want to track as Events." Additional events that you may want to track include form completions, scroll depth, outbound link tracking, and social sharing interactions.

The tracking of events, similar to the monitoring of downloads, requires us to modify the HTML code to let Google Analytics know what specific event has been "triggered." Before we address the HTML code itself, it is important to understand the types of information Google Analytics requires in order to track an event. The components of event tracking code are:

ga('send', 'event', 'category', 'action', 'label', value, {'nonInteraction': 1});

where:

- **ga** indicates that this is a Google Analytics command. This element is never modified.

- **send** directs the data to Google Analytics. This element is never modified.

- **event** indicates that the information being sent relates to an event. This element is never modified.

- **category, action, label,** and **value** provide details on the event taking place. Only **category** and **action** are required elements. The remaining two elements (**label** and **value**) are optional.

- **{'nonInteraction': 1}** indicates that the event, when activated, should not be treated as a user-site interaction.

This chapter discusses each of the components that provide the event's details and the ways in which event information is sent to Google Analytics. Subsequent chapters in this section provide examples of how events can be used to increase insights into user behavior, resulting in more effective strategic analysis and decision-making.

The Category parameter

The category parameter represents your highest level of event grouping and is a required element in all event statements. "Downloads", "Videos", and "Social Media Sharing" are examples of category parameters, although you can be as specific or broad as required by your strategic needs. You might, for example, need more specific information on videos viewed than simply collecting all event interactions within the single "Videos" event category. In this case, you could create more specific categories, for example:

- Videos - Movies
- Videos - Music
- Videos - Instructional
- Videos - Testimonial

Similarly, you might want to organize your blog entries and track the extent to which different types of entries are read by site users. Here, rather than having a single category named "Blog", you might create several categories to reflect the content of different blog posts, for example:

- Blog - Metrics
- Blog - HTML coding
- Blog - Research design

We highly recommend that you examine your site's goals and objectives, as well as your own information needs, prior to the creation of categories for use in event tracking. While new categories can always be added, it is a time-consuming process to create and analyze multiple categories and event triggers for essentially the same event. If, for example, you initially call your video tracking category "Video" and later forget and use the plural "Videos", you will have two separate categories for video tracking. A bit of pre-planning makes a major contribution to ease of analysis and application to decision-making.

The Action parameter

Every event command must contain an action parameter that names the specific interaction you are tracking. The action parameter appears right after the category parameter. You might, for example, want monitor when a video is started as a way of gauging site users' interest in the video's topic. In this circumstance, the category would be "video" and the action would be "play".

Similar to the category label, while you have complete control over the form and characteristics of the action name, it is always best to develop your naming strategy prior to (rather than during) implementation. In this regard, Google Analytics notes that during the planning process:

- *Action names should be relevant to your strategic information needs.*

  Google Analytics' event tracking combines metrics for the same action name across two different categories. If, for example, you associate the action label "Click" with both the "Downloads" category label and the "Videos" category label, the metrics for the "Click" in your reports appears with all interactions tagged with that same name. Thus, you should select different action labels for different categories of events. You might, for example, choose to use the action label "click" for gadget interactions, while reserving the action labels, "Play", "Pause", and "Stop" for video player interactions.

- *Use action names globally to either aggregate or distinguish user interaction.*

  For example, you can use "Play" as an action label in the "Videos" category for all videos on your website. In this model, the Top Actions report would provide aggregate data for events with the "Play" action, and you can see how this event for your videos compares to other events for all videos, such as "Pause" or "Stop."

Finally, keep in mind than an action name need not necessarily reflect an overt action. In some cases, such as tracking downloads as an event, the actual event or action name is not as meaningful as other information regarding the event, so you might use the action parameter to track other elements such as a topic or other strategically valuable pieces of information.

The Label parameter

The label parameter is an optional component in the event tracking code. Labels allow you to obtain additional information for events that you want to track, such as a video title, the source of the download (for example, text or image) or the video topic. Imagine, for example, that you have three videos on your site. With regard to event tracking, each one of these videos can use the "Videos" category name with the "Play" action, but each could also have a separate identifier (such as the video name or topic) so that they appear as distinct elements in your reports.

The Value parameter

The value parameter differs from the previous event command components in that it is a number rather than a word. As such, it is used when you need to assign a numeric value to a tracked event. You could, for example, use this parameter to record the number of seconds it takes for a video to load.

The value assigned to an event is interpreted as a number and, when Google Analytics reports an event's values, it reports values individually as well as the value's overall average. Imagine, for example, that you are monitoring video download time and that the download times for five unique views were: 5, 5, 8, 10 and 25. Google Analytics would report the average value for this event as 10.3.

The interaction parameter is an optional parameter that you can use with event tracking. This parameter allows you to determine how you want to calculate the bounce rate for pages on your site that include event tracking.

Google Analytics provides this scenario: Imagine, for example, that "you have a home page with a video embedded on it. It's quite natural that you will want to know the bounce rate for your home page, but how do you want to define that? Do you consider visitor interaction with the home page video an important engagement signal? If so, you would want interaction with the video to be included in the bounce rate calculation, so that sessions including only your home page with clicks on the video are not calculated as bounces. On the other hand, you might prefer a more strict calculation of bounce rate for your home page, in which you want to know the percentage of sessions including only your home page regardless of clicks on the video. In this case, you would want to exclude any interaction with the video from bounce rate calculation."

This where the non-interaction parameter comes into play. Remember that a bounce is defined as a session containing only one interaction hit, such as a single pageview. By default, the event hit sent by the **ga send event** command is considered an interaction hit, which means that it is included in bounce rate calculations. However, when **{'nonInteraction': 1}** is included in the event command, then the event trigger is not considered an interaction hit. Thus, Google Analytics notes that "including this command in a session containing a single page tagged with non-interaction events is counted as a bounce - even if the visitor also triggers the event during the session. Conversely, omitting this parameter means that a single-page session on a page that includes event tracking will not be counted as a bounce if the visitor also triggers the event during the same session." Thus, this command should only be used when the event triggers on a noninteraction event, such as an event that takes place when the page loads and therefore requires no active engagement on the part of the site user.[30]

Placing the event HTML code

Let's examine two common uses of event tracking: when a page loads[31] or when a user takes an action such a clicking on a link or starting a video play.

---

[30] The source used for the content and quotes in the value and interaction parameter discussion is Event Tracker Guide (https://developers.google.com/analytics/devguides/collection/gajs/eventTrackerGuide).

[31] While this type of event is most commonly associated with page loads, it can also be used to track any type of loading action, for example, the display of a particular image or a video load.

Sending event information when a page loads

Imagine that you want to use events to automatically monitor the characteristics of blog entries when each entry is viewed. You want to know, for each blog viewed, the author, topic, and month the blog was first posted. This information can be sent to Google Analytics via an event command when the page loads in a user's browser. This event command would have the following characteristics:

- **category** represents the author "Davis"

- **action** is the blog topic, in this case, "Analytics"

- **label** is the month of the original posting, in this case, "April"

- **value** is not relevant and is omitted

- **{'nonInteraction': 1}** is relevant as this event is triggered when the page loads without any overt user interaction

When an event is activated during a page load, it is typically attached to the **<body>** parameter using the **onload** HTML command. Given these parameters, the complete HTML statement that would activate the event would be:

<body onload = "ga('send', 'event', 'Davis', 'Analytics', 'April', {'nonInteraction': 1});">

The statement would replace the original **<body>** command in the HTML code.

Sending event information when an interaction occurs

When an event is triggered by an explicit user-site interaction such as a click on a link, the event code is typically attached to the relevant action using the **onClick** command. Let's imagine that you have a number of links that go to sites other than yours, and that you want to create an event whenever your site user clicks on one of these links. This will help you to gauge the relative use and appeal of these links. The event command for one of these links might have the following characteristics:

- **category** identifies the type of action, in this case labeled "Click External Link"

- **action** represents the interaction, in this case, "Click"

- **label** is the link's URL, in this case, "http://www.google.com/analytics"

- **value** is not relevant and is omitted

- **{'nonInteraction': 1}** is not relevant as this event is triggered by an overt user interaction and is omitted

Given these parameters, the complete HTML statement that would activate the event would be:

<a href = "http://www.google.com/analytics" onClick = "ga('send', 'event', 'Click External Link', 'Click', 'www.google.com/analytics');">Click here to go to Google Analytics</a>

This link would replace the normal link:

<a href = "http://www.google.com/analytics">Click here to go to Google Analytics</a>

Using javascript to send onClick event information

Visit the following page on my travel website:

http://www.googleanalyticsdemystified.com/xqanqeon/chap45.html

The page automatically sends a set of event information when the page loads. You can see the code for this event by looking at the <body> command within the page's HTML code. Clicking on the link sends you to Google Analytics. However, you'll note that rather than sending you directly, the page informs you that it is redirecting you to the new site. Why don't we send you directly without this notice?

You'll recall from Chapter 41 that there are differences across browsers in terms of how they interpret HTML commands. Thus, while the **onClick** command should always send event information directly to Google Analytics, the reality is that the event data may not always be sent and/or recorded. To avoid this problem, an alternative to the **onClick** format discussed previously is to use javascript to send the data associated with an **onClick** event. Similar to the use of javascript to track downloads, this approach is browser independent and has a much higher likelihood that your event data initiated by a link click will be recorded by Google Analytics.

This approach alters the form of the link and places a small javascript script in the <head> section of your page.

The javascript script needs to be placed in the HTML code on every page from which you want to track an **onClick** event. This script does not need to be on any other pages and it only needs to appear once a page's HTML code, regardless of the number of **onClick** events appearing on that page. The script should be placed directly after the opening <head> tag, as shown on the top of page 341 (for my site), where the Google Analytics tracking code is in the smaller type and the new javascript script is in larger type:

```
<head>

<script>
function redir(category, action, label, value, where)
{
ga('send', 'event', category, action, label, value);
alert("Redirecting");
(window.location=where);
}
</script>

[Additional HTML may appear here]

<script>

(function(i,s,o,g,r,a,m){i['GoogleAnalyticsObject']=r;i[r]=i[r]||function(){
(i[r].q=i[r].q||[]).push(arguments)},i[r].l=1*new
Date();a=s.createElement(o),
m=s.getElementsByTagName(o)[0];a.async=1;a.src=g;m.parentNode.insertBefore(
a,m)  })
(window,document,'script','//www.google-analytics.com/analytics.js','ga');
ga('create', 'UA-50182280-1', 'googleanalyticsdemystified.com');
ga('send', 'pageview');

</script>
```

Note that this script and others we provide do not conflict with each other. As a result, you can include this script and the download tracking script presented in Chapter 41 on the same page. Just place one after the other. The order does not matter.

Four instructions are embedded in the script.

- **function redir(category, action, label, value, where)** names the function and information to be collected. This line never needs to be changed.

- **ga('send', 'event', category, action, label, value);** sends the event information to Google Analytics. This line never needs to be changed.

- **alert("Redirecting")** uses a pop-up window to acknowledge the redirect. The time lag between the appearance of this window and the redirect allows time for all browsers to send the information to Google Analytics. You can customize the message by changing the text between the quotation marks. Make certain that any changes leave the beginning and ending quotation marks intact.

- **(window.location=where)** is the redirect location and should not be changed.

Next, you'll next need to create your link, which will be of the form:

```
<a href="javascript:redir('category', 'action', 'label', 0,'redirect URL')">Click Here</a>
```

The link carries all of the event and redirect information. When you use this link, leave all of the wording and punctuation as is except:

- replace the words **category** and **action** with your category and action names. Remember that both names are required.

- replace the word **label** with your label name parameter if one is being used. If you are not using a label parameter, then delete the word **label** leaving the ' ' punctuation.

- leave the 0 if your event has no value; otherwise replace the 0 with your event value.

- replace **redirect URL** with the full URL where the site user is being sent after clicking on the link.

You'll use this link format anywhere on your site where you want to use **onClick** to trigger an event whose data is sent to Google Analytics. Remember to replace **Click Here** with whatever text you want to appear as the text link.

Let's apply this approach to the same situation as described previously, where:

- **category** identifies the type of action, in this case labeled "Click External Link"

- **action** represents the interaction, in this case, "Click"

- **label** is location of the redirect, in this case, "google.com/analytics"

- **value** is zero

- **redirect URL** is `http://www.google.com/analytics`

In this case, the link would be:

```
<a href="javascript:redir('Click External Link', 'Click', 'google.com/analytics',
0,'http://www.google.com/analytics')">Click here to go to Google Analytics</a>
```

In contrast, if no label parameter were being used, the link would be:

```
<a href="javascript:redir('Click External Link', 'Click','',
0,'http://www.google.com/analytics')"> Click here to go to Google Analytics</a>
```

You have a `chap45.html` page in your travel site folder, which can be viewed by typing the full URL to the page into your browser. This page, at the moment, is identical to mine with the two types of links described on pages 340 to 342. You can use this page to experiment with **onClick** and **<body>** events. Use the **Real-Time > Events** menu option to monitor your results.

Events per session limit

Google Analytics places some limits on the collection of event data. Specifically, the first 10 event hits sent to Google Analytics are tracked immediately, after which the tracking rate is limited to one event hit per second.

As the number of events in a session approaches the Google Analytics overall data collection limits, additional events might not be tracked. For this reason, Google recommends that you:

-    avoid scripting a video to send an event for every second played and other highly repetitive event triggers,

-    avoid excessive mouse movement tracking, and

-    avoid time-lapse mechanisms that generate high event counts

46

Practice with Events

The questions and exercise in this chapter help to confirm that you understand the basics of creating events.

True/false and multiple choice

This first set of questions makes certain that you understand key concepts. Feel free to open and refer to Chapter 45. When you are finished, or if you are stuck, the answers can be found on our website beginning on page 619.

1. Below are the components of a Google Analytics event command. Which elements, when used, should never be changed; that is, they should appear exactly as shown below? (Click all that apply)

   a. ga

   b. send

   c. event

   d. category

   e. action

   f. label

   g. value

2. Which of the statements below are true? (Select all that apply)

   a. an event can be triggered when a link or other overt user-site interaction occurs

   b. an event can be triggered when a passive event such as a page load occurs

3. You have different videos that you want to monitor as events when played. You give each video an identifying name. *True of False:* When you create the event command, each video's name should appear as the <u>category</u> parameter.

4. Below are the components of a Google Analytics event command. Which elements are mandatory? (Select all that apply)

   a. ga

   b. send

   c. event

   d. category

   e. action

   f. label

   g. value

   h. {'nonInteraction': 1}

5. Which of the following represents the highest level of event grouping?

   a. category

   b. action

   c. label

   d. value

6. Imagine that you want to track the videos played anywhere on your blog and videos played on your home page so that you can better understand the differences in video plays across the two sources. All plays are considered interaction events. Which of the following would be an acceptable event command, assuming that the event will trigger when the video is played. (Select all that apply)

   a. Blog page: **ga('send', 'event', 'Video', 'Play', 'Blog', {'nonInteraction': 1});**

      Home page: **ga('send', 'event', 'Video', 'Play', 'Home', {'nonInteraction': 1});**

   b. Blog page: **ga('send', 'event', 'Video', 'Play', 'Blog');**

      Home page: **ga('send', 'event', 'Video', 'Play', 'Home');**

   c. Blog page: **ga('send', 'event', 'Blog', 'Video', 'Play');**

      Home page: **ga('send', 'event', 'Home', 'Video', 'Play');**

7. You create one event category named "Video" and a second event category named "Videos". *True or false:* Because the root category name is the same, Google Analytics will automatically combine both category's metrics together under the category name "Video*".

8. Which of the following actions can trigger an event? (Select all that apply)

   a. Clicking on a link to another of your website pages

   b. Clicking on a link to an external website

   c. Clicking on a link to download a PDF

   d. Starting a video play

   e. Stopping a video play

   f. Clicking on an email address

   g. Completing and sending a contact form

   h. Completing a site registration form

   i. Clicking on a social sharing icon

9. Consider this Google Analytics command for an interaction event with no value:

   ga(send, event, Video, Play, Analytics)

   True or False: This command is written correctly.

10. Imagine that you have a 20 minute video on your site and that you have written a javascript script to monitor site users' viewing. The script triggers an event at each two second interval during which the video is viewed. *True or False:* This approach has the potential to violate Google Analytics data limits.

Hands-on: Creating events

This exercise asks you to create your own events. If you are unsure or are having trouble with the solution see page 619.

Your travel website directory contains several pages that can only be reached by typing in the page's URL. These pages are designed to provide you with a context for specific exercises without cluttering your main travel site. One of the these pages is events. html which you can view by typing events.html at the end of your website's URL. Since, for example, my website URL is:

http://www.googleanalyticsdemystified/xqanqeon/

to see this page I would type:

http://www.googleanalyticsdemystified/xqanqeon/events.html

Visit your events page to confirm that it is accessible.

Next, you will need to add two events to the page. As the first step to accomplishing this, open the page in your HTML editing program.

The first event is passive and is activated when the page is loaded. Modify the page's HTML **<body>** command to activate this event when the body of the page begins to load. The parameters for the event are:

- **category** is "Event test"

- **action** is "Activates on page load"

- **label** is "Events page"

- **value** is not relevant and is omitted

- the event should **not** be treated as a user-site interaction

Page 339 provides direction on the correct format for transmitting this type of event.

The second event is active. It should be activated when a site user clicks on the link labeled **Click here to activate the event**. Clicking on the link should take the user to:

http://www.google.com

The link should replace the text **Click here to activate the event,** which has already been placed on the page.

Create this link's HTML code to activate this event when the link is clicked. The parameters for the event are:

- **category** is "Event test"

- **action** is "Activates on link click"

- **label** is "Events page"

- **value** is not relevant and is omitted

- the event should be treated as a user-site interaction

Pages 340 to 342 discuss both the javascript and link format for sending this type of event. Once both events have been added to the page, save your page under the same name and upload to your server.

You can confirm that your events are working by using the **Real-Time** menu's **Events** option. Log into your Google Analytics account and bring up the **Real-Time > Events** display. Click on **Events (last 30 min).** At the moment the display should be blank as no events have been activated. Now, in a separate browser window (or entirely separate browser), visit your `events.html` page. When you return to your analytics **Real-Time > Events** display, you should see evidence that the passive event has activated. The category label "Event test" should appear in the **Event Category** column (see below).

If all is working , clicking on the **Event test** link and then the **Events (last 30 min)** link (if it is not already selected) should confirm that the passive event has taken place (see below). The event action "Activates on page load" and label "Events page" should be displayed. Note that the number shown reflects the number of times your page loaded.

Next, return to your `events.html` page. Click on the link to activate the second event. When you return to your analytics **Real-Time > Events** display, you should see evidence that the link click event has activated, as shown below. Note that the new category action "Activates on link click" now appears in the **Event Action** column.

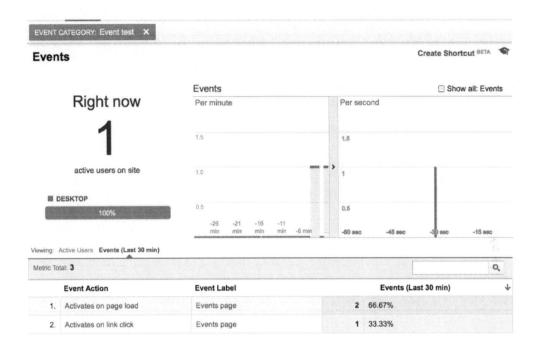

47
Events and Content Monitoring

The previous chapter illustrated how events can be used to monitor content consumption and link usage. This chapter and the next address each of these uses of events in more detail. We'll begin with a discussion of content consumption.

We've seen how Google Analytics provides a great deal of page specific information, for example, how often each page is viewed, time on page and bounce rate. This data, however, does not allow us to easily collapse similar types of pages to obtain an overview of how *types* of pages (as a group) are performing in terms of engagement and contribution to goals or transactions. Events allows us to accomplish this.

The first part of this chapter explains how to use events to monitor groupings of pages. The chapter ends with an opportunity for you practice creating this type of event

The scenario

Imagine that our website provides a significant amount of content related to budget travel and travel in Europe, Ireland, and Italy. Each topic is addressed with content created by one of two authors, as shown below:

Davis	Budget
Davis	Europe
Davis	Ireland
Rose	Budget
Rose	Europe
Rose	Italy

Looking across these writers and content, we want to know:

- Regardless of the author, which topics are most viewed and generate the most engagement and positive purchase behaviors?

- Regardless of the topic, which authors are most viewed and generate the most engagement and positive purchase behaviors?

We can use events to answer these strategic questions by placing two events on each page. When this page loads, one event automatically sends author information and the second event sends topic information.

The code used to signal our target events follows standard event code format. The code used to signal a page written by Davis would be:

ga('send', 'event', 'Written_By','Davis',{'nonInteraction': 1});

while the code for a page written by Rose would be:

ga('send', 'event', 'Written_By','Rose',{'nonInteraction': 1});

Notice that in both of these cases, since we only need to identify the author, the code only provides Category and Action information. No additional information is needed.

Similarly, the code used to signal the content of a specific page would be:

ga('send', 'event', 'Theme','Budget',{'nonInteraction': 1});

ga('send', 'event', 'Theme','Europe',{'nonInteraction': 1});

ga('send', 'event', 'Theme','Ireland',{'nonInteraction': 1});

ga('send', 'event', 'Theme','Scotland,{'nonInteraction': 1});

As with the code used to identify the page author, only the Category and Action information are required. We also identify each of these events as a noninteraction so as not to distort pageviews and bounce metrics.

Placing the code

We want both author and content information to be sent automatically to Google Analytics once the page loads in a site user's browser. As a result, we will attach both event commands to **<body>** using **onload**.

We have six author/topic combinations. The HTML event command for each author/topic combination would be placed on the appropriate page and would be of the form shown in the table on the top of page 352. Notice that there are two event commands attached to **onload**: one to identify author and one to identify topic.

Author/Topic Combination	HTML event code placed on page
Davis/Budget	\<body onload ="ga('send', 'event', 'Written_By','Davis',{'nonInteraction': 1}); ga('send', 'event', 'Theme','Budget',{'nonInteraction': 1});">
Davis/Europe	\<body onload ="ga('send', 'event', 'Written_By','Davis',{'nonInteraction': 1}); ga('send', 'event', 'Theme','Europe',{'nonInteraction': 1});">
Davis/Ireland	\<body onload ="ga('send', 'event', 'Written_By','Davis',{'nonInteraction': 1}); ga('send', 'event', 'Theme','Ireland',{'nonInteraction': 1});">
Rose/Budget	\<body onload ="ga('send', 'event', 'Written_By','Rose',{'nonInteraction': 1}); ga('send', 'event', 'Theme','Budget',{'nonInteraction': 1});">
Rose/Europe	\<body onload ="ga('send', 'event', 'Written_By','Rose',{'nonInteraction': 1}); ga('send', 'event', 'Theme','Europe'),{'nonInteraction': 1};">
Rose/Italy	\<body onload ="ga('send', 'event', 'Written_By','Rose',{'nonInteraction': 1}); ga('send', 'event', 'Theme','Ireland',{'nonInteraction': 1});">

Data analysis and insights

We begin by selecting **Top Events** from the **Behavior > Events** menu, which displays all of our event categories (see table on the top of the next page). The two event category parameters "Theme" and "Written_By" (see lines 8 and 9) correspond to the event categories in our event commands for tracking authors and content, so these are the event categories of interest. Since both the author and theme triggers are sent to Google Analytics at the same time, it is reassuring that both report the same number of events as shown in the **Total Events** column (21 for each in this example). Notice that the number of unique events is almost identical to the number of total events. This reflects the fact that almost all site users read only one blog.

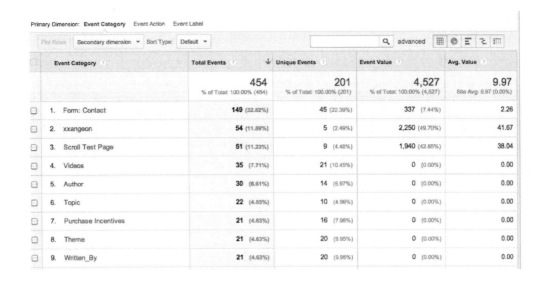

	Event Category ?	Total Events ?	↓ Unique Events ?	Event Value ?	Avg. Value ?
		454 % of Total: 100.00% (454)	**201** % of Total: 100.00% (201)	**4,527** % of Total: 100.00% (4,527)	**9.97** Site Avg: 9.97 (0.00%)
☐ 1.	Form: Contact	**149** (32.82%)	45 (22.39%)	337 (7.44%)	2.26
☐ 2.	xxangeon	**54** (11.89%)	5 (2.49%)	2,250 (49.70%)	41.67
☐ 3.	Scroll Test Page	**51** (11.23%)	9 (4.48%)	1,940 (42.85%)	38.04
☐ 4.	Videos	**35** (7.71%)	21 (10.45%)	0 (0.00%)	0.00
☐ 5.	Author	**30** (6.61%)	14 (6.97%)	0 (0.00%)	0.00
☐ 6.	Topic	**22** (4.85%)	10 (4.98%)	0 (0.00%)	0.00
☐ 7.	Purchase Incentives	**21** (4.63%)	16 (7.96%)	0 (0.00%)	0.00
☐ 8.	Theme	**21** (4.63%)	20 (9.95%)	0 (0.00%)	0.00
☐ 9.	Written_By	**21** (4.63%)	20 (9.95%)	0 (0.00%)	0.00

The selection of either **Theme** or **Written_By** from the list of Event Categories allows us to see more detailed information on that specific event category. Selecting **Theme** from the list brings up the table below, which shows that across authors Budget travel and Ireland are much more popular topics than Europe (as indicated in the counts in the Total Events column).

	Event Action ?	Total Events ?	↓ Unique Events ?	Event Value ?	Avg. Value ?
		21 % of Total: 4.63% (454)	**20** % of Total: 9.95% (201)	**0** % of Total: 0.00% (4,527)	**0.00** Site Avg: 9.97 (-100.00%)
☐ 1.	Budget_Travel	**10** (47.62%)	10 (47.62%)	0 (0.00%)	0.00
☐ 2.	Ireland	**8** (38.10%)	8 (38.10%)	0 (0.00%)	0.00
☐ 3.	Europe	**3** (14.29%)	3 (14.29%)	0 (0.00%)	0.00

Similarly, the selection of **Written_By** from the initial list of event categories brings up a table that shows that across topics, the materials written by Davis and Rose are read with about equal frequency (see below).

	Event Action ?	Total Events ?	↓ Unique Events ?	Event Value ?	Avg. Value ?
		21 % of Total: 4.63% (454)	**20** % of Total: 9.95% (201)	**0** % of Total: 0.00% (4,527)	**0.00** Site Avg: 9.97 (-100.00%)
☐ 1.	Davis	**11** (52.38%)	10 (50.00%)	0 (0.00%)	0.00
☐ 2.	Rose	**10** (47.62%)	10 (50.00%)	0 (0.00%)	0.00

While this information is helpful for future planning, it is not complete. We need to look at our author and content trends in terms of site engagement and subsequent transactions.

Let's return to the page displayed after one of the event categories is selected. The page below is shown when we select **Theme** from the **Behavior > Top Events** data display. On the top of this page, above the line chart (but beneath the **Explorer** tab) are additional data view options: Site Usage and Ecommerce (see below).

Clicking on **Site Usage** brings up the following table, in which we see that subsequent site engagement is different for each content area. Budget travel appears to motivate greater site engagement: users who read our blogs on this topic have more Pages/Session and spend more time on the site as reflected in Average Session Duration (see below).

We can conduct the same analysis for authors, which displays the following table. Here, we see mixed results with regard to each author's ability to motivate site engagement. Those who read Davis' blog view more site pages, but those who read Rose's blog spend more time on the site. (This may simply be a function of Rose's tendency to ramble.)

We can conduct a parallel analysis focused on transactions. Selecting **Ecommerce** from the **Explorer** options brings up the following table for the three types of content. Here, we can see that while Budget travel and Ireland are read at nearly equal levels, Budget travel is associated with significantly greater revenue versus the other two content areas.

Conducting a similar analysis for authors, we see that Davis' content has significantly greater association with better transactions versus content created by Rose (see table on the top of page 356). This is especially important since both authors are read at equal rates.

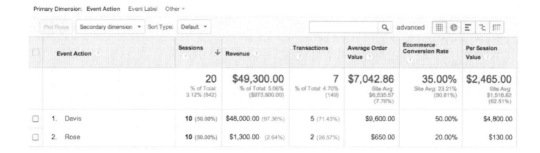

All in all, monitoring both authors and themes through events and relating these events to site engagement and purchase behaviors makes a significant contribution to future blog planning. We would likely want to publish relatively more blog entries written by Davis with a focus on budget travel.

Hands-on

With this material fresh in your mind, try this exercise.

As we noted in earlier, your travel website directory contains several pages that can only be reached by typing the page's URL directly into your browser. One of the these pages is `chap47.html`. You can view this page by typing `chap47.html` at the end of your website's URL. I would type:

`http://www.googleanalyticsdemystified.com/xqanqeon/chap47.html`

Visit your `chap47.html` page to confirm that it is accessible.

Imagine that your website has two authors, two topic areas, and two types of content presentation for your blog posts (resulting in eight different combinations). You want to use the **body onload** command to trigger an event that informs us of author, topic, and content associated with each blog post. One combination might be:

Written_By:	Davis
Topic:	Solo travel
Presentation:	Image dominant

Open the page in your HTML editing program. Generate and place the appropriate event HTML code on the web page `chap47.html` for the three event characteristics shown above. You can use the code on page 352 as a model, paying particular attention to the punctuation and placement of beginning and ending parentheses.

Once all events have been added to the page, save your page under the same name and upload to your server. You can confirm that your events are working (that is triggering when the page loads) by using the **Real-Time** menu's **Events** option. Log into your

Google Analytics account and bringing up the **Real-Time > Events** display. Click on **Events (last 30 min)**. At the moment, the display should be blank as no events have been activated. Now, in a separate browser window (or an entirely different browser, but preferably Chrome), visit your `chap47.html` page. Since all events should trigger when the page loads, you should see all three category action labels as shown below:

If your **onload** events are not displayed, compare your HTML code to the correct code shown below:

<body onload ="ga('send', 'event', 'Written_By','Davis',{'nonInteraction': 1}); ga('send', 'event', 'Topic','Solo Travel',{'nonInteraction': 1}); ga('send', 'event', 'Presentaton','Image dominant',{'nonInteraction': 1})">

48
Advanced Events: Link Tracking

Chapter 31 discussed how In-Page Analytics tells us how often each link on a page is clicked. However, In-Page Analytics cannot help us determine the ultimate effect of different link selections on an outcome variable such as purchase. Fortunately, event tracking allows us to transcend this limitation.

The first part of this chapter explains how to use events for link tracking.[32] The chapter ends with an opportunity for you to incorporate this type of event into your own travel website.

The scenario

Imagine that we want to learn which of three incentives is most likely to lead to purchase and which of the incentives leads to the highest travel purchase amount. The three incentives, each shown in a different link, are:

- 10% discount on day of purchase,

- free lifetime membership in the travel club, and

- free insurance.

All three incentives appear on the same page.

The Javascript and HTML event code

We're going to use the approach described on pages 340 to 342, a combination of java-script and link alteration.

The javascript is placed in the HTML code on the page containing the links we want to track. We place the script (shown on the top of page 359) directly after the Google Analytics tracking code. Note that the alert message now says: **Taking you to your special offer.**

---

[32] The techniques discussed in this chapter can be applied to any website link. An event can be created, for example, when a link to a downloadable PDF is selected or a link to an external website is used.

```
<script>
function redir(category, action, label, value, where)
{
ga('send', 'event', category, action, label, value);
alert("Taking you to your special offer");
window.location=where);
}
</script>
```

The links are placed on the appropriate place on the web page. Since there are three options, we will need three links, as shown below.

```
<a href="javascript:redir('Purchase Incentives', 'Click', '10% Off',
0,'purchase.html')"> 10% off today</a>

<a href="javascript:redir('Purchase Incentives', 'Click', 'Lifetime membership',
0,'purchase.html')"> Lifetime membership</a>

<a href="javascript:redir('Purchase Incentives', 'Click', 'Free insurance',
0,'purchase.html')"> Free insurance</a>
```

Each link is coded with the same destination page (`purchase.html`), as well as the same category and action name.[33] The label parameter differentiates the three events by explicitly naming the offer selected. Since we ultimately want to relate link selection with transaction amount event, value is set to zero.

Data analysis and insights

We begin by selecting **Top Events** from the **Behavior > Events** menu, which displays all of our event categories (see table on the top of page 360). Since we are interested in looking at link effectiveness we click on "Purchase Incentives", which is the event category parameter.

---

[33] The category name is "Purchase Incentives" and the action name is "Click". Note also that we avoid providing the full URL to the link destination because we are moving to another page on our site. Alternatively, if we desired, this link could be coded with the full URL with the same result. This latter coding would be, for example:

```
<a href="javascript:redir('Purchase Incentives', 'Click', '10% Off',
0,'http://www.googleanalytics.com/xqanqeon/purchase.html')"> 10% off today</a>
```

The full URL does need to appear in cases where the link takes the user to another website.

	Event Category	Total Events	↓ Unique Events	Event Value	Avg. Value
		188 % of Total: 100.00% (188)	**62** % of Total: 93.94% (66)	**4,284** % of Total: 100.00% (4,284)	**22.79** Site Avg: 22.79 (0.00%)
☐	1. xxangeon	**54** (28.72%)	5 (8.06%)	2,250 (52.52%)	41.67
☐	2. Scroll Test Page	**49** (26.06%)	8 (12.90%)	1,910 (44.58%)	38.98
☐	3. Form: Contact	**41** (21.81%)	19 (30.65%)	124 (2.89%)	3.02
☐	4. Purchase Incentives	**21** (11.17%)	16 (25.81%)	0 (0.00%)	0.00
☐	5. Download	**9** (4.79%)	9 (14.52%)	0 (0.00%)	0.00
☐	6. Videos	**8** (4.26%)	4 (6.45%)	0 (0.00%)	0.00
☐	7. Scroll Depth	**6** (3.19%)	1 (1.61%)	0 (0.00%)	0.00

The selection of an event category from the list allows us to see the actions associated with that category. In this case, there is only one action associated with the category "Purchase Incentives" (see below).

Primary Dimension: **Event Action**   Event Label   Other ▾

	Event Action	Total Events	↓ Unique Events	Event Value	Avg. Value
		21 % of Total: 4.64% (453)	**16** % of Total: 8.00% (200)	**0** % of Total: 0.00% (4,527)	**0.00** Site Avg: 9.99 (-100.00%)
☐	1. Click	**21**(100.00%)	16(100.00%)	0 (0.00%)	0.00

Clicking upon the **Event Action** "Click" brings up a chart of our three event labels (see below). Here, we can begin to see differences across offers, where "Lifetime Membership" appears to generate the least amount of interest, as reflected in its relatively low number of total and unique events. If you look at the HTML code for each link (shown on page 359), you'll notice that event value was set to zero. This decision is reflected in the **Event Value** and **Avg. Value** columns.

	Event Label	Total Events	↓ Unique Events	Event Value	Avg. Value
		21 % of Total: 11.17% (188)	**16** % of Total: 24.24% (66)	**0** % of Total: 0.00% (4,284)	**0.00** Site Avg: 22.79 (-100.00%)
☐	1. Free_Insurance	**10** (47.62%)	8 (44.44%)	0 (0.00%)	0.00
☐	2. 10%_Off	**7** (33.33%)	7 (38.89%)	0 (0.00%)	0.00
☐	3. Lifetime_Membership	**4** (19.05%)	3 (16.67%)	0 (0.00%)	0.00

We can look at the relationship between offer and transactions by selecting **Ecommerce** from the top of the page just beneath the **Explorer** tab (see below).

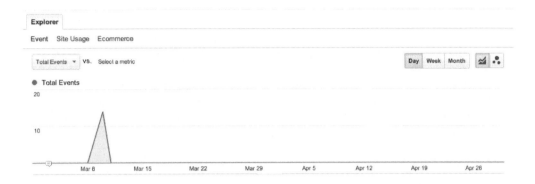

When **Ecommerce** is selected, the table shown below is generated (assuming that you are still on the **Event Label** display). This table shows our three label parameters where we can see significant differences across offers in terms of ultimate purchase behaviors. The number of sessions (equivalent to unique events in the earlier tables) is similar for "Free Insurance" and "10% Off". Both have nearly equal appeal. The effect of these links on purchase behaviors is, however, very different. The "Free Insurance" offer leads to higher overall revenue, more transactions per session, higher average order value, and higher per session value. Clearly this is the more powerful offer and should likely be the only one offered and emphasized.

Hands-on

While this material is fresh in your mind, try this exercise.

One of the pages we have provided you with is `chap48.html`. You can view this page by typing `chap48.html` at the end of your website's full URL. Visit this page to confirm that it is accessible.

We have already added the required javascript script to the page. You will need to add three link-triggered events to the page. The first step to accomplishing this is opening the page in your HTML editing program. As you review the HTML code you will see three instances of the following: REPLACE THIS WITH EVENT LINK TO PURCHASE PAGE. You'll need to replace each phrase with a different link-triggered event.

- All three of the events share the same category and action parameters: "Chapter 48" and "Click", respectively. The event labels are "Get an extra day free", "All meals paid", and "Free room upgrade."

Open the page in your HTML editing program. Generate and place the event HTML code in the web page. Once all three events have been added to the page, save your page under the same name and upload to your server. When you visit the page you should see the following, where your link order may be different than mine:

Welcome to Travel & Tour

As a special guest, choose one of the following:

This page sends one of three link triggered events to Google Analytics. The event sent reflects the link selected.

Get an extra day free

All meals paid

Free room upgrade

You can confirm that your events are working by using the **Real-Time** menu's **Events**. Log into your Google Analytics account and bring up the **Real-Time > Events** display. Click on **Events (last 30 min)**. At the moment, the display should be blank as no events have been activated. Now, in a separate browser window (or an entirely different browser, preferably Chrome), visit your chap48.html page. Click on each link, each of which should take you to the site's purchase page. When you return to your analytics **Real-Time > Events** display (after all three link clicks), you should see "Chapter 48" in the **Event Category** column. Click on **Events (last 30 min)** if it is not already selected and then click on "Chapter 48" to see the table of event actions and labels. If your link-activated events have worked properly, you should see each of the link-triggered events listed, as shown on the top of page 363. (If your links are not working, see the end of this chapter for the correct link form.)

Data generation is the next step. Visit `chap48.html` using your Chrome browser. On each visit click on one of the links. On some visits make a purchase. On other visits leave without making a purchase. Generate 25 to 30 visits and then try to answer the following questions using Google Analytics data to support your answer.

1. Which of the three links had the most appeal? Which had the least appeal?

2. Which of the three links had the greatest impact on site engagement? Which had the least impact?

3. Which of the three links had the greatest impact on purchase behaviors? Which had the lest impact?

4. Based on your responses to the prior questions, which, if any, link offer(s) would you continue to use?

The correct form for each of the three links is:

```
<a href="javascript:redir('Chapter 48', 'Click', 'Get an extra day free',
0,'purchase.html')">Get an extra day free</a>
```

```
<a href="javascript:redir('Chapter 48', 'Click', 'All meals paid',
0,'purchase.html')">All meals paid</a>
```

```
<a href="javascript:redir('Chapter 48', 'Click', 'Free room upgrade',
0,'purchase.html')">Free room upgrade</a>
```

49
Event Reporting

Chapters 47 and 48 introduced you to some of the event-related data reported by Google Analytics. This chapter takes a closer look at this data found within the **Behavior > Events** menu (see below.)

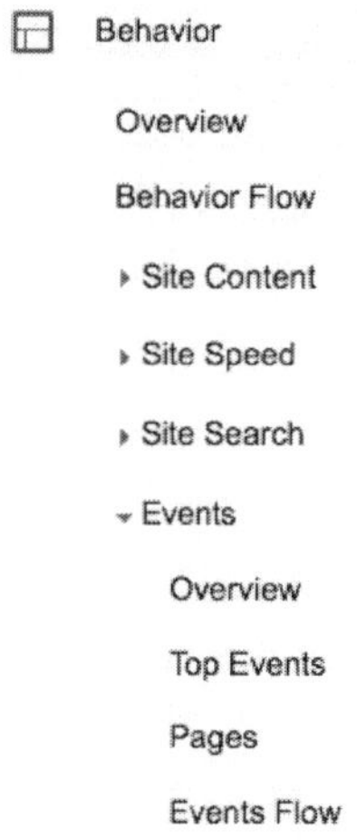

Behavior

    Overview

    Behavior Flow

    ▸ Site Content

    ▸ Site Speed

    ▸ Site Search

    ▾ Events

        Overview

        Top Events

        Pages

        Events Flow

Overview

The **Behavior > Events > Overview** report is organized similar to other overview reports, although the data reported here is focused on events. By default, the line chart on the top of the **Behavior > Events > Overview** page summarizes event activation for the total set of all events that occurred during the specified time period (see the display on the top of the next page). Keep in mind, however, that this is summative data that combines all events into a single display.

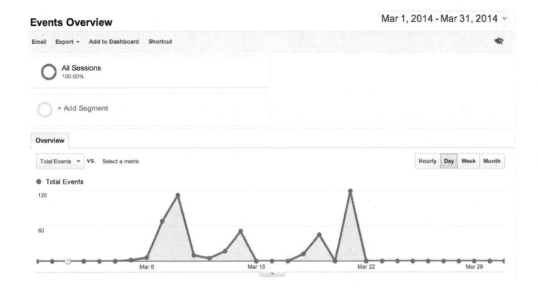

Beyond the default display of **Total Events**, you have the option of displaying additional event summary information by using the pull-down menu beneath **Overview** (see below).

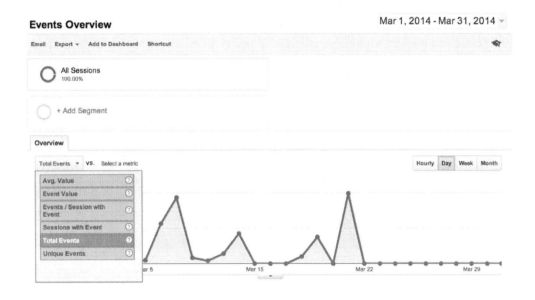

Selecting **Unique Events**, for example, displays the chart shown below.

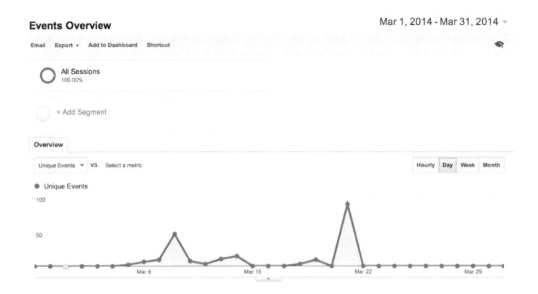

Finally, similar to all line charts, you can chart two dimensions at the same time by using the **Select a Metric** menu option. The chart shown below, for example, simultaneously charts "Unique Events" and "Total Events".

Google Analytics Demystified

The table on the middle of the **Behavior > Events > Overview** page provides numeric summary information for all events that have taken place during the specified time period (see below). Similar to other **Overview** pages, clicking on any small line graph changes the line chart display to that metric.

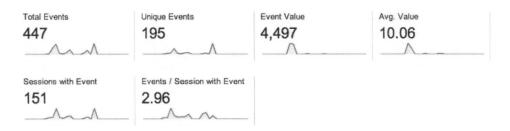

Total Events	Unique Events	Event Value	Avg. Value
447	195	4,497	10.06

Sessions with Event	Events / Session with Event
151	2.96

Once again, keep in mind that the preceding data may have limited value because they are summative and not specific to a single event.

You'll recall that you specify an event's category, action, and optional label when you create the event's HTML, for example:

ga('send', 'event', 'Videos', 'Play', 'Blog');

Here, "Videos" is the category, "Play" is the action, and "Blog" is the label.

Google Analytics uses this information to organize your event reports. The chart on the bottom of the **Behavior > Events > Overview** page provides insights into events organized by Category, Action or Label. By default, the display first focuses on events organized by Category parameters. The table shown below, for example, presents my ten categories of events with a percentage distribution by event category. This table is useful when you want to know which event categories are more or less likely to occur.

Top Events		Event Category	Total Events	% Total Events
Event Category	▸	1. Form: Contact	149	33.33%
Event Action		2. xxangeon	54	12.08%
Event Label		3. Scroll Test Page	49	10.96%
		4. Videos	35	7.83%
		5. Author	30	6.71%
		6. Topic	22	4.92%
		7. Purchase Incentives	21	4.70%
		8. Theme	20	4.47%
		9. Written_By	20	4.47%
		10. Download	14	3.13%

view full report

Clicking on the **Event Action** and **Event Label** links on the left-hand side of the table brings up similar charts, only now the charts present Action and Label metrics, as shown in the following two charts.

Top Events	Event Action	Total Events	% Total Events
Event Category	1. field filled	114	25.50%
Event Action ▶	2. scroll reach	103	23.04%
Event Label	3. Davis	52	11.63%
	4. submit	35	7.83%
	5. Play	26	5.82%
	6. Budget	25	5.59%
	7. Click	21	4.70%
	8. Ireland	14	3.13%
	9. Mexico-1	14	3.13%
	10. Budget_Travel	9	2.01%

view full report

Top Events	Event Label	Total Events	% Total Events
Event Category	1. Submit	51	15.89%
Event Action	2. click	35	10.90%
Event Label ▶	3. gender	23	7.17%
	4. http://www.youtube.com/watch?feature=player_embedded&v=ILDxENakeV8	23	7.17%
	5. 10%	19	5.92%
	6. 20%	19	5.92%
	7. 30%	17	5.30%
	8. email	17	5.30%
	9. name	13	4.05%
	10. 40%	10	3.12%

view full report

Top Events

The **Behavior > Events > Top Events** menu option repeats the list of events organized by event category, except now each event category is described not only in terms of total occurrence, but also, in terms of unique occurrence and value (see the table on the top of page 369). Similar to our analysis of pageviews, we can (for any individual event category) divide *total events* by *unique events*. The closer this ratio is to 1.0, the greater the proportion of that event triggered by different users.

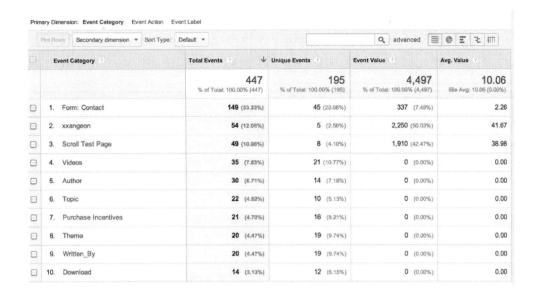

Primary Dimension: **Event Category** Event Action Event Label

	Event Category	Total Events ↓	Unique Events	Event Value	Avg. Value
		447 % of Total: 100.00% (447)	**195** % of Total: 100.00% (195)	**4,497** % of Total: 100.00% (4,497)	**10.06** Site Avg: 10.06 (0.00%)
☐	1. Form: Contact	**149** (33.33%)	45 (23.08%)	337 (7.49%)	2.26
☐	2. xxangeon	**54** (12.08%)	5 (2.56%)	2,250 (50.03%)	41.67
☐	3. Scroll Test Page	**49** (10.96%)	8 (4.10%)	1,910 (42.47%)	38.98
☐	4. Videos	**35** (7.83%)	21 (10.77%)	0 (0.00%)	0.00
☐	5. Author	**30** (6.71%)	14 (7.18%)	0 (0.00%)	0.00
☐	6. Topic	**22** (4.92%)	10 (5.13%)	0 (0.00%)	0.00
☐	7. Purchase Incentives	**21** (4.70%)	16 (8.21%)	0 (0.00%)	0.00
☐	8. Theme	**20** (4.47%)	19 (9.74%)	0 (0.00%)	0.00
☐	9. Written_By	**20** (4.47%)	19 (9.74%)	0 (0.00%)	0.00
☐	10. Download	**14** (3.13%)	12 (6.15%)	0 (0.00%)	0.00

Note that on the top of the above chart **Primary Dimension,** is set to **Event Category**. The other options for selecting the primary dimension allow you to see a chart focused on event actions or event labels, as shown in the following two tables.

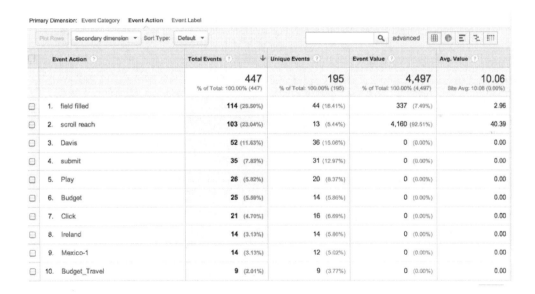

Primary Dimension: Event Category **Event Action** Event Label

	Event Action	Total Events ↓	Unique Events	Event Value	Avg. Value
		447 % of Total: 100.00% (447)	**195** % of Total: 100.00% (195)	**4,497** % of Total: 100.00% (4,497)	**10.06** Site Avg: 10.06 (0.00%)
☐	1. field filled	**114** (25.50%)	44 (18.41%)	337 (7.49%)	2.96
☐	2. scroll reach	**103** (23.04%)	13 (5.44%)	4,160 (92.51%)	40.39
☐	3. Davis	**52** (11.63%)	36 (15.06%)	0 (0.00%)	0.00
☐	4. submit	**35** (7.83%)	31 (12.97%)	0 (0.00%)	0.00
☐	5. Play	**26** (5.82%)	20 (8.37%)	0 (0.00%)	0.00
☐	6. Budget	**25** (5.59%)	14 (5.86%)	0 (0.00%)	0.00
☐	7. Click	**21** (4.70%)	16 (6.69%)	0 (0.00%)	0.00
☐	8. Ireland	**14** (3.13%)	14 (5.86%)	0 (0.00%)	0.00
☐	9. Mexico-1	**14** (3.13%)	12 (5.02%)	0 (0.00%)	0.00
☐	10. Budget_Travel	**9** (2.01%)	9 (3.77%)	0 (0.00%)	0.00

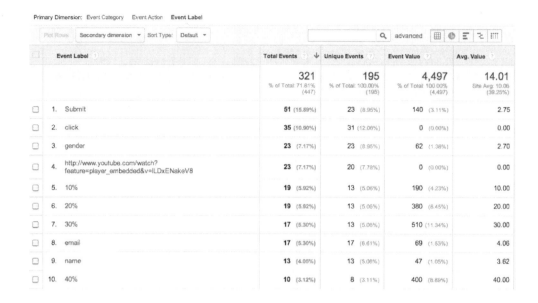

Primary Dimension: Event Category   Event Action   **Event Label**

	Event Label	Total Events ↓	Unique Events	Event Value	Avg. Value
		321 % of Total: 71.81% (447)	**195** % of Total: 100.00% (195)	**4,497** % of Total: 100.00% (4,497)	**14.01** Site Avg: 10.06 (39.25%)
☐ 1.	Submit	**51** (15.89%)	23 (8.95%)	140 (3.11%)	2.75
☐ 2.	click	**35** (10.90%)	31 (12.06%)	0 (0.00%)	0.00
☐ 3.	gender	**23** (7.17%)	23 (8.95%)	62 (1.38%)	2.70
☐ 4.	http://www.youtube.com/watch? feature=player_embedded&v=ILDxENakeV8	**23** (7.17%)	20 (7.78%)	0 (0.00%)	0.00
☐ 5.	10%	**19** (5.92%)	13 (5.06%)	190 (4.23%)	10.00
☐ 6.	20%	**19** (5.92%)	13 (5.06%)	380 (8.45%)	20.00
☐ 7.	30%	**17** (5.30%)	13 (5.06%)	510 (11.34%)	30.00
☐ 8.	email	**17** (5.30%)	17 (6.61%)	69 (1.53%)	4.06
☐ 9.	name	**13** (4.05%)	13 (5.06%)	47 (1.05%)	3.62
☐ 10.	40%	**10** (3.12%)	8 (3.11%)	400 (8.89%)	40.00

The advantage of the preceding three charts is that they provide information on all events in a single view. The disadvantage, however, is that the presence of multiple events in the same table makes it difficult to see the trends for just one single event category, action or label. Fortunately, this is easy to remedy.

You'll recall that selecting the **Behavior > Events > Top Events** menu option brings up a list of event categories (see the table on the top of the next page). The **Event Category,** "Topic", shown on line 6 of the table, relates to labeling of the topics of blog entries that can be read by site users. My site offers multiple blog entries addressing both budget travel and Europe. The goal is to see which topic, overall, is the most popular.

Two HTML event commands were used to collect the appropriate metrics:

ga('send', 'event', 'Topic', 'Budget');

ga('send', 'event', 'Topic', 'Europe');

The category "Topic" is the same for both events while the action parameter is used to label the topic as either "Budget" or "Europe."

The table below indicates that there have been 22 blog entries read (the number of total Topic events) with 10 of these being unique events. Thus, it appears that each site user read about two blog entries (as indicated in the ratio of total Topic events to unique Topic events).

Primary Dimension: **Event Category** Event Action Event Label

	Event Category ?	Total Events ?	↓ Unique Events ?	Event Value ?	Avg. Value ?
		447 % of Total: 100.00% (447)	195 % of Total: 100.00% (195)	4,497 % of Total: 100.00% (4,497)	10.06 Site Avg: 10.06 (0.00%)
☐ 1.	Form: Contact	149 (33.33%)	45 (23.08%)	337 (7.49%)	2.26
☐ 2.	xxangeon	54 (12.08%)	5 (2.56%)	2,250 (50.03%)	41.67
☐ 3.	Scroll Test Page	49 (10.96%)	8 (4.10%)	1,910 (42.47%)	38.98
☐ 4.	Videos	35 (7.83%)	21 (10.77%)	0 (0.00%)	0.00
☐ 5.	Author	30 (6.71%)	14 (7.18%)	0 (0.00%)	0.00
☐ 6.	Topic	22 (4.92%)	10 (5.13%)	0 (0.00%)	0.00

Clicking on the **Topic** category parameter in line 6 of the above table allows us to drill-down into the characteristics of just this one event category. After the category name is selected, a table presenting all actions associated with the category is displayed (see below). The table indicates that while both blog topics have been read, there is much more interest in budget versus European travel. Note that the **Event Action** labels are taken directly from the event's HTML commands.

Primary Dimension: **Event Action** Event Label Other ▼

	Event Action ?	Total Events ?	↓ Unique Events ?	Event Value ?	Avg. Value ?
		22 % of Total: 4.92% (447)	10 % of Total: 5.13% (195)	0 % of Total: 0.00% (4,497)	0.00 Site Avg: 10.06 (-100.00%)
☐ 1.	Budget	19 (86.36%)	8 (72.73%)	0 (0.00%)	0.00
☐ 2.	Europe	3 (13.64%)	3 (27.27%)	0 (0.00%)	0.00

Clicking on each link in the **Event Action** column brings up the list of **Event Labels** associated with that action, *if* this optional parameter has been used in the HTML code that provides the characteristics of the event. In this case, since no labels were used to describe this event, the resulting table presents no data, as shown below.

Primary Dimension: Event Action **Event Label** Other ▼

Event Label ?	Total Events ?	↓ Unique Events ?	Event Value ?	Avg. Value ?
	0 % of Total: 0.00% (9)	0 % of Total: 0.00% (0)	0 % of Total: 0.00% (0)	0.00 Site Avg: 0.00 (0.00%)

Pages

There are times when the same event is triggered from multiple pages. We could, for example, put event links for our special offers on four different pages of the website. In cases such as this, it is important to know the specific pages on which the event is taking place. This information is available though the **Behavior > Events > Pages** menu option, as shown below.

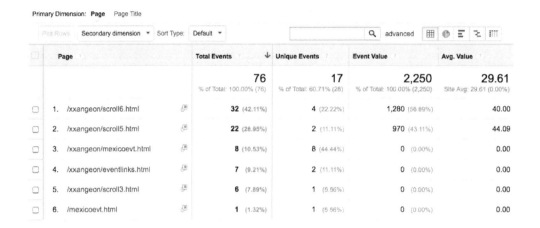

Clicking on the name of any individual page will bring up event information reports those events that occurred only on that page.

Events flow

The **Events Flow** chart (see top of page 373) is interpreted similarly to the flow charts discussed earlier, keeping in mind that the data reported here focus on the path to event triggers.

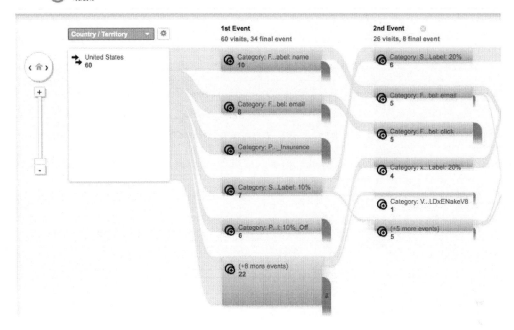

50
Events as Goals

Chapter 49 showed how events are reported as part of the **Behavior > Events** menu option. There are times, however, when you not only want to explore the data available through event reporting, but also, want to consider and examine events as website goals. Google Analytics allows you to do this.

> Your HTML code for naming and triggering the event should be present in your web page's HTML code prior to beginning goal creation.

Classifying events as goals

(The beginning of this section recaps the information from the goal creation discussion in Section VIII.)

You create goals through the **Admin** link on the top of every Google Analytics page. Once you click on this link, you'll see your administrator's page (see below). Make certain that the appropriate **Account, Property**, and **View** are displayed, and then click on the **Goals** link in the **View** column.

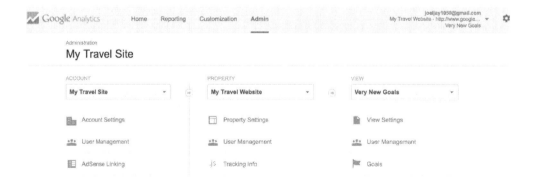

Your goals summary page will be displayed next (mine is shown below), showing all of the goals for the current view are displayed.

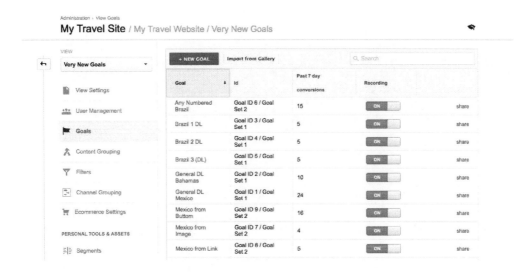

Clicking on **+ New Goal** brings us to the goal creation page (see below). The first step in creating an event-triggered goal is responding to the information requests in Step 1, **Goal description**. We give the goal a descriptive name by filling in the text box (in this case we'll call the goal "Any Mexico Download") and clicking on **Event** (under **Type**).

Clicking on **Next Step** brings up the display shown on the top of page 376 which collects the target event's characteristics.

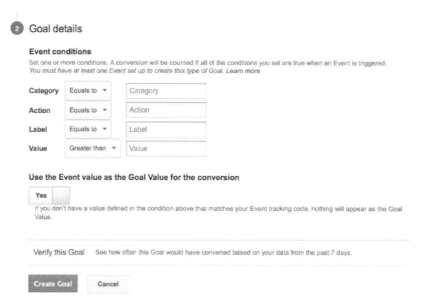

We fill in each text box with the event's characteristics, as shown below. Since there is no value associated with this goal, **Value** is left on the default **Yes**.

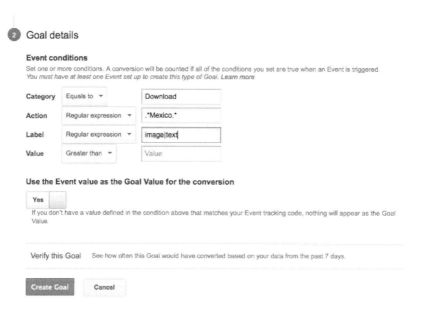

Note that we used regex in two places. First, since we are interested in any download containing the word "Mexico" we use regex to indicate this. Any action parameter containing "Mexico", for example, "Mexico1" or "3cMexico" will satisfy the action condition. Second, we are not interested in differentiating text from image links to the download, so we specify that either one qualifies for inclusion by using the regex | as the "or" statement., in this case "image|text".

Once we verify that all of the information is correct, we click on **Create Goal** to save the goal. The data relevant to this event-triggered goal will be reported identically to any other goals you created.

51
Events and Custom Segments

Chapter 39 discussed how goals can be used to create custom segments and how these segments inform strategic decision-making. Events can be used in a similar way.

Creating a custom segment using events

You create a custom segment using events similarly to the way you created custom segments using goals. You access segments via the **+Add Segment** option on the top of almost any page (located beneath the blue circle **All Sessions** identifier). When you click **+Add Segment**, the advanced segments page displays. You then begin the segment creation process by clicking the **+ New Segment** link. The segment creation page will then display.

Event metrics are incorporated into a segment's definition via the **Conditions** option, which is shown on the bottom left-hand side of the segment creation page. The selection of this option brings up the **Conditions** page, as shown below.

Pulling-down the menu currently labeled **Ad Content** displays both green and blue menu options. Within the green **Behavior** menu are three options related to events: Event Category, Event Action and Event Label (as shown on the top of the next page). The options are more easily found when you order the list alphabetically.

You can select any individual element or combination of elements to create the custom segment.

Let's illustrate the remainder of the process using two different types of events. One event triggers when the page is loaded, and the second event triggers from a link click. Both events have the same category and label:

- **category** is "Travel to Europe"

- **label** is "France"

The **action** for each event is different. The action for the page load event is "Activates on page load", while the action for the link-triggered event is "Activates on link click". We'll use these different actions to define our segments.

Let's create two custom segments based on these events using this scenario:

> Imagine that you have a blog page that describes travel to Europe, specifically France. You track those who visit the page through an event that triggers when the page is loaded. The page also provides a link to download a formatted, print-ready PDF of the blog. You track those who use this link through an event triggered when the link is clicked. Both events have the category, label, and action parameters described above. You want to be able to explore differences between those who visit the page and download versus those who visit the page and do not download.

The first custom segment will include those individuals who visited **both** the page (as this event was triggered automatically by a page visit) and clicked on the download PDF link (as this event was triggered by a user interaction on the same page).

On the initial **Conditions** screen, we begin by selecting **Event Action** from the pull-down menu. Next, we indicate the action that defines a visit to the blog page, as shown below:

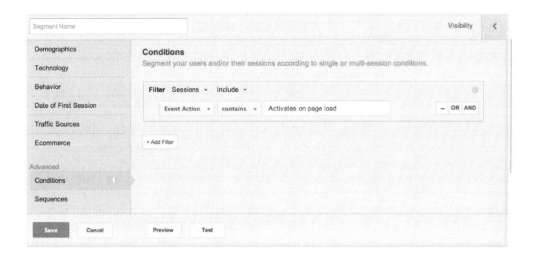

We leave **Sessions** and **Include** as the filters.

At the moment, the segment consists of all those who visited the page. We now need to restrict this segment to those who also downloaded the blog PDF. To do this, we click on **+Add Filter** which brings up the display shown below.

We now add the **Event Action** that signifies a download, i.e., "Activates on link click", as shown below. We leave **Sessions** and **Include** as the filters. We also name and test the segment, and if all looks correct we click **Save**.

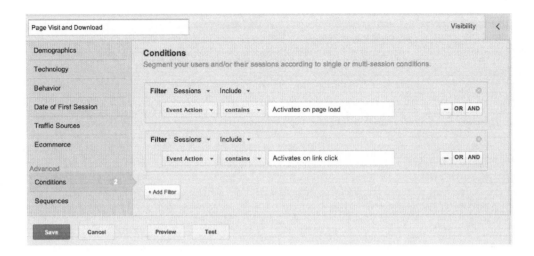

Let's now create the second custom segment. This segment will include all individuals who visited the page, but **did not** click on the link to download the PDF. We begin creating this segment in the same way as the previous segment, identifying all those who visited the page, as shown below.

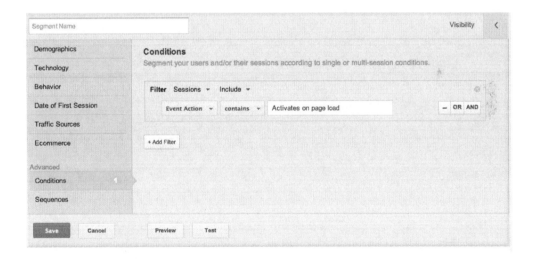

Now we need to now restrict this segment to those who did not download the PDF. To do this, we click on **+Add Filter** which brings up the display shown below.

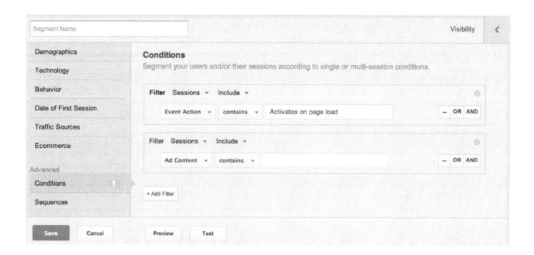

We add the **Event Action** that signifies a download, i.e., "Activates on link click", as shown below.

Now, however, while we once again leave **Sessions** as one of the filters, we select **Exclude** as the additional filter. As a result, the segment will contain only those who visited but did not download. We then name and test the segment, and if all looks correct we click **Save**.

Once created, event-related custom segments can be used in data analysis in the same way as goal-related custom segments.

52

Advanced Events: Page Scroll

You probably spend a lot of time planning your website or blog content. Ideally, by now you can see how Google Analytics can help you make better content-related strategic decisions by monitoring and reporting users' page and content interactions (for example, pages read, time spent on page, bounce rate, etc.). But without the use of events, Google Analytics cannot tell you *how much* of a page is actually read. This chapter explains how to set up and obtain data on "page scroll depth," the percentage of a page viewed by a site visitor.[34]

The first part of this chapter explains how to use events to monitor and analyze page scroll depth. The chapter ends with an opportunity for you practice creating this type of event yourself.

How the script works

The script first determines the total height of a web page and then divides the page into ten even splits (10% scroll). Next, the script finds the height of the site user's browser window and determines how many of those 10% splits the user can see when the page first loads. Finally, the script monitors the user's page scroll. When a user starts to scroll down the page, the script triggers an event when the user reaches each new 10% split.

The event command uses the following code format:

ga('send', 'event', title, 'scroll reach', '10%',10, {'nonInteraction': 1});

Title is the page title that the user is currently on and the 10% changes to reflect the split of the page to which the user has scrolled. The last field is set to **{'nonInteraction': 1}**, which tells Google Analytics to consider each event trigger a non-interaction event. This prevents distorting your pageview, bounce rate and related metrics.

---

[34] We will be using a script developed by Dave Taylor (http://dave-taylor.co.uk/blog/scroll-reach-tracking-in-google-analytics/) to track scroll depth. We have modified this script, however, to update the event commands to Universal Analytics.

One of your website pages that can only be reached by typing the page's URL directly into your browser is `chap52.html`. You can view this page by typing the page name at the end of your website's full URL. In my case, this is:

```
http://www.googleanalyticsdemystified.com/xqanqeon/chap52.html
```

Visit your `chap52.html` page to confirm that it is accessible.

We have already placed references to the two scripts you'll need to track scroll depth in the page's HTML code. The scripts themselves are already present on your site. You just need to do the following in order to use the scripts on your site.

1. Select the page you want to monitor, in this case `chap52.html`. Open the page in your HTML editing program. Make certain your Google Analytics tracking code is present on the page. Also make certain that you like the current page title, which is found between the **<title>** and **</title>** tags. You can change the title if you desire.

2. You need four lines of additional javascript on every page for which you want to track scroll depth. The lines are:

   <script src="https://ajax.googleapis.com/ajax/libs/jquery/1.7.2/jquery.min.js">

   </script>

   <script type="text/javascript" src="YOUR URL/google-analytics-scroll-tracking_ua.js">

   </script>

   As noted earlier, these lines have already been added to the page for you so that you can see their correct placement, which is just after the opening **<head>** command. All that you need to do is replace the phrase **YOUR URL** with the full URL to your site. Make certain that you use the full URL (that is, start with http://) and include the subdirectory, if one is used. My four lines of code would therefore look as follows:

   <script src="https://ajax.googleapis.com/ajax/libs/jquery/1.7.2/jquery.min.js">

   </script>

   <script type="text/javascript"
   src="http://www.googleanalyticsdemystified.com/xqanqeon/google-analytics-scroll-tracking_ua.js">

   </script>

3. Save the page and upload to your server. Do not change the page's name, that is, leave the page name `chap52.html`.

Once this is done, you can cut and paste the revised code to other pages for which you want to track scroll depth. Make certain that when you use this code on other pages, that you give each new page a descriptive title.

Interpreting the data

We access page scroll data through the **Behavior > Events > Top Events** menu which brings up a table similar to that shown below. Each website page containing the script will be listed using the page's title. In our case, the only page on which we incorporated the script is titled "Scroll Test Page." This page is shown in line three of the table shown below.

We click on the name of the page of interest to bring up the data related to this category's **Event Action** parameter (see below). The script automatically labels this "scroll reach."

Clicking on **scroll reach** brings up specific scroll information for the page, as illustrated in the table on the top of page 386. Note that the percentages are ordered in terms of **Total Events**, so they may not be listed in strict numeric order.

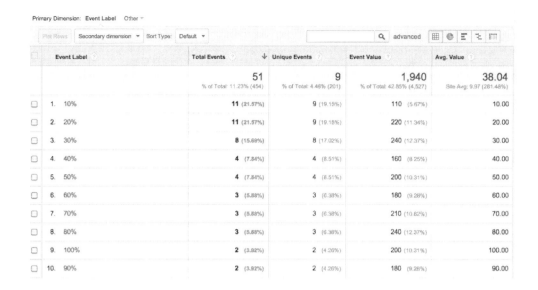

Primary Dimension: Event Label   Other ▾

Plot Rows   Secondary dimension ▾   Sort Type: Default ▾   🔍 advanced   ▦ ◐ ☰ ⇄ ⫼⫼⫼

	Event Label	Total Events ↓	Unique Events	Event Value	Avg. Value
		51 % of Total: 11.23% (454)	**9** % of Total: 4.46% (201)	**1,940** % of Total: 42.85% (4,527)	**38.04** Site Avg: 9.97 (281.48%)
☐ 1.	10%	11 (21.57%)	9 (19.15%)	110 (5.67%)	10.00
☐ 2.	20%	11 (21.57%)	9 (19.15%)	220 (11.34%)	20.00
☐ 3.	30%	8 (15.69%)	8 (17.02%)	240 (12.37%)	30.00
☐ 4.	40%	4 (7.84%)	4 (8.51%)	160 (8.25%)	40.00
☐ 5.	50%	4 (7.84%)	4 (8.51%)	200 (10.31%)	50.00
☐ 6.	60%	3 (5.88%)	3 (6.38%)	180 (9.28%)	60.00
☐ 7.	70%	3 (5.88%)	3 (6.38%)	210 (10.82%)	70.00
☐ 8.	80%	3 (5.88%)	3 (6.38%)	240 (12.37%)	80.00
☐ 9.	100%	2 (3.92%)	2 (4.26%)	200 (10.31%)	100.00
☐ 10.	90%	2 (3.92%)	2 (4.26%)	180 (9.28%)	90.00

Because of the way the script works, only some of the data is valuable. The **Average Value** on the right-hand side of the top line reports the average amount of page scrolling. In this case, the average depth of scrolling is 38.04%. So, only a bit more than one-third of the page (on average) is seen. This is not very good at all.

The **Total Events** column provides a distribution of how many individuals reached a certain point on the page. Since this data represents multiple scrolls for each individual, the key column is **Unique Events,** which reports the number of unique users reaching each scroll point. An **Event Label** of 10% or 20% (depending upon a page's total length) typically represents the number of pageviews, as this is the amount of the page that can typically be seen upon page load without the need for scrolling. The numbers decline moving down the **Unique Events** column, representing fewer and fewer individuals who scroll toward the end of the page. We can see that only three individuals read 80% of the page and only two scrolled to the bottom of the page reading 100% of the content. The content is simply not maintaining interest or engagement. We need a revised content strategy to increase the amount of content consumption.

Hands-on

While this material is fresh in your mind, let's confirm that your modifications to the javascript were correct.

You can always confirm that your scroll monitoring is working (that is, triggering when the page loads and is scrolled by a user) by using the **Real-Time** menu's **Events** option. Log into your Google Analytics account and bring up the **Real-Time > Events** display. Click on **Events (last 30 min)**. At the moment the display should be blank as no events have been activated. Now, in a separate browser window (or an entirely different browser, preferably Chrome), visit your chap52.html page that should be named "Scroll Test Page" unless you reamed the page following the directions on page 384. Begin to scroll down the page. Revisit your **Real-Time > Events** display where you should see a display similar to that shown below. It is only important that "Scroll Test Page" (or the renamed page title) appears in the **Event Category** column.

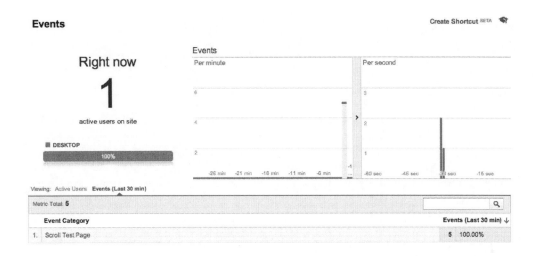

Click on **Scroll Test Page** (or the page title) to bring up the **Event Action** and **Event Label** display (see table below). If data appears in the two columns, then you have successfully monitored scroll depth.

53
Advanced Events:
Form Completion Monitoring

Forms, such as the one on our travel agency contact page, are an important way by which a website or blog begins to establish or reinforce a relationship with a site user. Google Analytics can tell us the number of people who send a form as well as the number of people who go to the form page without sending the form. Without events, however, Google Analytics cannot provide any diagnostics for the form itself. The use of events allows us to determine which fields (if any) are problematic and lead to form abandonment.[35]

How the script works

The script examines your form and identifies each field that needs a response. Every time a form user fills in a field, the script sends an event trigger to Google Analytics telling it that the field had been completed. In a perfect world, the number of pageviews for the page containing the form should equal the number of users completing every field on the form. The greater the discrepancy between the number of pageviews and form field completion, the greater the problem with that particular field.

Installing the script

Your website contact page (`contact.html`) contains a form with four fields. We have already placed the two scripts you'll need to track form completion in the page's HTML code. You just need to do the following in order to use the scripts on your site.

1. Select the page containing the form you want to monitor, in this case, `contact.html`. Open the page in your HTML editing program. Make certain your Google Analytics tracking code is present on the page. Also make sure that you like the current page title, which is found between the **\<title\>** and **\</title\>** tags. You can change the title if you desire.

---

[35] We will be using a script developed by Dave Taylor (http://dave-taylor.co.uk/blog/form-analytics-plugin-for-google-analytics/) to track form completion. We have modified this script, however, to make the event commands appropriate to Universal Analytics.

2. You need four lines of additional javascript on every page for which you want to track form completion. The lines are:

    <script src="https://ajax.googleapis.com/ajax/libs/jquery/1.7.2/jquery.min.js">

    </script>

    <script type="text/javascript" src="YOUR URL/form-tracking-google-analytics-v2.js">

    </script>

    As noted earlier, these lines have already been added to `contact.html` for you so that you can see the correct placement, which is just after the opening **<head>** command. All that you need to do is replace the phrase **YOUR URL** with the full URL to your site. Make certain that you use the full URL (that is, start with http://) and include the subdirectory, if one is used. My four lines of code would therefore look as follows:

    <script src="https://ajax.googleapis.com/ajax/libs/jquery/1.7.2/jquery.min.js">

    </script>

    <script type="text/javascript"
    src="http://www.googleanalyticsdemystified.com/xqanqeon/form-tracking-google-analytics-v2.js">

    </script>

3. Save the page and upload to your server. Do not change the page's name, which should remain `contact.html`.

Once this is done, you can cut and paste the revised code to other pages for which you want to track form completion. Make certain that when you use this code on other pages, that you give each new page a descriptive title.

Interpreting the data

Assume that we have placed the script on `contact.html`. We access form completion data through the **Behavior > Events > Top Events** menu option, which in this case brings up the table shown on the top of page 390.

The script automatically names the event category "Form: [Name of Page]", so in our case we are interested in the information relevant to the "Form: Contact" **Event Category**. Clicking on this link displays the page's **Event Action** table (see below).

We then click on the **field filled** link to bring up the following table. Because site users can fill in, leave and return to revise any field, we are interested in the **Unique Events** column rather than the **Total Events** column.

Each of the four fields in our contact form, as well as the submit button, are shown in the table. The data indicate problems with nearly all the form fields. The extent of these problems can be viewed in the context of the 23 people who submitted the form.

- The only information provided by all users was gender. Only about 74% of those submitting the form provided an email address. (This was calculated by dividing 17 by 23.) This is particularly distressing, as there is no opportunity to follow-up without an email address.

- The remaining two form fields, name and message, are even more problematic. Only about half of those submitting provided a name and only about one third provided a message.

Clearly our form isn't working. We need to redesign the form to facilitate the sending of complete information.

Hands-on

While this material is fresh in your mind, let's confirm that your form monitoring is working.

You can confirm that form monitoring is working (that is, triggering when a user completes a form field) by using the **Real-Time** menu's **Events** option. Log into your Google Analytics account and bring up the **Real-Time > Events** display. Click on **Events (last 30 min)**. At the moment, the display should be blank as no events have been activated. Now, in a separate browser window (or an entirely different browser, preferably Chrome), visit your contact page. Fill in the name form field and move to the email field. Now revisit your **Real-Time > Events** display. There you should see the display similar to that shown below, where "Form: name of your site - Contact" is shown in the **Event Category** column. (Ignore any prior events which might be displayed.)

Events   Create Shortcut BETA

	Event Category	Events (Last 30 min)	↓
1.	Form: Xqanqeon - Contact	1 100.00%	

Clicking on "Form: [Name of Page]" should display a table similar to the one shown below, where the first completed form field (shown in the **Event Label** column) is presented. Make certain that you select **Events (Last 30 min)** as the display parameter.

Now complete the form and press **Submit**. Revisit the **Real-Time** display after you see the contact confirmation page. You should see the following table indicating that all the fields have been completed and the form has been submitted.

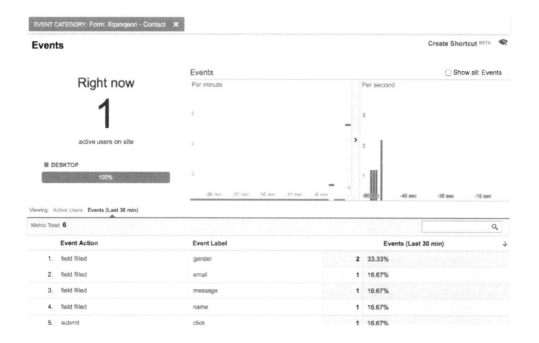

54

Advanced Events: Video Monitoring

The digital experience is moving from text to pictorial communication and as a result, increasing numbers of sites are integrating video and other visual elements into their websites and blogs. While Google Analytics can tell us the number of people who come to a page with video, without the use of events it cannot tell us whether the video was started and how much of the video was viewed.

How the script works

The script monitors a user's interaction with a video embedded on one of your website pages.[36] The script sends an event notification to Google Analytics when the video is started and at 25%, 50%, 75% and 100% of total video time actually viewed. The category label is set to "Video", the action label records the amount viewed, and the event label identifies the video by its YouTube identifier and name.

Installing the script

Your website "See a Video" page (`mediaplay.html`) contains a sample video and the scripts needed to monitor the video, as well as transmit the event information to Google Analytics. Visit the page to see the video and layout. You can access `mediaplay.html` via the link on the top of any travel agency site page.

You just need to do the following in order to use the script on your site.

1. Select the page containing the video you want to monitor, in this case, `mediaplay.html`. Open the page in your HTML editing program. Make certain your Google Analytics tracking code is present on the page. Also make sure that you like the current page title, which is found between the **<title>** and **</title>** tags. You can change the title if you desire.

---

[36] The script used to monitor video engagement was written by Stephane Hamel (http://www.cardinalpath.com/youtube-video-tracking-with-gtm-and-ua-a-step-by-step-guide). We have, however, made some modifications to eliminate the use of Google Tag Manager used in the original script in order to send event data to Google Analytics using the **ga (send, event)** command. We have also simplified/reduced the data sent to Google Analytics in an effort to simplify data interpretation. Finally, this script only works with YouTube video.

2. There is an extensive amount of javascript on the page, which is contained within two separate scripts. Both scripts appear in the page's HTML code just after the opening **<head>** tag. You do not need to customize any javascript in either of these scripts.

.

3. Find the line of HTML code that now reads:

    **<iframe width="420" height="315"
    src="http://www.youtube.com/embed/YTubeAddress?enablejsapi=1" frameborder="0"
    allowfullscreen></iframe>**

    The commands in this line pull the video from YouTube and place the video on your web page. Replace the phrase "YTubeAddress" with the unique address of the video when it plays at YouTube. For example, if you view a video at

    ```
    https://www.youtube.com/watch?v=MHgj2UzqMx0
    ```

    you would replace "YTubeAddress" with "MHgj2UzqMx0" and the line would read:

    **<iframe width="420" height="315"
    src="http://www.youtube.com/embed/MHgj2UzqMx0?enablejsapi=1"
    frameborder="0" allowfullscreen></iframe>**

    Complete this step with the video of your choice.

4. You have the option of altering the width and height of the video player by changing the width and height specifications in the beginning of the line. Leave the remainder of the line untouched.

5. Save the page and upload to your server. Do not change the page's name which should remain `mediaplay.html`.

You follow a similar procedure when you want to monitor videos on other pages. First, you need to place the javascript scripts immediately after the opening **<head>** tag. To facilitate this process, you can copy both scripts after the **<head>** tag on your `mediaplay.html` page onto your new page. Second, copy and paste the line of HTML code discussed in Step 3 in the place on the web page you want the video to appear. Make certain that you customize the line to incorporate the name of the video you want displayed.

Interpreting the data

We access the video interaction data through the **Behavior > Events > Top Events** menu option which brings up the display shown on the top of page 395. In this case, the only event listed in the Event Category column is named "Video", the category label used by the script. Note that since this script uses "Video" as the category label, you should avoid using this name to label other category events.

Primary Dimension: **Event Category**   Event Action   Event Label

	Event Category ?	Total Events ?	↓ Unique Events ?	Event Value ?	Avg. Value ?
		18 % of Total: 100.00% (18)	12 % of Total: 100.00% (12)	0 % of Total: 0.00% (0)	0.00 Site Avg: 0.00 (0.00%)
☐	1. Video	18 (100.00%)	12 (100.00%)	0 (0.00%)	0.00

The data presented in the table above is summative, that is, it reports metrics for all of the videos viewed on our site. We can see that there were twelve unique user sessions in which a video was started (as reported in the Unique Events column). Clicking **Video** brings up summary interaction information, as this information is reported via the Event Action (see table below). Again focusing on Unique Events, we can see that of the twelve people starting any video (as reported in the first line labeled 0%), only three watched at least 25% (as reported in line two) and only one made it all the way through (as reported in line 3).

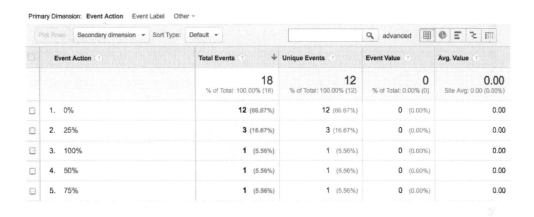

Primary Dimension: **Event Action**   Event Label   Other ▾

	Event Action ?	Total Events ?	↓ Unique Events ?	Event Value ?	Avg. Value ?
		18 % of Total: 100.00% (18)	12 % of Total: 100.00% (12)	0 % of Total: 0.00% (0)	0.00 Site Avg: 0.00 (0.00%)
☐	1. 0%	12 (66.67%)	12 (66.67%)	0 (0.00%)	0.00
☐	2. 25%	3 (16.67%)	3 (16.67%)	0 (0.00%)	0.00
☐	3. 100%	1 (5.56%)	1 (5.56%)	0 (0.00%)	0.00
☐	4. 50%	1 (5.56%)	1 (5.56%)	0 (0.00%)	0.00
☐	5. 75%	1 (5.56%)	1 (5.56%)	0 (0.00%)	0.00

Clicking on the Event Label option above the table allows us to see the specific videos viewed, as shown below.

Primary Dimension: Event Action   **Event Label**   Other ▾

	Event Label ?	Total Events ?	↓ Unique Events ?	Event Value ?	Avg. Value ?
		18 % of Total: 100.00% (18)	12 % of Total: 100.00% (12)	0 % of Total: 0.00% (0)	0.00 Site Avg: 0.00 (0.00%)
☐	1. QBQ63qb21po:Behold The Islands Of The Bahamas	12 (66.67%)	12 (66.67%)	0 (0.00%)	0.00
☐	2. _SPz_Jpf3aA:Mexico Tourism	2 (11.11%)	2 (11.11%)	0 (0.00%)	0.00
☐	3. nYihOr0pjT4:Atlantis, Paradise Island Bahamas	2 (11.11%)	2 (11.11%)	0 (0.00%)	0.00
☐	4. ro_88L1SkPg:Mexico City - Hidden America - TV Tourism Commercial - TV Advert - TV Spot - The Travel Channel	2 (11.11%)	2 (11.11%)	0 (0.00%)	0.00

While these summative findings are informative, we also want to look at the performance of individual videos. We can do this by using custom segments. Here, we create a segment to select only those individuals who visit the page hosting the video of interest. Let's focus on `mediaplay.html`, our "See a Video" page. We set up this custom segment, as shown below:

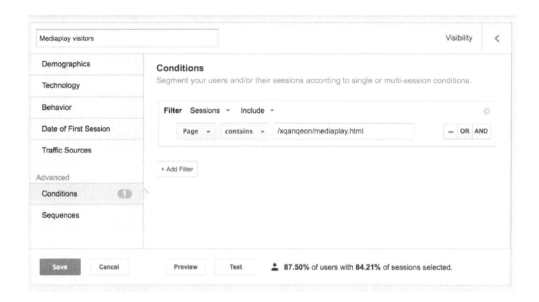

Then, when we select this segment as our sample, data is reported only for the video available on the page, as shown below:

Now that we've isolated a specific video, we can click on **Event Action** above the table to view engagement metrics, as shown on the top of page 397. The results are depressing. Again focusing on **Unique Events**, we can see that of the seven people who started this video (as reported in the first line labeled 0%) only two watched at least 25% (as reported in line two) and only one made it all the way through (as reported in line 3).

The final step puts our video interaction metrics in context by looking at behaviors specific to the page hosting the video. We can see how many users visited the page, as well as other important metrics, through the **Behavior > Site Content > All Pages** option (which generates the table shown below). These metrics reinforce our initial impression that this is an ineffective video. First, you'll recall that twelve people started the video, but we can now see (via the Unique Pageviews column) that 16 users visited the page. Thus, only three-quarters of page visitors even started the video. In addition, the vast majority of page visitors left our site from this page, indicating that the content, including the video, was of little interest and of little value for fostering further site engagement.

Hands-on

While this material is fresh in mind, let's confirm that your modifications to the HTML code were correct.

You can confirm that your video monitoring is working by using the **Real-Time** menu's **Events** option. Log into your Google Analytics account and bring up the **Real-Time > Events** display. Click on **Events (last 30 min)**. At the moment, the display should be blank as no events have been activated. Now, in a separate browser window (or an entirely different browser, preferably Chrome), visit your `mediaplay.html` page.

Watch the video all the way through. Now, revisit your **Real-Time > Events** display where you should see a display similar to that shown below.

Click on the **Video** link in the **Event Category** column. This should generate a table similar to that shown below. Here, in the **Event Action** column, you can see that one person started the video (as reflected in the top 0% line), and that one person watched the video all the way to the end (as reflected in the 25%, 50%. 75% and 100% lines). The name of the video being viewed is shown in the **Event Label** column.

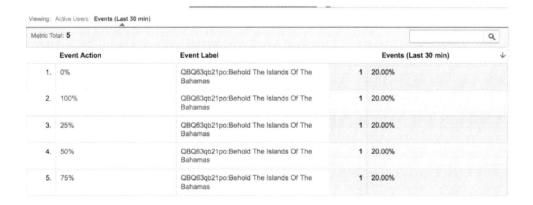

Section XI:
Referral Sources

One of the most powerful aspects of Google Analytics is the ability to track the origin of website users and to relate various origins to the broad range of data provided, including page interactions, goal conversions, conversion paths, user characteristics, and transactions. The chapters in this section help you better understand how to find and apply this data to your own strategic decision-making.

-   You will need to generate referral traffic to your site. Chapter 55 shows you how to create and generate data from sources external to your website.

-   Chapter 56 discusses the form, interpretation and application of data available through the Acquisition menu.

-   Chapter 57 shows you the power of treating your own links as referral sources.

-   Chapter 58 discusses the form, interpretation and application of data available through the Campaign menu.

-    Chapter 59 provides practice exercises to reinforce the content of the previous four chapters.

55

Generating Referral Sources

In order for you to explore Google Analytics' acquisition and social metrics, it's necessary to expand the range of external sources that send users to your site. This chapter shows you how to create these sources by opening accounts for your travel agency website at Wordpress and Facebook. You'll also post one or more comments at the Google+ account associated with the email address you created for this book.

Creating and using these referral sources will help you in two ways. First, they will allow you to generate data that will be used for later discussion of Google Analytics acquisition, social media, and attribution data. Second, the use of these sources will help you to better understand how to promote your real website or blog.

> ✓ You may already have accounts at one or both of these locations. Nevertheless, we recommend that you open new accounts so that your experimentation does not harm your real accounts or confuse those who visit those locations.

Wordpress

You register for a free Wordpress account at:

`https://signup.wordpress.com/signup/` as shown below.

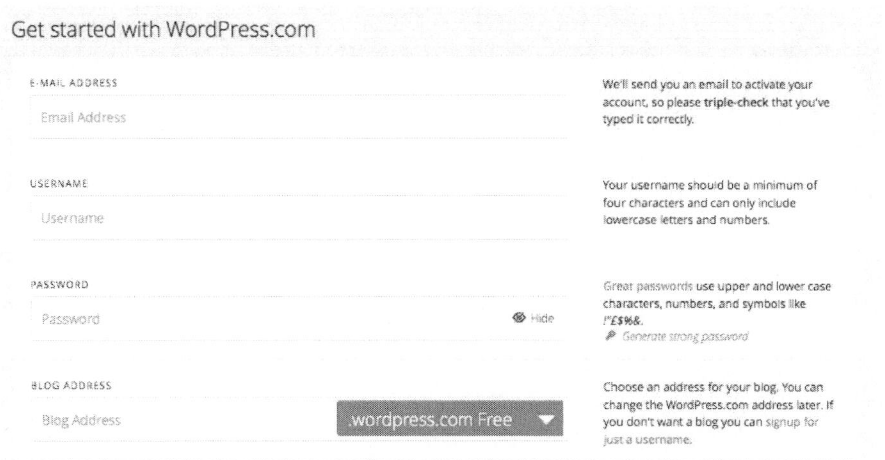

Get started with WordPress.com

E-MAIL ADDRESS
Email Address

We'll send you an email to activate your account, so please **triple-check** that you've typed it correctly.

USERNAME
Username

Your username should be a minimum of four characters and can only include lowercase letters and numbers.

PASSWORD
Password   👁 Hide

Great passwords use upper and lower case characters, numbers, and symbols like !"£$%&.
🔑 Generate strong password

BLOG ADDRESS
Blog Address   .wordpress.com Free ▼

Choose an address for your blog. You can change the WordPress.com address later. If you don't want a blog you can signup for just a username.

Complete the form with the following information:

- Use the Google email address you created for use with this book

- Pick any username and password that you can remember

- Use the unique name you created for your website for your blog address

When done, scroll to the bottom of the page and click **Create Blog** in the Wordpress.com **Beginner** column.

The next several pages provide your opportunity to create your blog. Do the following:

- The first page asks you to set up your blog. The default information prefilled on the page is fine. Click **Next Step**.

- On the next page (Step 2), choose your free theme and click **Next Step** (if you don't automatically move on to the next step after theme selection).

- The next page (Step 3) asks if you want to customize your blog. Since no customization is necessary, just click **Next Step**.

- There is no need to share on Facebook or Twitter, so just press **Next Step** for Step 4.

- Step 5 asks you to create your first post. Click on the **Text** icon. On the next page provide a title and the text for your post. (Mine is shown below.) Click **Next Step** when you are finished.

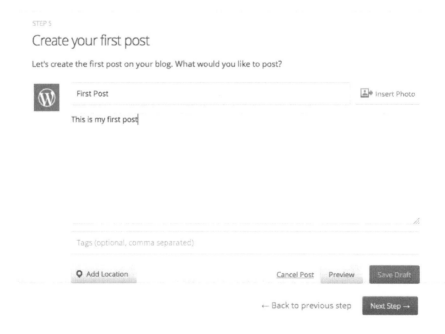

- Finally, on the next page, confirm your email address. Once your email is confirmed via the email sent to your account by Wordpress, you will see the page shown below . Be sure to check your spam folder if the email does not appear.

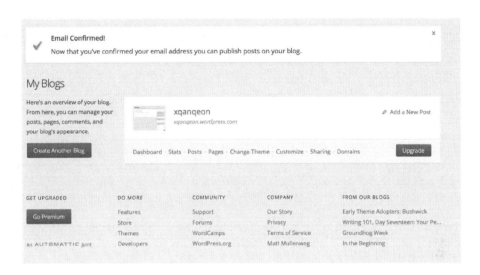

At this point sign out by moving your mouse over the picture icon on the top of the page (see below).

Now we're going to add two links that go from your Wordpress blog to your travel agency site. To begin this process, go to http://wordpress.com and sign in with your user-name or email address and password. On the top of the next page, click on **New Post**. Click on **Text**. If you don't see the opportunity to do this, then click on **My Blog** on the top of the page to continue. When asked "What do you want to post?" select **Text**. You goal for both approaches is the screen shown on the top of page 404.

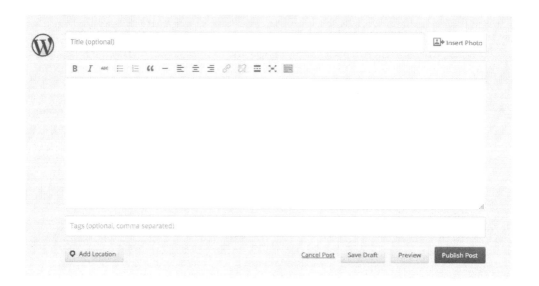

Type a title in the top text box. Your title should be: "Link to my travel site." In the large text box, type: "Here is a link to my home page" and "Here is a link to my purchase page" as shown below.

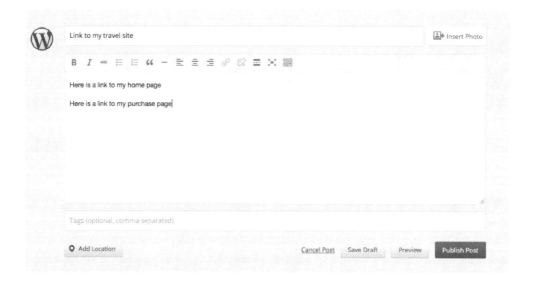

Highlight the first line of text and then click on the **Insert/Edit Link** icon, which is the fifth icon from the right above the large text box. A new pop up window will appear (see top of next page).

In the top text box type in the full URL to the homepage of your travel site. Leave the title blank and press **Add Link**. Do the same to change the second line to a link to your purchase page. This latter URL will consist of the full URL to your site followed by /purchase.html, as shown below for my site.

`http://www.googleanalyticsdemystified.com/xqanqeon/purchase.html`

When you are done, press **Publish Post** and you will see the confirmation page, as shown below.

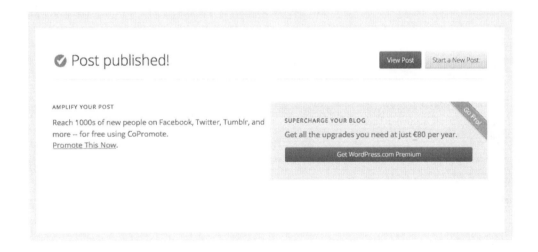

Click on **View Post** to see your post. My page looks like that shown on the top of page 406. (Note that your page may look different to reflect a different theme selection.)

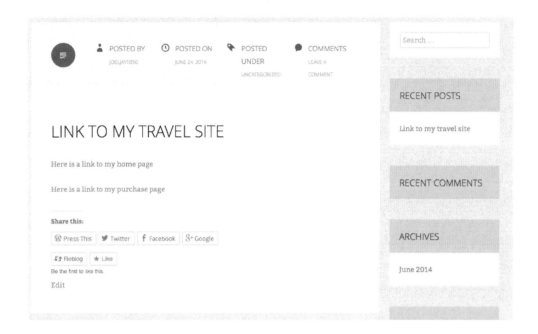

Check each link to make certain that it works as intended. If so, great. If not, click on **Edit** (beneath the **Share this** icons) to edit your links. Selecting this option may take you to a page resembling the initial page you used to create your links, or to a page resembling that shown below. In either case, the process is the same: highlight the link, click on the **Insert/Edit Link** icon, edit and save the link, and then save the revised post by selecting the **Update** option on the center, right-hand side of the page. The top of the page will then indicate that the post has been updated. Click on **View Post** (on the top of the page) to return to your blog.

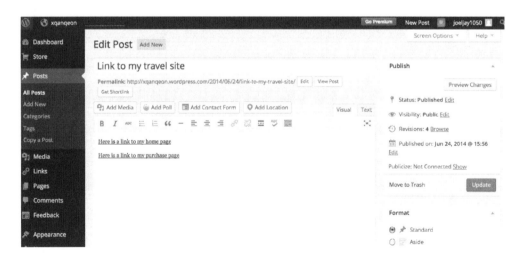

When you return to your blog, note the URL to this post. The full URL to my first blog page is:

`http://xqanqeon.wordpress.com/2014/06/24/link-to-my-travel-site/`

This full URL is what I give to those I want to visit this particular blog post. The beginning URL:

`http://xqanqeon.wordpress.com`

is what I give when I want them to visit my blog without a specific target page.

Facebook

Your second referrer will be your business Facebook page.

Open a new Facebook account using the gmail address you created for this book. You can register for Facebook at `https://www.facebook.com/r.php`.

Skip all informational pages following the main sign up page and you will eventually see your main Facebook page (shown below). Be certain to confirm your email address.

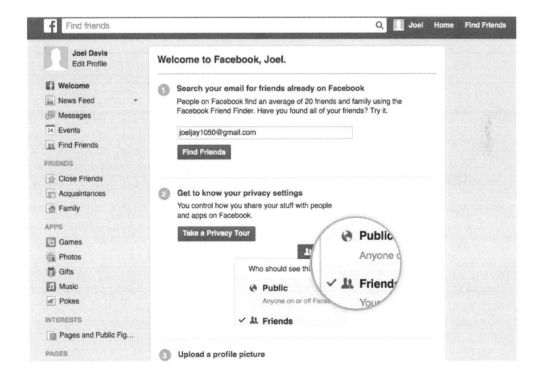

Now, while still logged into Facebook you'll need to create your business page. You get started at:

`https://www.facebook.com/pages/create/`

where you click on the icon labeled **Local Business or Place**. Doing so brings up the registration screen shown to the right. Select **Tours/Sightseeing** for business type. Use your web site's unique name for your business name. If you don't want to provide your own personal information to complete the form, you can use the information at Fake Name Generator instead.[37] When you are done, click **Get Started**.

Local Business or Place

| Choose a category ▼ |
| Business or Place Name |
| Street Address |
| City/State |
| Zip Code |
| Phone |

☐ I agree to Facebook Pages Terms

Get Started

The next page (shown below) asks for more information on your business. For category, type "Travel Agency" and for description put "Practice". Finally, put the full URL to your website's home page in the bottom text box and indicate that this is not a real organization. When done, select **Save Info**.

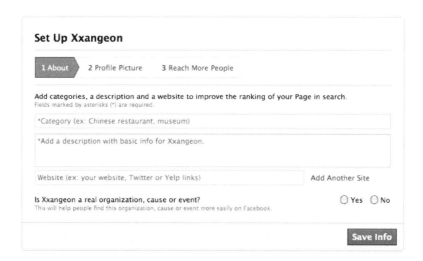

Skip the next three steps and you will arrive at your Facebook administrator's page. Scroll down until you see the text box that asks: "What have you been up to?" Click inside this box and you will see a screen similar to that shown on the top of the next page.

_____

[37] Fake Name generator is located at: http://www.fakenamegenerator.com/

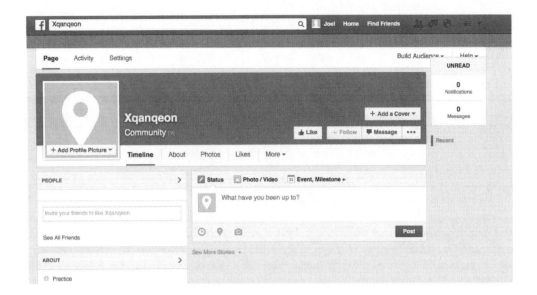

In the box type the following four lines:

> This is a URL to my homepage:
>
> http://www.googleanalyticsdemystified.com/xqanqeon
>
> This is a URL to my purchase page:
>
> http://www.googleanalyticsdemystified.com/xqanqeon/
> purchase.html

Press **Post** (in the lower right corner, see display above) when done. When the page updates you should see your post, as shown below.

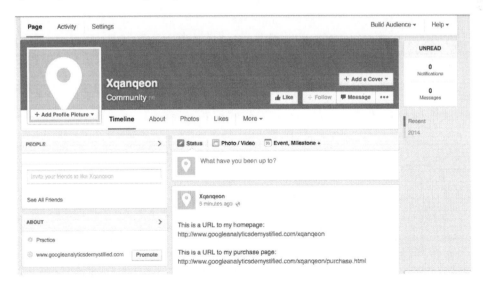

Now it's time to find your Facebook URL and test your first post. To find your URL, log into to Facebook using your normal Facebook account. Do a search for your company page. Once you arrive at the page, note the page's URL. My company page is located at:

`https://www.facebook.com/pages/Xqanqeon/1474258716149286`

Keep this handy for future reference. Then, check the links in your first post to make certain that they work as intended. Edit or leave as is, as appropriate.

Create a Google+ account

A series of icons appear on the top of your Gmail page to the right of the search bar. One of these will show your name with a plus in front. Click on this to begin the process of creating a Google+ account. Skip "Add People" and "Follow the things you love" by clicking on the **Continue** button on the bottom of the page. The, when asked, confirm that you don't mind being lonely. On the next page leave the page as is and click the **Finish** button. That's it.

Generating social referral data

The next several chapters will be more meaningful to you if you have your own data to examine. Now that you've set up your Wordpress and Facebook pages, share the addresses (URLs) with your friends. Ask them to select the link of their choice from each location and visit your site, perhaps making a purchase (or not). Try to get at least 50 or so referrals. In addition, ask your friends to type the unique name of your site into different search engines, visit your site through the search engine links, and then perhaps make a purchase (or not). Try to get at least 20 search engine referrals.

Google+ Comments

It will also be advantageous to have comments for Google+ to analyze. Click on the +[your name] on the top of your Gmail page. You'll be taken to a page similar in format to that shown below.

On the top left-hand side is a text box labeled "Share what's new." Select **Text** and then click in the box to see the overlay window shown on the top of the next page.

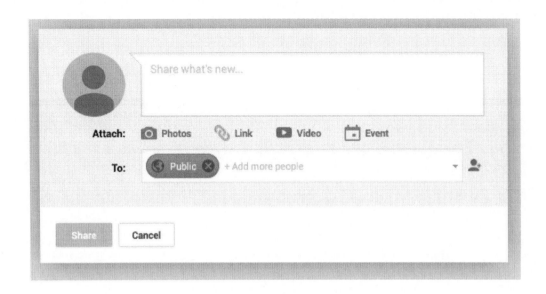

Type a comment about your travel website in the box making certain to use the unique name of the site in the comment. Leave **To:** set to public and click **Share**. Your comment should appear on the updated page. Leave two or three comments over the next several days. You can also encourage your friends who have Google+ accounts to log into Google+, do a search for your website's unique name, and leave a comment on your posts.

56
The Acquisition Menu

The **Acquisition** menu (see below) provides insights regarding the sources of your website users. While there is a significant amount of information available through this menu, we'll focus on uses that have more universal appeal, skipping metrics that relate to AdWords and paid advertising cost analysis.

Overview

Acquisition > Overview helps you understand how your website traffic is influenced by broad groupings of referral sources called **Channels**. These channels are predefined by Google Analytics and consist of the following:[38]

Direct	Sessions in which a user typed your website URL directly into his/her browser or who came to your site via a bookmark.
Email	Sessions that are manually tagged with a medium of "email". (Tagging is explained in the next chapter.)

---

[38] These existing channels should meet the needs of most websites and blogs. You can, however, visit and edit these channels by selecting **Channel Settings** in the **View** column of your Administrator's page. At this same location, if needed, you can create new channels that reflect your unique information or strategic needs. Source for channel definitions is "About MCF funnels" at: https://support.google.com/analytics/answer/1191184?hl=en.

Organic Search	Non-paid users to your site whose sessions begin at a search engine. Google tracks organic traffic from itself and most of the major search engines such as Bing and Yahoo. You can, if necessary, add additional search engines.
Paid Search	Traffic from the AdWords Search Network or other search engines identified as "cost per click" or "pay per click."
Referral	Traffic from other websites not identified as social that link to your site.
Social	Traffic from social media sites like Facebook, Linkedin and Twitter. Referrals from links tagged as ads are not considered a social referral.
Display	Interactions with a medium of "display" or "cpm". This channel also includes AdWords interactions with the ad distribution network set to "content" but excluding ad format of "text".
Paid Search	Traffic from the AdWords Search Network or other search engines, with a medium of "cpc" or "ppc" .
Other Advertising	Sessions that are tagged with a medium of "cpc", "ppc", "cpm", "cpv", "cpa", "cpp", "content-text", "affiliate" (excluding paid search).

There are two parts to the **Acquisition > Overview** display. The data on the top of the page provides summary data via pie and line charts (see below). By default, the pie chart displays the distribution of channels, while the line charts display sessions and transactions over time.

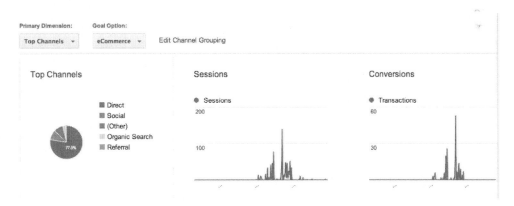

The data displayed in these charts are determined by the two pull-down menus on the top left-hand side of the page. The **Primary Dimension** menu allows you to change the data source from Channels to Sources/Mediums, as shown below.

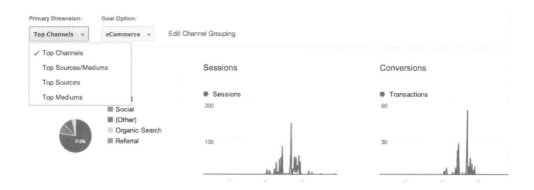

Selecting **Top Sources**, for example, changes the pie chart report to the distribution of specific sources that have initiated website referrals (see below).

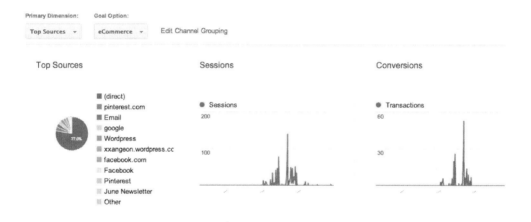

The **Goal Option** pull-down menu allows you to change the outcome measure to all goals or any specific goal (see the top of page 415).

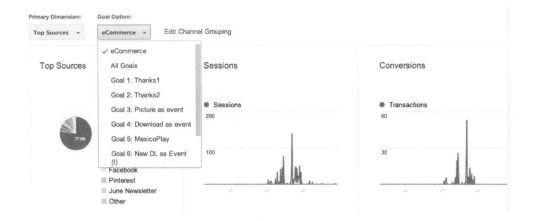

Selecting "Goal 1: Thanks 1", for example, changes the display to that shown below. This selection changes the line chart shown on the far right-hand side of the page as well as the Conversion data shown in the tables on the bottom of the **Acquisition > Overview** page.

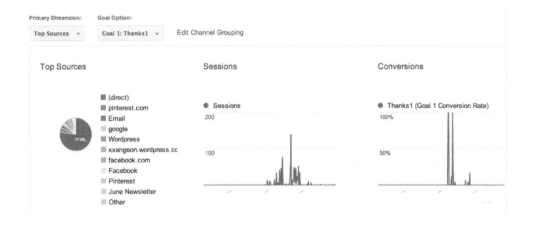

The numeric table shown on the bottom of **Acquisition > Overview** page provides detailed information on the selected Primary Dimension/Goal Option combination. The table shown on the top of page 416, for example, is the default table reporting **Top Channels** (from the Primary Dimension pull-down menu) and **Ecommerce** (from the Goal Option pull-down menu). Notice that three types of information are provided: Acquisition, Behavior and Conversion.

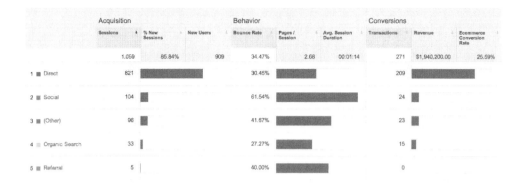

	Acquisition			Behavior			Conversions		
	Sessions	% New Sessions	New Users	Bounce Rate	Pages / Session	Avg. Session Duration	Transactions	Revenue	Ecommerce Conversion Rate
	1,059	85.84%	909	34.47%	2.68	00:01:14	271	$1,940,200.00	25.59%
1 ■ Direct	821			30.45%			209		
2 ■ Social	104			61.54%			24		
3 ■ (Other)	96			41.67%			23		
4 ■ Organic Search	33			27.27%			15		
5 ■ Referral	5			40.00%			0		

The top summary line indicates that overall, in terms of **Acquisition**, I've had 1,059 site sessions of which 85.84% were new sessions. This makes sense given that the vast majority of our site users (909) were new users. The **Behavior** block of data provides information on average bounce rate (34.47%), average pages per session (2.68), and average session duration (one minute and 14 seconds). Finally, the **Conversions** block of data provides information on total conversions (271), total revenue ($1,940,200), and average ecommerce conversion rate (25.59%).

Beneath the top summary line is a list of each referral source as defined by the Primary Dimension pull-down menu. Since the previous table was defined by **Top Channels**, each top referral channel is shown. (Note **(Other)** consists of sessions for which no referral source could be determined.) We can see that most of my site traffic is Direct, with Social providing some secondary support. Very little of my traffic is due to Organic Search or third-party referrals. These low levels might be unsatisfactory and we may need to develop strategies to increase referrals from these sources. We'll need more information, however, before we reach a final decision.

Clicking on the name of a channel or any of the bar charts brings up more detailed information relevant to that channel. Clicking on **Direct** (or any of it's bars), for example, brings up information on the landing pages used for direct access, as shown below.

Google Analytics Demystified

Clicking on **Social** provides more information on each social referrer (see below).

Primary Dimension: Social Network   Landing Page   Other ▾

Social Network	Acquisition			Behavior			Conversions eCommerce ▾			
	Sessions ↓	% New Sessions	New Users	Bounce Rate	Pages / Session	Avg. Session Duration	Transactions	Revenue	Ecommerce Conversion Rate
	104	78.85%	82	61.54%	2.35	00:00:21	24	$133,900.00	23.08%
	% of Total: 9.82% (1,059)	Site Avg: 85.84% (-8.14%)	% of Total: 9.02% (909)	Site Avg: 34.47% (78.55%)	Site Avg: 2.68 (-12.48%)	Site Avg: 00:01:14 (-72.00%)	% of Total: 8.85% (271)	% of Total: 6.90% ($1,940,200.00)	Site Avg: 25.59% (-9.82%)
1. Pinterest	41 (39.42%)	73.17%	30 (36.59%)	48.78%	2.63	00:00:42	10 (41.67%)	$61,300.00 (45.78%)	24.39%
2. WordPress	36 (34.62%)	86.11%	31 (37.80%)	52.78%	2.92	00:00:11	12 (50.00%)	$68,600.00 (51.23%)	33.33%
3. Facebook	27 (25.96%)	77.78%	21 (25.61%)	92.59%	1.15	00:00:01	2 (8.33%)	$4,000.00 (2.99%)	7.41%

Clicking on **Organic Search** provides more information on search terms used to find the site (when available), as shown below. We discuss the problems associated with **(not provided)** later, in the **Keywords** section of this chapter.

Primary Dimension: Keyword   Source   Landing Page   Other ▾

Keyword	Acquisition			Behavior			Conversions eCommerce ▾			
	Sessions ↓	% New Sessions	New Users	Bounce Rate	Pages / Session	Avg. Session Duration	Transactions	Revenue	Ecommerce Conversion Rate
	33	63.64%	21	27.27%	4.18	00:01:19	15	$226,200.00	45.45%
	% of Total: 3.12% (1,059)	Site Avg: 85.84% (-25.86%)	% of Total: 2.31% (909)	Site Avg: 34.47% (-20.87%)	Site Avg: 2.68 (55.99%)	Site Avg: 00:01:14 (6.97%)	% of Total: 5.54% (271)	% of Total: 11.66% ($1,940,200.00)	Site Avg: 25.59% (77.62%)
1. (not provided)	31 (93.94%)	67.74%	21 (100.00%)	25.81%	4.16	00:00:16	15 (100.00%)	$226,200.00 (100.00%)	48.39%
2. xxangeon	2 (6.06%)	0.00%	0 (0.00%)	50.00%	4.50	00:17:40	0 (0.00%)	$0.00 (0.00%)	0.00%

Finally, clicking on **Referral** displays the source(s) of third-party referrals, as shown below.

Primary Dimension: Source   Landing Page   Other ▾

Source	Acquisition			Behavior			Conversions eCommerce ▾			
	Sessions ↓	% New Sessions	New Users	Bounce Rate	Pages / Session	Avg. Session Duration	Transactions	Revenue	Ecommerce Conversion Rate
	5	40.00%	2	40.00%	7.20	00:01:02	0	$0.00	0.00%
	% of Total: 0.47% (1,059)	Site Avg: 85.84% (-53.40%)	% of Total: 0.22% (909)	Site Avg: 34.47% (16.05%)	Site Avg: 2.68 (168.57%)	Site Avg: 00:01:14 (-16.48%)	% of Total: 0.00% (271)	% of Total: 0.00% ($1,940,200.00)	Site Avg: 25.59% (-100.00%)
1. search.freefind.com	3 (60.00%)	33.33%	1 (50.00%)	66.67%	9.67	00:01:04	0 (0.00%)	$0.00 (0.00%)	0.00%
2. app.hublo.com	2 (40.00%)	50.00%	1 (50.00%)	0.00%	3.50	00:01:00	0 (0.00%)	$0.00 (0.00%)	0.00%

Channels

Selecting **Acquisition > Channels** displays the same broad channels as **Acquisition > Overview**, but more detailed data are provided for each channel grouping. You'll recall that the numeric table on the **Acquisition > Overview** page used bars to indicate relative size. The **Acquisition > Channels** option moves beyond this visual to display the underlying data, as shown below. Note that the three categories of data shown on the **Acquisition > Overview** page are also shown here.

Once again, we can see the dominance of Direct as the primary way users initiate site sessions and we can see the secondary importance of social referrals. Now, however, we can examine these findings in more detail. Here's is what we learn from the chart:

-   Direct site sessions are more likely to be new users versus all of the remaining referral sources.

-   The bounce rate for Social is much higher than all of the remaining referral sources.

-   The ecommerce conversion rate for Organic Search is much higher than for other sources while the conversion rate for Referrals is much worse than for the other referral sources.

-   In terms of gross revenue, Direct is clearly the most important, accounting for about 72.5% of all revenue.

We can focus more deeply on the site usage and ecommerce metrics by selecting each data view from the **Explorer** tab.

Selecting **Ecommerce** from the top of page **Explorer** tab displays the table shown on the top of page 419. Here, we find that while the overall share of revenue from Social referrals is relatively low, Social contributes a disproportionate share. This is a good source of ecommerce revenue and should be strategically strengthened. Third-party referrals, on the other hand, show the opposite pattern. The complete absence of revenue from this source indicates that sessions initiated from here are of little value, and little effort likely needs to be paid to increasing this source of site sessions. Finally, while the relative contribution of Organic Search is low, the per session value and average order value are much higher than that of other channels. Our business should improve dramatically if we were able to increase sessions from this channel.

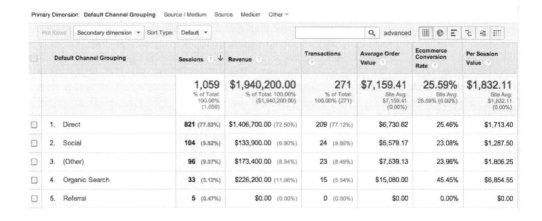

Default Channel Grouping	Sessions ⬇	Revenue	Transactions	Average Order Value	Ecommerce Conversion Rate	Per Session Value
	1,059 % of Total: 100.00% (1,059)	**$1,940,200.00** % of Total: 100.00% ($1,940,200.00)	**271** % of Total: 100.00% (271)	**$7,159.41** Site Avg: $7,159.41 (0.00%)	**25.59%** Site Avg: 25.59% (0.00%)	**$1,832.11** Site Avg: $1,832.11 (0.00%)
1. Direct	821 (77.53%)	$1,406,700.00 (72.50%)	209 (77.12%)	$6,730.62	25.46%	$1,713.40
2. Social	104 (9.82%)	$133,900.00 (6.90%)	24 (8.86%)	$5,579.17	23.08%	$1,287.50
3. (Other)	96 (9.07%)	$173,400.00 (8.94%)	23 (8.49%)	$7,539.13	23.96%	$1,806.25
4. Organic Search	33 (3.12%)	$226,200.00 (11.66%)	15 (5.54%)	$15,080.00	45.45%	$6,854.55
5. Referral	5 (0.47%)	$0.00 (0.00%)	0 (0.00%)	$0.00	0.00%	$0.00

Selecting **Site Usage** from the top of page **Explorer** tab displays the following table, which helps to explain the high value obtained from sessions initiated through Organic Search. These sessions show much higher engagement as Pages/Session is relatively higher than for other channels while the Bounce Rate is much lower.

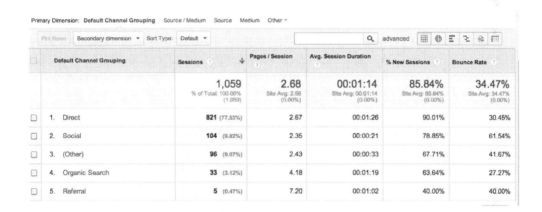

Default Channel Grouping	Sessions ⬇	Pages / Session	Avg. Session Duration	% New Sessions	Bounce Rate
	1,059 % of Total: 100.00% (1,059)	**2.68** Site Avg: 2.68 (0.00%)	**00:01:14** Site Avg: 00:01:14 (0.00%)	**85.84%** Site Avg: 85.84% (0.00%)	**34.47%** Site Avg: 34.47% (0.00%)
1. Direct	821 (77.53%)	2.67	00:01:26	90.01%	30.45%
2. Social	104 (9.82%)	2.35	00:00:21	78.85%	61.54%
3. (Other)	96 (9.07%)	2.43	00:00:33	67.71%	41.67%
4. Organic Search	33 (3.12%)	4.18	00:01:19	63.64%	27.27%
5. Referral	5 (0.47%)	7.20	00:01:02	40.00%	40.00%

As with **Acquisition > Overview**, clicking on any named channel brings up more detailed information on just that channel.

All traffic

The **Acquisition > All Traffic** report provides user referral metrics categorized by:

- **Source**: This is the search engine or referring domain from which traffic to your site originated, for example, *google* (the search engine) or *google.com* (the domain). Direct traffic that does not originate from search-engine results or a referring link in a domain is identified as *(direct)*.

- **Medium**: The type of web content that contained the link to your site. For example, when traffic originates from links in organic search results, then the medium is identified as *organic*; when the traffic originates from links in banner ads, then the medium is identified as *banner*. The medium for direct traffic for which there is no originating link is identified as *(none)*.

This is illustrated by the combinations shown in the first column of the table shown below. Here, as we've seen on earlier charts, the overwhelming source of my site sessions is Direct/(none) which means that individuals are most likely to come to my site either by typing the URL directly into their browser or by using a bookmark to the site. All other specific Source/Medium combinations play a secondary role.

An understanding of site traffic origins helps you make better informed decisions about where to focus your marketing efforts.

All referrals

The information in the **Acquisition > All Referrals** report (see the top of page 421) lets you see which domains (and pages in those domains) are referring traffic to your site, how much traffic they're referring, which landing pages are the most popular referral destinations, and the extent to which those referred visitors interact with your site. As a result, this report not only lets you see traffic levels from expected sources, but also lets you see whether there are unexpected sources (such as a review, blog post, or news story) you didn't know about.

Google's shift to secure, encrypted search in late 2013 has resulted in many Google Analytics users seeing the largest segment of their Keyword report being **(not provided)**. This is because encrypted Google searches don't pass the keyword data through to websites, eliminating the ability to see which keywords are bringing users to the site or blog. The table below illustrates this phenomenon.

Several individuals have proposed workarounds to this problem. Their recommendations can be found at:

Google '(Not Provided)' Keywords: 10 Ways to Get Organic Search Data at:

http://searchenginewatch.com/article/2297674/
Google-Not-Provided-Keywords-10-Ways-to-Get-Organic-Search-Data

Smarter Data Analysis of Google's https (not provided) change: 5 Steps at:

http://www.kaushik.net/avinash/google-secure-search-keyword-
data-analysis/

How to Unlock Your 'Not Provided' Keywords in Google Analytics at:

http://blog.kissmetrics.com/unlock-keyword-not-provided/

57
Tagging Links

Chapter 56 illustrated how Google Analytics tracks and reports the sources of your website or blog users. While this information helps you assess the relative use and value of different referral sources, it does not provide the depth of data needed to determine the relative value of specific pages or links from individual referral sources. For example, Google Analytics can tell you the number of people visiting your website via your blog, but without your assistance it cannot easily tell you which individual posts are generating relatively more or less referrals. Similarly, without your assistance Google Analytics will have difficulty determining how many visits are generated from different emails or from different links within the same email. Fortunately, this assistance is easy to provide.

One way that you can help Google Analytics collect more detailed information on referral sources is by tagging your links. This chapter explains the value of tagged links and how to create this type of link.

The value of tagged links

Imagine that email is an important way by which you communicate with current and potential site users. Every week you send out an email that features a different cruise package. There are three links placed at different points in the email (the beginning, middle and end) and all three links take the user to the same page on your website. This page has been specially created to work with the email and is only accessible via the links within the email. You invest a lot of time and money in developing the email promotions, which are designed to drive traffic to the special offer page. Given this goal, you need to answer two strategic questions:

- Overall, how effective is the email in generating site visits?

- Which link placement is the most effective in generating site visits?

These questions cannot be answered when untagged links are used. A click on a normal (i.e., untagged link) will only bring the email recipient to the appropriate page on your site and Google Analytics will treat all three links in exactly the same way. It will not identify which link was used nor will it give the link in the email credit for the site referral. This is illustrated on the top of page 423, where we are using the **Real-Time > Traffic Sources** menu to see the source of site sessions. A click on an untagged link in an email shows that Google Analytics records this as a direct referral, the same type of referral as when one types the page URL directly into a browser. (This can be seen by the information provided beneath the number of active users on the left-hand side of the display). As a result this classification does not allow us to answer either of the prior two strategic questions.

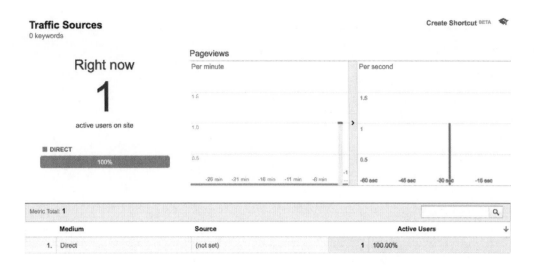

Link tagging allows us to add additional information to a link so that Google Analytics can more precisely track how a site user came to the site. In this example, we can tell Google Analytics to treat each link as if it were part of a marketing campaign, to record that the campaign was conducted via email, and that each link has a specific placement in the email. We'll see how to do this later in this chapter, but for now, let's create these labels for each link using the Google Analytics terms "Source," "Medium", and "Campaign".

Link #1

Source	June 23 Cruise Offer
Medium	Email
Campaign	Top of page

Link #2

Source	June 23 Cruise Offer
Medium	Email
Campaign	Middle of page

Link #3

Source	June 23 Cruise Offer
Medium	Email
Campaign	Bottom of page

Note how all links share common Source and Medium labels. This is because all appear in the same email and all relate to the same cruise offer. We use the campaign slot to label link placement within the email.

The **Real-Time > Traffic Sources** display shown below is what appears when we click on the data related to Link #1. Note how the display has changed from the previous in several important ways. First, Google Analytics notes that the user came to the site as part of a campaign, rather than directly. (This can be seen by the label beneath the number of active users.) Second, our labels for the referral's Medium and Source are shown in the Medium and Source columns. We now know exactly where the user is coming from.

Imagine that email recipients continue to click through to the site, resulting in ten visits, as shown in the figure on the top of page 425. As we continue to monitor this data, we can *begin* to answer the first question posed earlier: "Overall, how effective is the email in generating site visits?" Over the next few days, after more data has been collected, we will examine the data available through the **Acquisition > Campaign** menus to try to definitively answer this question.[39]

---

[39] The next chapter discusses how to access tagged link data from Google Analytics menus and provides direction for the analysis of this data. At the moment we are using Real Time data just to illustrate the type of data available through tagged links.

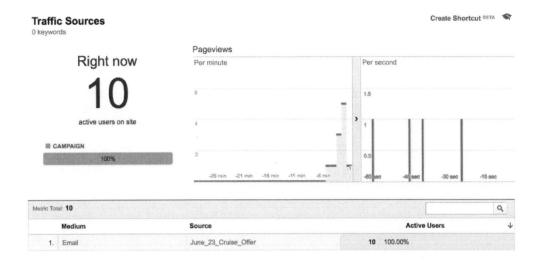

A click on "Email" in the **Medium** column brings up the display shown below.

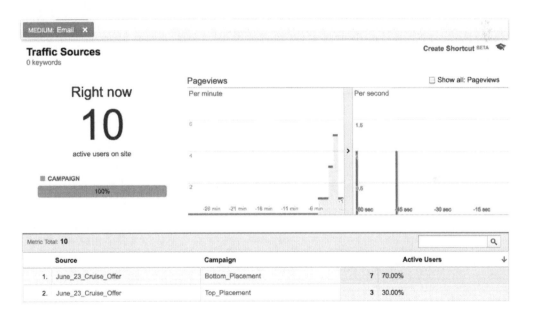

Note that the source of the data, the June 23 cruise offer, is shown in the **Source** column. The **Campaign** column displays link placement. In both cases, the names shown reflect how we labeled each link on page 423. The **Active Users** column shows the distribution of email recipients who clicked on one of the email links. Note: (1) how the link placed on the bottom of the email drives much more traffic to the site and (2) the absence of "Middle Placement" in the list, indicating that no one clicked on the link placed in the middle of the email. As noted earlier, our analysis would continue through the **Behavior > Campaigns** menu option as more data is collected.

As you know, text links typically appear on a digital property as a colored underlined word or phrase. Consider the link "learn about email". You would expect that a click on this link would take you to a page that explains email basics. While "learn about email" is what is displayed, the actual command for taking you to the linked page is hidden in the HTML code.

The HTML code for the "learn about email" link would be:

<a href = http://www.mysite.com/email/email.html><learn about email</a>

where the link's destination is: `http://www.mysite.com/email/email.html` and the text that appears on the web page is: **learn about email**.

A Google Analytics tag adds additional information to the end of a standard URL link. All tags in Google Analytics start with a question mark and utm_ followed by the name of the tag, an equal sign, and the tag label. Google Analytics allows a tag to contain up to five types of information. The table below provides the three types of information Google Analytics requires all tags to contain. Since you will have only occasional opportunities to use the remaining two tags, these are omitted from the discussion.

Tag Name	Tag	Definition	Example
Source	utm_source	The marketing vehicle or source of the referral	June Newsletter Wordpress Facebook Pinterest
Medium	utm_medium	The digital medium that conveyed the link	Email Blog post
Campaign	utm_campaign	The identifier for the specific referral source	Spring sale 10% off offer

Let's incorporate each of the prior example's link characteristics into this table:

Tag Name	Tag	Definition	Label
Source	utm_source	The marketing vehicle or source of the referral	June 23 cruise offer
Medium	utm_medium	The digital medium that conveyed the link	Email
Campaign	utm_campaign	The identifier for the specific referral source	Top_placement, or Middle_placement, or Bottom_placement

Using this information, Link #1 would appear as follows, where all the recipient would see is "Visit Now" and selecting the link would take the user to the page at `purchase1. html`.

<a href = http://www.googleanalyticsdemstified.com/xqanqeon/purchase1.html?utm_source=June_ 23_cruise_offer&utm_medium=Email&utm_campaign=Top_placement>Visit Now</a>

Fortunately, we don't have to create these links manually. Google provides a link tag generator that allows us to type in our labels and destination URL after which Google generates a fully tagged link. The link tag generator is located at:

`https://support.google.com/analytics/answer/1033867?hl=en`

The first screen you'll see when you visit the tag generator is shown below. This screen provides a text field for you to input the full URL of the link's target page, as well as each of the link parameters you want to use. Note that the three parameters discussed earlier are required and are marked with an asterisk.

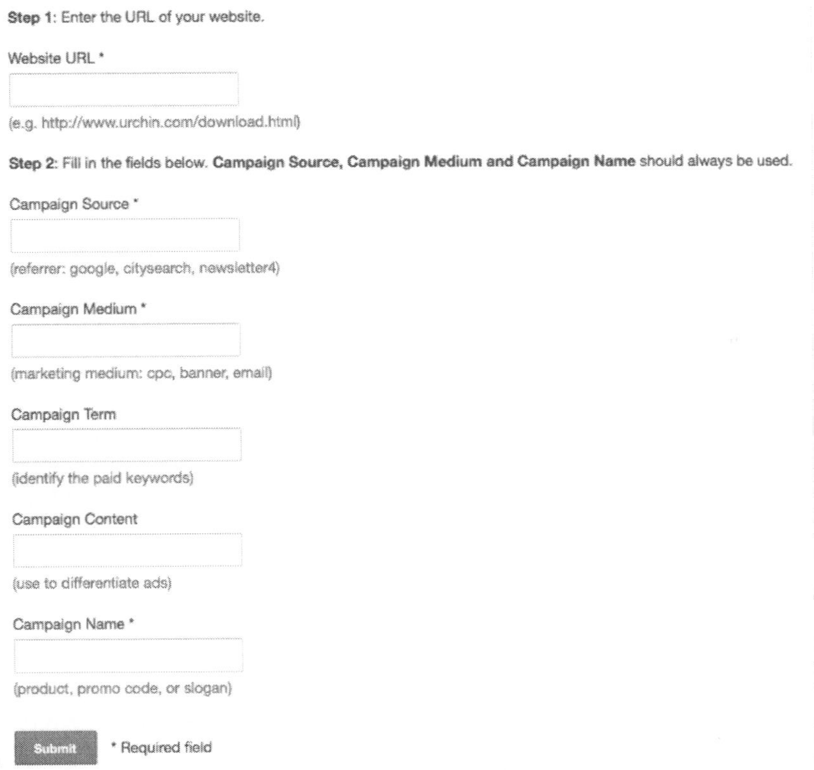

Step 1: Enter the URL of your website.

Website URL *

(e.g. http://www.urchin.com/download.html)

Step 2: Fill in the fields below. **Campaign Source, Campaign Medium and Campaign Name** should always be used.

Campaign Source *

(referrer: google, citysearch, newsletter4)

Campaign Medium *

(marketing medium: cpc, banner, email)

Campaign Term

(identify the paid keywords)

Campaign Content

(use to differentiate ads)

Campaign Name *

(product, promo code, or slogan)

[Submit]   * Required field

The display below illustrates how the link generator form looks when we type in the information for Link #1 from the example on page 426.

Step 1: Enter the URL of your website.

Website URL *

> .com/xqanqeon/purchase1.html

(e.g. http://www.urchin.com/download.html)

Step 2: Fill in the fields below. **Campaign Source, Campaign Medium and Campaign Name** should always be used.

Campaign Source *

> June_23_cruise offer

(referrer: google, citysearch, newsletter4)

Campaign Medium *

> Email

(marketing medium: cpc, banner, email)

Campaign Term

(identify the paid keywords)

Campaign Content

(use to differentiate ads)

Campaign Name *

> Top_placement|

(product, promo code, or slogan)

[Submit]   * Required field

Clicking on **Submit** provides the full tagged link below. Just copy and use this link where appropriate.

[Submit]

http://www.googleanalyticsdemystified.com/xqanqeon/purchase1.html?utm_source=June_23_cruise%20offer&utm_medium=Email&utm_campaign=Top_placement

58

The Campaigns Menu

The **Acquisition > Campaigns** menu (see below) allows you to see data related to your tagged links. This menu option does not have any submenus.

We'll explore the type of data provided from this menu option in the context of the following scenario.

The scenario

Consider a situation in which you promote a special offer through your Facebook page, your blog, and an email newsletter. The offer is communicated through a video post that offers individuals a two cabin upgrade if they buy a tour through the use of one of these links. Each of these links takes the user to a special purchase page. You want to determine which referral source is better at driving traffic to the site and fostering positive purchase behaviors.

You'll monitor each referral source via tagged links that have the following characteristics: the Source tag will be different for each link, but all three links will have the same Medium and Campaign tags. The Source tag identifies the referral source.

Source	utm_source	The marketing vehicle or source of the referral	Facebook, or Blog, or Email
Medium	utm_medium	The digital medium which conveyed the link	Video Post
Campaign	utm_campaign	The identifier for the specific referral source	2 cabin upgrade

All three links are generated with Google's link tag generator as shown below:

<a href =
http://www.googleanalyticsdemstified.com/xqanqeon/sale1.html?utm_source=Facebook
&utm_medium=Video_Post&utm_campaign=2_cabin_upgrade>Visit Now</a>

<a href =
http://www.googleanalyticsdemstified.com/xqanqeon/sale1.html?utm_source=Blog&utm
_medium=Video_Post&utm_campaign=2_cabin_upgrade>Visit Now</a>

<a href =
http://www.googleanalyticsdemstified.com/xqanqeon/sale1.html?utm_source=Email&ut
m_medium=Video_Post&utm_campaign=2_cabin_upgrade>Visit Now</a>

Campaign metrics

Clicking on **Acquisition > Campaigns** brings up a summary display of all campaigns initiated during the specified time period. The display on the top of the page contains important information (see below). First, the **All Sessions** graphic (on the top, left-hand side of the page) indicates the size of the session base underlying all of the campaign-related data reports. In this case, 73.33% of all site sessions were related to one or more campaigns.

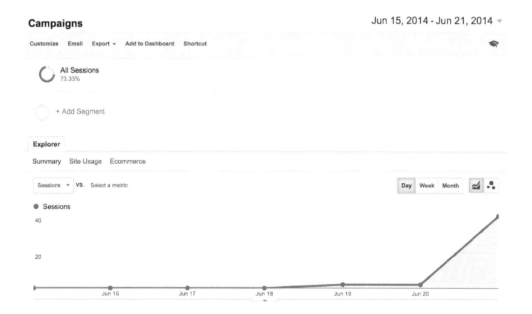

Second, there are three data display options beneath the **Explorer** tab on the left-hand side of the page. Each option changes both the line chart and the tabular data display shown on the bottom of the **Acquisition > Campaigns** page. All three options present data for each campaign conducted during the specified time period. The **Summary** option summarizes acquisition, behavior and conversion metrics (see top table below). The **Site Usage** option summarizes site behavior and engagement metrics (see middle table below). Finally, the **Ecommerce** option provides ecommerce-specific metrics (see bottom table below).

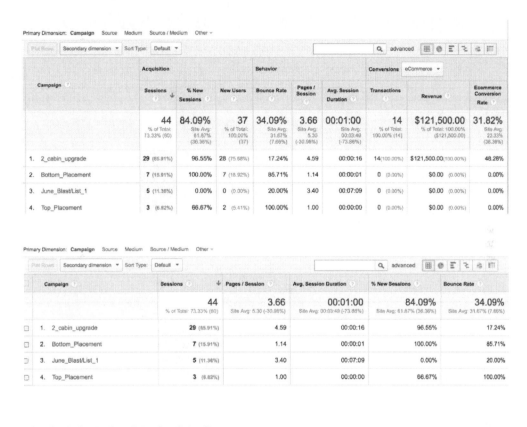

Primary Dimension: **Campaign**   Source   Medium   Source / Medium   Other ▾

Campaign	Acquisition			Behavior			Conversions eCommerce ▾		
	Sessions ↓	% New Sessions	New Users	Bounce Rate	Pages / Session	Avg. Session Duration	Transactions	Revenue	Ecommerce Conversion Rate
	44 % of Total: 73.33% (60)	84.09% Site Avg: 61.87% (36.36%)	37 % of Total: 100.00% (37)	34.09% Site Avg: 31.87% (7.66%)	3.66 Site Avg: 5.30 (-30.98%)	00:01:00 Site Avg: 00:03:49 (-73.86%)	14 % of Total: 100.00% (14)	$121,500.00 % of Total: 100.00% ($121,500.00)	31.82% Site Avg: 23.33% (36.36%)
1. 2_cabin_upgrade	29 (65.91%)	96.55%	28 (75.68%)	17.24%	4.59	00:00:16	14 (100.00%)	$121,500.00 (100.00%)	48.28%
2. Bottom_Placement	7 (15.91%)	100.00%	7 (18.92%)	85.71%	1.14	00:00:01	0 (0.00%)	$0.00 (0.00%)	0.00%
3. June_Blast/List_1	5 (11.36%)	0.00%	0 (0.00%)	20.00%	3.40	00:07:09	0 (0.00%)	$0.00 (0.00%)	0.00%
4. Top_Placement	3 (6.82%)	66.67%	2 (5.41%)	100.00%	1.00	00:00:00	0 (0.00%)	$0.00 (0.00%)	0.00%

Primary Dimension: **Campaign**   Source   Medium   Source / Medium   Other ▾

Campaign	Sessions	Pages / Session ↓	Avg. Session Duration	% New Sessions	Bounce Rate
	44 % of Total: 73.33% (60)	3.66 Site Avg: 5.30 (-30.98%)	00:01:00 Site Avg: 00:03:49 (-73.86%)	84.09% Site Avg: 61.87% (36.36%)	34.09% Site Avg: 31.87% (7.66%)
1. 2_cabin_upgrade	29 (65.91%)	4.59	00:00:16	96.55%	17.24%
2. Bottom_Placement	7 (15.91%)	1.14	00:00:01	100.00%	85.71%
3. June_Blast/List_1	5 (11.36%)	3.40	00:07:09	0.00%	20.00%
4. Top_Placement	3 (6.82%)	1.00	00:00:00	66.67%	100.00%

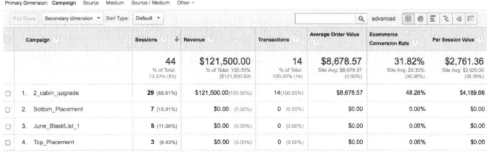

Primary Dimension: **Campaign**   Source   Medium   Source / Medium   Other ▾

Campaign	Sessions	Revenue ↓	Transactions	Average Order Value	Ecommerce Conversion Rate	Per Session Value
	44 % of Total: 73.33% (60)	$121,500.00 % of Total: 100.00% ($121,500.00)	14 % of Total: 100.00% (14)	$8,678.57 Site Avg: $8,678.57 (0.00%)	31.82% Site Avg: 23.33% (36.36%)	$2,761.36 Site Avg: $2,025.00 (36.36%)
1. 2_cabin_upgrade	29 (65.91%)	$121,500.00 (100.00%)	14 (100.00%)	$8,678.57	48.28%	$4,189.66
2. Bottom_Placement	7 (15.91%)	$0.00 (0.00%)	0 (0.00%)	$0.00	0.00%	$0.00
3. June_Blast/List_1	5 (11.36%)	$0.00 (0.00%)	0 (0.00%)	$0.00	0.00%	$0.00
4. Top_Placement	3 (6.82%)	$0.00 (0.00%)	0 (0.00%)	$0.00	0.00%	$0.00

Taken together, these three charts provide important insights into the overall response to the "2 cabin upgrade" campaign.

- This is the most successful campaign run during this time period. Nearly two thirds of all sessions (29 of 44) were related to this campaign.

- Almost all sessions (96.55%) were new sessions primarily from new site users.

- Site engagement generated by the campaign had several positive outcomes, in particular: the number of pages per session was quite high and the bounce rate was quite low.

- The campaign was by far the most successful in revenue generation. In fact, it was the only campaign to generate revenue.

All of these positive outcomes describe overall campaign impact. However, you'll recall that the campaign consisted of three elements: a Facebook post, a blog post, and an email. We need to determine the extent to which each of these elements contributed to this campaign's success.

We begin by clicking on the name of the campaign in any of the prior tables. Clicking on the campaign name from the Summary table brings up the summary display for each of the source/medium combinations used in the campaign (see below).

The data in this table indicates that each of the sources resulted in about the same number of sessions, the vast majority of which were new sessions. There were, however, significant differences across the three campaign sources in terms of the campaign objective: cruise purchase. The blog post was clearly the strongest referral source while Facebook was clearly the weakest. Those who came to the website from the blog post had more transactions and generated more revenue. This relationship between campaign source and transactions can be seen in more detail when we select Ecommerce from below the **Explorer** tab. This brings up the table shown on the top of page 433, where we can see that average purchase rate, conversion rate, and per session value are all the highest for the blog campaign source.

Source / Medium	Sessions ↓	Revenue	Transactions	Average Order Value	Ecommerce Conversion Rate	Per Session Value
	29 % of Total: 48.33% (60)	$121,500.00 % of Total: 100.00% ($121,500.00)	14 % of Total: 100.00% (14)	$8,678.57 Site Avg: $8,678.57 (0.00%)	48.28% Site Avg: 23.33% (106.90%)	$4,189.66 Site Avg: $2,025.00 (106.90%)
1. Blog / Video_Post	10 (34.48%)	$84,000.00 (69.14%)	8 (57.14%)	$10,500.00	80.00%	$8,400.00
2. Email / Video_Post	10 (34.48%)	$30,500.00 (25.10%)	4 (28.57%)	$7,625.00	40.00%	$3,050.00
3. Facebook / Video_Post	9 (31.03%)	$7,000.00 (5.76%)	2 (14.29%)	$3,500.00	22.22%	$777.78

Selecting **Site Usage** from below the **Explorer** tab provides data that helps to explain this outcome. Individuals who came to site from the blog post were more engaged with site content. These individuals viewed more pages per session, had longer average session duration and a nonexistent bounce rate.

Source / Medium	Sessions ↓	Pages / Session	Avg. Session Duration	% New Sessions	Bounce Rate
	29 % of Total: 48.33% (60)	4.59 Site Avg: 5.30 (-13.47%)	00:00:16 Site Avg: 00:03:49 (-92.82%)	96.55% Site Avg: 61.67% (56.57%)	17.24% Site Avg: 31.67% (-45.55%)
1. Blog / Video_Post	10 (34.48%)	7.10	00:00:27	100.00%	0.00%
2. Email / Video_Post	10 (34.48%)	4.60	00:00:16	100.00%	0.00%
3. Facebook / Video_Post	9 (31.03%)	1.78	00:00:05	88.89%	55.56%

An alternative way to obtain campaign data

You'll recall that when we accessed **Acquisition > Channels** the list of channels included **(Other)**, as shown below.

Default Channel Grouping	Acquisition			Behavior			Conversions eCommerce ▼		
	Sessions ↓	% New Sessions	New Users	Bounce Rate	Pages / Session	Avg. Session Duration	Transactions	Revenue	Ecommerce Conversion Rate
	1,060 % of Total: 100.00% (1,060)	85.85% Site Avg: 85.85% (0.00%)	910 % of Total: 100.00% (910)	34.53% Site Avg: 34.53% (0.00%)	2.68 Site Avg: 2.68 (0.00%)	00:01:14 Site Avg: 00:01:14 (0.00%)	271 % of Total: 100.00% (271)	$1,940,200.00 % of Total: 100.00% ($1,940,200.00)	25.57% Site Avg: 25.57% (0.00%)
1. Direct	822 (77.55%)	90.02%	740 (81.32%)	30.54%	2.66	00:01:26	209 (77.12%)	$1,406,700.00 (72.50%)	25.43%
2. Social	104 (9.81%)	78.85%	82 (9.01%)	61.54%	2.35	00:00:21	24 (8.86%)	$133,900.00 (6.90%)	23.08%
3. (Other)	96 (9.06%)	67.71%	65 (7.14%)	41.67%	2.43	00:00:33	23 (8.49%)	$173,400.00 (8.94%)	23.96%
4. Organic Search	33 (3.11%)	63.64%	21 (2.31%)	27.27%	4.18	00:01:19	15 (5.54%)	$226,200.00 (11.66%)	45.45%
5. Referral	5 (0.47%)	40.00%	2 (0.22%)	40.00%	7.20	00:01:02	0 (0.00%)	$0.00 (0.00%)	0.00%

The **(Other)** channel, shown in line three, represents our tagged campaigns. The relative rank of these campaigns shows its effectiveness in generating referrals versus the other channels. In this case, our tagged campaigns are our third largest source of site sessions.

Clicking on **(Other)** brings up the display of all of our tagged campaign sources, as shown below.

Selecting **Acquisition > Source/Medium** from the secondary dimension pull-down menu brings up detailed information on each tagged campaign, as shown below.

Finally, clicking on the top grey **Source/Medium** box alphabetizes the source of your tagged campaign referrals, allowing you to easily see the relative effectiveness of campaigns from the same source, as shown below.

	Source	Source / Medium	Acquisition			Behavior			Conversions eCommerce ▾		
			Sessions	% New Sessions	New Users	Bounce Rate	Pages / Session	Avg. Session Duration	Transactions	Revenue	Ecommerce Conversion Rate
			96	67.71%	65	41.67%	2.43	00:00:33	23	$173,400.00	23.96%
			% of Total: 9.00% (1,080)	Site Avg: 85.85% (-21.12%)	% of Total: 7.14% (910)	Site Avg: 34.53% (20.67%)	Site Avg: 2.68 (-9.41%)	Site Avg: 00:01:14 (-55.87%)	% of Total: 9.49% (971)	% of Total: 8.94% ($1,940,200.00)	Site Avg: 25.87% (-6.39%)
1.	Email	Email / February	14 (14.58%)	100.00%	14 (21.54%)	14.29%	3.36	00:00:14	6 (26.09%)	$32,200.00 (18.57%)	42.86%
2.	Email	Email / February_Newsletter	18 (18.75%)	100.00%	18 (27.69%)	61.11%	2.94	00:00:05	4 (17.39%)	$31,600.00 (18.22%)	22.22%
3.	Email	Email / Post	4 (4.17%)	75.00%	3 (4.62%)	0.00%	3.00	00:00:06	0 (0.00%)	$0.00 (0.00%)	0.00%
4.	Facebook	Facebook / Post	7 (7.29%)	71.43%	5 (7.69%)	57.14%	1.71	00:00:17	0 (0.00%)	$0.00 (0.00%)	0.00%
5.	Facebook	Facebook / Text_link	5 (5.21%)	100.00%	5 (7.69%)	60.00%	1.40	00:00:28	1 (4.35%)	$1,000.00 (0.58%)	20.00%
6.	June Newsletter	June Newsletter / Email	8 (8.33%)	25.00%	2 (3.08%)	37.50%	2.88	00:02:35	0 (0.00%)	$0.00 (0.00%)	0.00%
7.	My_Wordpress	My_Wordpress / Post	1 (1.04%)	0.00%	0 (0.00%)	100.00%	1.00	00:00:00	0 (0.00%)	$0.00 (0.00%)	0.00%
8.	Pinterest	Pinterest / (not set)	4 (4.17%)	50.00%	2 (3.08%)	100.00%	1.00	00:00:00	0 (0.00%)	$0.00 (0.00%)	0.00%
9.	Pinterest	Pinterest / PictureMex	5 (5.21%)	100.00%	5 (7.69%)	60.00%	1.40	00:00:03	2 (8.70%)	$2,000.00 (1.15%)	40.00%
10.	Wordpress	Wordpress / Post	19 (19.79%)	5.26%	1 (1.54%)	47.37%	2.26	00:01:04	0 (0.00%)	$0.00 (0.00%)	0.00%

59

Practice with Acquisition, Link Tags, and Campaigns

This chapter presents exercises to help you apply and extend your knowledge of the **Acquisition** menu, link tags, and the **Campaigns** menu.

True/false and multiple choice

This first set of questions makes certain that you understand key concepts related to the **Acquisition** and **Campaigns** menus and link tags. Feel free to open and refer to the previous chapters or access your analytics account. When you are done, or if you are stuck, the answers can be found beginning on page 620.

1. *True or False:* A **composite** is the label that Google Analytics applies to a collection of similar referral sources.

2. Which of the following are Google Analytics channels? (Select all that apply.)

    a. Direct

    b. Indirect

    c. Organic search

    d. Social

    e. Multi-step

3. Think about the **Acquisition > Overview** page. *True or False:* The **Primary Dimension** menu allows you to change the source from Channels to Sources.

4. Think about the **Acquisition > Overview** page. *True or False:* The **Outcome Measure** menu allows you to change the outcome measure to all goals or any individual goal.

5. Imagine that you are looking at the table on the bottom of the **Acquisition > Overview** page. *True or False:* Clicking on **Organic Search** and **Direct** will bring up the same data display.

6. Think about the **Acquisition > Overview** page. Which of the following types of metrics are shown in the bottom of page table. (Select all that apply.)

   a. Acquisition

   b. Behavior

   c. Conversions

7. A site session is initiated via an untagged link in an email. Google Analytics will record the referral source as _____.

   a. Email

   b. Not set

   c. Direct

   d. Social

8. Which of the following are required elements of a link tag? (Select all that apply.)

   a. Source

   b. Author

   c. Content

   d. Medium

   e. Campaign Name

9. *True or False:* The tagged link shown below is acceptably formatted.

   <a href = http://www.googleanalyticsdemstified.com/xqanqeon/sale/?source=Cruise_offer&medium=Email&campaign=Top_Placement>Visit Now</a>

10. *True or False:* The tagged link shown below is acceptably formatted.

    <a href = http://www.googleanalyticsdemstified.com/xqanqeon/sale/?utm_source=Cruise_offer&utm_medium=Email>Visit Now</a>

11. Metrics related to tagged links and campaigns can be found in what main menu?

    a. Acquisition

    b. Behavior

    c. Conversion

12. You decide to examine campaign data and select the **Campaigns** menu option. *True or False:* The initial data display will show the percentage of sessions accounted for by campaigns during the specified time period.

13. The **Acquisition >** _____ report automatically categorizes user referral metrics by Source/Medium.

    a. All traffic

    b. All referrals

    c. All visits

    d. All sessions

14. You decide to examine campaign data and select the **Campaigns** menu option. Beneath the **Explorer** tab are options for examining the data. Which, if any, of the following options are provided? (Select all that apply)

    a. Summary

    b. Engagement

    c. Site usage

    d. Ecommerce

    e. Reverse funnel

Application

Imagine that you have created a campaign to determine which blog topic leads to greater site engagement and positive purchase behaviors. You create three blog entries, each of which is on a different topic (cruise cost, chilling-out on a cruise, and cruise activities) and each of which contains a tagged link to a special purchase page on your travel site.

You'll monitor each referral source via tagged links that have the following characteristics. All three links will have the same Source and Campaign tags:

| **Source** | utm_medium | The digital medium which conveyed the link. | Blog |
| **Campaign** | utm_campaign | The identifier for the specific referral source. | May 15 |

The Medium will identify the source of the referral as: "Post_Cost," "Post_Chill" or "Post_Refresh".

Examine the data shown below to determine the outcome of the campaign. What was the overall effectiveness of the campaign? Did all links work equally well? What would be your recommendations for future campaigns? When you are done, or if you are stuck, you can see our analysis beginning on page 620.

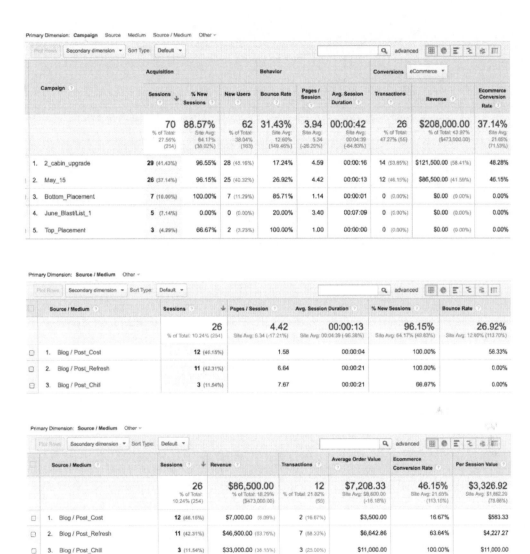

Hands-on (I)

Divide your email list of friends into two groups: male and female. Send each group an email asking them to visit your site and perhaps make a "purchase." Place a tagged link in each email that should be used to initiate the site visit.

After a week or so, examine the data. What are the similarities and differences between the two groups? Which group was the better group of "customers?"

Hands-on (II)

Provide a comprehensive analysis of traffic patterns to your travel website focusing on all channels except (Other). Using your own site's data, address the following questions:

-   Which are the primary and secondary referral channels?

-   What are the relative strengths and weaknesses of each channel?

-   What is your recommendation for future action? Which channels should be given the same, increased or decreased emphasis?

Section XII:
The Social Menu

Social media continue to grow as an important source of website and blog referrals. Fortunately, Google Analytics provides the means to examine both the extent to which specific social platforms generate traffic and the ability of these platforms to help you achieve your unique goals and objectives. The two chapters in this section help you understand how to obtain, interpret and apply Google Analytics social media metrics. Chapter 60 discusses social referral metrics, while Chapter 61 provides practice exercises to help reinforce key concepts.

60

The Social Menu

We saw in Chapter 56 that the **Acquisition > Channels** menu options provide important information on the role of social channels and specific social platforms in referring users to your site. The **Acquisition > Social** menu options shown below allow you to focus on social referrals in greater depth.

Overview

The **Acquisition > Social > Overview** report allows you to quickly see conversion metrics generated from social channels. The default view, shown on the top of page 444, displays total conversions and conversion value, that is, the sum of all ecommerce and goal metrics. This is indicated by the Conversions pull-down menu (located on the top of the page beneath **Overview** and **Add to Dashboard**) which is currently set to "All".

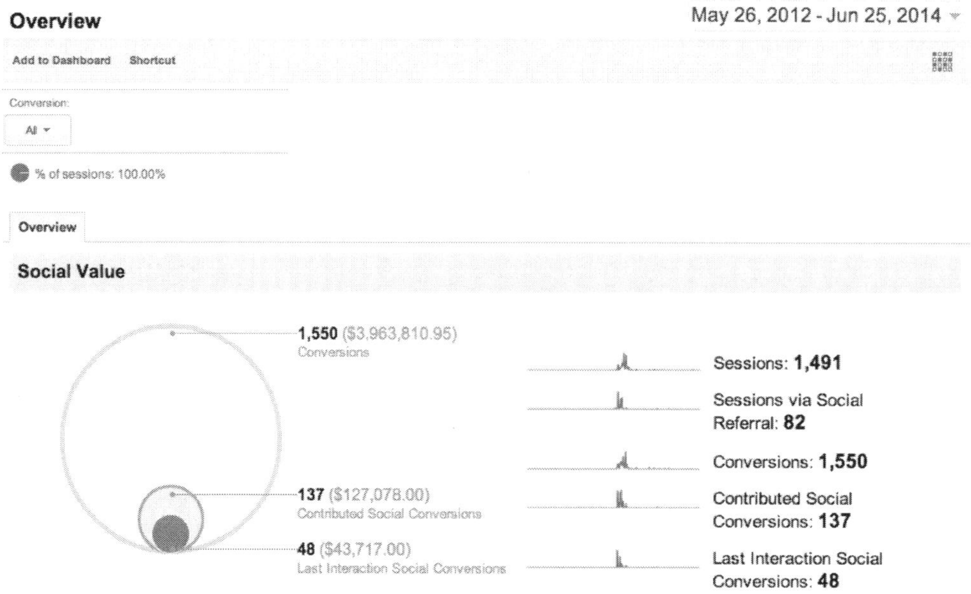

Add to Dashboard   Shortcut

Conversion:

All ▾

● % of sessions: 100.00%

Overview

Social Value

1,550 ($3,963,810.95)
Conversions

137 ($127,078.00)
Contributed Social Conversions

48 ($43,717.00)
Last Interaction Social Conversions

Sessions: **1,491**

Sessions via Social
Referral: **82**

Conversions: **1,550**

Contributed Social
Conversions: **137**

Last Interaction Social
Conversions: **48**

The **Social Value** graph and numeric report compare the total number and monetary value of goal completions and/or ecommerce conversions to those that resulted from social referrals. (The chart above focuses on ecommerce conversions.) Before we look at these metrics, it is important to keep in mind that a visit from a social referral may result in a conversion immediately, or it may assist in a conversion that occurs at a later date. Referrals that generate conversions in the same session as the referral are labeled **Last Interaction Social Conversions**. However, if a referral from a social source does not immediately generate a conversion, but the visitor returns later and converts, the referral is included in **Contributed Social Conversions**. Looking at both types of conversions is essential to understanding the role that social referrals play in helping you to achieve your strategic objectives.

As noted, the display can focus on either goals or ecommerce. When the focus is on goals, we believe that the display has only moderate value because the overall summative measures may mask significant differences across contributing individual goals. Additionally, not all goals may be of equal importance. We recommend, therefore, that you focus this table and subsequent analyses on the specific goals of interest. This is accomplished via the **Conversion** pull-down menu. Selecting this menu (see the top of page 445) allows us to select just ecommerce and/or goals of interest. We just revise the checkmarks to leave only the items(s) of interest checked.

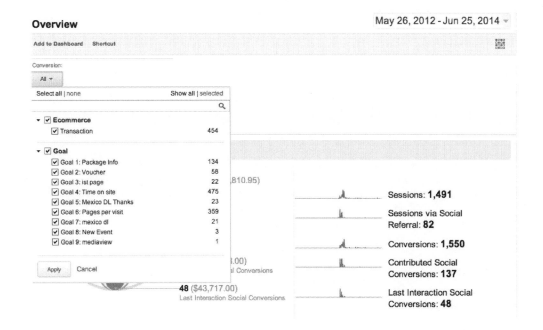

Checking only **Transaction** revises the display to that shown below. Note how the total number of conversions and the two social metrics (**Contributed Social Conversions** and **Last Interaction Social Conversions**) have changed to reflect this narrower focus.

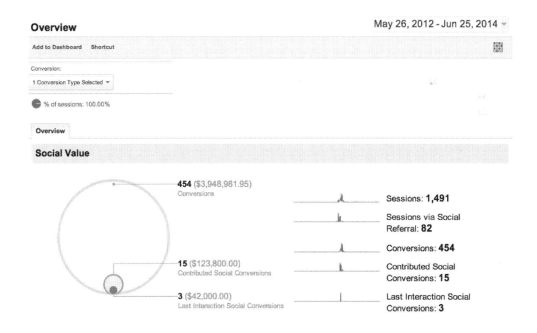

Now we can more clearly see the extent to which social referrals contribute to ecommerce success. Beginning with the data on the right-hand side, we see that of 1,491 total sessions, only 82 were initiated via a social referral. This percentage (5.5%) indicates that social overall plays a minor role in driving traffic to our site. In addition, social's role in conversions is even lower. Social contributed to 15 conversions out of the total 454 (3.3%). Perhaps more importantly, only 18% of all social referrals resulted in a transaction (15 ÷ 82), which is below our site average conversion rate of 30.4% (454 ÷ 1491).

The circular chart on the left-hand side of the previous display provides data related to ecommerce conversion value. Overall, the 454 conversions resulted in just over $3.9 million in sales, of which social contributed $123,800. We can compare social's share of all ecommerce conversions (3.3%) to its share of conversions value (3.1%, calculated as 123,800 ÷ 3,948,982). Thus, social's contribution to sales is about what we would expect given its share of referrals.

Overall, our social efforts appear to be problematic. Our rate of social referral is very low and the overall conversion rate and monetary conversion amounts for social-initiated sessions are very low when compared to our overall site averages. Later, we'll see if this conclusion is true of all social networks.

The table on the bottom of **Acquisition > Social > Overview** (see below) presents a list of data selection options (on the left-hand side) and social networks involved in site sessions (on the right-hand side). We can see that sessions have been initiated by four social networks, with Pinterest accounting for the most sessions and Facebook generating the least number of sessions.

Social Sources		Social Network	Sessions	% Sessions
Social Network	▸	1. Pinterest	28	34.15%
Pages		2. YouTube	20	24.39%
Shared URL		3. WordPress	19	23.17%
Social Plugins		4. Facebook	15	18.29%
Social Source				

view full report

Network Referrals

The **Acquisition > Social > Network Referrals** report provides two types of data (see the top of page 447). The line charts on the top of the report allow you to compare the number of sessions via a social referral to the number of all sessions. At first glance, the similarity in the two line charts might lead us to believe that almost all sessions were initiated via social referrals. However, note the scale on the left-hand side of each line chart. The inconsistency in scales makes it very hard to use and interpret these charts.

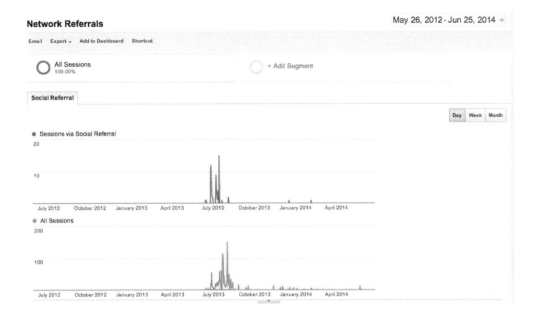

The table on the bottom of the **Acquisition > Social > Network Referrals** report is much more useful and allows you to examine and compare engagement metrics for each social network which has initiated referrals (see below). Here, in addition to the number of sessions, you can see total pageviews, average session duration, and average number of pages/session. These data indicate that user engagement differs across social networks. Users referred by YouTube appear to have the highest engagement with our travel site, while users referred by Facebook appear to have the lowest engagement. Soon we'll examine these metrics in the context of conversions and conversion value.

Clicking on the name of any social network displays information on the path taken from the social referrer to your website, as shown for YouTube on the top of page 448. Two things are noteworthy. First, almost all referrals from YouTube are to my site home page. Second, even though the samples are small, it appears that site engagement after a YouTube referral differs depending upon the URL to which the referral took place. We would want to monitor this trend and, if warranted, to try to increase the number of referrals to pages with higher engagement but only if those pages were important contributors to conversions. We can explore that aspect of social referrals via the **Acquisition > Social > Conversions** menu option described next.

Secondary dimension ▼				advanced ⊞ ◉ Ξ ᴛ

Shared URL	Sessions ↓	Pageviews	Avg. Session Duration	Pages / Session
1. www.classmatandread.net/462site/	15 (75.00%)	67 (58.26%)	00:03:22	4.47
2. www.classmatandread.net/462site/contact.html	2 (10.00%)	28 (24.35%)	00:01:15	14.00
3. classmatandread.net/462site/	1 (5.00%)	2 (1.74%)	00:00:39	2.00
4. classmatandread.net/462site/mediaplay.html	1 (5.00%)	15 (13.04%)	00:02:00	15.00
5. www.classmatandread.net/462site/mexico1a.html	1 (5.00%)	3 (2.61%)	00:00:42	3.00

Conversions

The **Acquisition > Social > Conversions** report allows you to move beyond engage-ment metrics to quantify the monetary value of social network referrals. This report shows the total number of conversions and the monetary value of conversions that occurred as a result of referrals from each social network. Conversions are treated and defined similarly to those on the **Acquisition > Social > Overview** page:[40]

- *First Click Conversions* and *First Click Conversion Value* represent the number and monetary value of sales and conversions the channel initiated. This is the first interaction on a conversion path. The higher these numbers, the more im-portant the channel's role in initiating new sales and conversions.

- *Last Click or Direct Conversions* and *Last Click or Direct Conversion Value* repre-sent the number and monetary value of last click conversions. When someone visits your site from a social network and converts in the same session, the visit is considered a last click. The higher these numbers, the more important the so-cial network's role is in driving completion of sales and conversions.

- *Assisted Conversions* and *Assisted Conversion Value* are the number and mone-tary value of sales and conversions that the social network assisted. An assist occurs when someone visits your site after a social network referral, leaves without converting, but returns later to convert during a subsequent visit. The higher these numbers, the more important the assist role of the social network is in completing a conversion.

- *Assisted/Last Click or Direct Conversions* and *First/Last Click or Direct Conver-sions* summarize a social network's overall role. A value close to 0 indicates that the social network functioned primarily in a last click capacity. A value close to 1 indicates that the social network functioned equally in an assist and a last click capacity. The more this value exceeds 1, the more the social network func-tioned in an assist capacity.

---

[40] *Analyzing channel contribution*
(https://support.google.com/analytics/answer/1191204?hl=en)

The figure shown below is the initial display when **Acquisition > Social > Conversions** is selected. Note that the **Conversions** pull-down menu below the **Explorer** tab (on the top left-hand side) is by default set to "All". Thus, without changing this setting, the report will provide summative measures similar to the default view on the **Acquisition > Social > Overview** page.

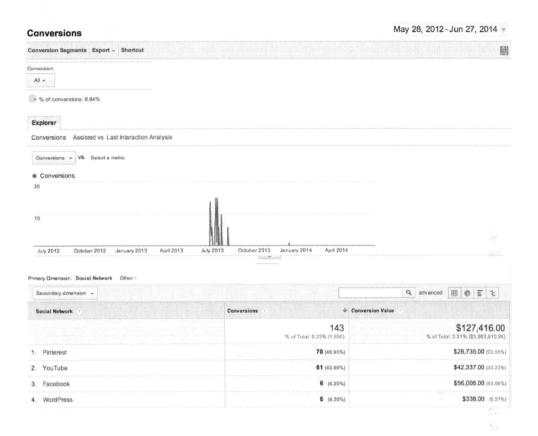

As with the prior **Acquisition > Social > Overview** data, we recommend focusing on ecommerce alone or on specific goals. We can focus on ecommerce by checking only **Transaction**, as shown below.

The display shown below is the result of our focus on ecommerce transactions. The numeric table on this page provides insights into each social network's role in ecommerce conversions. The top summary line chart repeats the data shown on the **Acquisition > Social > Overview** page. Each row beneath this summary provides information on a specific social network, specifically the total number of conversions and the conversion value associated with that network.

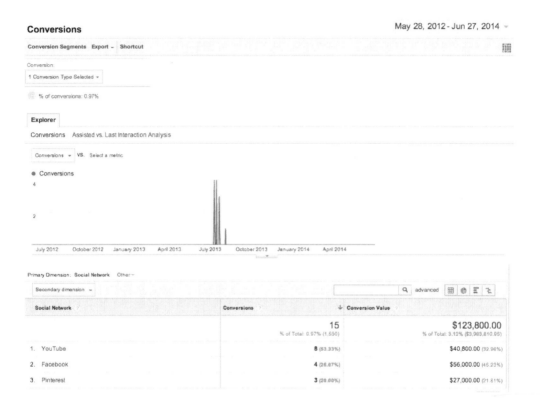

At this point, it is useful to create a summary table of our own. This table puts conversions in context by combining the session information from the **Acquisition > Social > Overview** report with the conversion information in the previous report. We also calculate, for each social network, the percentage of all sessions that resulted in a conversion. This table is shown on the following page.

Network	Sessions	Conversions	% Sessions Converted
Pinterest	28	3	10.7%
YouTube	20	8	40.0%
Wordpress	19	0	0.0%
Facebook	15	4	26.7%

The data in this table indicate that not all social referrals are equally valuable. While Pinterest has the most referrals (i.e., initiates the greatest number of sessions), it has a very low conversion rate, indicating that most people who arrive at our site via Pinterest leave without a purchase. At this point we would conclude that these are not valuable referrals. The conversion rates for Facebook and YouTube are much higher, indicating that these network referrals are more likely to make a purchase. Based on this information, we would conclude that YouTube and Facebook referrals are better, more valuable referrals. Finally, note Wordpress, where the number of sessions are relatively high but the conversion rate is 0%, No one referred by Wordpress made a purchase. Clearly, we would need to examine our Wordpress content strategy to see why this is the case.

We can continue to differentiate referrals from different social networks by modifying the previous table, this time examining conversion value per session and average conversion value. This new table is shown below for the three networks that generated conversions.

Network	Sessions	Conversions	Average Conversion $/ Session[41]	Average $/ Conversion[42]
Pinterest	28	3	$954	$9,000
YouTube	20	8	$2,040	$5,100
Facebook	15	4	$3,733	$14,000

This data indicates that the relative contribution of each social network is more complex than originally thought. As such, each may require a different strategy.

- The conversion rate for Pinterest is indeed quite low (as indicated in the first table) and the resulting **Average Conversion $/Session** is also low as a result. However, when individuals referred by this network do make a purchase, it is a

---

[41] This metric is calculated by dividing Conversion Value by Sessions.

[42] This metric is calculated by dividing Conversion Value by Conversions.

large one. Overall, these are valuable customers, and our goal would be to increase conversions/session.

- YouTube makes a different type of contribution to our ecommerce success and therefore requires a different strategy. Individuals referred by YouTube are the most likely to convert but their financial contribution is relatively low. We can try to increase the number of referrals from YouTube (accepting the current financial contribution) and/or attempt to increase the average purchase amount.

- Facebook referrals have a relatively high conversion rate and they generate the highest **Average Conversion $/Session** and **Average $/Conversion.** These are very valuable customers, and our strategic goal would be to increase referrals from Facebook, assuming that the conversion rate and purchase amount would remain the same.

One last insight into the strategic contribution of different social networks can be found by clicking on the **Assisted Versus Last Interaction** link beneath the **Explorer** tab. This brings up the table shown below.

This table indicates that our current content strategy at YouTube and Pinterest works to drive users to the site, but these users never make a purchase on the same visit. Therefore, we might want to modify content at these sites to encourage a purchase during their initial referred visit. Facebook, on the other hand, sends a different type of individual to our site. These users are much more likely to make a purchase and to make this purchase during their initial referred visit. Thus, when it works, the content appears to be effective. But, the breadth of appeal of this content may be relatively low, as indicated in the low number of overall sessions initiated by Facebook. As a result, our initial hunch is supported - we would want to examine our content strategy to try to increase the referral rate from Facebook (assuming consistency in purchase behaviors once they arrive).[43]

---

[43] Assisted and last click conversions provide important insights into a social network's contribution to ecommerce success and goal attainment. Attribution allows us to look even more deeply at social network performance and to place this performance in the context of other channels. Attribution is discussed in Section XIV.

The **Acquisition > Social > Plugins Report** focuses on site buttons such as Google +1 and Facebook Like. From a content management perspective, it is important to know which buttons are being clicked and for which content. For example, if you publish articles on your site, you'll want to know which articles are most commonly "liked" or shared, and from which social networks they're being shared (for example, Google+ or Facebook). You can use this information to create more of the type of content that's popular with your visitors. Also, if you find that some buttons are rarely used, you may wish to remove them to reduce clutter.

Google Analytics notes that no setup is required to track Google +1 interactions that occur on your site, but additional technical setup is required to track other Social interactions.

Data hub activity

When data are available, **Acquisition > Social > Data Hub Activity** shows you how people are engaging with your site content on social networks. You can see the most recent URLs people shared, how and where they shared (via a "reshare" on Google+, for example), and what they said. The information comes from Google's Social Data Hub where social networks send activity streams to the hub and this information is then organized and presented in Google Analytics.

An example of data hub activity is shown below, where the two social conversations about my travel site are reported.

It is easy to see all of the conversations in this example. However, if there were many conversations, then I could use the top **All networks** pull-down menu to isolate conversations from one or a subset of social sources (as shown on the top of page 454).

Finally, there is a pull-down menu to the right of each conversation (see below). You can use these menu options to see the extent to which a conversation has been shared (**View Ripple**) or you can view the original conversation in context (**View Page**).

Landing Pages

Acquisition > Social > Network Referrals allowed us to see the specific landing pages referred to by each individual social network. The **Acquisition > Social > Landing Pages** report (shown below) displays engagement metrics (sessions, pageviews, average session duration, and average pages per session) organized by landing page and summed across all social networks. Keep in mind that because these are summative measures, the overall average may not reflect the characteristics of a specific social network. Note that a metric new to this table is Data Hub Activities, which reports data hub conversations and events associated with each social referral landing page.

	Shared URL	Sessions		Pageviews		Avg. Session Duration	Data Hub Activities		Pages / Session
1.	www.classmatandread.net/462site/	39	(47.56%)	165	(55.18%)	00:01:29	0	(0.00%)	4.23
2.	www.classmatandread.net/462site/purchasef.html	13	(15.85%)	15	(5.02%)	00:00:03	0	(0.00%)	1.15
3.	www.classmatandread.net/462site/mexico.html	8	(9.76%)	28	(9.36%)	00:01:36	0	(0.00%)	3.50
4.	www.classmatandread.net/462site/thanks_p.html	8	(9.76%)	15	(5.02%)	00:00:05	0	(0.00%)	1.88
5.	www.classmatandread.net/462site/package.html	5	(6.10%)	22	(7.36%)	00:00:59	0	(0.00%)	4.40
6.	www.classmatandread.net/462site/contact.html	2	(2.44%)	28	(9.36%)	00:01:15	0	(0.00%)	14.00
7.	www.classmatandread.net/462site/indexa.html	2	(2.44%)	3	(1.00%)	00:00:08	0	(0.00%)	1.50
8.	www.classmatandread.net/462site/mediaplay.html	2	(2.44%)	3	(1.00%)	00:02:39	0	(0.00%)	1.50
9.	classmatandread.net/462site/	1	(1.22%)	2	(0.67%)	00:00:39	0	(0.00%)	2.00

The **Acquisition > Social > Trackbacks** report shows you which sites are linking to your content, and in what context. This can help you replicate successful content and build relationships with those users who frequently link to your site. This report presents each endorsing URL's page title and publication date, as well as the number of visits that it sends to your site.

The **Acquisition > Social > Social Users Flow** is identical to other flow charts, except here the focus is on social networks (see the chart below). Similar to other user flow reports, you can select and highlight the user path for traffic beginning from a single source, in this case a specific social referrer. The chart on page 456, for example, shows users flow for those referred to my site from YouTube.

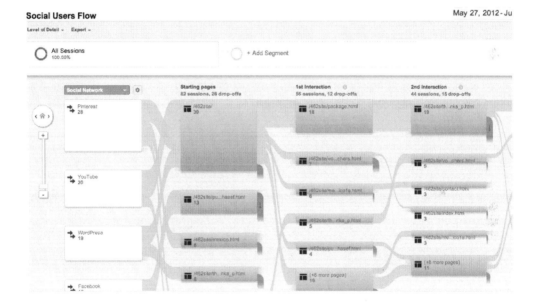

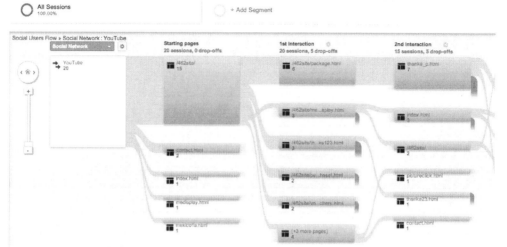

61

Practice with the Social Menu

This chapter presents questions and an exercise to help you apply and extend your knowledge of social analytics.

True/false and multiple choice

This first set of questions makes certain that you understand key concepts. Feel free to open and refer to Chapter 60 or access your analytics account. When you are done, or if you are stuck, the answers can be found on page 622.

1. *True or False:* The default **Acquisition > Social > Overview** report presents summative metrics for all goals and transactions.

2. *True or False:* Social referrals that generate a transaction or goal conversion in the initial site visit are called **Finishing Interaction Conversions.**

3. Imagine that Wordpress sends a user to your site. The user leaves the site and returns the next day to make a transaction. *True or False:* This is called a **Delayed Social Conversion.**

4. *True or False:* The **Acquisition > Social > Network Referrals** report allows you to examine and compare engagement metrics for each social network that has initiated referrals to your site.

5. Which of the following metrics are included on the **Acquisition > Social > Network Referrals** report? (Select all that apply.)

    a. Sessions

    b. Pageviews

    c. Goal conversions/session

    d. Average session duration

    e. Pages/Session

    f. Pages/Conversion

6. The **Acquisition > Social >** _____ report allows you to move beyond engagement metrics to quantify the value of social network referrals.

    a. Continuum

    b. Conversions

    c. Contact

    d. Content

7. The **Acquisition > Social >** _____ **Report** focuses on site buttons such as Google "+1" and Facebook "Like".

    a. Premium

    b. Power

    c. Plugins

    d. Precision

8. When data are available, **Acquisition > Social >** _____ **Activity** shows you how people are engaging with your site content on social networks.

    a. Data Hub

    b. Dynamics

    c. Decision

    d. Domain

Application

Page 459 presents tables from the **Acquisition > Social** menu. All focus on ecommerce transactions. Examine these tables and then provide a point of view (1) regarding the strengths and weaknesses of each social network and (2) strategies to improve your social referral program. Make certain to use data to support your point of view. When you are done, or if you are stuck, you can read our analysis on page 622.

Social Value

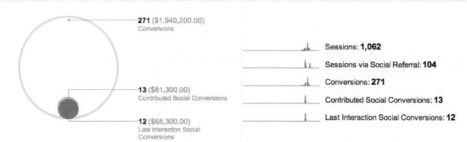

271 ($1,940,200.00)
Conversions

Sessions: **1,062**

Sessions via Social Referral: **104**

Conversions: **271**

13 ($81,300.00)
Contributed Social Conversions

Contributed Social Conversions: **13**

12 ($65,300.00)
Last Interaction Social
Conversions

Last Interaction Social Conversions: **12**

Primary Dimension: Social Network

Secondary dimension ▾   [ ] 🔍 advanced

Social Network ?	Sessions ↓	Pageviews	Avg. Session Duration	Pages / Session
1. Pinterest	41 (39.42%)	108 (44.26%)	00:00:42	2.63
2. WordPress	36 (34.62%)	105 (43.03%)	00:00:11	2.92
3. Facebook	27 (25.96%)	31 (12.70%)	00:00:01	1.15

Primary Dimension: Social Network   Other ▾

Secondary dimension ▾   [ ] 🔍 advanced

Social Network ?	Conversions ?	Conversion Value ?
	13 % of Total: 2.80% (465)	$81,300.00 % of Total: 4.19% ($1,940,200.00)
1. Pinterest	11 (84.62%)	$77,300.00 (95.08%)
2. Facebook	2 (15.38%)	$4,000.00 (4.92%)

Google Analytics Demystified

Section XIII:
The Ecommerce Menu

Integrating ecommerce functionality into your site can be a daunting task. The task becomes even more complex when you decide to send ecommerce data to Google Analytics. Given the multiple approaches that can be used to accomplish these tasks and the need to customize the approach selected to your specific needs, we are not going to discuss how to install ecommerce on your site. Rather, our focus is on the analysis of ecommerce data, helping you to understand the types of information available and the strategic insights this information provides.

- Chapter 62 describes the process by which ecommerce data is sent to Google Analytics.

- Chapter 63 discusses the various ways ecommerce data can be viewed, analyzed and applied to strategic decision-making.

- Chapter 64 provides practice exercises to help reinforce and extend your understanding of ecommerce metrics.

Google Analytics Demystified

Sending Ecommerce Data to Google Analytics

A website would typically use a data base, shopping cart, and server-side programs to implement ecommerce. So, you may be wondering how we are generating ecommerce data on your site without the use of any of these things. The answer is: we cheated. We've hardcoded the ecommerce information onto specific web pages that send this information to Google Analytics. Here is how it works:

- Your purchase page provides six tour purchase options. Each tour option takes a site user to a different thank you page.

- Hardcoded into each thank you page is the information Google Analytics needs to record the specifics of the selected ecommerce transaction. Let's see the types of data provided in this hardcoding, as it is this information that is displayed in the Google Analytics ecommerce reports.

Google Analytics ecommerce data

The format of the ecommerce transmission is identical across all six tour options. The content differs with regard to tour specifics. The source code used to send ecommerce data to Google Analytics for the 10 day Bahamas tour package is shown below.

```
ga('require', 'ecommerce', 'ecommerce.js');

ga('ecommerce:addTransaction',
{   'id': '1234',                          // Transaction ID. Required.
    'affiliation': 'Travel Tour',          // Affiliation or store name.
    'revenue': '9000.00',                  // Grand Total.
    'shipping': '0',                       // Shipping.
    'tax': '0'                             // Tax. });

ga('ecommerce:addItem',
{   'id': '1234',                          // Transaction ID. Required.
    'name': '10 Day Tour Package',         // Product name. Required.
    'sku': 'B10',                          // SKU/code.
    'category': 'Bahamas',                 // Category or variation.
    'price': '9000.00',                    // Unit price.
    'quantity': '1'                        // Quantity. });

ga('ecommerce:send');
```

There are four parts to this block of code. The first line, **ga('require', 'ecommerce', 'ecommerce.js');**, sends a request to Google Analytics for the ecommerce javascript necessary to process the data. This line of code is required.

The second block of code is summary information for the entire transaction, which would normally be calculated by the shopping cart. It is common practice to send information that provides the store name, the grand total, shipping, and tax. In our case, because we are only selling tour packages, shipping and tax are set to zero and the total revenue equals the price of the selected tour.

The third block of code is generated for every item placed in the shopping cart. Since we are only purchasing one tour package there is only one item listed. Google Analytics requires that we provide the transaction ID (which is the same as that reported in the summary information) and the product name. We've also named each tour package in terms of the number of tour days. Providing the remaining information in this block of code allows us to look more deeply at our ecommerce outcomes in Google Analytics' ecommerce reports. Each tour is therefore also given a SKU code and category.

- The SKU code indicates the tour destination and number of days. The B10 in this example indicates that the tour is for 10 days in the Bahamas. A code of M02 would indicate a 2 day Mexico tour.

- The category indicates the destination without worrying about days. Two categories are used: Bahamas and Mexico.

Finally, we provide price and quantity information for the specific item.

The last line of code, **ga('ecommerce:send');** sends all of the information to Google Analytics.[44] This line of code is required.

As noted earlier, the format remains the same while the specifics change for each tour package. Information on a fifteen day tour to Mexico would be sent to Google Analytics as follows:

```
ga('require', 'ecommerce', 'ecommerce.js');

ga('ecommerce:addTransaction',
{    'id': '1234',                    // Transaction ID. Required.
     'affiliation': 'Travel Tour',    // Affiliation or store name.
     'revenue': '15000.00',           // Grand Total.
     'shipping': '0',                 // Shipping.
     'tax': '0'                       // Tax. });
```

---

[44] If you are adventurous, you can edit each tour thank you page to change any of these parameters. You can, for example, change the price, descriptions, etc.

```
ga('ecommerce:addItem',
{    'id': '1234',                        // Transaction ID. Required.
     'name': '15 Day Tour Package',       // Product name. Required.
     'sku': 'M15',                        // SKU/code.
     'category': 'Mexico',                // Category or variation.
     'price': '15000.00',                 // Unit price.  '
     quantity': '1'                       // Quantity. });

ga('ecommerce:send');
```

The following table provides the information sent to Google Analytics for each of the six tour packages available on your travel website. With this information in mind, the next chapter introduces you to ecommerce reporting options.

ID	Name	SKU	Category	Price	Quantity
1234	2 Day Tour Package	M02	Mexico	$2,000	1
1234	10 Day Tour Package	M10	Mexico	$9,000	1
1234	15 Day Tour Package	M15	Mexico	$15,000	1
1234	2 Day Tour Package	B02	Bahamas	$2,000	1
1234	10 Day Tour Package	B10	Bahamas	$9,000	1
1234	15 Day Tour Package	B15	Bahamas	$15,000	1

63
Ecommerce Metrics and Reporting

Ecommerce reporting options and metrics are found in the **Conversions** menu, shown below.

Overview

The **Conversions > Ecommerce > Overview** display is similar in format to other Overview pages, except here the focus is on ecommerce metrics. The line chart on the top of the overview page (see display on the top of page 477) displays one of six core ecommerce metrics for the selected time period. My ecommerce conversion rate by day is displayed. The specific data displayed in this chart are noted just above the line graph.

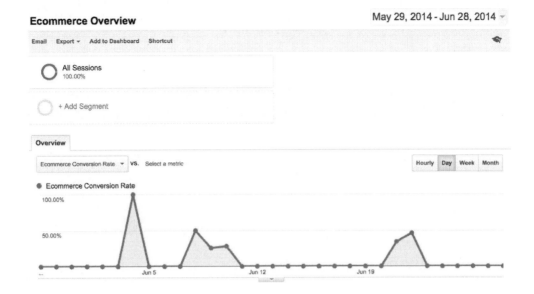

These data are interesting, informing me that on some days everyone who initiated a session on my site made a transaction while on other days where very few users converted. We would certainly want to explore this trend in greater depth to see if an explanation could be found, for example, if the lower conversion rates were associated with website or browser problems.

We can use the pull-down menu just beneath the **Overview** tab to explore the trend in other ecommerce metrics (see below).

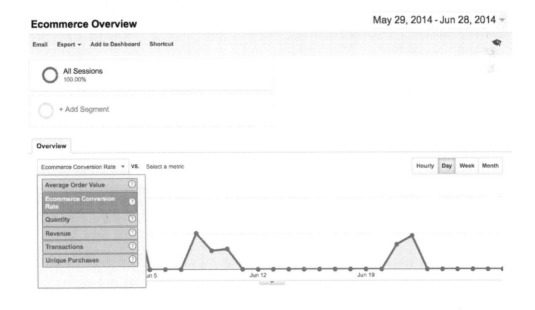

Beneath the line chart are two groups of data. Immediately below the chart are summary ecommerce metrics (see below). Here, the ecommerce conversion rate, number of transactions, unique purchases, total revenue and average order value are reported. The bottom table reports names of products sold and the total quantity of each. You can use the options on the left-hand side to change the listing to reflect Product SKU, Product Category, and Source/Medium. The product-related names, SKU and category come from the ecommerce information sent to Google Analytics, as discussed Chapter 62.

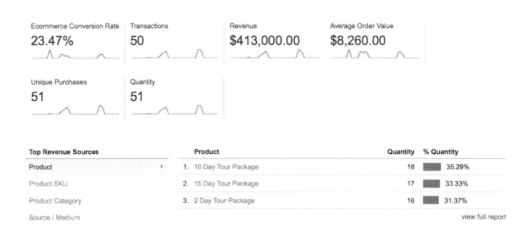

It is often informative to use the **Conversions > Ecommerce > Overview** presentation to compare two time periods. Imagine, for example, that we select the period of May 22 to June 9 as our baseline, which we will use to provide context for interpreting the period of June 10 to June 28. Both periods contain 19 days. It was in this latter period that we modified the site in an attempt to increase our sales conversion rate while simultaneously maintaining levels of revenue and average order value. The figure below shows that this comparison has been selected.

Summary statistics are shown on the top of page 469. All of the transaction measures show improvement after we modified the site, especially the ecommerce conversion rate, number of transactions (which more than doubled), and revenue. This is great. However, it is important to note that the significant gain in revenue came in spite of a slight decline in order value. However, given that transactions more than doubled and that revenue nearly doubled, this is not a cause of concern.

Ecommerce Conversion Rate	Transactions	Revenue	Average Order Value
54.17%	105.56%	82.39%	-11.27%
25.00% vs 16.22%	37 vs 18	$305,500.00 vs $167,500.00	$8,256.76 vs $9,305.56

Unique Purchases	Quantity
94.74%	94.74%
37 vs 19	37 vs 19

The bottom tabular chart (see below) allows us to see the specific source of increased revenue. These data indicate that the rise in revenue is due to an increase in the number of two and especially ten day tour packages. This explains the slight drop in average order value noted earlier.

Top Revenue Sources

- Product ►
- Product SKU
- Product Category
- Source / Medium

Product	Quantity	% Quantity
1. 10 Day Tour Package		
Jun 10, 2014 - Jun 28, 2014	15	40.54%
May 22, 2014 - Jun 9, 2014	3	15.79%
% Change	400.00%	156.76%
2. 15 Day Tour Package		
Jun 10, 2014 - Jun 28, 2014	11	29.73%
May 22, 2014 - Jun 9, 2014	11	57.89%
% Change	0.00%	-48.65%
3. 2 Day Tour Package		
Jun 10, 2014 - Jun 28, 2014	11	29.73%
May 22, 2014 - Jun 9, 2014	5	26.32%
% Change	120.00%	12.97%

The **Conversions > Ecommerce > Product Performance** menu option provides summary ecommerce metrics for each product sold, in our case, the three tours of different durations: 2, 10, and 15 days (see table below). We can see that all three packages are purchased with about equal frequency, and therefore (not surprisingly) the 15 day package makes the largest contribution to overall revenue (48.34%).

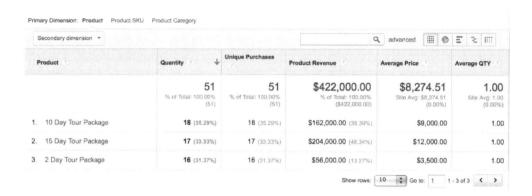

It is often useful to examine ecommerce product data in the context of a secondary dimension. The table below, for example, looks at product performance in the context of user type: new versus returning user. Here we can see that our repeat business is quite poor, with new visitors accounting for the vast majority of purchases. We placed user type in alphabetical order by clicking on the **User Type** header box.

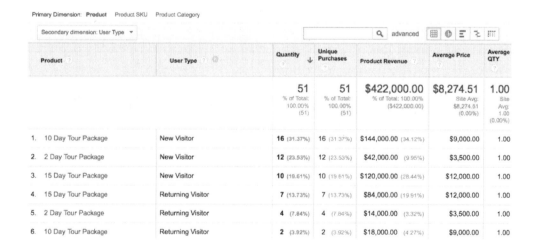

The table below examines product performance in the context of source (which we have placed in alphabetical order by clicking in the **Source** header box). We can see that both direct site access and referrals from our blog are important sources of transactions and revenue. Email and Facebook are not very effective in stimulating transactions or sales during this period.

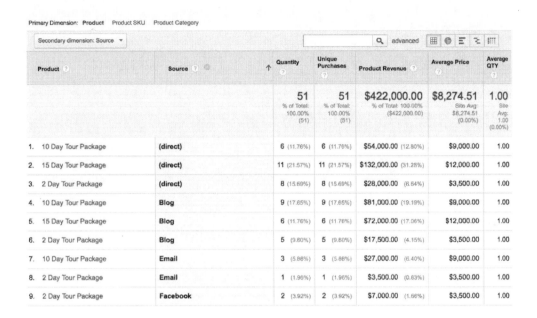

Product	Source	Quantity	Unique Purchases	Product Revenue	Average Price	Average QTY
		51 % of Total: 100.00% (51)	51 % of Total: 100.00% (51)	$422,000.00 % of Total: 100.00% ($422,000.00)	$8,274.51 Site Avg: $8,274.51 (0.00%)	1.00 Site Avg: 1.00 (0.00%)
1. 10 Day Tour Package	(direct)	6 (11.76%)	6 (11.76%)	$54,000.00 (12.80%)	$9,000.00	1.00
2. 15 Day Tour Package	(direct)	11 (21.57%)	11 (21.57%)	$132,000.00 (31.28%)	$12,000.00	1.00
3. 2 Day Tour Package	(direct)	8 (15.69%)	8 (15.69%)	$28,000.00 (6.64%)	$3,500.00	1.00
4. 10 Day Tour Package	Blog	9 (17.65%)	9 (17.65%)	$81,000.00 (19.19%)	$9,000.00	1.00
5. 15 Day Tour Package	Blog	6 (11.76%)	6 (11.76%)	$72,000.00 (17.06%)	$12,000.00	1.00
6. 2 Day Tour Package	Blog	5 (9.80%)	5 (9.80%)	$17,500.00 (4.15%)	$3,500.00	1.00
7. 10 Day Tour Package	Email	3 (5.88%)	3 (5.88%)	$27,000.00 (6.40%)	$9,000.00	1.00
8. 2 Day Tour Package	Email	1 (1.96%)	1 (1.96%)	$3,500.00 (0.83%)	$3,500.00	1.00
9. 2 Day Tour Package	Facebook	2 (3.92%)	2 (3.92%)	$7,000.00 (1.66%)	$3,500.00	1.00

Let's return to the original table displayed when **Conversions > Ecommerce > Product Performance** is selected from the left-hand menu (see below). Above the chart are three display options, where **Product** is currently selected.

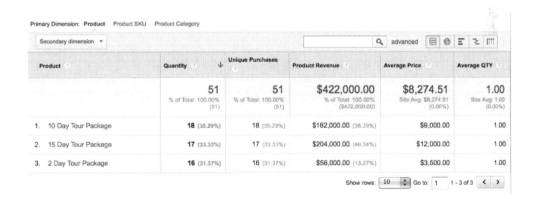

Product	Quantity	Unique Purchases	Product Revenue	Average Price	Average QTY
	51 % of Total: 100.00% (51)	51 % of Total: 100.00% (51)	$422,000.00 % of Total: 100.00% ($422,000.00)	$8,274.51 Site Avg: $8,274.51 (0.00%)	1.00 Site Avg: 1.00 (0.00%)
1. 10 Day Tour Package	18 (35.29%)	18 (35.29%)	$162,000.00 (38.39%)	$9,000.00	1.00
2. 15 Day Tour Package	17 (33.33%)	17 (33.33%)	$204,000.00 (48.34%)	$12,000.00	1.00
3. 2 Day Tour Package	16 (31.37%)	16 (31.37%)	$56,000.00 (13.27%)	$3,500.00	1.00

Show rows: 10   Go to: 1   1 - 3 of 3

Selecting **Product SKU** changes the display to that shown below. This more detailed table tells us which specific products are most popular and each product's contribution to revenue. As with the product names, the SKUs come from the information sent to Google Analytics when a transaction takes place. We can see that all Mexico products (those with SKUs beginning with an "M") are of relatively equal appeal; all Bahamas products (those with SKUs beginning with an "B") are also of equal appeal. We can also see that regardless of tour duration, Mexico products are much more popular than Bahamas products.

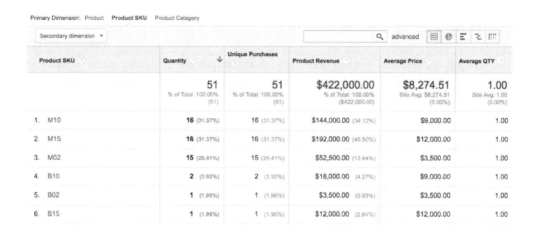

Primary Dimension: Product **Product SKU** Product Category

Product SKU	Quantity	Unique Purchases	Product Revenue	Average Price	Average QTY
	51	51	$422,000.00	$8,274.51	1.00
	% of Total: 100.00% (51)	% of Total: 100.00% (51)	% of Total: 100.00% ($422,000.00)	Site Avg: $8,274.51 (0.00%)	Site Avg: 1.00 (0.00%)
1. M10	16 (31.37%)	16 (31.37%)	$144,000.00 (34.12%)	$9,000.00	1.00
2. M15	16 (31.37%)	16 (31.37%)	$192,000.00 (45.50%)	$12,000.00	1.00
3. M02	15 (29.41%)	15 (29.41%)	$52,500.00 (12.44%)	$3,500.00	1.00
4. B10	2 (3.92%)	2 (3.92%)	$18,000.00 (4.27%)	$9,000.00	1.00
5. B02	1 (1.96%)	1 (1.96%)	$3,500.00 (0.83%)	$3,500.00	1.00
6. B15	1 (1.96%)	1 (1.96%)	$12,000.00 (2.84%)	$12,000.00	1.00

This preference for Mexican tour packages can also be seen when we select **Product Category** from the link options appearing above the table. Here we can see that Mexico packages account for the overwhelming share of both sales (92.16%) and revenue (92.06%). We would certainly want to determine the strategic implications of these disproportionate sales.

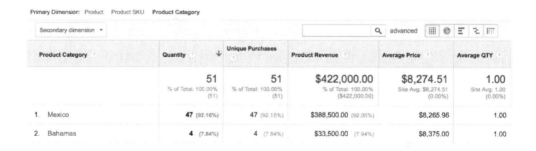

Primary Dimension: Product Product SKU **Product Category**

Product Category	Quantity	Unique Purchases	Product Revenue	Average Price	Average QTY
	51	51	$422,000.00	$8,274.51	1.00
	% of Total: 100.00% (51)	% of Total: 100.00% (51)	% of Total: 100.00% ($422,000.00)	Site Avg: $8,274.51 (0.00%)	Site Avg: 1.00 (0.00%)
1. Mexico	47 (92.16%)	47 (92.16%)	$388,500.00 (92.06%)	$8,265.96	1.00
2. Bahamas	4 (7.84%)	4 (7.84%)	$33,500.00 (7.94%)	$8,375.00	1.00

Let's return one last time to the initial table displayed by the **Conversions > Ecommerce > Product Performance** menu option (see below).

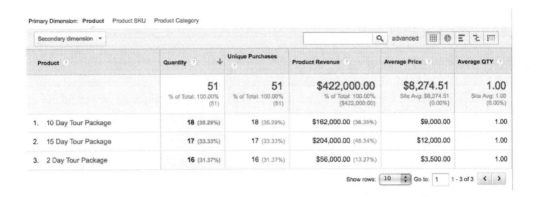

Primary Dimension: **Product**   Product SKU   Product Category

Product	Quantity ↓	Unique Purchases	Product Revenue	Average Price	Average QTY
	51	51	$422,000.00	$8,274.51	1.00
	% of Total: 100.00% (51)	% of Total: 100.00% (51)	% of Total: 100.00% ($422,000.00)	Site Avg: $8,274.51 (0.00%)	Site Avg: 1.00 (0.00%)
1. 10 Day Tour Package	18 (35.29%)	18 (35.29%)	$162,000.00 (38.39%)	$9,000.00	1.00
2. 15 Day Tour Package	17 (33.33%)	17 (33.33%)	$204,000.00 (48.34%)	$12,000.00	1.00
3. 2 Day Tour Package	16 (31.37%)	16 (31.37%)	$56,000.00 (13.27%)	$3,500.00	1.00

Show rows: 10   Go to: 1   1 - 3 of 3   <   >

Clicking on the name of any specific product brings up a display of information specific to that product, in this case 10 day tour packages. The initial display after the selection of "10 Day Tour Package" is a table that shows SKU-associated revenue metrics (see first chart below). Here we can see that there were 16 Mexican 10 day tours sold versus two 10 day Bahamas tours. This information is summarized in terms of product category in the second table below. This latter table is generated by clicking on the **Product Category** link on the top of the table.

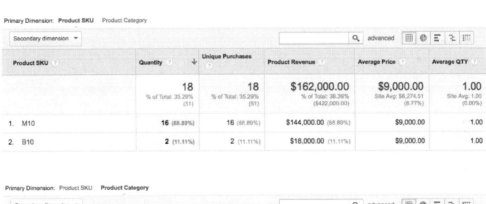

Primary Dimension: **Product SKU**   Product Category

Product SKU	Quantity ↓	Unique Purchases	Product Revenue	Average Price	Average QTY
	18	18	$162,000.00	$9,000.00	1.00
	% of Total: 35.29% (51)	% of Total: 35.29% (51)	% of Total: 38.39% ($422,000.00)	Site Avg: $8,274.51 (8.77%)	Site Avg: 1.00 (0.00%)
1. M10	16 (88.89%)	16 (88.89%)	$144,000.00 (88.89%)	$9,000.00	1.00
2. B10	2 (11.11%)	2 (11.11%)	$18,000.00 (11.11%)	$9,000.00	1.00

Primary Dimension: Product SKU   **Product Category**

Product Category	Quantity ↓	Unique Purchases	Product Revenue	Average Price	Average QTY
	18	18	$162,000.00	$9,000.00	1.00
	% of Total: 35.29% (51)	% of Total: 35.29% (51)	% of Total: 38.39% ($422,000.00)	Site Avg: $8,274.51 (8.77%)	Site Avg: 1.00 (0.00%)
1. Mexico	16 (88.89%)	16 (88.89%)	$144,000.00 (88.89%)	$9,000.00	1.00
2. Bahamas	2 (11.11%)	2 (11.11%)	$18,000.00 (11.11%)	$9,000.00	1.00

Selecting **Conversions > Ecommerce > Sales Performance** generates the a table similar to that shown below. Here, revenues by day of sale are placed in descending order of revenue generated.

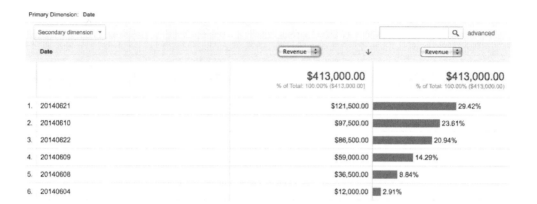

This chart can be organized by descending or ascending date, as shown in the chart below. This view is particularly useful for helping you see how revenue grows or declines over time. Fortunately, in our case, revenue is increasing as time goes on. We put the dates in sequence by clicking in the **Date** box on the top of the table.

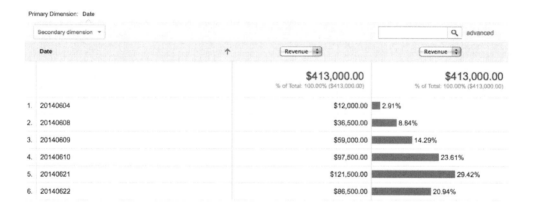

The **Conversions > Ecommerce > Transactions** menu option is similar to the previous display, except now revenues are reported in terms of your Transaction ID which, as discussed in Chapter 62, is sent to Google Analytics as part of the ecommerce data transmission. There is only one Transaction ID listed in the chart, as all of our transactions are hardcoded to use the same ID.

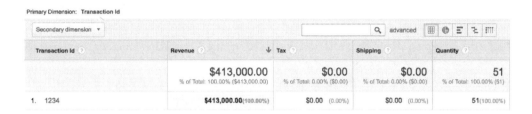

Time to Purchase

Finally, the **Conversions > Ecommerce > Time to Purchase** menu option provides two data displays. The specific display is selected via the options presented beneath the **Distribution** tab.

Days to Transaction reports the number of days that pass between the initial site session and an ecommerce transaction. This table (shown below) indicates that most transactions (84%) are made on the same day as the initial session. Most of the remaining transactions show a gap of at least fourteen days from initial session to final transaction.

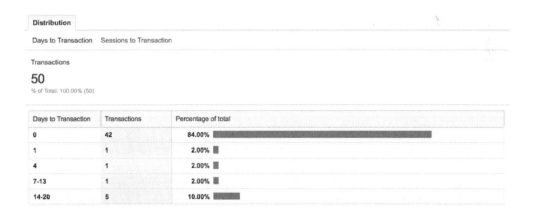

Sessions to Transaction reports the number of sessions that pass between the initial site session and the session with a transaction. When interpreted in conjunction with the previous table, this table (see below) shows that not only is a transaction made on the day of the first session, but it is also made *during* the first session.

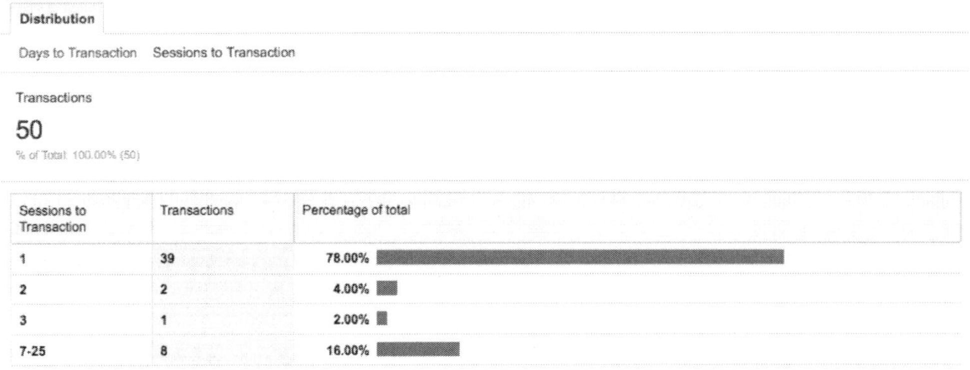

Distribution

Days to Transaction   Sessions to Transaction

Transactions

50

% of Total: 100.00% (50)

Sessions to Transaction	Transactions	Percentage of total	
1	39	78.00%	
2	2	4.00%	
3	1	2.00%	
7-25	8	16.00%	

Google Analytics Demystified

64

Practice With Ecommerce

This chapter presents two sets of exercises to help you apply and extend your knowledge of ecommerce metrics.

True/false and multiple choice

This first set of questions makes certain that you understand key concepts. Feel free to open and refer to the previous chapters or access your analytics account. When you are done, or if you are stuck, the answers can be found on page 623.

1. The initial line in the block of code used to send ecommerce data to Google Analytics is: **ga('require', 'ecommerce', 'ecommerce.js');** *True or False:* This line of code is optional and can be deleted if space is limited.

2. Consider the block of code shown below. Based on the discussion in Chapter 62, what mandatory item(s) is/are missing? Select all that apply.

```
ga('ecommerce:addTransaction',
'affiliation': 'Travel Tour',      // Affiliation or store name.
'shipping': '0',                   // Shipping.
'tax': '0'                         // Tax.
});
```

   a. Order revenue (grand total)

   b. Order confirmation page URL

   c. Transaction ID

   d. Site session number

   e. Thank you page URL

3. *True or False:* Ecommerce data should never be viewed in the context of a secondary dimension.

4. *True or False:* The **Conversions > Ecommerce > Sales Performance** menu option allows you to view total revenue by day of sale.

5. *True or False:* The **Conversions > Ecommerce > Transactions** menu option allows you to view total revenue by Transaction ID.

6. Consider the block of code shown below. Based on the discussion in Chapter 62, what *mandatory* item(s) is/are missing? Select all that apply.

```
ga('ecommerce:addItem',
{  'id': '1234',                    // Transaction ID. Required.
'sku': 'B10',                       // SKU/code.
'category': 'Bahamas',              // Category or variation.
'price': '9000.00',                 // Unit price.  });
```

    a.   Product name

    b.   URL of product description page

    c.   Number of pageviews leading to purchase

    d.   Referral channel

7. You access the **Conversions > Ecommerce > Overview** menu option. Which of the following metrics are available to chart in the top of page line graph? Select all that apply.

    a.   Average order value

    b.   Average pageviews/dollar

    c.   Average pageviews/conversion

    d.   Quantity

    e.   Revenue

    f.   Transactions

8. *True or False:* Google Analytics automatically assigns a Transaction ID to all ecommerce sales. As a result, this piece of sales information is not a required element of the data sent to Google Analytics.

9. Which of the following are provided as part of the **Conversions > Ecommerce > Time to Purchase** menu option? Select all that apply.

    a.   Number of days to transaction

    b.   Number of pageviews to transaction

    c.   Number of sessions to transaction

    d.   Time (in session minutes) to transaction

Imagine that you are the sales manager for your travel website. New management has arrived and has asked you for an analysis of ecommerce trends over the past month. Provide a point of view on the strengths and weaknesses of the site. What appears to be working? What needs improvement? Where would you focus upcoming strategic efforts? Be certain to use the data provided to support your point of view and recommendations.

Section XIV:
Attribution and ROI

In today's digital world, consumers encounter a number of touchpoints on their way to a conversion, for example, purchasing a product. A typical consumer, for example, might first learn about a product via an email, then read reviews, then read about the product on several blogs, then visit the product's website, then read more reviews, then see an AdWords ad, and then finally purchase the product. Attribution is the process by which a marketer assigns a value to each of these touchpoints in order to determine the relative contribution of each touchpoint to the final conversion. The four chapters in this section lead you through the process of working with and applying attribution models.

- Chapter 65 discusses the strengths and weaknesses of the primary types of attribution models.

- Chapter 66 illustrates how to obtain and apply Google Analytics attribution data to your own strategic information needs.

- Chapter 67 illustrates how attribution can help you better understand your return on investment in various marketing channels.

- Chapter 68 provides exercises to reinforce and extend the attribution concepts raised in the three previous chapters.

65

Attribution Models

Chapter 60 described how we determine which (if any) social networks served as a referral source immediately prior to a site session. But for many sites and blogs, the path to visitation or conversion is longer, containing many different channels in addition to social media, (e.g., paid and organic search, display advertising, and email).

Imagine, for example, Betsy's search for a new espresso machine:

- Betsy starts by reading reviews in her favorite online food blogs. She begins to create a list of brands in which she is interested. One of the blogs has a link to a review site, which Betsy visits.

- The next day, Betsy does a Google search for "espresso machines" and for each of the brands on her list. She clicks on several of the organic search terms, as well as several of the paid ads.

- Betsy narrows her list to two brands. She does another search to focus on just these two brands. The results show that there are YouTube videos related to each brand. She views the videos. Later that same day, while visiting her favorite food websites, she sees display advertising that describes a sale currently occurring at Best Buy. An espresso machine is featured in one of the ads. She clicks on the ad to visit the Best Buy site.

- Finally, Betsy decides on the brand she wants. She does another Google search to find the best price. She clicks on a paid search ad that takes her to Best Buy's website, where she buys a $500 machine.

This is a complicated but not unrealistic path to conversion. We have two options for determining the contribution of each channel or digital encounter to the final sale (i.e., conversion). On the one hand, we can decide that the last click prior to conversion gets all the credit for the conversion. Since Betsy's last click prior to conversion was the paid ad, Best Buy would give all the credit for the sale to this ad. But this just doesn't feel right because it ignores all of the exposure and influence of everything Betsy saw prior to the purchase. On the other hand, we can spread out credit for the conversion to all channels encountered prior to the conversion. This seems much more reasonable and this is what attribution modeling allows us to do.

Attribution models are a way to distribute the value of a conversion across all of the channels an individual encountered prior to the conversion. In Betsy's case, the $500 she spent on the espresso machine would be distributed across the following channels: social, organic search, paid display advertising, and direct site access.

Attribution models make us strategically smarter about individual channel contributions to the path to conversion, which in turn helps us determine whether our efforts and associated spending to influence consumers reflect consumers' actual behaviors. Once we know this, we can answer marketers' most fundamental question: What is our return on investment across all of the digital channels in which we are engaged? (This topic is explored in Chapter 68.)

Google Analytics performs three of the data-intensive jobs that allow us to accomplish a distribution of conversion credit across digital channels:

- it tracks consumers' journey to purchase;

- for each consumer, it records exposure to different channels during that journey; and

- it does the math that allocates conversion value across channels.

Our very important job is to tell Google Analytics how to perform the allocation. We accomplish this through the selection of one or more attribution models.

We begin by determining which attribution model(s) make the most sense for our brand, website, or blog. The model(s) we select represent our current understanding of the value of each sequential digital encounter during the consumers' path to conversion. Google Analytics provides seven predefined models from which we can choose.[45] We'll illustrate each model with the path to conversion shown below. We'll update this path as we discuss each attribution model available in Google Analytics.

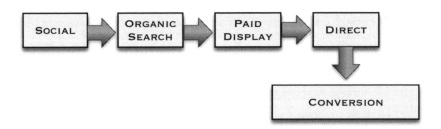

Last Interaction attribution model

This model assumes that only one channel influences the conversion and that this channel was the one encountered immediately preceding the conversion. No channel other than the one immediately prior to conversion is believed to exert any influence.

---

[45] We explore six of these models, ignoring the AdWords-focused model as this model applies only to AdWords advertisers.

It is now almost universally believed that this attribution model oversimplifies the conversion process and distorts the influence of all channels encountered prior to the conversion. As a result, this model has extremely limited usefulness and should only be used when it is assumed that:

- the path to conversion is short, with little to no consideration or evaluation taking place prior to conversion, and

- all channels are believed to exert the same level of influence when they occur immediately prior to the conversion.

The Last Interaction attribution model is illustrated below where 100% of the credit for the conversion is given to direct site access. The influence of all other channels encountered prior to this access are ignored to reflect the assumption that the consumer decided to access the site directly without being influenced by any other channels.

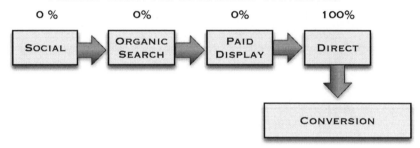

Last Non-Direct Click attribution model

This is a variation of the Last Interaction model. This model assumes that:

- direct site access and a subsequent conversion represent consumers who have already been influenced through a different channel prior to direct site access, and

- conversion can be attributed entirely to the last channel encountered prior to direct site access, and

- all channels are believed to exert the same level of influence when they occur immediately prior to the conversion.

This model is illustrated on the top of page 486, where 100% of the credit for the conversion is given to paid display, the last channel encountered prior to direct site access. The influence of all other channels prior to paid display are ignored.

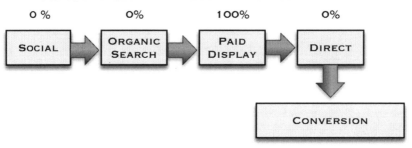

First Interaction attribution model

This model is a mirror image of the Last Interaction model and, as a consequence, reflects an opposite set of assumptions. The First Interaction attribution model assumes that only the first channel encountered in the path to conversion exerts any influence, regardless of the length of that path.

The First Interaction attribution model is illustrated below where 100% of the credit for the conversion is given to Social. The influence of all other channels are ignored because no channel other then the first one encountered is believed to exert any influence.

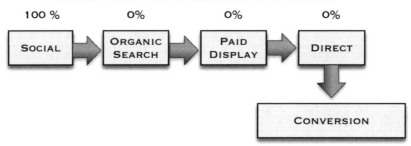

Linear Attribution model

This model deviates from the previous models in its beliefs that:

- all channels prior to a conversion are important,

- every channel exerts an equal amount of influence, and therefore,

- each channel deserves an equal amount of credit for the conversion.

The Linear Attribution model is illustrated below where credit for the conversion is allocated equally across all four channels encountered prior to the conversion, resulting in each channel being given 25% of the credit for the conversion.

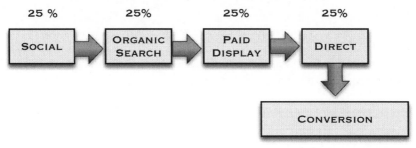

In the absence of other strategic information to inform your judgment regarding influences on the path to conversion, this and the next model are the recommended models to apply to your conversion data.

Time Decay model

The Time Decay model, illustrated below assumes that all channels encountered prior to conversion exert some influence, *and* that this influence increases as the consumer moves closer to the conversion. Thus, channels encountered closer to the conversion are given relatively more credit for that conversion.

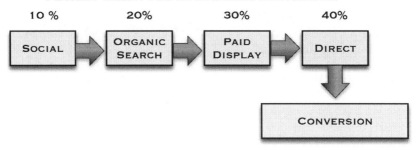

Google Analytics explains this model as follows: "This model is based on the concept of *exponential decay* and most heavily credits the touchpoints [i.e. channels] that occurred nearest to the time of conversion. The Time Decay model has a default *half-life* of 7 days, meaning that a touchpoint occurring 7 days prior to a conversion will receive 1/2 the credit of a touchpoint that occurs on the day of conversion. Similarly, a touchpoint occurring 14 days prior will receive 1/4 the credit of a day-of-conversion touchpoint."

Position Based model

This is a hybrid model, reflecting the assumptions of several of the previously discussed models. This model assumes that:

- all channels prior to a conversion are important, but

- the first and last encounter are relatively more important and therefore,

- the first and last encounter deserve to be given most of the credit for the conversion.

The Position Based model is illustrated below, where the first and last channels encountered are each given 40% of the credit for the conversion, while the remaining credit is distributed across the remaining channels.

PERCENT CREDIT FOR INFLUENCING CONVERSION:

40 %	10%	10%	40%
SOCIAL	ORGANIC SEARCH	PAID DISPLAY	DIRECT

CONVERSION

Attribution in practice

Once we specify a model, Google Analytics does all of the number crunching. Specifically, Google Analytics keeps track of every site users' path to conversion and then applies the model's credit allocation framework to that path.

Imagine, for example, that we want to use the Last Interaction attribution model to evaluate contributions to conversion. For simplicity, we'll apply this model to two site users, each of whom bought a $100 tour. Each user, however, took a different path to conversion, as shown below.

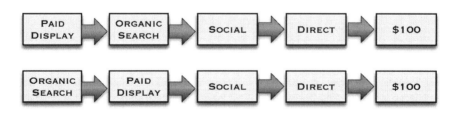

In each case, Google Analytics would allocate 100% of the credit for the conversion to the last channel encountered, which in both cases is Direct. Our Google Analytics report would state that $200 of the total $200 conversion value should be given to Direct. We would then assume that we don't need to invest in any other channels, as all of our sales are credited to Direct.

This outcome illustrates the flaw in the Last Interaction attribution model. Notice that multiple channels are encountered prior to conversion, and that Social always precedes conversion. Certainly, these channels, especially Social, deserve some credit. We can see the influence of the channels encountered prior to conversion by changing our model to the Time Decay attribution model. This model would result in the following credit to each channel:

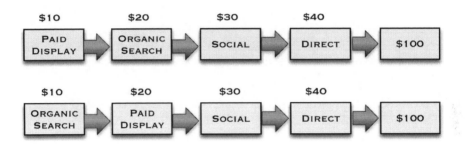

Adding the allocations for each channel results in the following:

Channel	Total $ Allocation	% of Total
Direct	$80	40%
Social	$60	30%
Paid Display	$30	15%
Organic Search	$30	15%

This outcome seems much more reasonable. Direct is given the most credit relative to the other channels, because it is the channel encountered immediately prior to the final conversion. Social's important role in always leading to the final channel is reflected in its high, but not highest, conversion credit. Finally, both Paid and Organic Search show relatively low levels of conversion credit given their relative distance from the final conversion.

The take away from this example is hopefully clear. The model we select to allocate credit for conversions has a direct impact on the conclusions we draw. Our use of the Last Interaction attribution model would lead us to believe that no channels other than Direct have any value to our business success. This conclusion would likely lead to disaster. The Time Decay attribution model, on the other hand, is much more likely to lead to business success, where we acknowledge the importance of Direct as the final channel encounter, but also note how Social plays an important role in leading to this final channel encounter and ultimate conversion.

66

Working With Attribution Models

We access Google Analytics attribution data from the **Conversions > Attribution > Model Comparison** menu option, shown below.

Clicking on **Model Comparison** brings up the display shown below. Before examining the data, however, we need to make certain that all of the settings are appropriate to our strategic information needs.

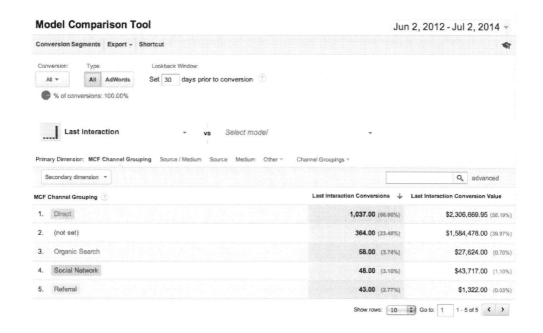

The very top of the page presents three options for data examination (see below).

- Within the **Conversion** pull-down menu (currently labeled "All") is a list of all web site goals and ecommerce transactions. Use this menu to select only those items of interest. In our case, we'll focus on ecommerce transactions.

- The middle display, labeled **Type**, asks you to select the data of interest. Here you can decide to examine all data or to isolate the data associated with your AdWords campaigns. We'll leave the default select **All**.

- **Lookback Window** is the final option. This setting determines the amount of time Google Analytics will track channel encounters prior to the conversion. You can increase or decrease the Lookback Window by clicking in the numeric display window (which is set by default to 30) and then using the resulting slider bar to increase or decrease the window to reflect your assumptions as to the length of the consideration phase leading to conversion (see below). A window of 30 days is the generally accepted time frame.

Once these settings are finalized, you can move on to interacting with the attribution models.

The initial data displayed after selecting **Conversions > Attribution > Model Comparison** is generated using the assumptions inherent in the Last Interaction attribution model (see below).

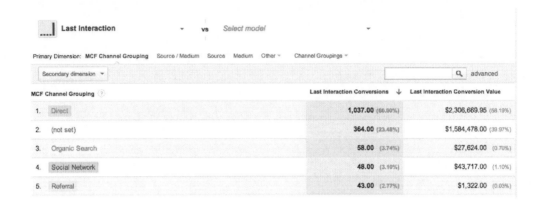

We know that the data represents the Last Interaction model because of the label immediately above the data display as well as the labels for the two data columns. This chart is interpreted as follows:

- The first column, labeled **MCF Channel Grouping**, shows all of the channels encountered prior to purchase. In our case, users encountered our site directly, and also used organic search, social networks, and referrals. Note that "(not set)" means that Google Analytics could not determine a specific channel.

- The middle column, labeled **Last Interaction Conversions**, reports the number of times each channel was given credit as the last channel encountered prior to conversion.

- The last column, labeled **Last Interaction Conversion Value**, presents the allocated conversion dollar value for each channel, where this amount is allocated according to the assumptions of the model selected. In this case, each channel is given 100% of its conversion value when it was the last channel encountered prior to conversion.

The data derived in this model would lead to the conclusion that only Direct is important and that it is a waste of time to place any effort in other channels.

We can test this conclusion by altering the model used to generate the data. Above the table (on the left-hand side) is a chart description currently labeled **Last Interaction**. This is actually a pull-down menu (see below) that allows you to change the model.

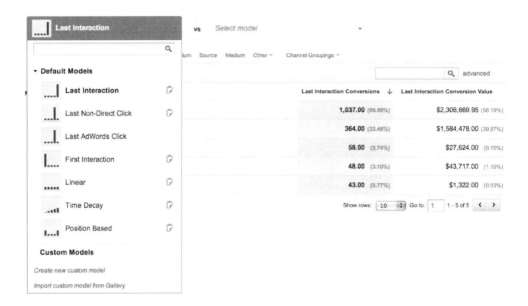

Selecting **Position Based**, for example, changes the data display to that shown below.

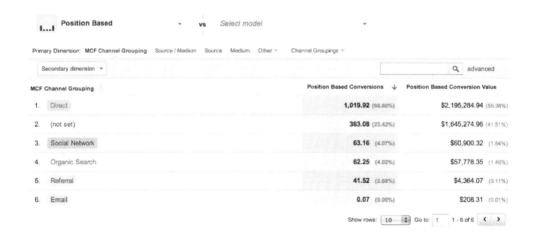

The outcomes derived from this model's assumptions appear (not unexpectedly) to be different than those shown in the **Last Interaction** model. However, it's hard to keep all the numbers in your head to make a direct comparison. Fortunately, Google Analytics simplifies this task for you.

In the previous section we saw how Google Analytics allows you to change the model being displayed. We can use this same portion of the display to simultaneously select, view, and compare two or three models in the same display.

To the right of the currently selected model name is a pull-down menu labeled **Select Model**. You can see this option just to the right of the **Last Interaction** label in the display shown below.

This pull-down menu labeled "Select model" also displays a list of attribution models (see below).

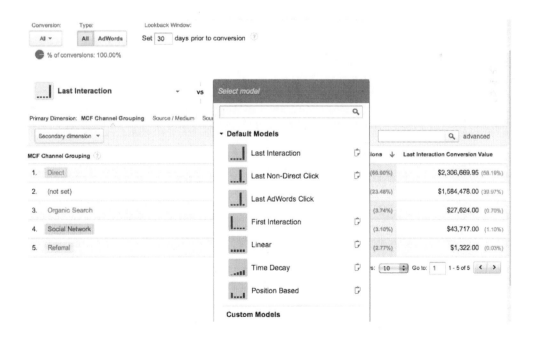

Selecting a model from this list, in this case **Position Based**, changes the data display to that shown below. Note that the names of both of the selected attribution models are now displayed above the numeric table.[46]

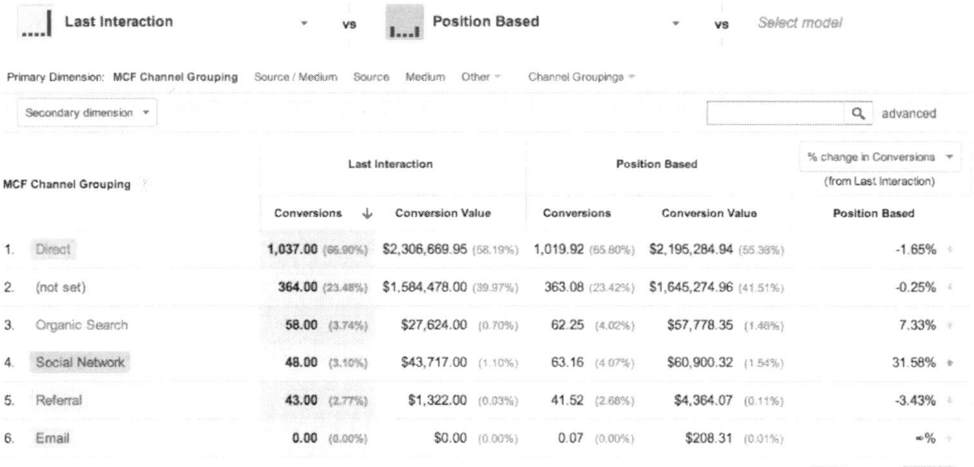

MCF Channel Grouping	Last Interaction		Position Based		% change in Conversions ▾ (from Last Interaction)
	Conversions ↓	Conversion Value	Conversions	Conversion Value	Position Based
1. Direct	**1,037.00** (66.90%)	$2,306,669.95 (58.19%)	1,019.92 (65.80%)	$2,195,284.94 (55.38%)	-1.65%
2. (not set)	**364.00** (23.48%)	$1,584,478.00 (39.97%)	363.08 (23.42%)	$1,645,274.96 (41.51%)	-0.25%
3. Organic Search	**58.00** (3.74%)	$27,624.00 (0.70%)	62.25 (4.02%)	$57,778.35 (1.46%)	7.33%
4. Social Network	**48.00** (3.10%)	$43,717.00 (1.10%)	63.16 (4.07%)	$60,900.32 (1.54%)	31.58%
5. Referral	**43.00** (2.77%)	$1,322.00 (0.03%)	41.52 (2.68%)	$4,364.07 (0.11%)	-3.43%
6. Email	**0.00** (0.00%)	$0.00 (0.00%)	0.07 (0.00%)	$208.31 (0.01%)	∞%

The table simultaneously presents data generated from both attribution models. The format is the same as the single model display. The first column displays channels encountered on the path to conversion, while the next two pairs of columns present conversions and conversion amounts for each attribution model. The last column allows us to compare the outcomes of the two models.

At the moment, the last column is labeled **% Change in Conversions** via a pull-down menu, and this change is relative to our first selected model: **Last Interaction**. Given how this comparison is calculated, make certain that the attribution model that you are using as your frame of reference model is always selected first. Notice how changing the model changes the conclusions we draw about the relative contribution of different channels. Direct remains the most important channel, but the number of conversions attributed to organic search and especially social network referral increased substantially when we shift to the Position Based model.

We can change the right-hand comparison from conversions to conversion value by selecting the pull-down menu currently labeled **% Change in Conversions** and selecting **% Change in Conversion Value**. This changes the previous display to that shown on the top of page 497. Once again we see the importance of the Direct channel, but the remaining channels are now significantly more important in terms of their contribution to conversion amount.

Once again, we can see how the model we select has a direct influence on how we interpret the success of our efforts and formulate subsequent strategic decisions.

---

[46] This example compares two models. You can, however, compare three models at the same time by using the Select Model pull-down menu to add a third model to the display,

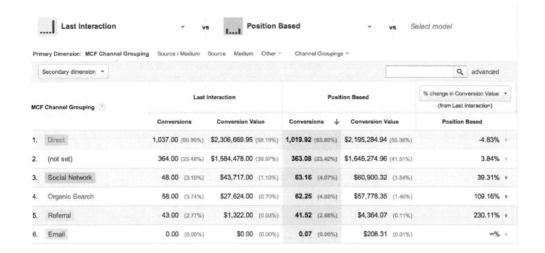

MCF Channel Grouping	Last Interaction		Position Based		% change in Conversion Value (from Last Interaction)
	Conversions	Conversion Value	Conversions ↓	Conversion Value	Position Based
1. Direct	1,037.00 (66.90%)	$2,306,669.95 (58.19%)	1,019.92 (65.80%)	$2,195,284.94 (55.38%)	-4.83%
2. (not set)	364.00 (23.48%)	$1,584,478.00 (39.97%)	363.08 (23.42%)	$1,645,274.96 (41.51%)	3.84%
3. Social Network	48.00 (3.10%)	$43,717.00 (1.10%)	63.16 (4.07%)	$60,900.32 (1.54%)	39.31%
4. Organic Search	58.00 (3.74%)	$27,624.00 (0.70%)	62.25 (4.02%)	$57,778.35 (1.46%)	109.16%
5. Referral	43.00 (2.77%)	$1,322.00 (0.03%)	41.52 (2.68%)	$4,364.07 (0.11%)	230.11%
6. Email	0.00 (0.00%)	$0.00 (0.00%)	0.07 (0.00%)	$208.31 (0.01%)	∞%

Custom attribution models

After you work with Google Analytics standard attribution models for a while, you may decide that you need to create your own model, one that reflects your own unique business situation and your specific customers' paths to conversion. Fortunately, Google Analytics makes this easy to accomplish.

Let's imagine that the standard **Position Based** attribution model best fits your analytical needs, but that it could nevertheless be fine-tuned to better describe your customers' paths to conversion. You begin the customization process by activating the pull-down menu attached to the current attribution model's name, as shown on below.

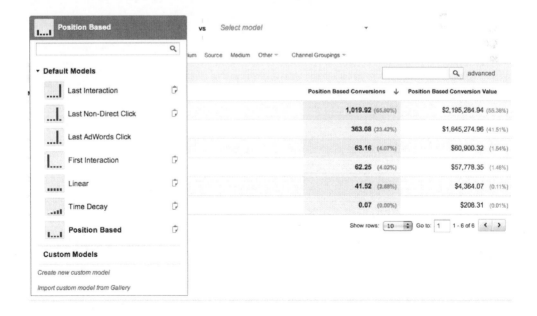

On the very bottom of the menu is a link labeled **Create new custom model**. Clicking on this link brings up the display shown below.

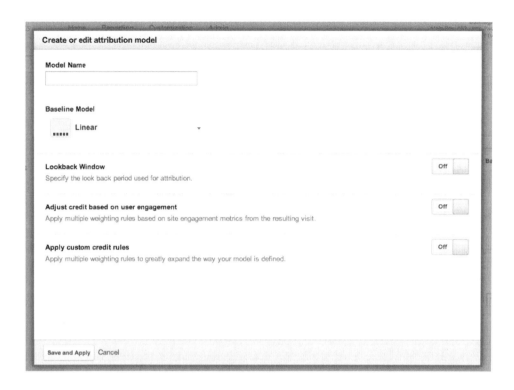

We'll name the file "Modified Position Based Model" and select **Position Based** from the **Baseline Model** pull-down menu. The display then changes to items relevant to the Position Based model, as shown page 499.

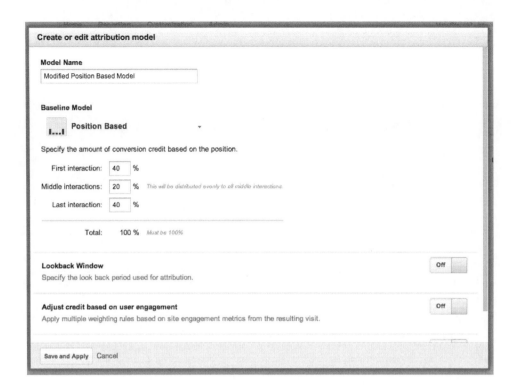

The standard Position Based model's assumptions for distributing conversion credit are shown in the middle of the display. The model currently uses a 40 - 20 - 40 percent distribution. But, we want this new model to distribute conversion credit as 50 - 35 - 15 percent. So, we change the percentages shown to these new percentages. Next, we turn the **Lookback Window** "On" and then use the slider or text box to indicate 30 days. Finally, we leave the last two settings turned "Off". All of these settings are shown on the top of page 500. When we are satisfied with our settings, we click **Save and Apply**. The custom attribution model is then applied to the current data set.

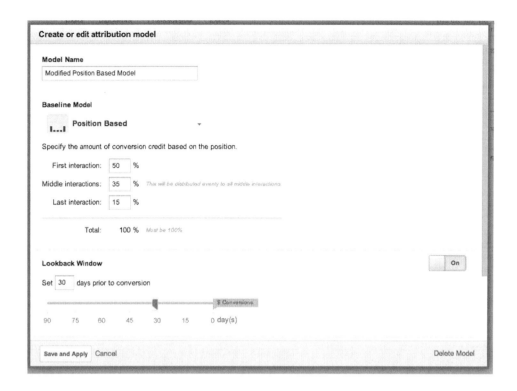

The tables below and on the top of page 501 compare our Modified Position Based model to the standard Position Based model. Both tables indicate that our change in how conversion credit is allocated affects both conversion credit (the table below) and especially conversion amount (the table on the top of page 501).

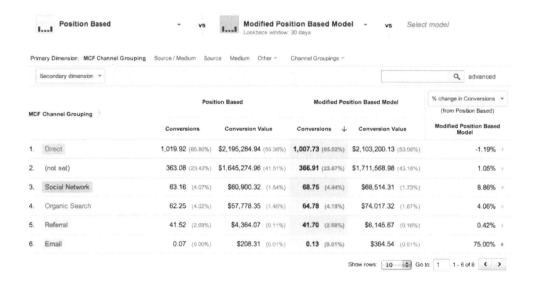

MCF Channel Grouping	Position Based		Modified Position Based Model		% change in Conversions ▼ (from Position Based)
	Conversions	Conversion Value	Conversions ↓	Conversion Value	Modified Position Based Model
1. Direct	1,019.92 (65.80%)	$2,195,284.94 (56.38%)	1,007.73 (65.02%)	$2,103,200.13 (53.06%)	-1.19%
2. (not set)	363.08 (23.42%)	$1,645,274.96 (41.51%)	366.91 (23.67%)	$1,711,568.98 (43.18%)	1.05%
3. Social Network	63.16 (4.07%)	$60,900.32 (1.54%)	68.75 (4.44%)	$68,514.31 (1.73%)	8.86%
4. Organic Search	62.25 (4.02%)	$57,778.35 (1.46%)	64.78 (4.18%)	$74,017.32 (1.87%)	4.06%
5. Referral	41.52 (2.68%)	$4,364.07 (0.11%)	41.70 (2.69%)	$6,145.67 (0.16%)	0.42%
6. Email	0.07 (0.00%)	$208.31 (0.01%)	0.13 (0.01%)	$364.54 (0.01%)	75.00%

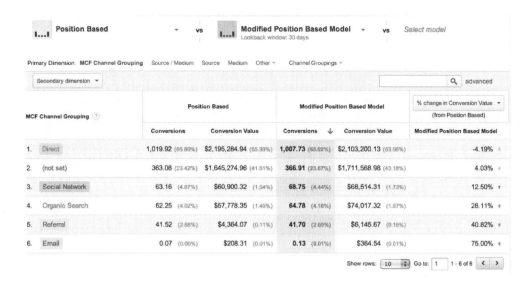

MCF Channel Grouping ?	Position Based		Modified Position Based Model		% change in Conversion Value ▼ (from Position Based)
	Conversions	Conversion Value	Conversions ↓	Conversion Value	Modified Position Based Model
1. Direct	1,019.92 (65.80%)	$2,195,284.94 (55.36%)	1,007.73 (65.02%)	$2,103,200.13 (53.06%)	-4.19% ↓
2. (not set)	363.08 (23.42%)	$1,645,274.96 (41.51%)	366.91 (23.67%)	$1,711,568.98 (43.18%)	4.03% ↑
3. Social Network	63.16 (4.07%)	$60,900.32 (1.54%)	68.75 (4.44%)	$68,514.31 (1.73%)	12.50% ↑
4. Organic Search	62.25 (4.02%)	$57,778.35 (1.46%)	64.78 (4.18%)	$74,017.32 (1.87%)	28.11% ↑
5. Referral	41.52 (2.68%)	$4,364.07 (0.11%)	41.70 (2.69%)	$6,145.67 (0.16%)	40.82% ↑
6. Email	0.07 (0.00%)	$208.31 (0.01%)	0.13 (0.01%)	$364.54 (0.01%)	75.00% ↑

You can select, edit, or share custom attribution models by using the attribution model pull-down menu and scrolling down (if necessary) to **Custom Models**, as shown below.

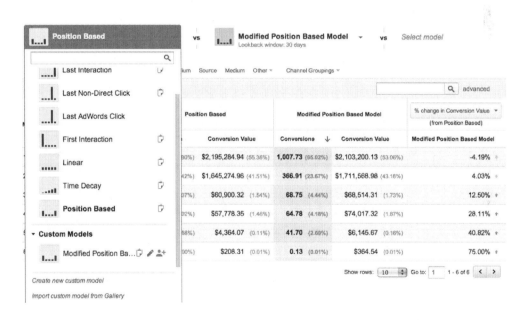

We don't need to end model customization with just the percentage allocation for conversion credit and conversion value. We can select and give extra credit to a channel that we believe deserves extra credit regardless of its position in the conversion path. Imagine, for example, that we think the Social channel exerts an important influence at any point in the conversion path in which it appears, and as a result, we want our model to take this into account when calculating credit for conversions and conversion amounts.

We begin by selecting **Create new custom model** in the model pull-down menu (see the bottom of the lower figure on page 501). This model begins the same as the previous model, only this time with a new name. We'll call this new model "Social Bonus Modified Position Based". Next, we select Position Based as our baseline model, change the percentages shown to 50 - 35 - 15, turn the **Lookback Window** "On", and then use the slider or text box to indicate 30 days. Finally, we scroll to the bottom of the page and turn **Adjust custom credit rules** "On". The figure shown below will then appear.

The top pull-down menu (currently labeled **Position in Path**) allows us to choose the type of interaction to which we want to allocate extra credit. We select **MCF Channel Grouping** from this menu and **Social Network** from the menu to its immediate right. Then, on the bottom of the display we set the credit display to "10" to indicate that we want Social Network to have ten times the credit of other channels in the path to conversion (see below). When done, we select **Save and Apply** from the bottom of the page (which is not shown below).

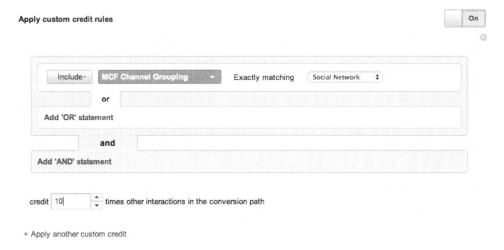

The table below displays the conversion amount credit assigned by the original **Position Based** model and the **Social Bonus Modified Position Based** model. Notice how all channels are affected, some much more than others, as we change the underlying assumptions of the model. This is why, from a strategic perspective, it is so important to develop a model that fits your unique set of conversion circumstances.

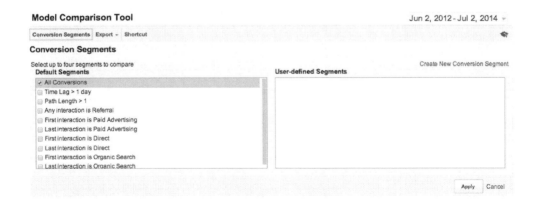

MCF Channel Grouping	Position Based		Social Bonus Modified Position Based		% change in Conversion Value ▼ (from Position Based)
	Conversions	Conversion Value	Conversions ↓	Conversion Value	Social Bonus Modified Position Based
1. Direct	1,019.92 (65.80%)	$2,195,284.94 (55.36%)	982.27 (63.37%)	$2,089,385.24 (52.71%)	-4.82% ↓
2. (not set)	363.08 (23.42%)	$1,645,274.96 (41.51%)	365.99 (23.61%)	$1,698,799.35 (42.86%)	3.25% ↑
3. Social Network	63.16 (4.07%)	$60,900.32 (1.54%)	97.55 (6.29%)	$95,171.78 (2.40%)	56.27% ↑
4. Organic Search	62.25 (4.02%)	$57,778.35 (1.46%)	63.02 (4.07%)	$74,003.58 (1.87%)	28.08% ↑
5. Referral	41.52 (2.68%)	$4,364.07 (0.11%)	41.05 (2.65%)	$6,123.64 (0.15%)	40.32% ↑
6. Email	0.07 (0.00%)	$208.31 (0.01%)	0.11 (0.01%)	$327.37 (0.01%)	57.15% ↑

Refining the data

We can not only change the underlying assumptions of an attribution model, but we can also change the data to which the model is applied.

It is often useful to restrict the data displayed after an attribution model is selected. These restrictions allow you to more precisely focus on specific aspects of the path to conversion. This is accomplished by using the **Conversion Segments** pull-down menu just below the page title. Selecting a single option from this menu restricts the data set to only those paths to conversion that match your selected criteria. Clicking on this box brings up the display shown below where "All Conversions" is checked by default.

As an example, I can choose to view conversion values for any path beginning with Organic Search or only those paths that are longer than a single encounter. Let's explore the first option.

Checking "First Interaction is Organic Search" and unchecking "All Conversions" in the pull-down menu restricts the data being analyzed to just the paths to conversion that begin with Organic Search. These data are shown below for the First Interaction attribution model.

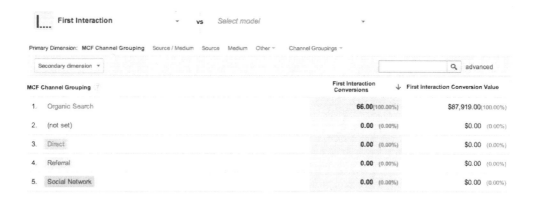

Here we learn that there were 66 conversions in which the path to conversion began with Organic Search. These conversions were worth $87,919. But how did these paths end? We can answer this question by adding the Last Interaction Attribution Model to the table. This new table is shown below.

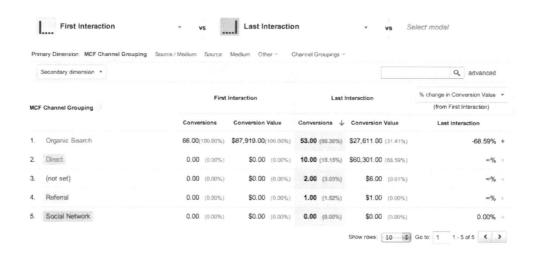

With this chart, we acquire a very important insight into the path to conversion when the path begins with Organic Search. Of the 66 conversions begun with Organic Search, 53 of these ended with organic search, indicating a path length of just this single encounter. However, 10 of the remaining paths begun with Organic Search ended with Direct. While this might seem a small number, look at the conversion column. The ten paths involving Direct as the final encounter generate significantly more revenue than when Organic Search is the only channel encountered. We would certainly want to explore this trend to determine how we can capitalize on the Organic Search to Direct path to conversion.

67

Attribution Data and Return on Investment

Attribution data provides the information marketers need to determine the return from their time and financial investment overall and in different channels. This chapter begins with a basic discussion of the return on investment calculation. It then moves on to an illustration of how this calculation can be performed using attribution data. Finally, the chapter closes with a discussion of the strategic application of this calculation to channel support. This discussion illustrates how you can conduct your own Return on Investment analysis.

Return on Investment defined

Return on Investment (ROI) is a calculation that places the revenue you receive from marketing efforts in the context of how much you spent to obtain those revenues. ROI is calculated as follows:

First, calculate your Net Revenue (NR) by subtracting Total Costs from Total Revenue: $NR = \text{Total Revenue} - \text{Total Costs}$

Next, divide NR by Total Costs to obtain percent gain/loss (%GL) $\%GL = (NR \div \text{Total Costs})$

Finally, obtain ROI by multiplying %GL by 100 and adding the percent sign $ROI = \%GL * 100$

Imagine, for example, that your total marketing expenditures for the year are $100,000 and that total revenues for the period are $250,000. Your return on investment would be calculated as follows:

First, calculate your Net Revenue (NR) by subtracting Total Costs from Total Revenue:	NR = Total Revenue – Total Costs	NR = 250,000 - 100,000 = **150,000**
Next, divide NR by Total Costs to obtain percent gain/loss (%GL)	%GL = NR / Total Costs	%GL = 150,000 ÷ 100,000 = **1.5**
Finally, obtain ROI by multiplying %GL by 100 and adding the percent sign	ROI = %GL * 100	ROI = 1.5 * 100 = **150%**

The ROI in this example indicates that we have made a 150% return on investment, that is, for every dollar spent we made $1.50. Thus, interpreting an ROI calculation is straight forward: a positive ROI means that we made money, a negative ROI means that we lost money.

Overall ROI

Our goal is to determine both overall and channel specific ROI. We'll use the data collected by Google Analytics to represent revenue. With this information, we'll calculate overall ROI first.

Two pieces of data are required for the computation of overall ROI: total revenues and total costs. We'll use the **Conversions > Ecommerce > Overview** report to find total revenue, which is $3,948,981.95 (this is the same number as adding the individual channels in the Conversion Value column in any of the **Conversions > Attribution > Model Comparison** reports). We'll round total revenues to $3,950,000. Our marketing expenditures for the same time period for all channels and activities were, in total, $3,750,000. We calculate overall ROI as follows:

First, calculate your Net Revenue (NR) by subtracting Total Costs from Total Revenue:	NR = Total Revenue – Total Costs	NR = ($3,950,000 - 3,750,000) = **200,000**
Next, divide NR by Total Costs to obtain percent gain/loss (%GL)	%GL = NR / Total Costs	%GL = 200,000/3,750,000 = **.05333**
Finally, obtain ROI by multiplying %GL by 100 and adding the percent sign	ROI = %GL * 100	ROI = .05333 * 100 = **5.33%**

Overall, not a great year for ROI. The revenue generated by all of our marketing activities just very barely exceeded our marketing expenditures.

The overall ROI results are pretty depressing. An examination of ROI by channel may provide insights into this outcome.

In order to examine ROI by channel we need to determine channel specific expenditures and revenue for each channel. Channel-specific expenditures come from our internal records. Channel-specific revenues come from our selected attribution model report. We'll use the Social Bonus Modified Position Model created in Chapter 66 and shown below.

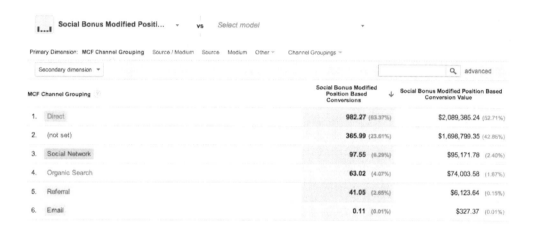

First, we create a table that provides revenues, expenditures, and net revenues by channel. Note that: (1) we include only those channels for which we have revenue estimates, (2) the **(not set)** channel grouping has been eliminated as we don't know the specific channel(s) that are reported here, and (3) the total of these channel expenditures does not equal the total expenditures shown in the previous section because those expenditures included activities beyond these specific channels. This table is shown below where all revenue numbers have been rounded.

Channel	Expenditures	Revenue	Net Revenue
Direct	$2,500,000	$2,089,390	- $410,610
Social Network	$50,000	$95,170	+ $45,170
Organic Search (for SEO)	$30,000	$74,000	+ $44,000
Referral	$9,000	$6,120	- $2,880
Email	$1,000	$330	- $670

All that remains is to use the ROI formula presented earlier to calculate ROI by channel. The results of these calculations have been added to the prior table, as shown below.

Channel	Expenditures	Revenue	Net Revenue	Channel ROI
Direct	$2,500,000	$2,089,390	- $410,610	-16.4%
Social Network	$50,000	$95,170	+ $45,170	+90.3%
Organic Search (for SEO)	$30,000	$74,000	+ $44,000	+146.7%
Referral	$9,000	$6,120	- $2,880	-32.0%
Email	$1,000	$ 330	- $670	-67.0%

The analysis shows that investments in different channels have different outcomes. At the moment, we are losing money in three channels (Direct, Referral, and Email) and making money (i.e., a profit) in two channels (Social Network and Organic Search). The strategic implications of these findings are discussed next.

Strategic ROI

The overall ROI calculation shows that we are just breaking even. The above analysis by channel shows us how well each channel is performing. The ROI by channel analysis also provides insights into how overall ROI can be improved.

- Direct conversions comprise the overwhelming majority of sales. But, the negative ROI indicates that we are losing money on this channel. We can use the **Conversions > Ecommerce > Overview** menu option combined with custom segments to discover that our conversion rate (18.6%) and average sale ($3,200) for this channel are both relatively low. We need to develop a strategic plan to increase both of these metrics. Beyond this, we need to become more efficient with regards to our marketing efforts in this channel. Decreasing expenditures while improving conversion rate and increasing average sale amount should reverse the negative ROI observed in this channel.

- Two channels, Social Network and Organic Search, show significant promise. At the moment, the overall dollar revenue from these channels is relatively low, but their ROI is very high. Investing marketing support in these channels, given their high ROI, should help our overall ROI improve. This is especially true given that these channels' conversion rates are very high (34.5% and 42.8%, respectively) as are their average sales ($5,100 and $6,500, respectively). Clearly, a strategic plan that provides greater support for these two channels is needed.

- Two channels, Referral and Email, appear to negatively impact our overall ROI. Revenue from these two channels is not only very low, but there also appears to be little motivation for us to invest in these channels given their negative ROI. Marketing support for these two channels should probably be eliminated and these funds should instead be invested in other areas where there is a greater likelihood of a positive return..

68

Practice with Attribution and ROI

This chapter presents three sets of exercises to help you apply and extend your knowledge of attribution and ROI.

True/false and multiple choice

This first set of questions makes certain that you understand key concepts. Feel free to open and refer to the relevant chapters or access your analytics account. When you are done, or if you are stuck, the answers can be found on page 624.

1. *True or False:* **Attribution modeling** allows us (if we desire) to spread out credit for a conversion to all channels encountered prior to the conversion.

2. Which of the following are standard attribution models provided by Google Analytics? (Select all that apply)

    a. Pageview Dominance model

    b. Last Interaction model

    c. Time Decay model

    d. Conversion Click model

    e. Linear model

3. *True or False:* The **Last Interaction** attribution model should be used when there is a great deal of consideration/evaluation prior to the point of actual purchase.

4. *True or False:* Attribution models can only be used when the path to conversion consists of four or fewer touchpoints.

5. *True or False:* It is recommended that Paid Display advertising always be given 25% of the credit for a conversion.

6. *True or False:* It is recommended that Social only be given credit for a conversion when it is the first touchpoint in the conversion path.

Use the figure and options shown below to answer Questions 7 to 10.

Response options:

    a.   Last Interaction model

    b.   Last Non-Direct Click model

    c.   First Interaction model

    d.   Linear model

    e.   Time Decay

    f.   Position Based

7.   Which attribution model(s) would give all the credit for the conversion to Organic Search?

8.   Which attribution model(s) would give all the credit for the conversion to Paid Advertising?

9.   Which attribution model(s) would give equal credit to each of the touchpoints prior to conversion?

10. Which attribution model(s) would give more credit to Social and Paid Display and less credit given to Direct and Organic Search?

The figure shown below displays two paths to conversion used by two different users. Use this figure to answer Questions 11 to 13.

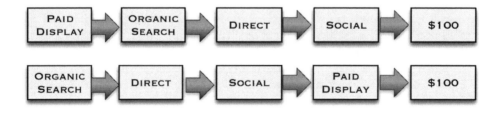

11. Using the Linear Attribution model, what percent of the total conversion value would be given to Direct?

    a. 0%

    b. 20%

    c. 25%

    d. 35%

    e. 50%

12. Using the Position Based model, what percent of the total conversion value would be given to Social?

    a. 0%

    b. 20%

    c. 25%

    d. 35%

    e. 50%

13. Using the Last Interaction Attribution model, what percent of the total conversion value would be given to Organic Search?

    a. 0%

    b. 20%

    c. 25%

    d. 35%

    e. 50%

14. *True or False:* Google Analytics will only allow you to view two attribution models at the same time.

15. *True or False:* The Google Analytics **Model Comparison Tool** allows you to only see data relevant to ecommerce transactions.

16. *True or False:* Thirty days is the maximum amount of time for a **Lookback Window**.

17. *True or False:* A **Custom Attribution** model allows you to specify conversion credit for each touchpoint in the path to conversion.

18. *True or False:* ROI stands for "Return on Investment."

19. *True or False:* An ROI of 175% means that you made $17.50 for every dollar spent.

20. What would the ROI be for the situation shown below?

Net Revenue: $500

Total Costs: $300

    a.   6.7%

    b.   16.0%

    c.   66.7%

    d.   96.7%

    e.   200.0%

Hands-On: Attribution models

This set of exercises makes certain that you understand attribution models. Use your own site data to respond to each exercise. Feel free to open and refer to the previous chapters or access your analytics account when working through the exercises.

1. Compare the Last Interaction and First Interaction models in terms of conversions and conversion value. What, if any, are the significant differences between the two models' channel credit allocation?

2. Compare the Linear, Time Decay, and Position Based models in terms of conversions and conversion value. What, if any, are the significant differences between the three models' channel credit allocation?

3. Based on questions 1 and 2, which model do you think best represents your site users' path to conversion?

4. Repeat questions 1 through 2 setting your view to **Path Length > 1**. What additional insights, if any, are obtained via this option?

5. Repeat questions 1 through 2 setting your view to **Time Lag > 1 Day**. What additional insights, if any, are obtained via this option?

6. Create a custom attribution model using the **Position Based** model as the baseline. Set the relative percentages to 30 - 20 - 50. Set the **Lookback Window** to 15 days. Give Social 5x extra credit.

Imagine that you have the responsibility to analyze and make recommendations with regard to the various channels that drive traffic to your site. Which attribution model do you think best describes channel influence? Why do you recommend that particular model? Using the insights provided by your selected attribution model, prepare a point of view that identifies channels that merit additional support and channels for which support should be reduced or eliminated. (You can make up the dollar amount of marketing support given to each channel.) Be certain to support your recommendations with Google Analytics engagement, conversion, and conversion value data.

Google Analytics Demystified

Section XV:
Experiments

We often use our best informed judgment to make decisions with regard to site design and content. There are times, however, where important insights and direction come from a more objective source - data gathered via an experiment. An experiment allows us to ask a question, manipulate appropriate stimuli, and then collect data to see how the manipulations affect the outcome. We could, for example, develop three alternative versions of our home page and use judgment to pick the "best." Or, we could conduct an experiment, expose the pages to site visitors in a systematic way, and then use Google Analytics data to see the relationship between alternative page design and subsequent conversions. The latter approach is more likely to lead to a better decision.

The four chapters in this section introduce you to experiments and explain how you can conduct experiments with Google Analytics.

- Chapter 69 provides an introduction to experiments and experimental planning.

- Chapter 70 leads you through the steps required to create an experiment with Google Analytics.

- Chapter 71 discusses how to manage experiments and interpret the data collected through experiments.

- Chapter 72 provides practice exercises to reinforce the discussion in Chapters 69, 70 and 71.

Introduction to Experiments

The process of website or blog development typically begins with informed judgment. We apply what we know about our business, competitors, and target audience to decisions related to design and content. Google Analytics provides descriptive data hat facilitates insights into the strengths and weaknesses of these decisions.

There are times and situations, however, when descriptive data are not enough, especially when we need the answers to "how does" questions, for example:

-   How does moving our sharing icons from the right- to left-hand side of the page affect the percentage of site visitors clicking to share?

-   How does changing the placement of our "Register Now" button affect registration rate?

-   How does changing the length and style of our home page headline affect bounce rate?

-   How does changing our call-to-action from text to image affect the rate of contact?

-   How does altering our check-out process from three steps to two steps affect shopping cart abandonment and transaction completion?

-   How does changing the images on our tour selection page from places to people affect transaction completion and amount?

All of these questions imply that we are seeking to determine causality - the effect of changes in one area on one or more other areas. The best way to determine causality is through an experiment.

The use of experiments to determine causality makes a significant contribution to successful website or blog planning and revision. Fortunately, Google Analytics provides an easy way to conduct experiments. Before discussing the specific types of experiments that can be conducted, however, one additional insight into experimental planning is necessary.

The planning stage of an experiment is crucial to the experiment's ability to provide insightful, actionable information. Thus, when planning an experiment it is necessary to explicitly answer the following questions prior to initiating the experiment:

- What is the background, that is, what concerns or information needs are motivating the experiment?

- What do we need to manipulate?

- How will we measure to outcome of the manipulation?

- Is the manipulation reasonable, that is, why do we believe that there is a relationship between what we are manipulating and what we are measuring as the outcome(s)?

The use of these questions in experimental planning is illustrated below.

What is the background and how does this lead to what we specifically need to learn?	The bounce rate of our home page is unacceptably high (42%) and has consistently remained at this level over the past three months. It has been proposed that the font used on this page is both too small and too dense in layout, discouraging visitors from staying and engaging with the content. We need to learn whether altering the type appearance on the home page reduces the bounce rate.
What do we need to manipulate?	We need to manipulate the type style and density. Specifically, we will increase the type size from 9 point to 11 point and at the same time we will move from single to double spacing. Content will remain unchanged.
How will we measure the outcome of the manipulation?	We will evaluate the effect of the manipulation in terms of bounce rate, comparing the bounce rate of the original page to that of the revised page. Data on both pages will be collected at the same time, keeping the effect of any external influences on the outcome consistent across both pages.
Is the manipulation reasonable?	It is believed that the effect of type size and density on bounce rate is reasonable, as competitive sites all use less dense approaches to content presentation.

An A/B experiment is the simplest form of experimental design.

An A/B test evaluates the effect of a **single** revision or change on your outcome measure(s), where "A" refers to your original stimulus and "B" refers to your altered stimulus. An A/B test, for example, might alter the color of a "register now" button while leaving placement and all other page elements the same. Alternatively, an A/B test might alter the headline on the page, once again leaving all other elements the same. Thus, in an A/B test it is crucial that only one revision be made at a time, allowing any differences in outcome between the A and B versions to be attributed to the single change. Given a single change, the execution of an A/B test is straightforward, as illustrated in the above figure: half of site visitors are randomly assigned to view the "A" version while the remaining half view the "B" version.

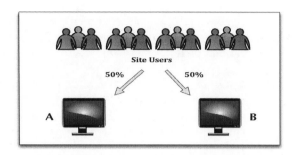

Every A/B test is unique in that it is designed to satisfy a specific set of strategic information needs. However, across websites and blogs, the following are commonly addressed issues:

- the wording, size, color and placement of calls-to action
- the placement and size of sharing icons
- the wording and appearance of a headline or product description
- the layout of page functional elements such as menus, content, and images
- form layout and field sequence
- types, size and placement of images

There are better and worse ways to conduct an A/B test. .[47]

Things to do:

- *Know how long to run a test.* Ending the test too early can lead to false conclusions because you may have gotten different results had you waited a little longer to obtain more data from a larger sample. Ending the test too late isn't good either, because poorly performing variations could cost you conversions and sales. You can estimate how long to run a test by using a calculator like the

---

[47] Adapted from Smash Magazine, http://www.smashingmagazine.com/2010/06/24/the-ultimate-guide-to-a-b-testing/

one provided by Visual Website Optimizer[48] or you can keep running the test until you find a statistically significant difference between the A and B variations.

- *Show repeat visitors the same variations.* You should have a mechanism for remembering which variation a visitor has seen. This prevents visitor confusion when, for example, the same visitor is shown different visuals, prices, offers, or content on different visits.

- *Make your A/B test consistent across the whole website.* If you are testing a sign-up button that appears in multiple locations, then a visitor should see the same variation everywhere. Showing one variation on your home page and another variation on the registration page will confuse the visitor and skew the results.

Things not to do:

- *Never wait to test the variation until after you've tested the original.* Always test both versions simultaneously. If you test one version one week and the second variation the next week, extraneous variables may be the real influence on the outcome. It's possible, for example that the "B" version is actually less effective than the "A" version in motivating sales, but you had better sales while testing it because a huge snowstorm kept people indoors during use of this version. Always split traffic between two versions at the same time.

- *Don't surprise regular visitors.* If you are testing a core part of your website, include only new visitors in the test. This can be done through the use of cookies outside of Google Analytics. You want to avoid shocking regular visitors, especially because the variations may not ultimately be implemented.

- *Don't let your gut feeling overrule test results.* The winners in A/B tests are often surprising or counter-intuitive. On a green-themed website, a stark red button could emerge as the winner, even if the red button isn't easy on the eye. Don't reject an outcome simply because you disagree with or predicted different results.

Finally, there are two important things to keep in mind with regard to A/B testing. First, A/B tests are not restricted to websites. You can use the same approach to test the comparative impact of alternative approaches within email, blog posts, and similar digital communications. Second, it is possible to test three (or more) variations of the same change at the same time. Imagine, for example, that you wanted to test the impact of photos of people (the original) versus pets (revision "B") versus scenery (revision "C"). Since only one element is changing across variations (i.e., image subject matter), this would simply be an A/B/C test.

---

[48] See http://visualwebsiteoptimizer.com/ab-split-test-duration/

A/B tests explore the effect of a single revision on one or more outcome measures. Sometimes, though, it is necessary to simultaneously measure the effects of two manipulations at the same time. We choose this approach when we think that there may be some interaction or interplay between the two manipulations. Let's illustrate this approach with an example.

Imagine a home page with a high bounce rate. This page is visually quite dense, with a display that includes many small pictures and uses very small type. You want to know whether a change in just pictures *or* just type *or* both pictures and type at the same time will affect the bounce rate. This information need can be answered with a factorial design.

Once the planning questions have been answered, a factorial design experiment begins with the identification of factors and levels. A factor is a manipulation. We have two factors in this example, pictures and text. Each factor consists of two or more levels (also referred to as options), which represent the actual manipulations. In this case, each factor has two levels. The levels for pictures will be Eight (the number of pictures on the current home page) and Four (the number of pictures on the revised page). The levels for text will be Small (as on the current page) and Large (as on the revised page).

The number of stimuli needed for a factorial design experiment is determined by multiplying the numbers of levels across all factors. In this case we would need four stimuli (obtained by multiplying 2 x 2; 2 levels of pictures x 2 levels of type). We then create one stimuli for each combination of levels. This is illustrated in the grid shown below where the numbers refer to variation numbers.

	Factor 1	
	Small Type	Large Type
Eight pictures	1	2
Factor 2		
Four pictures	3	4

The four numbered variations in the grid will have the following characteristics:

Variation 1:	Small type, Eight pictures
Variation 2:	Large type, Eight pictures
Variation 3:	Small type, Four pictures
Variation 4:	Large type, Four pictures

This experiment would be executed similarly to an A/B test, except here site visitors would be randomly assigned to view one of the four test stimuli, keeping in mind and applying the do's and don'ts for A/B testing discussed earlier.

70

Creating an Experiment With Google Analytics

Before launching a Google Analytics experiment, it is necessary to have all stimulus pages loaded on your server and accessible online. Once this is done, you begin the process by selecting **Behavior > Experiments**. Selecting this option brings you to the page which lists all of your experiments. The page shown below will display if you have not yet created any experiments.

The display changes after you create your first experiment. Now, all of your current and past experiments are listed, as shown below for the experiments being conducted on my website. When examining the list keep in mind that experiments are view specific, so an experiment will only be shown in the view in which it was created.

Experiments are initiated by clicking on **Create experiment**. The next display (see below) presents an overview of the four steps we need to go through to create an experiment.

This first step asks you to provide a descriptive name for the experiment (we'll call ours "Purchase Page Image Test") and to identify your outcome measure via the pull down **Select a metric** menu. We'll choose **Revenue** within the **Ecommerce** menu, keeping in mind that an outcome measure does not have to be transactions or, in fact, any ecommerce measure. Different experimental objectives might require the use of a goal as the outcome measure. Next, we determine the percentage of website traffic we want to participate in the experiment. The greater the percentage, the quicker results can be obtained. However, if your experiment involves drastic or risky changes, you might want to include only a small proportion of your site's traffic in the experiment. We'll set this parameter to 100%, allowing all site visitors to participate. Since we don't need any email notifications we leave this set to "Off" and select **Next Step**.

Step 2 asks us to identify the test materials (see the display on the top of page 526). We type in the full URL to our current and test page and give each page a descriptive name. We use the displayed images to confirm that the correct pages have been selected. Since we are running a simple A/B test, just the two pages shown are required. If we were running an experiment with more variations, we would click on the **+Add Variation** link to add additional test variations. In either case, when done we select the **Next Step** link.

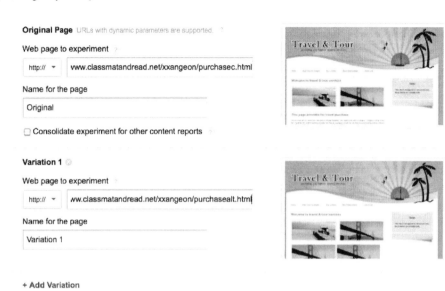

Step 3 asks us how we want to handle the tracking code necessary for the experiment to run and for Google Analytics to collect data (see below).

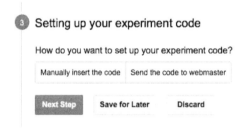

Since we are doing this ourselves, we click on **Manually insert the code**, after which we see the display shown on the top of page 527.

Adding script code to your page ⓘ

1. Make sure your original and variation pages have Google Analytics tracking code installed.
2. Then, paste this experiment code immediately after the opening head tag at **the top** of your original page.

```
<!-- Google Analytics Content Experiment code -->
<script>function utmx_section(){}function utmx(){}(function(){var
k='80466313-19',d=document,l=d.location,c=d.cookie;
if(l.search.indexOf('utm_expid='+k)>0)return;
function f(n){if(c){var i=c.indexOf(n+'=');if(i>-1){var j=c.
indexOf(';',i);return escape(c.substring(i+n.length+1,j<0?c.
length:j))}}}var x=f('__utmx'),xx=f('__utmxx'),h=l.hash;d.write(
'<sc'+'ript src="'+'http'+(l.protocol=='https:'?'s://ssl':
'://www')+'.google-analytics.com/ga_exp.js?'+'utmxkey='+k+
'&utmx='+(x?x:'')+'&utmxx='+(xx?xx:'')+'&utmxtime='+new Date().
valueOf()+(h?'&utmxhash='+escape(h.substr(1)):'')+
'" type="text/javascript" charset="utf-8"><\/sc'+'ript>')})();
</script><script>utmx('url','A/B');</script>
<!-- End of Google Analytics Content Experiment code -->
```

Additional information for your experiment code:

> **Experiment ID:** PYfum_W_SmePjEH6teDzCQ
> **Experiment Key:** 80466313-19

Publish experiment pages

> Publish your original and variation pages to the web.
> When you're done - Click **Next Step** to continue.

The directions ask us to place the code shown in the box immediately after the opening <head> tag of our original page, which in this case is **purchasec.html**. We open the page in our HTML editor, paste the code into the page where directed, upload the page to the server, and then press **Next Step**. Note that this page now contains both the GATC code and the above experiment-specific code. Only our original page contains the experiment-specific code.

If all has gone well, we'll then see the confirmation shown below. Clicking on **Start Experiment** activates data collection and begins the experiment.

④ **Review and start**

Experiment Code Validation

✓ Original: Two Pictures: Experiment code found. Google Analytics code found.

✓ Test: Six Pictures: Google Analytics code found.

Notes for this experiment

```
┌─────────────────────────────────┐
│                                 │
│                                 │
│                                 │
│                                 │
└─────────────────────────────────┘
```

| Start Experiment | Save for Later | Discard |

Random assignment to experimental groups

A typical experiment uses pure random assignment to determine which variation an individual will see. Thus, in a typical A/B/C test, each respondent will have a 33.3% chance of being assigned to each group.

Google Analytics experiments use a different random assignment technique. You can read about this approach here:

https://support.google.com/analytics/answer/
2844870?hl=en&ref_topic=2844866

71

Managing Experiments and Interpreting Outcomes

After your first experiment has been created, selecting **Behavior > Experiments** takes you to the experiment summary page, as shown below for my experiments.

All Experiments

Experiment Name	Status	Details	Sessions	Start Date	End Date
Newest A/B/C	◎ Ended	Stopped manually	36	Aug 8, 2013	Aug 10, 2013
A/B/C: Aust	◎ Ended	Stopped manually	8	Aug 6, 2013	Aug 8, 2013
Purchase 2 x 2 -e	◎ Ended	Time limit reached	207	Jul 31, 2013	Oct 30, 2013
2 x 2 Purchase Page - Europe	◎ Ended	Stopped manually	11	Jul 31, 2013	Jul 31, 2013
Individual Transactions	◎ Ended	Stopped manually	16	Jul 25, 2013	Jul 27, 2013
2x2 Purchase Page	◉ Ended	Winners found	204	Jul 22, 2013	Aug 20, 2013
Home Page	◉ Ended	Winner found	96	Jul 19, 2013	Aug 2, 2013

Show rows: 10   Go to: 1   1 - 7 of 7   <   >

Summary information is provided for each current and past experiment associated with the current view. The display provides information regarding status (in development, running, or ended), outcome details (stopped manually, time limit reached, or winner found), number of sessions, and start/end date. Clicking on the name of any specific experiment brings up a detailed data display for that experiment.

Let's look at the types of data provided and data analysis for A/B and factorial experiments.

The background and specifics of this A/B test are as follows::

What is the background and how does this lead to what we specifically need to learn?	When we look at all site users and the average revenue per session, we find an average of about $3,000 per user over the past six months. The goal is to raise this average amount. It has been proposed that by adding additional pictures to the purchase page, users will be subconsciously motivated to purchase longer vacations.
What do we need to manipulate?	We need to manipulate the number of pictures on the page, increasing the number from two to six. Other content and the purchase process will remain unchanged.
How will we measure the outcome of the manipulation?	We will evaluate the effect of the manipulation in terms of average transaction per session.
Is the manipulation reasonable?	We have observed significantly more pictures on competitive sites, especially on the purchase page. As a result, we believe that there may be a relationship between picture quantity and average transaction amount.

Given this situation, we'll create one new version of the purchase page (with six pictures) and test this page against the current purchase page (which has two pictures). For purposes of labeling within Google Analytics reporting, we'll call the original page "Original: Two Pictures" and the alternative version "Test: Six Pictures". We can access current reports of experimental results by selecting **Behavior > Experiments** and then, on the experiments summary page, clicking on the name of the experiment.

The report shown on the top of page 531 is the default view shown when we first access our experiment's data. Since the focus is on conversions, these data can always be viewed by selecting the **Conversions** link on the top of the page (beneath the **Explorer** tab). The top and side of the page provide important context for data interpretation:

- The message in the center of the display indicates that we stopped the experiment manually before Google Analytics chose a "winner." In our view, the data trend indicated that we would cause significant harm to our company by continuing the research.

- The data on the upper right-hand side of the display indicates that the outcome represents 91 days of data collection during which there were 206 experimental sessions.

There are two sets of data displayed: the upper line chart and the bottom tabular data. We ignore the useless line chart on the top of the page and focus on the data reported in the bottom table.

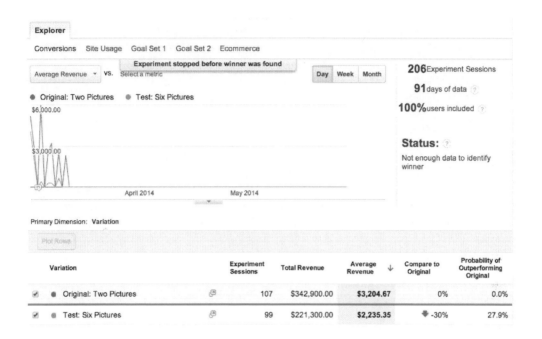

The two line table on the bottom of the page presents conversion data on our original purchase page (the top line of the table) and the test page (the bottom line of the table). We can see that the number of Experiment Sessions for each page are roughly equivalent. With regard to Average Revenue (calculated by dividing Total Revenue by Experiment Sessions) we find that while the original page is equivalent to the historical average (about $3,000), the test page is performing significantly less well, generating about 30% less revenue per session. This metric rather than Total Revenue is the more meaningful, as it adjusts for different numbers of sessions on the original and test page. Finally, Google Analytics predicts that there is a very low probability that the test page will eventually outperform the original.

Selecting **Ecommerce** from beneath the **Explorer** tab displays additional detail on the ecommerce performance of the original and test page, as shown below.

Primary Dimension: Variation

Variation		Experiment Sessions ↓	Revenue	Transactions	Average Order Value	Ecommerce Conversion Rate	Per Session Value
☑ ● Original: Two Pictures		107	$342,900.00	52	$6,594.23	48.60%	$3,204.67
☑ ● Test: Six Pictures		99	$221,300.00	48	$4,610.42	48.48%	$2,235.35

This table repeats several of the metrics reported in the **Conversions** table, with slight changes in how the metrics are named.

- Experiment Sessions are reported with the same label.

- The Revenue column reports the same data as the Total Revenue column in the **Conversions** table.

- Per Session Value reports the same data as the Average Revenue in the **Conversions** table.

The table also reports three valuable new metrics. The Transactions and Ecommerce Conversion Rate columns provide the absolute number of transactions and, more importantly the percentage of sessions resulting in a transaction. In this experiment, these metrics are equivalent across the original and test page. In both cases, about half of all sessions resulted in a sale. The final metric, Average Order Value, reports the average sales amount (calculated by dividing Total Revenue by Transactions). Once again, the original purchase page is outperforming the test page. In fact, both the average sale (i.e., Average Order Value) and average per session (i.e., Per Session Value) are higher for the original purchase page.

Beyond the experimental manipulation, insights into the reasons for differences across pages used in an experiment can sometimes be found by selecting **Site Usage** from beneath the **Explorer** tab. This selection results in the table shown below, which indicates that, in this case, engagement metrics did not differ across the two pages.

Primary Dimension: Variation

Plot Rows

Variation	Experiment Sessions ↓	Pages / Session	Avg. Session Duration	% New Sessions	Bounce Rate
● Original: Two Pictures	107	1.63	00:00:08	97.17%	47.17%
● Test: Six Pictures	99	1.52	00:00:05	98.98%	50.00%

In sum, the experiment demonstrated that our hypothesis with regard to the effect of number of pictures on the purchase page was not validated. Our current page is the more powerful design when compared to the page with additional pictures. While the conversion rate for the two pages is nearly identical, the Average Order Value and Average Session Value for our current page is significantly higher than that of the test page. It's best that we keep our current page as is and run another experiment to determine if a stronger page can be designed.

This experiment is similar to the factorial experiment discussed on page 523. Here we are looking at the simultaneous influence of two factors on engagement, conversion, and transaction metrics. The first factor explores the influence of picture type with two levels: pictures of people and pictures of scenery. The second factor looks at type of call to action (i.e., the link to purchase), again with two levels: image and text. The factorial design for this experiment is summarized below.

		Factor 1: Type of Picture	
		People	Scenery
	Image	1	2
Factor 2:			
Call to Action			
	Text	3	4

Similar to all experiments, we access the data for this experiment through the list of experiments displayed after **Experiments** is selected from the **Behavior** menu. Clicking on the name of the experiment first brings up the data summary shown below. Note that the data relates to transactions, as this was set as our primary outcome measure when we created the experiment.

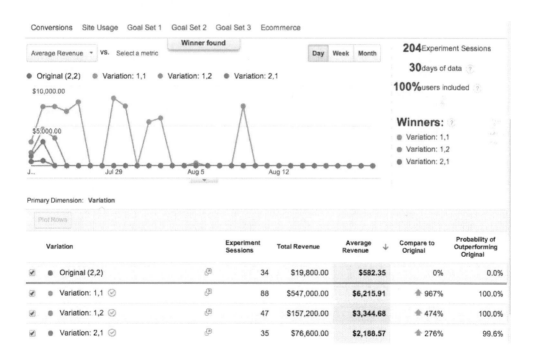

Variation	Experiment Sessions	Total Revenue	Average Revenue ↓	Compare to Original	Probability of Outperforming Original
● Original (2,2)	34	$19,800.00	$582.35	0%	0.0%
● Variation: 1,1 ⊘	88	$547,000.00	$6,215.91	▲ 967%	100.0%
● Variation: 1,2 ⊘	47	$157,200.00	$3,344.68	▲ 474%	100.0%
● Variation: 2,1 ⊘	35	$76,600.00	$2,188.57	▲ 276%	99.6%

The characteristics of each stimulus shown in the previous table are provided below.

	Factor 1: Type of Picture	
	People	Scenery
Image	1 (1,1)	2 (2,1)
Factor 2:		
Call-to-Action		
Text	3 (1,2)	4 (2,2)

Variation (1,1):	People in picture, image call to action
Variation (1,2):	People in picture, text call to action
Variation (2,1):	Scenery in picture, image call to action
Original (2,2):	Scenery in picture, text call to action

Let's first look at what the reported results tell us about our experimental manipulations. First, the experiment has run long enough and has collected enough data for Google Analytics to declare a winner, which is noted on the top right-hand side of the page. This decision was made after 204 experimental visits took place over a 30 day period. The report indicates that:

- All three variations performed significantly better than the original, in both a practical and statistical sense, as reflected in the data reported in the Average Revenue column. In all three cases, our confidence that each variation outperformed the original in terms of average revenue generated per session is at or near 100%. (Typically, any confidence level over 95% is considered statistically significant.)

- While all three variations outperformed the original, there do appear to be important differences within the set of three variations. The average transaction generated by Variation (1,1) appears to be much higher than the average transaction generated by the remaining two variations, which are quite close to one another.

We can look at these trends from a different perspective if we put the Average Revenue per session amounts within each cell of our table, as shown below.

	Factor 1: Type of Picture	
	People	Scenery
Image	$6216	$2189
Factor 2:		
Call-to-Action		
Text	$3345	$582

The data, when examined in this way, provides three important insights.

- First, regardless of the type of call-to-action, pictures of people generated higher average revenue versus pictures of scenery.

- Second, regardless of the type of picture, an image call-to-action always resulted in higher revenue versus a text call-to-action.

- Finally, there seems to be an interaction or cumulative effect of the factors tested. The combination of people + image call-to-action shows that both elements work together to produce a result that is much stronger than the contribution of each factor independently. This latter insight is only available through a factorial design, and would not occur if we conducted two sequential A/B tests (one test to explore pictures and a second test to explore the call-to- action).

Selecting the **Ecommerce** option beneath the **Explorer** tab displays the chart shown below. While the **Per Session Value** is the same as the prior table, note the data reported in the **Average Order Value** column. The superiority of the people + image approach (Variation 1,1) is again apparent: the **Ecommerce Conversion Rate** and **Average Order Value** for this variation are significantly higher than the other variations, especially the original home page.

Variation	Experiment Sessions ↓	Revenue	Transactions	Average Order Value	Ecommerce Conversion Rate	Per Session Value
Original (2,2)	34	$19,800.00	13	$1,523.08	38.24%	$582.35
Variation: 1,1	80	$547,000.00	39	$14,025.64	48.75%	$6,837.50
Variation: 1,2	47	$157,200.00	18	$8,733.33	38.30%	$3,344.68
Variation: 2,1	35	$76,600.00	13	$5,892.31	37.14%	$2,188.57

72
Practice with Experiments

This chapter presents two sets of exercises to help you apply and extend your knowledge of experiments.

True/false and multiple choice

This first set of questions makes certain that you understand key concepts. Feel free to open and refer to the previous chapters or access your analytics account. When you are done, or if you are stuck, the answers can be found on page 625.

1. *True or False:* Experiments allow us to determine <u>causality</u> - the effect of changes in one area on one or more other areas.

2. Which of the following are required questions to consider when planning an experiment. (Select all that apply).

    a. What is the background and how does this lead to what we specifically need to learn?

    b. What do we need to manipulate?

    c. How will we measure to outcome of the manipulation?

    d. Is the manipulation reasonable?

3. *True or False:* An A/B test permits the manipulation of up to three different changes from the original "A" page at one time. You could, for example, create a "B" version that simultaneously differs from "A" in terms of background color, font, and headline.

4. *True or False:* When conducting an A/B test you are restricted to a single outcome measure.

5. *True or False:* A factorial experimental design allows you to manipulate two or more variations at the same time.

6. Which of the following are recommended guidelines for an A/B test? (Select all that apply)

   a. An A/B test should always run at least two weeks.

   b. Repeat site vistors should always be shown the same variation.

   c. Make the A/B test consistent across the entire website.

   d. A/B tests should only be conducted when the outcome measure is related to ecommerce.

   e. Always test both the "A" and "B" versions at the same time.

   f. Don't surprise regular site visitors.

   g. Send a maximum of 10% of site traffic to the "B" version.

7. You want to conduct a factorial experiment. You want to test the effect of three differrent headlines and four different offers. In order to conduct the test you would need _____ variations.

   a. 3

   b. 4

   c. 7

   d. 12

8. *True or False:* Before launching a Google Analytics experiment, it is necessary to have all stimulus pages loaded on your server and accessible online.

9. *True or False:* Experiments are view specific.

10. *True or False:* When creating an experiment, you control the percentage of site sessions that will participate in the experiment.

11. *True or False:* Goals can be used as an outcome measure for an experiment.

12. *True or False:* The code snippet required to run an experiment must appear on every page involved with the experiment.

Application

This second set of questions makes certain that you understand how to interpret Google Analytics experimental data. Feel free to open and refer to the previous chapters or access your analytics account when working through the exercises. When you are done, or if you are stuck, our response can be found beginning on page 625.

1. The two tables below report the data obtained for an A/B experiment. The experiment compared the original home page (which contained pictures and text integrated into the same paragraph) with a variation of the home page (which presented text on the top of the page and pictures on the bottom of the page). You want to see the ultimate effect of this variation on purchase behaviors. Use this data to answer the following questions:

- Was a winner found?

- Which of the two home pages, if any, would be the stronger page to place on your site? Why?

- How does site engagement data provide insights into what may influence the difference between the two pages?

Primary Dimension: Variation

Plot Rows

Variation		Experiment Sessions	↓ Pages / Session	Avg. Session Duration	% New Sessions	Bounce Rate
☑ ● Original ⊘		73	3.41	00:00:50	79.70%	18.05%
☑ ● Variation		14	1.88	00:00:04	80.00%	20.00%

Primary Dimension: Variation

Plot Rows

Variation		Experiment Sessions	↓ Revenue	Transactions	Average Order Value	Ecommerce Conversion Rate	Per Session Value
☑ ● Original ⊘		73	$537,900.00	43	$12,509.30	58.90%	$7,368.49
☑ ● Variation		14	$15,600.00	8	$1,950.00	57.14%	$1,114.29

2. The following table reports the data obtained for a factorial experiment that explored reactions to four different purchase pages where we manipulated two factors: text color (all black, black and color) and text font size (medium, large). Four stimuli are needed, as shown below:

		Factor 1: Text Color	
		All Black	Black and Color
	Medium	1 (1,1)	2 (2,1)
Factor 2: Text Size			
	Large	3 (1,2)	4 (2,2)

Variation (1,1):   All black, medium font size
Variation (1,2):   All black, large font size
Variation (2,1):   Black and color, medium font size
Original (2,2):   Black and color, large font size

- Was a winner found? If not, would you recommend continuing or stopping the experiment?

- Regardless of text size, what is the effect of text color on key ecommerce metrics?

- Regardless of a text color, what is the effect of font size on key ecommerce variables?

- Is there an interaction between font size and font color?

Primary Dimension: Variation

Plot Rows

Variation		Experiment Sessions ↓	Revenue	Transactions	Average Order Value	Ecommerce Conversion Rate	Per Session Value
☑ ● Original (2,2)		93	$635,100.00	43	$14,769.77	46.24%	$6,829.03
☑ ● Variation 2 (1,2)		48	$207,600.00	24	$8,650.00	50.00%	$4,325.00
☑ ● Variation 3 (2,1)		45	$152,000.00	22	$6,909.09	48.89%	$3,377.78
☑ ● Variation 1 (1,1)		19	$6,000.00	7	$857.14	36.84%	$315.79

Google Analytics Demystified

Section XVI:
Data Management

There is no shortage of data in Google Analytics. Therefore, it is important for you to manage your data in a way that allows you to focus on important issues and facilitates application to strategic decision-making. The five chapters in this section discuss three techniques that can help you manage your data.

-   Chapters 73 and 74 discuss two types of Google Analytics intelligence events: automatic and custom alerts and notifications. Chapter 75 provides practice in using these data management techniques.

-   Chapter 76 discusses shortcuts and downloads, and their use in easing data management and analysis burdens.

-   Chapter 77 discusses the creation and use of dashboards.

Google Analytics Demystified

73

Automatic Alerts and Diagnostic Messages

Like a good analyst, Google Analytics monitors your website users' characteristics and behaviors in order to detect and bring to your attention significant statistical variations. Google brings these variations to your attention either through automatic alerts and notifications or custom alerts.

Automatic alerts and notifications are generated whenever Google Analytics detects a significant change in the traffic or engagement patterns on your site. These items are generated by Google Analytics without the need for any input on your part.

Custom alerts are triggered when user characteristics or engagement patterns reach a specific threshold you specify. For example, you can set a custom alert to appear when traffic from a particular city or country decreases by more than 20%. You can view these alerts via the **Intelligence Events** menu or you can opt to receive email or text message notifications, so you'll know when the event happens, even if you're not checking your reports.

Examining the information provided in both types of reports can help you acquire insights into important trends that you otherwise might have missed. This chapter explains automatic alerts. The next chapter provides direction for creating custom alerts.

Here is how Google describes alerts:[49]

> How would you like to have 24-hour a day access to a dedicated assistant who is focused exclusively on your site's analytics? Your assistant would be so diligent and detailed that they wouldn't miss a thing. Sound too good to be true? We're giving you one. Say "Hello" to Analytics Intelligence.

> Analytics Intelligence can't replace you or a professional analyst. But, it can find key information for you and your professional analysts -- so that your team can focus on making strategic decisions, instead of sifting through an endless sea of data.

---

[49] Intelligence Basics at:
https://support.google.com/analytics/answer/1011414?hl=en&ref_topic=1032994

Analytics Intelligence constantly monitors your website's traffic. Anytime something significant happens, it adds an automatic alert in your Intelligence reports. If your bounce rate suddenly jumps on one of your referrals, Analytics Intelligence creates an alert. Of course, it's up to you to go find out that the bounce rate jumped because someone inadvertently changed the landing page. But you might not have noticed that there was a problem that needed fixing if your trusty assistant hadn't alerted you.

Behind Analytics Intelligence is a sophisticated algorithmic intelligence engine that detects any anomalies in your traffic patterns. That means it's smart enough to know the difference between a change that's actually part of a larger trend versus a change that you might need to look into. But, from a user perspective, Analytics Intelligence couldn't be simpler.

Navigate to the Intelligence reports and you'll see three reports -- Daily Alerts, Weekly Alerts, Monthly Alerts. Daily Alerts contains all the alerts that are based on daily data. Weekly Alerts contains alerts based on weekly data. Monthly Alerts contains, you guessed it, alerts based on monthly data.

When you look at your alerts, you'll notice that your trusty assistant has already gone through your historical data and posted alerts. This highlights a key feature of Analytics Intelligence: you don't have to do anything -- alerts automatically get posted to your account.

Accessing automatic alerts

Your primary access point for automatic alerts is through **Intelligence Events > Overview**. We recommend that you check for these alerts at least once per day. This will bring up one of two types of displays.

The display shown below appears if Google Analytics has not identified any variations it considers worth mentioning.

The display shown on the top of page 545 appears whenever Google Analytics has identified a statistical variation of note. In this case, it has examined the totality of my website traffic and has noted important changes in the past week (as reported in the period and date columns) in terms of three metrics: goal conversion rate, average visit duration, and bounce rate.

Automatic Alerts   Custom Alerts

	Metric	Segment	Period	Date	Change	Importance ↓	
1.	Goal Conversion Rate	All Traffic	Weekly	Mar 9, 2014 - Mar 15, 2014	>500%		Details
2.	Avg. Visit Duration	All Traffic	Weekly	Mar 9, 2014 - Mar 15, 2014	307%		Details
3.	Bounce Rate	All Traffic	Weekly	Mar 9, 2014 - Mar 15, 2014	-34%		Details

These alerts are good news - things are looking up. My overall goal conversion rate has increased over 500%, average site visit duration has increased 307% and my bounce rate has declined by 34%.

Clicking on **Details** for any specific report brings up more information. The table below, for example, is displayed when **Details** is selected for the **Goal Conversion Rate** automatic alert.

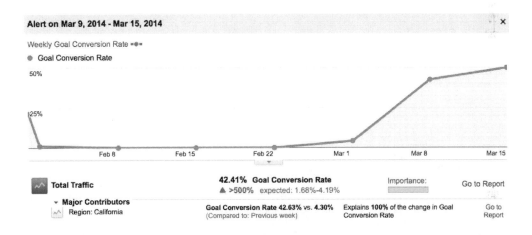

The line chart displays my historic goal conversion rate, where you can see the rapid increase beginning March 8. Beneath the chart is more detailed information regarding this event. The line immediately beneath the chart (on the line labeled Total Traffic) conveys why Google believes this trend is a significant variation. Our expected goal completion rate is 1.68% to 4.19%; our conversion rate for the week beginning March 9 was 42.41%. Importantly, as noted on the bottom line, much of this rise in goal conversion rate was the result of a change in Californians' behavior, among whom the goal conversion rate was 42.63% versus 4.30% in the prior week.

The display below is the detail report for bounce rate change noted in the automatic alert.

Once again, the top line (labeled Total Traffic) compares the target week to the overall website average. Here, last week's bounce rate of 29.32% is significantly below the site average of 40.71% to 46.52%. The bottom portion of the display informs us that this lower bounce rate is driven by two groups: new visitors and Californians. Good news, indeed.

Diagnostic messages

Similar to automatic alerts, diagnostic messages are designed to highlight and bring to your attention a situation which Google Analytics perceives to be an important problem, for example:

- when your current tracking code is not present, configured properly and/or readable, or

- when there are odd data trends, such as when conversions stop occurring.

Diagnostic notifications are accessed through the "bell" on the upper right-hand side of any report page (see below) by any user with Edit permission.

When there is a number on the bell, as in this example, clicking on the bell brings up a list of current and past notifications (see below). Selecting any of the options in a notification block (such as **Details**) allows you to better understand the perceived problem, see Google Analytics' recommendation, and plan a response.

Custom Alerts allow you to identify a set of conditions related to user characteristics and behaviors. Google Analytics then posts to your Google Analytics account or sends you an email when one of your specified conditions is met.

Imagine, for example, that the bounce rate of your home page has been an ongoing problem, and that you have just redesigned the page in an effort to reduce the bounce rate. You can set up a custom alert that would have Google Analytics inform you whenever something good or something bad happens on this page, for example, a decrease or an increase of 10% or more in the page's bounce rate.

There are two different circumstances in which custom alerts are very valuable. First, alerts can be used to provide ongoing monitoring of website health. Second, alerts can be created to monitor the results of a specific campaign. We'll look at custom alerts for both situations later in this chapter.

Creating custom alerts

Custom alerts are view specific, that is, the alert will only appear within that view or any other views with which you share the alert.

You begin the alert creation process by selecting any of the time-related options from the **Intelligence Events** menu (which is located on the left-hand side of any data reporting page). I've selected Daily Events, which brings up the display shown below. Note that this display and process is the same should you select the Weekly or Monthly Events options.

Intelligence Events Overview   Feb 19, 2014 - Mar 21, 2014

Automatic Alerts   Custom Alerts

	Metric	Segment	Period	Date	Change	Importance ↓	
1.	Goal Conversion Rate	All Traffic	Weekly	Mar 9, 2014 - Mar 15, 2014	>500%		Details
2.	Avg. Visit Duration	All Traffic	Weekly	Mar 9, 2014 - Mar 15, 2014	307%		Details
3.	Bounce Rate	All Traffic	Weekly	Mar 9, 2014 - Mar 15, 2014	-34%		Details

Scrolling down the new page locates a display similar to that shown below.

You create a new custom alert by clicking on **+Create a Custom Alert** on the right-hand side in **Custom Alerts** row. When you do so, the following overlay is shown. This is where you will specify the alert parameters.

This form is completed as follows.

- You enter a descriptive name for your custom alert in the **Alert Name** text box.

- The **Apply to:** field is used to indicate the view(s) for which you want to apply the alert. The current view is shown by default in bold type. If you want to apply the alert to additional views, use the pull-down menu and check each view to which you want to apply the alert. The alert is then available to you in any of the other views you select. Nothing needs to be done if you want the custom alert to only apply to the current view.

- Use the **Period** pull-down menu to indicate the frequency at which the alert should be generated. You can select Day, Week, or Month.

-   Use the next set of check boxes to indicate how (if at all) you want to be notified when the custom alert is generated. Note that when you choose to receive a notice by email, you can have others informed at the same time.

-   You use the green and blue pull-down menus to specify the alert's conditions. The top (green) pull-down menu allows you set the focus of the alert (options are shown on the left, below), while the bottom (blue) pull-down menu allows you select the metric of interest (options are shown on the right, below).

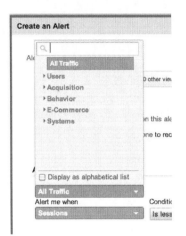 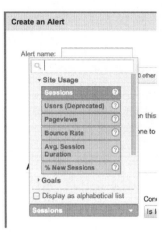

-   Finally, specify the **Condition** and **Value** (see chart on page 548), and when all looks right, click **Save Alert**. If there are no errors, Google Analytics will indicate that the alert was successfully created.

The remainder of this chapter discusses situations in which custom alerts provide important strategic insights.[50]

Using custom alerts to monitor website health

Unfortunately, we don't always know when there are problems on our site, for example, when the server is down or when other network issues prevent access. A **daily** custom alert can be used to monitor the site and inform you when there are access issues as reflected in an absence of traffic. The parameters shown in the display on the top of page 550 shows how this custom alert can be created.

---

[50] Source material and further examples can be found at: *Top 15 Google Analytics Custom Alerts*: http://www.6smarketing.com/blog/top-15-google-analytics-custom-alerts-to-set-up/; *55 Google Analytics Custom Alerts*: http://www.lunametrics.com/blog/2012/09/24/55-google-analytics-custom-alerts-check-engine-light-data/.

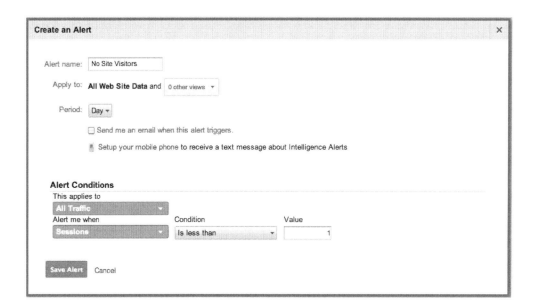

This alert is, in fact, one of two user specific custom alerts I've set up for my travel site. On days when there are no visitors, I receive the email notification shown below.

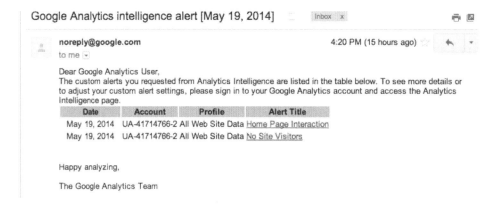

Clicking on either of the alert titles brings up the custom alert page (if you are signed into your Google ID) where you can find links to more detailed information, as shown on the top of page 551.

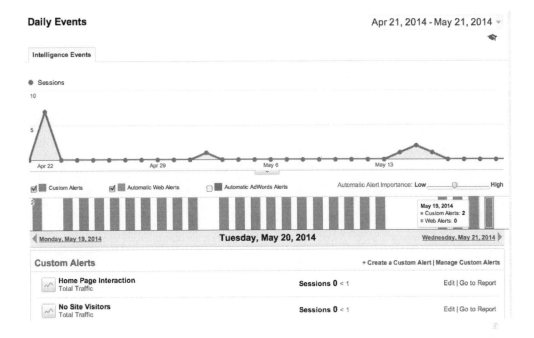

Intelligence Events

● Sessions

10

5

Apr 22   Apr 29   May 6   May 13

☑ Custom Alerts   ☑ Automatic Web Alerts   ☐ Automatic AdWords Alerts   Automatic Alert Importance: Low _____ High

May 19, 2014
▪ Custom Alerts: 2
▪ Web Alerts: 0

◁ Monday, May 19, 2014   **Tuesday, May 20, 2014**   Wednesday, May 21, 2014 ▷

Custom Alerts   + Create a Custom Alert | Manage Custom Alerts

| | **Home Page Interaction** Total Traffic | **Sessions 0** < 1 | Edit | Go to Report |
| | **No Site Visitors** Total Traffic | **Sessions 0** < 1 | Edit | Go to Report |

Using custom alerts to monitor
important groups of users

Custom alerts are an excellent way to monitor key user characteristics related to your strategic objectives, for example, monitoring changes in returning visitors and visitor location. The examples on pages 552 and 553 show how **weekly** custom alerts are created for each of these situations. In both cases:

- the time period is set to weekly because we don't want the alert to be influenced by random daily fluctuations.

- we create two alerts for each situation, one to signal a positive trend and the second to signal a negative trend.

- each alert looks at relative percentage change rather than an absolute percentage.

The displays below show the parameters of the two custom alerts created to monitor *new site sessions*. The first alert triggers with a significant increase in sessions, while the second alert triggers with a significant decrease.

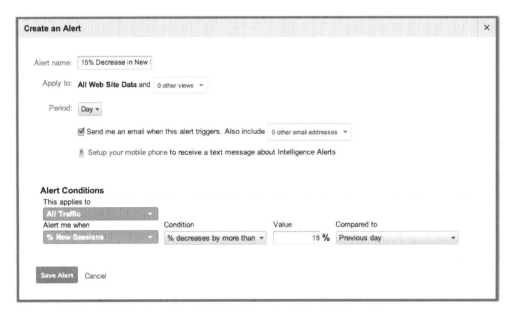

The displays below show the parameters of two custom alerts created to monitor *new site visitors from England,* one of our important geographic source of sales. Again, we create one alert that triggers on a significant increase, and another alert that triggers on a significant decrease.

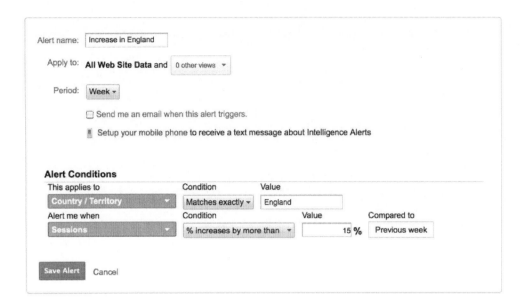

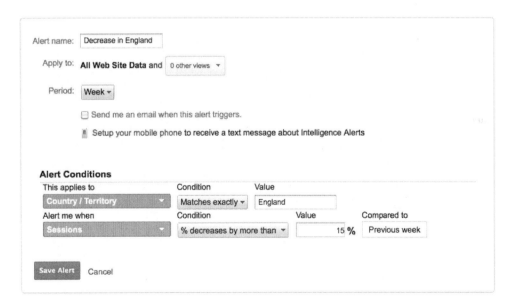

Strategic planning is always facilitated when you understand how users find your website. Imagine that you have made a significant investment in search engine optimization, specifically Google and Bing. You can monitor the impact of this investment by creating a custom alert that monitors changes in referrals from these sources to your site. You can create an alert to monitor search referrals as a group (shown in the first figure below) or referrals from a specific source (shown in the second figure below).

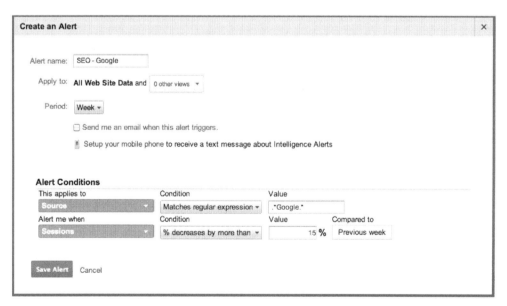

Custom alerts are appropriate for tracking changes in site engagement. You can, for example, look at changes in your bounce rate and average visit duration. However, you are not limited to overall site metrics. You can monitor the bounce rate or other engagement metrics for one or more specific pages.

The example below shows how we monitor the bounce rate for an individual page, in this case our purchase page. Since the alert is looking at bounce rate, we are only interested in knowing when bounce rate increases beyond the absolute level we consider acceptable.

We can use custom alerts to monitor changes in important metrics such as revenue, purchase conversion rate, and total revenue. The two figures shown on page 556 illustrate the creation of two custom ecommerce alerts. The first (top figure) alerts us when total revenue drops by 15% or more. The second (bottom figure) alerts us when revenue generated by a specific category, in this case Bahamas tours, declines more than 15%. Both comparisons are on a week to week basis.

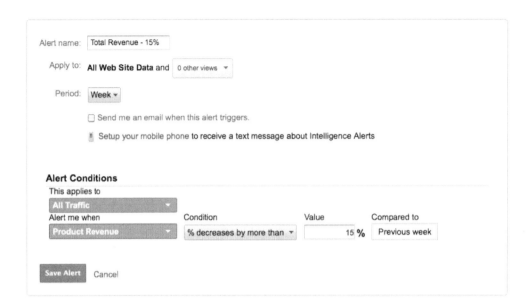

Managing custom alerts

You manage alerts by selecting any of the time-related options from the **I**ntelligence **Events** menu. For our example, we'll select **Daily Events**, which brings up the display shown on the top of page 557. Note that this display and process is the same should you select the Weekly or Monthly Events options.

Clicking on **Custom Alerts** on the top of the page brings up the display shown below.

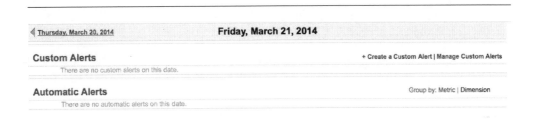

Selecting **Manage Custom Alerts** (on the right-hand side) displays a listing of all your custom alerts, as shown below.

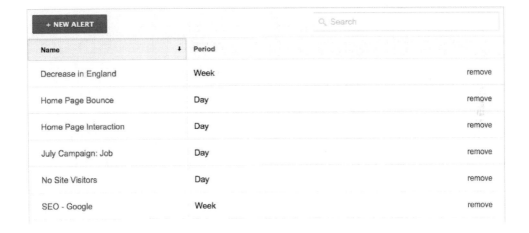

You can remove any alert by clicking on the **remove** link associated with the alert. Clicking on the name of any specific alert allows you to edit the alert's characteristics.

75

Practice With Alerts

This chapter's three sets of exercises address automatic and custom alerts. All of the information and procedures you'll need to respond to these exercises are presented in Chapters 73 and 74.

True/false and multiple choice

This first set of exercises explores your understanding of alerts. You can check your answers on page 627. Feel free to refer to **Intelligence Events** on your own site as you answer the following questions.

1. *True or False:* Automatic alerts are generated only for accounts that have 50 or pageviews per day.

2. *True or False:* Custom alerts are available only to accounts that pay Google Analytics a monthly fee.

3. *True or False:* Automatic and custom alerts can be viewed via the **Intelligence Events > Overview** data reporting menu option.

4. What type of alert uses email to communicate with you?

   a. Automatic

   b. Custom

5. *True or False:* Custom alerts can only be used to monitor ecommerce-related metrics.

6. What time periods are used by custom alerts? (Select all that apply.)
   a. Hourly
   b. Daily
   c. Weekly
   d. Biweekly
   e. Monthly
   f. Semi-monthly
   g. Annually

7. *True or False:* Custom alerts are set at the property, and as a result, apply to all views within that property.

8. You want to set a custom alert that monitors the percentage of returning users to the site. Which of the following would be permitted? (Select all that apply.)

   a. Send an alert when the absolute number of returning users is less than 20.

   b. Send an alert when the percentage of returning users decreases by more than 20%.

9. You want to create a series of custom alerts based on specific user characteristics and behaviors. Which behaviors below could be selected? (Select all that apply.)

   a. Users who purchased a specific product

   b. Users who came to the site from a specific referral source

   c. Users from a specific city

   d. Users visiting the site via mobile

10. You want to create a series of custom alerts based on engagement metrics. Which metrics can be used as the basis of a custom alert? (Select all that apply.)

   a. Pageviews

   b. Bounce rate

   c. Sessions

   d. Average session duration

Hands-on

This second set of exercises explores how well you can create custom alerts. You can check your answers beginning on page 627. Feel free to delete all alerts when you are done.

1. Create a weekly alert that monitors the percentage of new site sessions. Name this alert Exercise 1. You want to be alerted when the relative percentage of new site sessions drops by more than 10% when compared to the prior week.

2. Create a daily alert that monitors the number of unique purchases for a product category named "Mexico". There are typically 50 purchases per day and you want to be alerted when the number of purchases rises or declines by more than 20% when compared to the previous day. Name this alert Exercise 2.

3. Create a weekly alert that monitors views to either of the following two pages. You want to be alerted when the total number of pageviews declines by more than 15% or more when compared to the previous week. Name this alert Exercise 3. The pages are:

   `www.googleanalyticsdemystified.com/xqanqeon/thanksp2m.html`

   `www.googleanalyticsdemystified.com/xqanqeon/thanksp10m.html`

4. Create a daily alert that monitors the number of sessions for all users visiting your site. You typically have about 300 sessions per day and want to know when the number of sessions drops below this amount. Name this alert Exercise 4.

Application

This third set of exercises explores how well you can strategically apply the concept of custom alerts.

Examine your travel website. Think of three strategic uses of custom alerts to help you monitor important site developments. Name and describe each alert, provide a strategic rationale, and then actually create the alert.

76

Shortcuts and Exports

Shortcuts and exports are two powerful ways to reduce your data-related workload.

Creating shortcuts

A shortcut is a quick way for you to access one or more of the Google Analytics reports you use most often. Creating a shortcut to a report uses the same logic as keyboard shortcuts, that is, they are a way of accomplishing more by doing less.

Below is a typical Google Analytics report, in this case a focus on new versus returning users. The link **Shortcuts** appears in two places: near the top of the left-hand margin and above the line chart beneath the chart title. The former allows you to access all of the shortcuts you created, the latter allows you to create a shortcut.

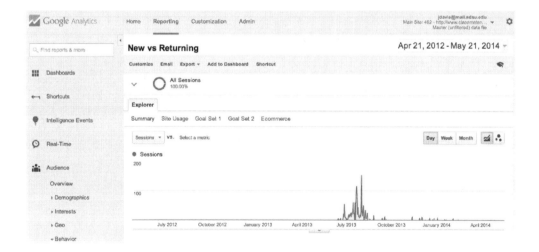

You create a shortcut directly from the data report of interest by clicking on the **Short-cut** link beneath the report title. Doing so brings up an overlay where you can accept the proposed name or rename the shortcut. Clicking **OK** creates the shortcut and places the shortcut name beneath the **Shortcuts** main menu option (in the left-hand margin) as shown on the top of page 562. Clicking on any shortcut name brings up the appropriate report.

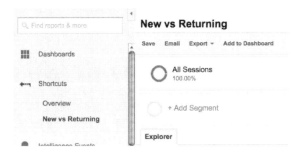

While shortcuts allow you to instantly access frequently used reports, their real power comes from the additional information that is saved as part of the shortcut. Google notes that:

> Any setting you apply to a report, like adding an advanced segment or a new metric, stays applied in a shortcut until you manually change the settings. The settings are saved even if you sign out and sign back in to your account. All report customizations and settings are saved in a shortcut except the date range. Check the dates each time you use a shortcut to make sure the time period you need is applied.[51]

As a result, you do not have to repeat time consuming actions in order to drill-down into important metrics. All of the drill-down behaviors are saved along with the shortcut.

Managing shortcuts

You access all of your shortcuts through the Shortcuts main menu option in the left-hand margin. Clicking **Shortcuts > Overview** brings up a list of all of the shortcuts you've created, as shown below.

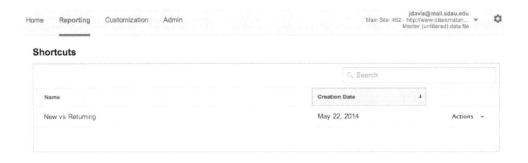

---

[51] *Shortcuts* at: https://support.google.com/analytics/answer/2676996?hl=en

On the far right hand side there is an **Actions** menu for each shortcut. Pulling-down this menu displays shortcut management options that you can use to view the report, rename, or delete the shortcut (see below).

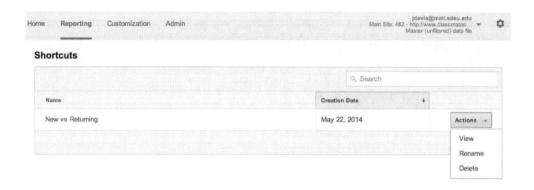

Exporting reports

You have two options with regard to exporting Google Analytics reports. You can download the report to view and manipulate offline or you can email the report to others.

Downloading a report

At the top of almost every report is an option to export the report. This option, labeled **Export**, is on the line directly beneath the report title (on the same line as the **Shortcut** link). Pulling-down the **Export** menu displays the various formats in which data can be downloaded (see below).

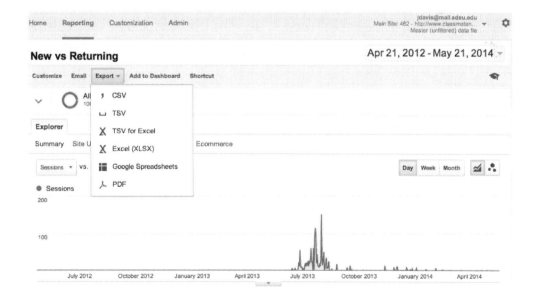

Note that the PDF download is an exact representation of the data displayed in the online view and that this download contains a link back to the original online report.

Emailing a report

The option to email a report or its underlying data, labeled **Email**, is located to the left of the **Export** option (beneath the chart title). Selecting this link brings up the overlay shown below.

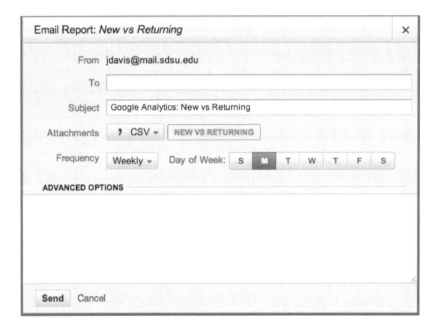

Your email address and subject are automatically filled in the form. You'll need to fill out the rest of the parameters (recipient, attachment format, email frequency, and day of the week to email). Once this is done, just click **Send** to initiate the email process.

> Emails will continue to be sent until canceled. If you know in advance how long you want the emails sent, select the appropriate time period from the email form's **ADVANCED OPTIONS**.

77

Dashboards

A dashboard is a visual display of metrics that relate to a specific strategic information need, property goal, or strategic objective. You can, for example, create a dashboard that will focus on the conversion of specific goals, the outcome of a specific marketing campaign, ecommerce data, referral sources, site health, or website or blog engagement. This chapter discusses the procedures for creating and editing your own dashboards as well as for acquiring dashboards created by others.

You access dashboards through the **Dashboards** menu option that appears on the upper left-hand side of any report page (see opposite). Here you can either see dashboards which are associated with the current view (**Private**) or you can create a new dashboard (**+New Dashboard**).

At the moment, I have two dashboards in the current view, as listed beneath **Dashboard > Private**. "My Dashboard" is the default starter dashboard created by Google Analytics, while the "Site Performance" dashboard is a dashboard I created.[52]

Let's look at the "Site Performance" dashboard in order to see a dashboard's primary components.

An example dashboard

The dashboard shown on the top of page 566 focuses on website health. We access this dashboard through the **Dashboards > Private > Site Performance** menu option. Note how each displayed metric is relevant to website health.

Dashboards can be used to track any time period, but are best used when they display recent data, typically either the past week or previous day. Since the maintenance of site health is of critical importance, we've set up this dashboard to report only the prior day's data (as indicated by the date range shown on the upper right-hand corner).

---

[52] Dashboards are view and user specific. So, unless you share your dashboards across views and users, any individual dashboard will only appear in the view in which it was created, accessed by the individual who created it. Later in this chapter we'll discuss how to share dashboards with others who have permission to access the view.

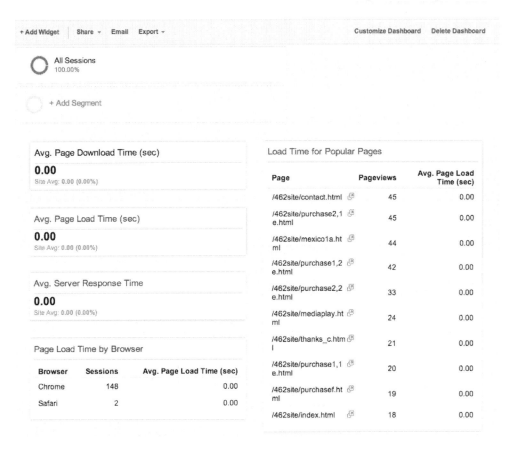

Site Performance Dashboard

Aug 1, 2013 - Aug 1, 2013

+ Add Widget   Share ▾   Email   Export ▾   Customize Dashboard   Delete Dashboard

All Sessions
100.00%

+ Add Segment

Avg. Page Download Time (sec)

0.00
Site Avg: 0.00 (0.00%)

Avg. Page Load Time (sec)

0.00
Site Avg: 0.00 (0.00%)

Avg. Server Response Time

0.00
Site Avg: 0.00 (0.00%)

Page Load Time by Browser

Browser	Sessions	Avg. Page Load Time (sec)
Chrome	148	0.00
Safari	2	0.00

Load Time for Popular Pages

Page	Pageviews	Avg. Page Load Time (sec)
/462site/contact.html	45	0.00
/462site/purchase2,1 e.html	45	0.00
/462site/mexico1a.ht ml	44	0.00
/462site/purchase1,2 e.html	42	0.00
/462site/purchase2,2 e.html	33	0.00
/462site/mediaplay.ht ml	24	0.00
/462site/thanks_c.htm l	21	0.00
/462site/purchase1,1 e.html	20	0.00
/462site/purchasef.ht ml	19	0.00
/462site/index.html	18	0.00

Creating a dashboard

Let's create a dashboard from scratch. This will allow us to see the options for data selection and visual appearance. Our dashboard will focus on website engagement for the previous seven days. This time range is easily set through the use of the pull-down menu in the date range settings (see below).

Site Engagement

Jul 28, 2013 - Aug 3, 2013

The first step to dashboard creation is clicking on **Dashboards > +New Dashboard** which brings up the overlay screen shown below.

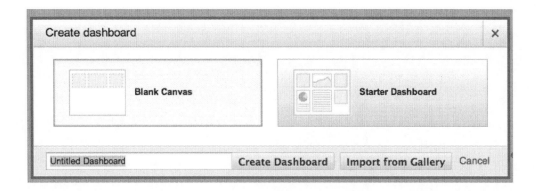

Here we select "Blank Canvas" to create an entirely customized new dashboard. We name the dashboard "Site Engagement" and press **Create Dashboard**. (We'll discuss the **Import from Gallery** option later in this chapter.) At this point the name of the new dashboard is added to the **Dashboards > Private** menu options and the overlay screen shown below is displayed. Note that "New Widget" is the default name that will remain until you rename the dashboard element.

There are two rows of available metrics: **Standard** and **Real-Time**. **Standard** metrics are displayed for a requested time period while **Real-Time** metrics pull data to reflect what is happening now. Your choice of metrics depends upon your strategic information needs. Our site engagement dashboard will only use **Standard** metrics.

We begin by clicking in the **2.1 Metric** box in the **Standard** row, thereby indicating that we want to display a single numeric metric. The desired metric is selected through the use of the pull-down menu beneath **Show the following metric**. Our first engagement metric is **Average Session Duration**. When we select this metric from the menu, the screen changes to that shown below. Note that the widget name has automatically been changed to reflect our selection.

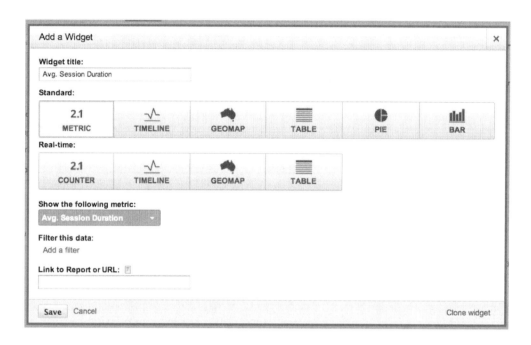

When we press **Save,** the metric is added to our dashboard as shown below. Note how the data includes both the numeric summary for the time period and a line graph of the underlying data.

Once our first metric is added to the dashboard, additional metrics can be added by clicking on **+Add Widget** on the top left of the display. (Each item displayed in the dashboard is called a "widget".) The preceding process then repeats. The figure shown below illustrates dashboard appearance after adding two more engagement metrics in the same way as just described.

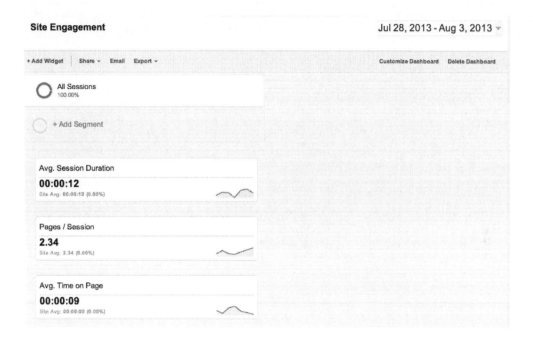

After the addition of several metrics to the dashboard, it is often beneficial to modify the dashboard's visual appearance by rearranging the widgets. We accomplish this as follows: First we click on the **Customize Dashboard** option on the top of the dashboard. This brings up the overlay page shown opposite that allows us to determine the number and size of columns in which widgets are displayed.

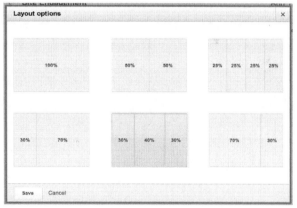

Selecting the bottom row middle option (and then pressing **Save**) returns us to our original dashboard display.

We have the option of moving metric displays into one of three rows and manipulating the order if desired. To move a widget, we simply click in the line containing the widget's name, and then drag and drop the widget into its desired place, as shown below.

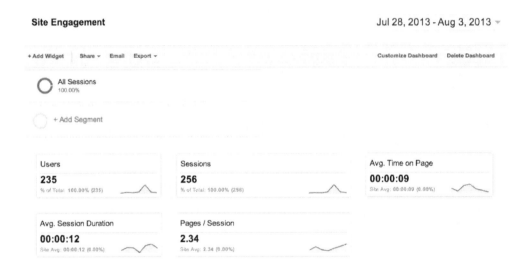

So far so good, but something is missing. There is no context to interpret any of these metrics. Are they based on 1,000 sessions or 10 sessions? 100 users or 5 users? As a result, we recommend including both sessions and users metrics on all dashboards, as shown below. These are added in the same way as the previous metrics.

Let's add one last single metric. As before, we click on **+Add Widget** to add a metric and then, on the overlay, we add **Goal Conversion Rate** as an additional 2.1 Metric. Now that we know the overall conversion rate, let's see the trend that relates goal conversion rate to the overall number of goals started. We can look at the relationship between two metrics by clicking in the **TIMELINE** box made available after **+Add Widget** is selected. This changes the display to that shown on the top of page 571.

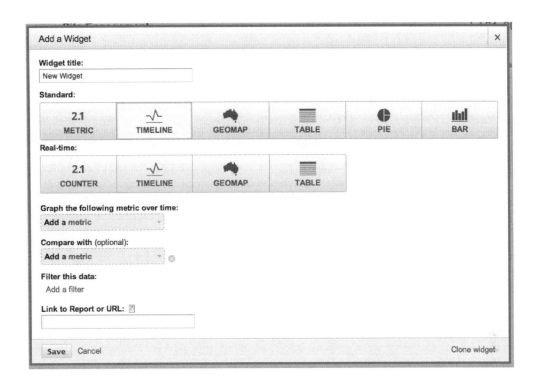

Notice how the selection options have changed to reflect our desire to create a timeline. We can look at the relationship between goal conversions and goal starts by first selecting **Goal Conversion** rate from the **Graph the following metric over time:** pulldown menu and by selecting **Goal Starts** from the **Compare with (optional)** pull-down menu. This adds the timeline data to our dashboard, as shown on the top of page 572.

The timeline display for the two selected metrics is shown in the second row of the dashboard. Note how displaying both the average conversion rate metric and the timeline provides insights beyond those provided by each individually. The **Goal Conversion Rate** metric is high at 51.17%, indicating that just over half of all goals started are completed. This is good, but because it is an average, it is important to look at the underlying data, which are provided by the timeline. You can see that early in the week, the number of goal starts was quite low, and the conversion rate was declining. We then tried, in the middle of the week, to improve both measures. On the next day (August 1) both measures improved, after which the conversion rate remained very high, but the number of goals started significantly declined. We appear to have overcompensated and need to determine a way to increase goal starts while maintaining the high goal completion rate.

We'll skip the **GEOMAP** display since all of our visitors are from the United States and we are not interested in engagement by geographic region.

The **TABLE** option allows us to display tables similar to those provided in standard Google Analytics reports. When we click in the **TABLE** box, the following is displayed. Note how the metric selection options have again changed to reflect that we are constructing a table.

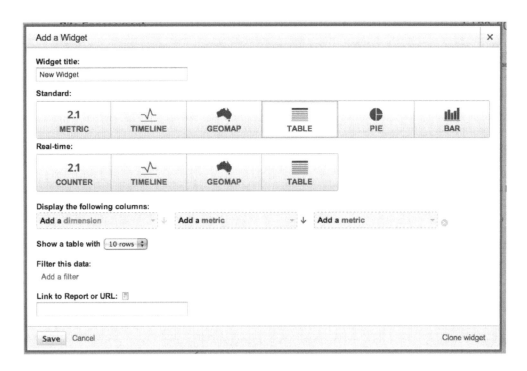

The engagement behaviors of new versus returning users have always been a concern, so we are going to construct a table that looks at this relationship. As illustrated below, we select our dimension of interest (in this case **User Type** from the first pull-down menu) and our two metrics of interest from the middle and right pull-down menus (in this case, the two engagement metrics **Avg. Time on Page** and **Avg. Session Duration**).

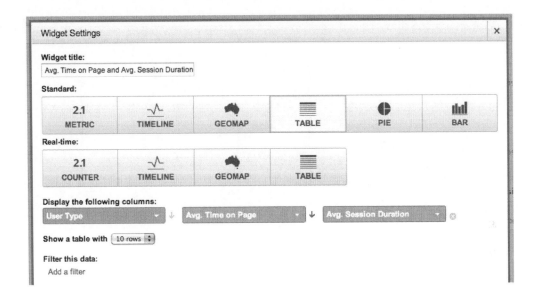

Pressing **Save** adds the table to our dashboard which, after rearranging the display, appears on the bottom of the middle column, as shown below.

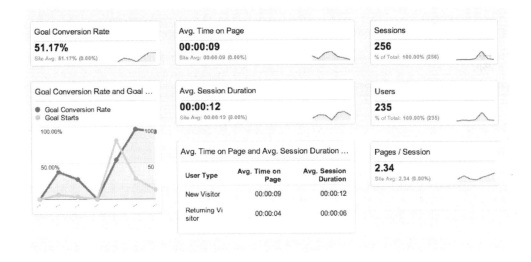

We can continue our focus on new versus returning visitors by selecting the **PIE** chart option, as shown below. Notice, that once again the options have changed to reflect **PIE** chart selection.

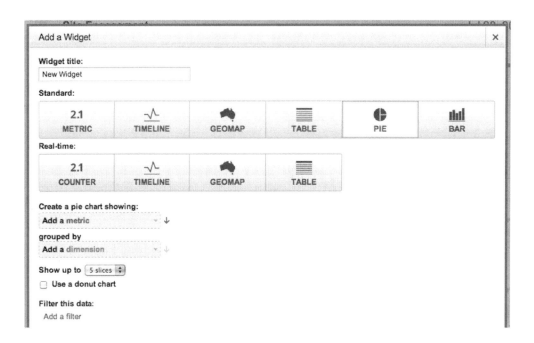

We select our engagement metric, **Unique Pageviews**, from the top pull-down menu and **User Type** from the bottom pull-down menu, as shown below.

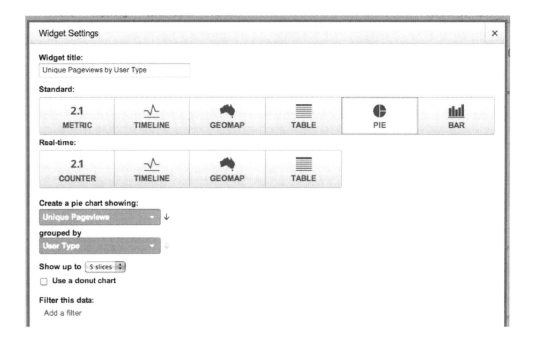

Pressing **Save** adds the pie chart to our dashboard which, after rearranging the display, appears on the bottom of the right-hand column as shown below.

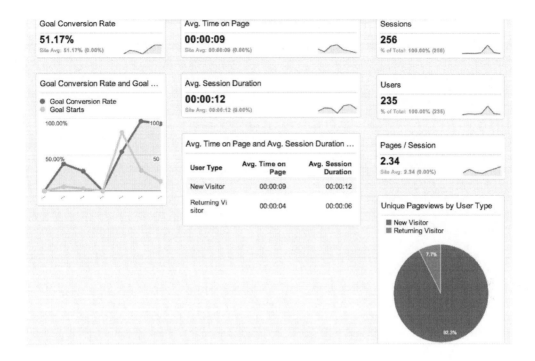

BAR charts are the last metric display option. When we select this option, similar to the other display choices, the options change to reflect bar chart creation (see the top of page 576). We need to specify the metric we want displayed and the grouping dimension. This is accomplished through the use of two pull-down menus, where the metric is selected from the top **Create a bar chart showing:** pull-down menu and the grouping dimension is selected from the **grouped by** pull-down menu.[53]

---

[53] There are many more options for widget display beyond the basics we discuss in this chapter. We encourage you to play with these options, keeping in mind that any widgets created but unwanted can be edited or deleted, as discussed shortly.

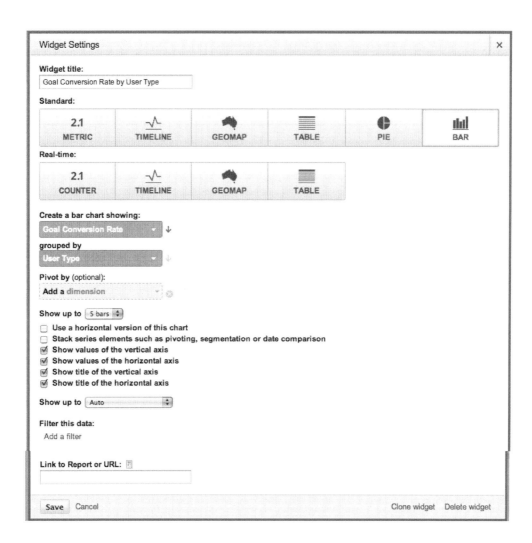

Pressing **Save** adds the table to our dashboard which, after rearranging the display, appears on the bottom of the first column, as shown on the top of page 577.

Our dashboard is now complete. We've added all the core metrics to allow us to quickly evaluate site engagement on a rolling seven day basis. One final observation on the dashboard's organization is needed, however. This dashboard, similar to others you create, should allow for the quick observation of related measures. As a result, metrics should be displayed in a logical way. In our case, we've grouped related measures within the same column. The left-hand column presents measures related to conversion rate; the middle column presents timing and view measures; and the right-hand column provides information related to new versus returning users.

Editing or deleting dashboard elements

You can edit or delete any dashboard display.

As shown opposite, every display contains an edit option (the pencil) and a delete option (the "x") which appear when you roll your mouse over the display's title.

Clicking on the "x" initiates the deletion process, which is finalized when you confirm the deletion. Clicking on the pencil takes you to the same overlay page in which the display was created. Here, any of the display options can be edited.

You can edit the name of a dashboard by clicking in the dashboard's title frame, as shown below. Then, just type the new name and press **Save**.

| Campaign Evaluation Dashboard | Save | cancel |

Jun 29, 2014 - Jul 29, 2014 ▾

Custom segments can be applied to a dashboard by clicking on **+Add a Segment**, which appears on the top of the page just beneath **All Sessions**.

The figure below shows the addition of the custom segment, **Sessions with Transactions**, to the dashboard display. Note how each widget now reports data for both all sessions and sessions with transactions.

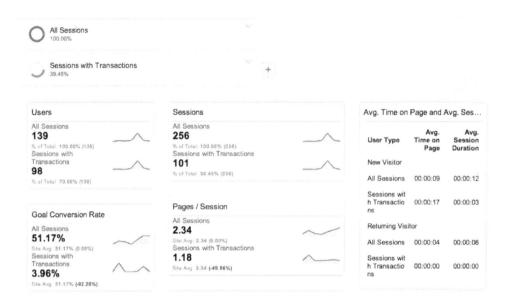

This display, however, feels a bit crowded. We can make things easier to read and better focused on the segment of interest by eliminating the **All Sessions** data. This allows the display to present only the data relevant to **Sessions with Transactions**, as shown below. This display allows us to much more easily focus on the characteristics of just this segment of site users.

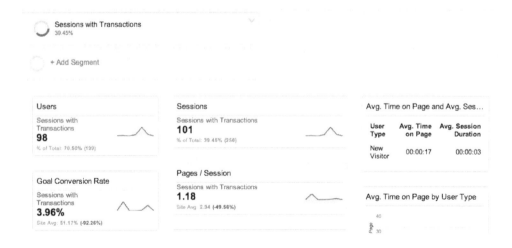

One very beneficial use of applying custom segments to dashboards is the monitoring of marketing campaigns. You'll recall that we can tag campaigns with source, medium, and campaign parameters (see Chapter 57). We can create a dashboard designed to present key metrics related to campaigns, and then use custom segments to focus the dashboard on the campaign of interest. This is accomplished as follows.

Determine the link tags

Campaign links are tagged so that Google Analytics can identify the source of the referral. Imagine that we are going to send out a campaign with the following characteristics:

Tag Name	Tag	Definition	Label
Source	utm_source	The marketing vehicle or source of the referral	May 10% off offer
Medium	utm_medium	The digital medium that conveyed the link	Facebook
Campaign	utm_campaign	The identifier for the specific referral source	Video post

Create the dashboard

We create a dashboard that focuses on the essential metrics needed to evaluate the campaign. This dashboard is shown below. Note that any data shown in the dashboard reflect the current time period and not the upcoming campaign.

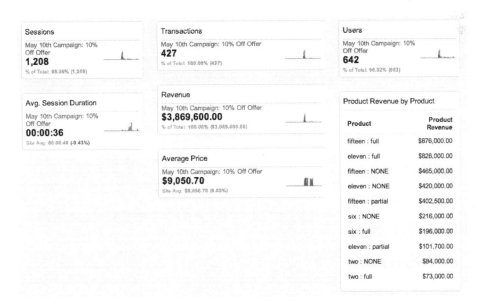

Create a custom segment to identify users referred by the campaign.

We click on **+Add Segment** (on the top of the dashboard page) and then **+New Segment** to begin the segment creation process. On the next screen we click on **Traffic Sources** to define our segment in terms of the upcoming campaign. This brings up the display shown below.

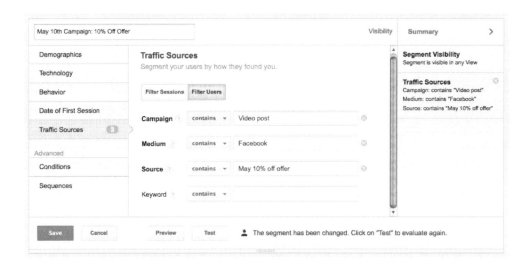

We'll define the segment by using the **Source** and **Medium** parameters provided on page 579. Adding these parameters and naming the segment results in the display shown below. Clicking **Save** stores the segment and adds the segment to our list of available segments.

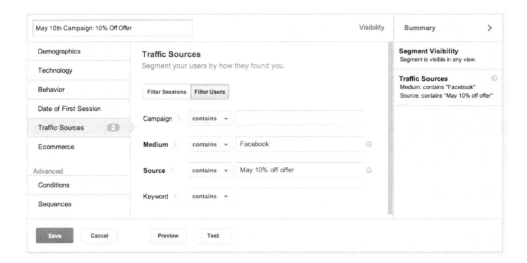

Apply the segment to the dashboard

Once the campaign starts, we load the **Dashboards > Private > Campaign Evaluation Dashboard** and then apply the custom segment. In our case, this results in the dashboard shown below, where we can quickly examine the campaign's effect on generating traffic and sales.

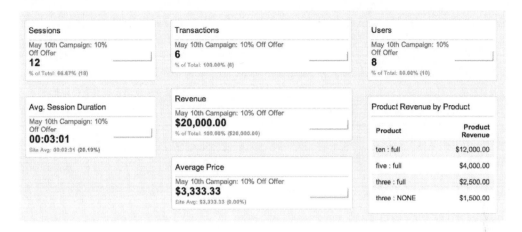

Sharing dashboards

We noted earlier that dashboards are, by default, available only within the view in which they were created and are viewable only by the person who created the dashboard. You have two options, however, for sharing your dashboards with others who have account access.

On the top of the dashboard, next to **+Add Widget**, is a sharing pull-down menu with three options (as shown below). The options are displayed when **Share** is selected.

The **Share Object** option allows everyone with access permission to the current view to see the dashboard. These individuals merely go to **Dashboards > Shared** and click on the dashboard name to view the data for the selected date range. The figure opposite shows my two shared dashboards.

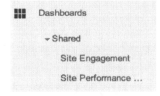

The second option in the **Share** pull-down menu, **Share template link,** allows you to share the dash-board with any Google Analytics user. Clicking on **Share template link** brings up an overlay page with a custom link. You can send the link to others whom you want to be able to see the dashboard. When they click on this link, the page shown below displays, which asks the individual to assign the dashboard to one of his/her views via the **Select a view** pull-down menu, as illustrated below. Selecting a view adds the dashboard to that view. Note that when you share a dashboard in this way only the display is shared; your data remains confidential.

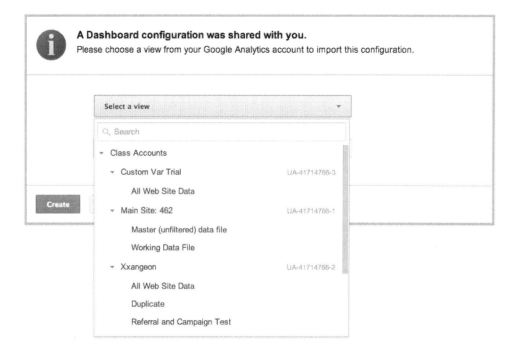

The final way to share a dashboard is through the **Share in Solutions Gallery** option. This option places your dashboard in the Google Analytics Solution Gallery for anyone to use. As with the link sharing option, only your dashboard configuration is shared; your data remains confidential and is not shared.

Importing dashboards

While you may wish to share your dashboards with others via the Google Analytics Solutions Gallery, other Google Analytics users have already decided to share their dashboards with you. You can import dashboards from the Google Analytics Solutions Gallery by selecting **Import from Gallery** when the initial create dashboard window is displayed (see the top graphic on page 567). You will then see the dashboards that are available for import.

Finally, there are dashboards available for import outside of the Google Analytics Solutions Gallery. The following, for example, are excellent sources of dashboard ideas, all of which can be imported and then edited to meet your specific strategic information needs.

- Econsultancy, *10 Useful Google Analytics Custom Dashboards*, at:
  `https://econsultancy.com/blog/62828-10-useful-google-analytics-custom-dashboards#i.ie2lm07nwewwyz`

- Dashboardjunkie, Free Google Analytics Dashboards, at:
  `http://www.dashboardjunkie.com/`

- Zeta, Zeta's Ten Best Free Google Analytics Dashboards, at:
  `http://www.zeta.net/10-free-google-analytics-dashboards/`

Answers to Practice Exercises

Answers to Chapter Eight

1. either **a** or **b** will work, but **b** is the better approach
2. true
3. false
4. a
5. false
6. false
7. true
8. c
9. false
10. g
11. false
12. false

Hands-on

Step by step instructions for addressing each exercise can be found on the following pages.

1. See pages 32 - 34
2. See pages 34 - 35
3. See pages 35 - 36
4. See pages 19 - 20
5. See page 37
6. See pages 38 - 39
7. See page 38
8. See pages 38 - 39
9. See pages 39 - 40
10. See pages 40 - 41

79
Answers to Chapter Ten

True/false and multiple choice

1. None. She would not have access to any levels above View.
2. true
3. true
4. Edit
5. false
6. true
7. false
8. true

Application

1. Tom's intern status would preclude granting him any level of permission where he could harm the integrity of the data. Permission at the **Read & Analyze** level would be appropriate and would allow him to perform his expected job function.

2. Kate's position in the company and her desire to be actively involved merit permission at the highest level: **Edit.** Given Kate's belief that she should have full administrative capabilities, including adding and deleting users, she should also be granted the ability to **Manage Users**.

3. Amanda's responsibilities and position as well as her creativity in data analysis and view creation would indicate that **Edit** permission is appropriate.

4. Ken should likely not be given any permission. He can be placed on an email list to receive PDFs of Google Analytics reports for analysis. If permission is granted, it should be at the lowest level: **Read & Analyze**.

Hands-on

The procedures needed to complete this exercise are described on pages 46 to 50.

Answers to Chapter Twelve

True/false and multiple choice

1. b
2. c
3. false
4. false
5. true
6. true
7. false
8. b
9. b
10. a
11. c

Hands-on

1.

Filter Information

Filter Name   Exercise 1

Filter Type   ⦿ Predefined filter   ○ Custom filter

| Exclude ⬍ | traffic from the IP addresses ⬍ | that begin with ⬍ |

IP address   208 . 87 . 149 .   ☐ IPv6
(e.g. 74.125.19.103 or 2001:db8::1)

2. From the listing of filters, click on "Exercise 1". On the next page, change the filter's characteristics to those shown below.

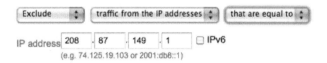

| Exclude ⬍ | traffic from the IP addresses ⬍ | that are equal to ⬍ |

IP address   208 . 87 . 149 . 1   ☐ IPv6
(e.g. 74.125.19.103 or 2001:db8::1)

3.

Filter Information

Filter Name   Exercise 3

Filter Type   ⦿ Predefined filter   ○ Custom filter

[Include only ⬍] [traffic from the ISP domain ⬍] [that contain ⬍]

From ISP Domain   wordpress.com
(e.g. mydomain.com)

Case Sensitive   ○ Yes   ⦿ No

4.

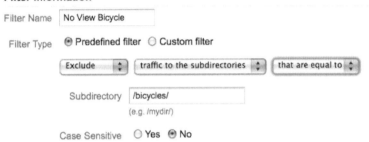

Filter Information

Filter Name   No View Bicycle

Filter Type   ⦿ Predefined filter   ○ Custom filter

[Exclude ⬍] [traffic to the subdirectories ⬍] [that are equal to ⬍]

Subdirectory   /bicycles/
(e.g. /mydir/)

Case Sensitive   ○ Yes   ⦿ No

5.

Filter Information

Filter Name   Exercise 5

Filter Type   ⦿ Predefined filter   ○ Custom filter

[Include only ⬍] [traffic to the subdirectories ⬍] [that contain ⬍]

Subdirectory   art
(e.g. /mydir/)

Case Sensitive   ○ Yes   ⦿ No

6.

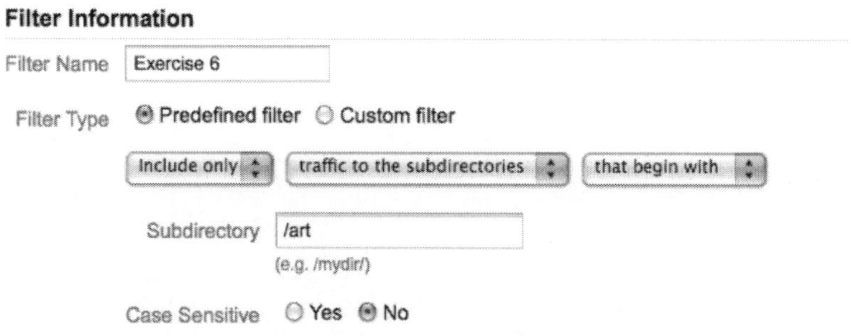

Filter Information

Filter Name | Exercise 6

Filter Type ◉ Predefined filter ○ Custom filter

[Include only ⬍] [traffic to the subdirectories ⬍] [that begin with ⬍]

Subdirectory | /art
(e.g. /mydir/)

Case Sensitive ○ Yes ◉ No

7. First, from the listing of filters, select the **Assign Filter Order** option. On the next screen, highlight "No View Bicycle". Then press the **Move Up** button until the "No View Bicycles" filter is on the top of the list. Press **Save** and you should see the revised filter order with "No View Bicycle" in the first position.

8. From the listing of filters, click on the **remove** button on the line containing "Exercise 3". On the next page, confirm that you want to remove the filter.

Application

Answers will vary.

81
Answers to Chapter Fourteen

We recommend using RegexPal (http://www.regexpal.com) to check your answers, keeping in mind that your answer may be different from ours, but still correctly respond to the task.

1. **art|cup**

2. **art.***

3. **.*art.***

4. **.*art.*s**

5. **cup|.*art.***

6. **.***

7. **man*kind**

8. **.**.***

9. **59|78|159**

10. **(history|med)2(4[89]|5[0-9]|6[0-3])**

11. **google\.com?\.(uk|de)**

12. **.*(pdf|xcl|doc)**

13. **Voda(ph|f|pf|)one**

82

Answers to Chapter Sixteen

True/false and multiple choice

1. a, c, d, f
2. c
3. false
4. false
5. false
6. d
7. false
8. b
9. false
10. false

Hands-on

1.

Filter Information

Filter Name   Mobile-Sam

Filter Type   ○ Predefined filter   ◉ Custom filter

   ○ Exclude
   ◉ Include
   ○ Lowercase
   ○ Uppercase
   ○ Search and Replace
   ○ Advanced

   Filter Field   Mobile brand name ▲▼

   Filter Pattern   Samsung

   Case Sensitive   ○ Yes   ◉ No

2. We first use Regex_For_Range (http://utilitymill.com/utility/Regex For Range) to obtain the regex code needed. Once the code is generated, we ignore the beginning and ending **/b** and copy the remainder of the output. This output is then used in custom filter creation, as shown on the top of the next page.

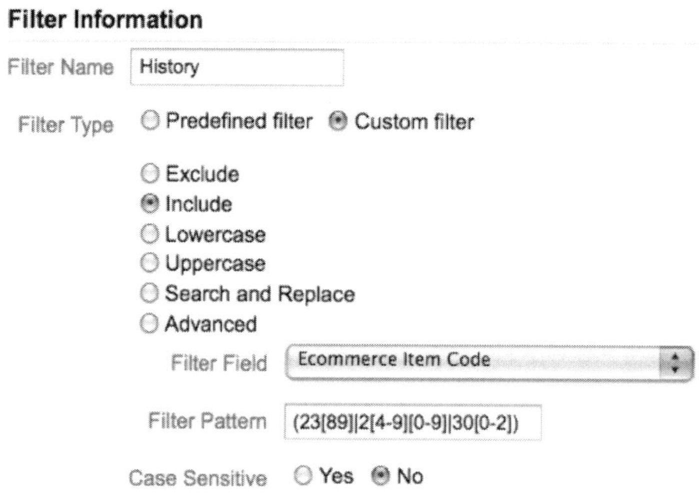

Filter Information

Filter Name   History

Filter Type   ○ Predefined filter   ● Custom filter

       ○ Exclude
       ● Include
       ○ Lowercase
       ○ Uppercase
       ○ Search and Replace
       ○ Advanced

         Filter Field   Ecommerce Item Code

         Filter Pattern   (23[89]|2[4-9][0-9]|30[0-2])

       Case Sensitive   ○ Yes   ● No

3.

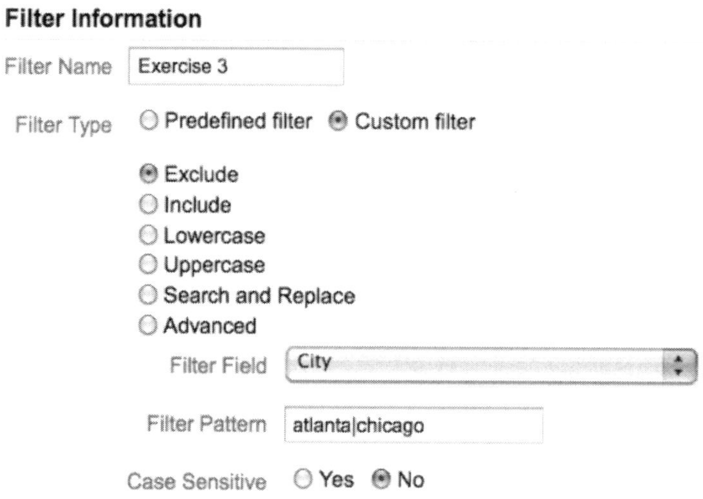

Filter Information

Filter Name   Exercise 3

Filter Type   ○ Predefined filter   ● Custom filter

       ● Exclude
       ○ Include
       ○ Lowercase
       ○ Uppercase
       ○ Search and Replace
       ○ Advanced

         Filter Field   City

         Filter Pattern   atlanta|chicago

       Case Sensitive   ○ Yes   ● No

4.

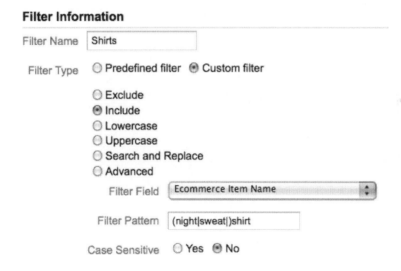

Filter Information

Filter Name   Exercise 4

Filter Type   ○ Predefined filter ● Custom filter

    ○ Exclude
    ● Include
    ○ Lowercase
    ○ Uppercase
    ○ Search and Replace
    ○ Advanced

Filter Field   Request URI

Filter Pattern   .*/tpage.*

Case Sensitive   ○ Yes ● No

5. First we must determine the correct regex statement, which is **(night|sweat|)shirt**. We can confirm this at RegexPal (http://regexpal.com/). Next, we apply the regex to custom filter creation, as shown below

.

Filter Information

Filter Name   Shirts

Filter Type   ○ Predefined filter ● Custom filter

    ○ Exclude
    ● Include
    ○ Lowercase
    ○ Uppercase
    ○ Search and Replace
    ○ Advanced

Filter Field   Ecommerce Item Name

Filter Pattern   (night|sweat|)shirt

Case Sensitive   ○ Yes ● No

6. First we must determine the correct regex statement, which is **(air|tri|bi|)planes?**. We can confirm this at RegexPal (http://regexpal.com/). Next, we apply the regex to custom filter creation, as shown on the top of the next page.

Filter Information

Filter Name   Plane

Filter Type   ○ Predefined filter   ◉ Custom filter

     ○ Exclude
     ◉ Include
     ○ Lowercase
     ○ Uppercase
     ○ Search and Replace
     ○ Advanced

Filter Field   Search Term

Filter Pattern   (air|tri|bi|)planes?

Case Sensitive   ○ Yes   ◉ No

83

Answers to Chapter Eighteen

Application (I)

1. metric
2. dimension
3. dimension
4. metric
5. dimension
6. metric
7. dimension
8. dimension
9. dimension
10. dimension
11. dimension

Application (II)

Note that other insights and follow-up questions are possible.

1. Country/Territory is a dimension.

    Insights include:

    -   Most site sessions originate in Germany or the United States.

    -   Sessions primarily originate in six countries (Italy is excluded)

    -   Among the top four countries (ranked by sessions), the United States has the lowest percentage of new sessions (which means that it has the highest percentage of returning sessions); Germany has the highest percentage of new sessions

    -   Bounce rate is comparable across the top six countries except for Australia, which seems to have a significantly higher bounce rate

    -   Sessions originating in the United States have higher engagement, with a relatively higher average number of pages/session and average session duration

Follow-up questions include:

- What can we learn from the United States that will help us increase the percentage of returning sessions (i.e., non-new sessions) in other countries?

- What can we learn from Germany to increase the absolute number of site sessions in other countries?

- What is going wrong in Australia to account for the relatively higher bounce rate?

- What can we learn from the United States in order to increase site engagement in other countries?

2. Browser is a dimension.

Insights include:

- The vast majority of site sessions take place via the Chrome browser.

- There is significant variation in site behaviors across browser types.

- Chrome sessions are almost all new sessions with a relatively lower bounce rate

- Firefox and especially Safari sessions show a much lower rate of new sessions, and as a result, a much higher percentage of sessions initiated by returning users

- Engagement (pages/session and average session duration) is much higher for sessions conducted via Firefox

Follow-up questions include:

- Why is there a relationship between new/returning sessions and browser type? Does understanding this relationship have a strategic impact on our future business success?

- Why is there a relationship between engagement and browser type? Does this relationship have a strategic impact on our future business success?

- What can we learn from Firefox sessions so that we can increase levels of engagement with sessions conducted via other browsers?

3. Referral Source and Browser are both dimensions.

Insights include:

- Most site sessions originate from a user typing our website URL directly into their browser (or using a bookmark). As a result of the large number of direct sessions, this type of session accounts for about half of all revenue and transactions

- Among the primary referral sources, average order value is a bit higher for those referred to the site by either Wordpress or Google

- The ecommerce conversion rate is lower for direct users (and very low for Google referrals); higher for those referred to the site by Facebook, Wordpress, and YouTube

- The prior two points indicate that Wordpress is a very valuable referral source

- Among those who accessed the site directly, browser used appears to have a significant impact on transaction completion. No one using Firefox or Internet Explorer completed a transaction.

Follow-up questions include:

- How can we increase referrals from Facebook, YouTube, and especially Wordpress?

- Why are average purchase amounts and ecommerce conversion rates higher for those referred from Facebook and Wordpress? How can we use the answer to the prior question to increase average purchase amount and transaction rate for those who access the site directly?

- Why can't/don't those using Firefox or Internet Explorer complete a transaction? How can we fix this?

4. User Type is a dimension.

Insights include:

- The vast majority of site visitors are "new" versus "returning."

- New versus returning visitors show different site behaviors. New visitors show a lower bounce rate, but a much lower average session duration versus returning visitors.

- Returning visitors have a higher average order value but lower conversion rate versus new visitors

Follow-up questions include:

- Why don't we attract more returning site visitors? How can we increase the relative percentage of this type of visitor?

- Among new visitors, how can we explain the combination of low bounce rate (typically a good thing) and low session duration (generally a bad thing)? What are the implications of this explanation for our future business success?

- What can we learn from returning visitors with regard to their higher order value so that we can increase order value among new visitors? What can we learn from new visitors with regard to their higher conversion rate so that we can increase conversion rate among returning visitors?

84

Answers to Chapter Twenty

1. false
2. false
3. a, b, d, e
4. false
5. true
6. true
7. a, b, d, f
8. true
9. b

Application (I)

Time Period	Pageviews	Session Number	Session Length	Explanation
Monday				
09:00 - 09:20	1	1	0 min.	Since there was no page engagement or other pages viewed, there was no ending time for the session, which is why session length is set to zero.
10:00 - 10:11	4	2	8 min.	The session begins with the first pageview at 10:00 and ends when the final page viewed is loaded at 10:08.
23:59- 00:00	1	3	0 min.	There has been no engagement or further pageviews, so no session end time can be calculated. The session ends at midnight.
Tuesday				
00:01 - ?	1	4	0 min.	Since there is no end time to this session, it times out at 30 minutes and session length is set to zero.
06:00 - 06:11	4	5	6 min.	The session begins with the first pageview at 06:00 and ends when the final page viewed is loaded at 06:06.
Totals	**11**	**5**	**14 min.**	

Application (II)

The graphs reflect the trend in user interactions with my travel agency website. We want to evaluate the effectiveness of an email campaign. Emails were sent on July 9, July 16, July 21, and July 28. As annotated in the top chart, the campaign had two goals: to increase the proportion of new sessions and to increase users' engagement with the site.

The first chart relates to the first objective. It appears that the first, second and fourth emails all improved the proportion of new sessions. In all three cases, the impact was nearly immediate. The long-term effects, however, differed across emails. The first email had a dramatic and continuing effect which the second email accelerated. The fourth email also had an immediate effect, but this effect appeared to last much shorter than the first two emails. The third email, mailed on July 21, had an effect counter to our objective. This email failed to capitalize on the momentum created by the prior two emails and, after its mailing, the percentage of new sessions actually decreased slightly.

The second and third charts relate to the second objective: to increase user engagement with the website. Two audience metrics were selected as the evaluative criteria: **Average Session Duration** and **Pages/Session**. Taken together, the two charts indicate that only the first email had an overall positive impact on user engagement by improving both metrics. However, this impact does appear to be short-lived, declining rapidly in less than a week after emailing. The second and third emails appear to have little effect on either metric. Finally, while the last email does appear to have a positive (although short-term) effect on Pages/Session, this increase is not accompanied by an increase in Session Duration, indicating that little real engagement is taking place.

In sum, it appears that only the first email allows us to simultaneously achieve both objectives, and we would recommend that the approach and content of this email be used to address these objectives in the future.

Application (II)

Answers will vary.

85

Answers to Chapter Twenty Three

1. d
2. false
3. false
4. false
5. a, b, c, d
6. false
7. b
8. true
9. false
10. a, b
11. false
12. true
13. true

Application

1. Chrome is by far the most commonly used browser, responsible for about 90% of all sessions. Internet Explorer accounts for too few sessions and will be omitted from further analysis. While **Pages per Session** does not vary across the three remaining browsers, **Average Session Duration** does vary, with this metric significantly lower for Chrome. The use of Chrome is also associated with a much higher proportion of **New Sessions**, that is, Chrome users are much less likely to return. In sum, given the extremely high use of Chrome to access the site, we need to see if there are any Chrome-specific issues that are degrading the users' website experience.

2. While Chrome is associated with the greatest number of sessions (91.2%), perhaps more importantly it is associated with all (100%) of transactions and website revenue. Our first priority would be to determine why there is a complete absence of transactions with other browsers and to immediately address any identified browser-specific issues. Our second priority is to address the relatively low Chrome conversion rate.

3. The two time periods are shown below.

Jan 1, 2014 - Jan 31, 2014
Compare to: Dec 1, 2013 - Dec 31, 2013

Website traffic and site usage showed a marked decline in January versus December. The negative numbers for **Sessions**, **Users**, and **Pageviews** all indicate that these metrics were lower in January than in December. The large positive percentage for **% New Sessions**, when examined in the context of the underlying percentages, indicates that our session base significantly changed from a relatively even mix of new and returning sessions to predominantly new sessions. This shift might explain the positive increase in metrics related to site engagement (**Pages/Session** and **Avg. Session Duration**).

4. The first two tables indicate that Poway is the most important city in terms of the reported metrics: **Sessions** and **Revenue.** We can put these metrics for Poway and the remaining two cities into perspective by calculating an index that relates sessions to revenue, as shown below.

Relationship of Sessions and Revenue in Top Three Calif. Cities

City	% Sessions	% Revenue	Index
Poway	69.27%	76.91%	111
San Diego	21.69	10.30	47
Rancho Santa Fe	4.96	9.30	188

The indices indicate that both Poway and Rancho Santa Fe are performing better than would be expected given each city's share of sessions. In both cases, the share of revenue is higher than the share of sessions. San Diego is underperforming, generating only about half the percentage of revenue that would be expected given its share of sessions.

The third table reports transaction conversion rate. Here, our best city is San Francisco, with a conversion rate over 50%. We would certainly want to see what is working there so that we could apply it to other cities. We would also want to capitalize on this high rate by proactively trying to increase sessions in San Francisco. What is of concern is the low conversion rate in Poway. This is surprising given Poway's very high contribution to revenue. Clearly, our business would significantly improve if we could increase the Poway conversion rate.

Hands-on

Answers will vary.

1. false
2. true
3. true
4. a, c, e, f
5. true
6. false
7. a, b, c, d
8. true
9. true

1. Both tables demonstrate the importance of Ireland over Germany for business success. Ireland accounts the vast majority of sessions (96.71%) and revenue (97.32%). The importance of Ireland is further supported when we adjust for the different number of sessions through **Average Order Value.** Ireland has a much value. The difference between the two countries might be attributable to differences in site engagement, where sessions originating in Ireland show much greater engagement: **Pages/Session** and **Avg. Session Duration** are higher; **Bounce Rate** is lower.

2. The vast majority of site revenue comes from new visitors who account for 85.49% of sessions and 96.04% of revenues. The much higher share of revenues accounted for by new visitors (versus this group's share of sessions) is the result of their significantly higher **Ecommerce Conversion Rate** and **Per Session Value**. It appears that returning visitors do spend more time on site and read more pages, but the outcome is not very positive. Clearly, we need to better understand how the site can better meet the needs of these individuals without jeopardizing sales from new visitors.

3. While the number of sessions and pageviews have increased after changes were implemented, the underlying pattern of engagement shows a dismal picture. Website engagement is actually worse after the changes. With regard to **Session Duration**, prior to the changes about 57% of site sessions were ten seconds or less (149 ÷ 259). After the changes this percentage rose to 81% (456 ÷ 561). The same pattern is seen for **Page Depth**. Prior to the changes about 49% of site sessions were one page (126 ÷ 259). After the changes this percentage rose to 70% (393 ÷ 561).

Answers will vary.

87

Answers to Chapter Twenty Eight

True/false and multiple choice

1. b
2. a, c, d
3. b
4. a, b, c
5. a
6. c
7. true
8. true
9. a, b

Application

All site users enter through the home page. None exit after viewing this page, which is very good. From the home page, site users seek more information: about half move on to the mediaplay page to see a video and about half move on to the "more information" page. None leave after viewing either of these pages, which means that the information provided is relevant and motivating to continue the purchase process. Both of the prior pages lead to the purchase page on which tours are described and selected for purchase. This page appears to be problematic. Only 25% of those who arrive on this page actually finalize a purchase. The remainder either go to the contact page (70%) or use the site search function (5%). We would speculate that there is important information missing from this page, which motivates individuals to abandon the purchase process and initiate a contact or search. Our priorities, therefore, should be to determine what this missing information is and to revise the purchase page to explicitly and clearly provide this information.

Hands-on

Answers will vary.

88

Answers to Chapter Thirty

1. false
2. false
3. a, b, d
4. true
5. false
6. true
7. true
8. a
9. true

Application

1. Overall, all of the pages load in less than the three second industry recommended average and the overall average for the site is very low (.81 seconds). This is very good. All of the pages do exhibit room for improvement, with no page receiving a score over 91. This is also good. We can make pages working quite well even better. Let's look at each page individually.

   The first page listed is one of our purchase pages. While the load time for this page is acceptable, there is still room for improvement, as Google Analytics gives the page a score of 91 with four speed improvement suggestions. Improvement for this page is important as the bounce rate (39.71%) and especially % Exit (95.56%) indicate that a significant number of site users are having difficulty with this page. The fact that this is one of our purchase pages reinforces the need to shorten the page's load time and reduce bounce rate. Additionally, we should examine page content, layout, and purchase process in order to significantly reduce the % Exit rate.

   The second page listed is the site's home page. The load time for this page is acceptable (1.93 seconds) and there is some room for improvement. Fortunately, the bounce rate and % Exit rates for this page are low. We would want to explore and implement Google Analytics' suggestions for improving load time as we want the lowest possible load time for our home page. Implementing these changes should also (hopefully) reduce the bounce rate and % Exit rate.

   The next two pages have too few pageviews to provide reliable metrics and so are eliminated from the analysis.

The final purchase page loads very quickly, but still has some room for improvement. Improving the load speed for this page would be a lower priority than the prior purchase pages. However, we would want to examine content, layout and the purchase process in order to reduce the bounce rate and especially the % Exit rate.

2. The consultant's changes have been a disaster. The website's most important speed-related metrics are significantly poorer in the period in which the changes were implemented versus the prior period. In particular, Average Page Load Time is 15.9% poorer (1.26 versus 1.09 seconds), Average Redirection Time is 203.98% poorer (.54 versus .18 seconds) and Average Page Download Time is 115.33% slower (.02 versus .01 seconds). While the decline in any single measure may not cause a user to have a significantly poorer experience, the fact that all three measures are worse post-change is very bad indeed. The positive changes in the other measures are minimally important in an absolute sense and do not overshadow the poor performance in measures directly related to website revision.

Hands-on

Answers will vary.

89

Answers to Chapter Thirty Two

1. false
2. false
3. true
4. true
5. a, c
6. true
7. true
8. c
9. a, f

Application

1. Site users appear to have a "let's get down to business" mindset. The only links clicked are those that allow product purchase or provide additional information (via a video or a more information page). As a next step, we would want to explore the use of these links by any specific user. If each user, over the course of a visit, uses only one link, then cumulatively the levels of use are likely acceptable. If, however, individual users are clicking on more than one link (by returning to the home page), then there are likely fundamental problems with overall site navigation, which should be quickly addressed. We should also try to find a way to improve navigation and link labels to respond to users' desire for information and immediate purchase. Finally, no home page user clicked on the "Contact Us" link. We should determine if a visit to the home page is too early in the process for this link's usage, or if another link to contact should be provided in a different location on the page.

2. While we have no pre-revision data to use as context, a look at the absolute levels of provided data indicate that the page is still very weak in spite of any prior revisions. First, the relatively high time on page (which is typically a good thing) coupled with the very high bounce rate indicates that this page is likely confusing and/or not providing the information that site users seek and value. The low use of links to the purchase and information pages and the relatively high use of "Contact Us" further reinforce the hypothesis that home page content and/or navigation are very problematic. A full review of home page content and layout should be undertaken.

Hands-on

Answers will vary.

90
Answers to Chapter Thirty Four

True/false and multiple choice

1. true
2. false
3. false
4. false
5. b
6. c
7. false
8. a, b, c, d
9. false
10. false
11. false
12. false
13. true
14. a, c
15. false

Application

1.

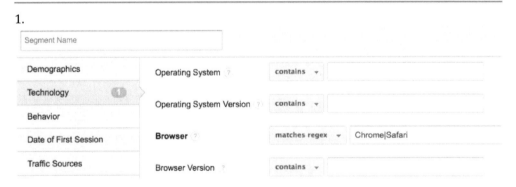

2.

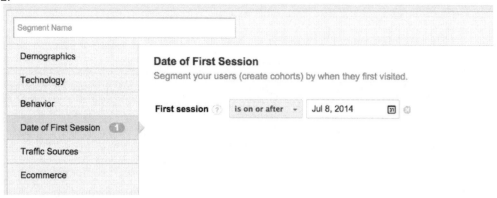

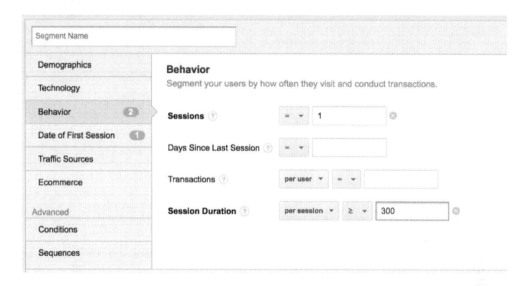

3.

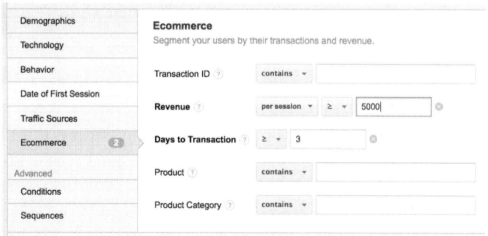

4.

Demographics	**Filter** Sessions ▾ Include ▾
Technology	
Behavior	Landing Page ▾ exactly matches ▾ Welcome
Date of First Session	**Filter** Sessions ▾ Include ▾
Traffic Sources	
Advanced	Quantity ▾ per session ▾ ≥ ▾ 2
Conditions ③	**Filter** Sessions ▾ Include ▾
Sequences	Source ▾ matches regex ▾ [W|w]ordpress

5. Answers will vary.

Hands-on

Answers will vary.

91

Answers to Chapter Forty

1. a, b, d
2. false
3. true
4. false
5. false
6. a, b, c
7. b
8. false
9. false
10. false
11. true
12. true
13. false
14. b
15. d
16. false
17. a
18. d
19. true
20. false
21. a, b, d, e
22. false

Application

We'll need to calculate some data manually. The goal conversion rate is quite low with only 134 sessions out of a total of 1,491 sessions (8.99%). Few sessions, therefore, participate in viewing the tour package. The relative proportion of new users in the Failure and Success groups is not significantly different: 83.5% (1133 ÷ 1397) of the Failure group and 78.4% (105 ÷ 134) of the Success group. The major difference between the two groups lies in site engagement, where the Success group is much more engaged. The Success group's bounce rate is lower, and its Pages/Session and Average Session Duration are much higher.

Next steps should use funnels and path analyses as well as **Behavior** and **Conversion** metrics to determine the reasons for the Failure group's lower site engagement. Additionally, we should explore differences in transaction value across the two groups.

1. Select **Goals** from the Admin View display

   Step One: Select **+ New Goal** or **Custom** (as appropriate)

   Step Two: **Name** is: Exercise 1
   Type is: Destination

   Step 3:   See below

   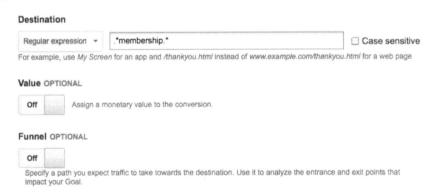

   ③ Goal details

   Destination

   | Equals to ▾ | /mediaplay.html | ☐ Case sensitive |

   For example, use *My Screen* for an app and */thankyou.html* instead of *www.example.com/thankyou.html* for a web page

   Value OPTIONAL

   Off | Assign a monetary value to the conversion.

   Funnel OPTIONAL

   Off | Specify a path you expect traffic to take towards the destination. Use it to analyze the entrance and exit points that impact your Goal.

2. Step One: Select **+ New Goal** or **Custom** (as appropriate)

   Step Two: **Name** is: Exercise 2
   Type is: Destination

   Step 3:   See below

   ③ Goal details

   Destination

   | Regular expression ▾ | .*membership.* | ☐ Case sensitive |

   For example, use *My Screen* for an app and */thankyou.html* instead of *www.example.com/thankyou.html* for a web page

   Value OPTIONAL

   Off | Assign a monetary value to the conversion.

   Funnel OPTIONAL

   Off | Specify a path you expect traffic to take towards the destination. Use it to analyze the entrance and exit points that impact your Goal.

3. Step One: Select **+ New Goal** or **Custom** (as appropriate)

   Step Two: **Name** is: Exercise 3
   Type is: Destination

   Step 3: See below

   ### ③ Goal details

   Destination

   | Equals to ▾ | /purchase.html | | ☐ Case sensitive |

   For example, use *My Screen* for an app and */thankyou.html* instead of *www.example.com/thankyou.html* for a web page

   Value OPTIONAL

   [Off] Assign a monetary value to the conversion.

   Funnel OPTIONAL

   [On]

   Use an app screen name string or a web page URL for each step. For example, use *My Screen* for an app and */thankyou.html* instead of *www.example.com/thankyou.html* for a web page.

Step	Name	Screen/Page	Required?
①	Home	/index.html	No
②	Media	/mediaplay.html	⊗

   [+ Add another Step]

4. Step One: Select **+ New Goal** or **Custom** (as appropriate)

   Step Two: **Name** is: Exercise 4
   Type is: Duration

   Step 3: See below

   ### ③ Goal details

		Hours	Minutes	Seconds
Duration	Greater than ▾	0	5	0

   Value OPTIONAL

   [Off] Assign a monetary value to the conversion.

5. Step One: Select **+ New Goal** or **Custom** (as appropriate)

    Step Two: **Name** is: Exercise 5
                 Type is: Pages/Screens per session

    Step 3:   See below

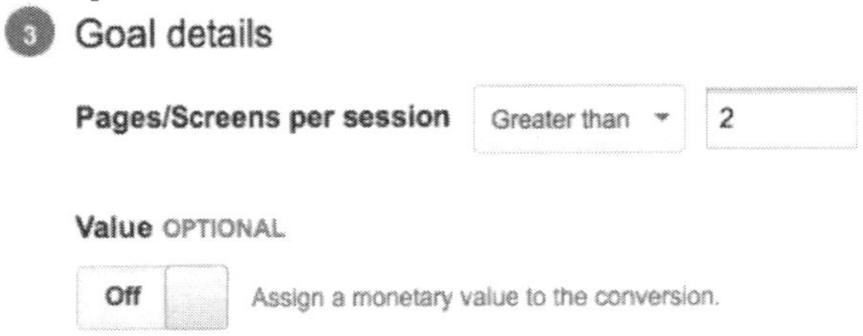

    ③ Goal details

    Pages/Screens per session | Greater than ▾ | 2 |

    Value OPTIONAL

    | Off | Assign a monetary value to the conversion.

Hands-on (II)

Answers will vary.

Answers to Chapter Forty Two

1. true
2. a, b, c, d
3. a, b, c
4. false
5. false
6. false
7. false
8. true
9. false
10. true

The form of the text link is:

<a href="javascript:download('/brochure/bahamas_dl_text.pdf')">Click Here</a> to obtain a brochure on Bahamas travel

The form of the image link is:

**<a href="javascript:download('/brochure/bahamas_dl_image.pdf')">
<img src="images/bahamas1.jpg"></a>**

The form of the button link is:

**<a href="javascript:download('/brochure/bahamas_dl_button.pdf')">
<img src="images/dl.jpg"></a>**

93
Answers to Chapter Forty Four

Answers will vary.

Answers to Chapter Forty Six

1. a, b, c
2. a, b
3. false
4. a, b, c, d, e
5. a
6. b
7. false
8. all options can trigger an event
9. false
10. true

Hands-on

The form of the **\<body\>** code is:

 \<body onload = "ga('send', 'event', 'Event test', 'Activates on page load', 'Events page', {'nonInteraction': 1});"\>

The form of the **\<onClick\>** link is:

\<a href="javascript:redir('Event test', 'Activates on link click', 'Events page', 0,'http://www.google.com/analytics')"\>Click here to go to Google Analytics\</a\>

95
Answers to Chapter Fifty Nine

True/false and multiple choice

1. false
2. a, c, d
3. true
4. false
5. false
6. a, b, c
7. c
8. a, d, e
9. false
10. false
11. a
12. true
13. a
14. a, c, d

Application

Let's address the tables in the order presented.

The first table places the current campaign in the context of prior campaigns. With regard to the total number of sessions generated (26), this campaign was very strong, placing just behind the most successful campaign, which generated 29 sessions.

The second table reports sessions by blog post topic. The Cost and Refresh campaigns generated significantly more sessions versus Chill (12, 11, and 3 sessions, respectively). Site engagement across these campaigns varied significantly. Both the Refresh and Chill campaigns generated better engagement versus Cost: the number of Pages/Session and Average Session Duration were much higher; the Bounce Rate was much lower. Thus, it appears that while Cost strongly motivated users to visit the site, they were very displeased when they arrived, as demonstrated by much poorer engagement metrics.

The third table presents ecommerce metrics for each blog topic. Given the differences in engagement metrics, it is not surprising that Average Order Value and the Ecommerce Conversion Rate were much higher for Refresh and Chill versus Cost. Chill's ecommerce metrics are particularly noteworthy. While this topic generated the fewest number of sessions, it had the highest Ecommerce Conversion Rate (100%) and highest Average Order Value ($11,000). It appears that while this topic does not appeal to everyone, those to whom it does appeal are very important to site success.

In sum, we would recommend abandoning future blog topics focused on Cost. We would allocate our emphasis 70%/30% on Refresh and Chill, respectively. Refresh will generate a high number of site referrals and sales, while Chill will send a smaller but very important group of users to the site.

Hands-on (I) and (II)

Answers will vary.

Answers to Chapter Sixty One

True/false and multiple choice

1. true
2. false
3. false
4. true
5. a, b, d, e
6. b
7. c
8. a

Application

The three tables provide insights into social media's contribution to overall business success and differences in site engagement across individual social media referral sources.

From the top table we learn that social media account for relatively few sessions (9.8%) and contributions to conversions (4.8%). Given these metrics, it is not surprising that social referrals only contribute to about 4.2% of all revenue.[1]

The middle table provides insights into sessions generated from specific social referral sources. Pinterest and Wordpress account for about the same number of sessions (41 and 36 respectively), with Facebook accounting for fewer sessions (27). Engagement differs across the three referral sources. Those referred by Pinterest show the most engagement, with relatively high session duration and number of pages/session. Those referred by Wordpress have moderate site engagement, with low session duration but a high number of pages/session. Those referred by Facebook show the least engagement, with very short session duration and few pages viewed per session.

The bottom table shows that Pinterest is the social referral source responsible for almost all conversions (84.62%) and revenue (95.08%). This is not surprising given Pinterest's much higher level of site engagement.

---

[1] The percentage of sessions is calculated as 104 ÷ 1062. The percentage of contribution to conversions is calculated as 13 ÷ 271. Contribution to revenue is calculated as 81,300 ÷ 1,940,200.

Answers to Chapter Sixty Four

1. false
2. c
3. false
4. true
5. true
6. a
7. a, d, e, f
8. false
9. a, c

Hands-on

Answers will vary.

98
Answers to Chapter Sixty Eight

True/false and multiple choice

1. true
2. b, c, e
3. false
4. false
5. false
6. false
7. c
8. a, b
9. d
10. e
11. c
12. c
13. a
14. false
15. false
16. false
17. true
18. true
19. false
20. c

Hands-on: Attribution models and analysis

Answers will vary.

Answers to Chapter Seventy Two

1. true
2. a, b, c, d
3. false
4. false
5. true
6. b, c, e, f
7. d
8. true
9. true
10. true
11. true
12. false

Application

1. No winner was found, although the very large difference in Average Order Value would indicate that the original home page was the stronger of the two.

   Based on this data, we would leave the original home page on the site, as this page was stronger in terms of both ecommerce and site engagement.

   - As mentioned, the ecommerce metrics (Average Order Value as well as Per Session Value) are much stronger for the original home page.

   - Site engagement metrics are also much stronger for the original home page, specifically, Pages/Session and Avg. Session Duration.

2. No winner was found, although Average Order Value and Per Session Value would indicate that the original home page was the strongest variation tested. In light of this large original home page advantage, we would recommend stopping the experiment.

   Variations (1,1) and (1,2) used black font while Variations (2,1) and (2,2) used black and color. The Average Order Values for each group are shown on the next page.

Type of Font	Average Order Value
Black	$4,763
Black and Color	$10,840

Thus, regardless of font size, the Black and color approach is associated with higher Average Order Value.

Variations (1,1) and (2,1) used the medium font size option while Variations (1,2) and (2,2) used the larger font size option. The Average Order Values for each group are shown below.

Size of Font	Average Order Value
Medium	$3,938
Large	$11,710

Thus, regardless of font color, larger font size is associated with higher Average Order Value.

The Average Order Value for each individual variation is shown below.

		Factor 1: Text Color	
		All Black	Black and Color
	Medium	$857	$6,909
Factor 2: Text Size			
	Large	$8,650	$14,770

There does appear to be an interaction between the two factors tested. All Black/ Medium font size is very weak. The presence of *either* color or larger type results in a large improvement. The presence of color with larger type is the strongest combination, resulting in a significantly larger improvement over all other variations.

100

Answers to Chapter Seventy Five

True/false and multiple choice

1. false
2. false
3. true
4. b
5. false
6. b, c, e
7. false
8. a, b
9. a, b, c, d
10. a, b, c, d

Hands-on

Answers will vary. Example responses follow.

1.

2.

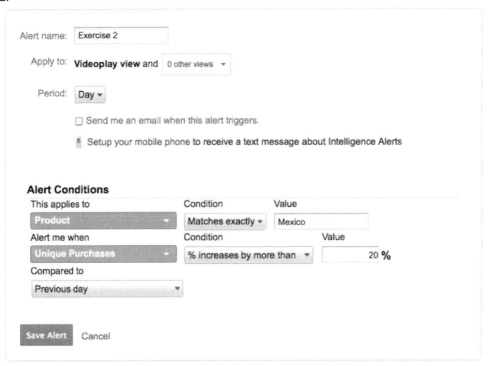

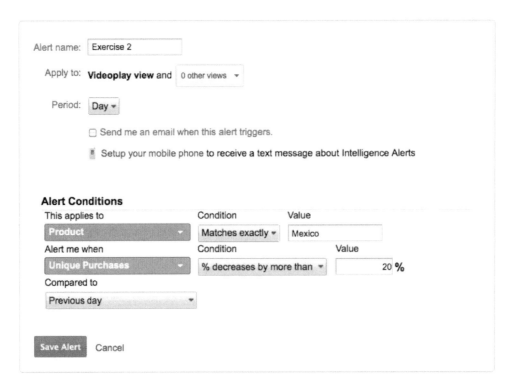

3.

4.

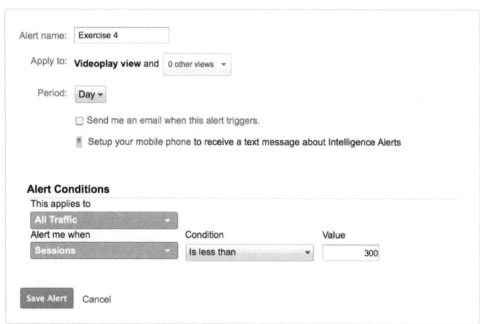

Answers will vary.

Index

9382488R00362

Printed in Great Britain
by Amazon.co.uk, Ltd.,
Marston Gate.